TULAPAI TO TOKAY:

A BIBLIOGRAPHY OF ALCOHOL USE AND ABUSE AMONG NATIVE AMERICANS OF NORTH AMERICA

compiled by
PATRICIA D. MAIL and DAVID R. McDONALD

With a Foreword and Literature Review by JOY H. LELAND
and Indexes by SANDRA NORRIS

HRAF PRESS
New Haven
1980

INTERNATIONAL STANDARD BOOK NUMBER: 0-87536-253-2
LIBRARY OF CONGRESS NUMBER: 80-81243
© 1980
HUMAN RELATIONS AREA FILES, INC.
ALL RIGHTS RESERVED
PRINTED IN THE UNITED STATES OF AMERICA

Tulapai, also known as Tizwin, was an alcoholic beverage made originally by the Apaches. Tokay, an inexpensive wine, is frequently consumed by contemporary Native Americans. The title, <u>Tulapai to Tokay</u>, symbolizes the changes that have occurred over time in the pattern of alcohol use among Native Americans, and reflects the historical range of alcohol use among them.

This book is dedicated to

those Native Americans

who are winning the battle with the bottle;

who are helping in the battle;

and to the memory of those who lost the battle,

but in whose name the fight continues.

TABLE OF CONTENTS

Abbreviations vi

Foreword by Joy H. Leland vii

Preface xii

Native American Alcohol Use: 1
A Review of the Literature
   Joy H. Leland

Bibliography 57

Author Index 290

Subject Index 317

ABBREVIATIONS

AA	Alcoholics Anonymous
BIA	Bureau of Indian Affairs
CHMP	Community Health Maintenance Program
DHEW	Department of Health, Education, and Welfare, U.S. Government (recently changed to the Department of Health and Human Services)
DWI	Driving While under the Influence, usually of alcohol
GAO	General Accounting Office
G.E.D.	General Equivalency Degree
IHS	Indian Health Service
NCAI	National Clearinghouse for Alcohol Information, U.S. Government
NIAAA	National Institute on Alcohol Abuse and Alcoholism
N.W.T.	Northwest Territories
P.H.S.	Public Health Service
T.B.	Tuberculosis
U.M.	University Microfilms, a publishing company located in Ann Arbor, Michigan
USDHEW	U.S. Department of Health, Education and Welfare
USHIS	U.S. Indian Health Service
USNCAI	U.S. National Clearinghouse for Alcohol Information
USPHS	U.S. Public Health Service
V.A.	Veterans Administration
VISTA	Volunteers in Service to America

FOREWORD

The qualifier "selected" in the title of a bibliography guards against charges of incompleteness, after the inevitable omissions have been discovered. Instead of using this hedge, Mail and McDonald candidly admit that the entries in this book represent every item on Native American alcohol use that they had discovered by their cut-off date. Such comprehensive coverage makes the contents very useful, but hard to characterize briefly and summarize. The works included vary greatly in their objectives, intended audience, quality of execution and pertinence to an understanding of Native American drinking.

One way to suggest the variability in the literature covered by this bibliography is to look at the authors. They represent a broad range of training, experience, ethnicity and disciplinary perspective. Mail and McDonald have helpfully indicated authors' specialties in the annotations.

A multidisciplinary literature has the advantage of a variety of perspectives and the disadvantages of communication and coordination problems. Dissimilar authors choose different places to publish their work. The consequent scattering discourages most researchers from becoming familiar with the entire body of material.

Mail and McDonald's bibliography provides an overview of the literature in the annotations, and a guide to more detailed reading on specific topics in the comprehensive index. A novice can become familiar with the available information in an afternoon.

Mail and McDonald have included unpublished work in the bibliography. This portion of the literature (about one-third) consists of such items as workshop pep talks, student term papers, reports by bureaucrats, M.A. theses, Ph.D. dissertations, and scholarly papers ranging from rough drafts to final texts as delivered to colleagues at professional meetings.

Ordinarily, work which is not promptly published is assumed to have been judged unworthy. This is not true in the Native American alcohol field, where many contributors are not academics and the idea of publishing simply does not occur to some of them. Much of the unpublished material has been prepared for treatment and other action programs, often before an adequate theoretical and empirical foundation has emerged. Some of the letters and informal reports, discussions at workshops and other meetings are a rich source of new ideas and data.

We need summaries to help us fit this unpublished work into the published segment, while pointing out its special features, particularly Native American viewpoints on alcoholism. This bibliography will greatly facilitate reviews of the literature. Fortunately, Mail and McDonald have spared us frustration in obtaining copies of these unpublished items. The Preface tells how the reader may get them.

Although excellent work on Native American use of alcohol exists, even a casual reading of the annotations suggests some serious weaknesses in the literature--especially the thin coverage on the range of variation in Native American alcohol use. The literature concentrates too much on the raucous, visible public drinking style which admittedly is popular with many Native Americans. Over-documentation of this behavior pattern has produced a falsely homogeneous picture. Other styles of handling liquor deserve more attention (as in Leland 1975). The major omission is those Native Americans who can drink without getting into trouble. First of all, we need to document their existence; then we should explore their drinking behavior, attitudes, personal histories, strategies for resisting peer pressure to drink dangerously, and methods for avoiding problems when they do drink. Their techniques for steering clear of alcohol abuse in a milieu where it is prevalent could serve as practical guides to others, Native American and non-Native American, who are struggling with the problem. The middle-aged Native American male who seemingly has grown out of problem drinking deserves our careful study. Abstainers also are of interest, though that solution probably has somewhat less potential appeal as a Native American role model than the example of people who can handle liquor without giving it up completely.

We have very few studies in which drinking attitudes and practices are investigated by the same authors using the same methods among more than one group of Native Americans. Levy and Kunitz (1974) have made a valuable contribution of this kind, but many more comparisons among and within tribes are needed before we could begin to generalize to Native Americans as a whole with reasonable confidence.

Research on the drinking behavior and attitudes of young Native American people is urgently needed. There is growing evidence that patterns of alcohol use are largely learned early from peers and families; that Native American youth begin drinking earlier than either whites or the previous generation of Native Americans; that the Native American population contains a high proportion of young people; and that the proportion of Native Americans in the total population is growing rapidly and steadily.

The drinking behavior of urban Native Americans needs more documentation. We need to scrutinize the alleged association between urban residence and excessive drinking by Native Americans. The notion that city dwelling exacerbates Native American drinking must be demonstrated, not presumed.

The role of alcohol in the lives of Native American women needs more attention. We know little about their drinking, since the literature deals almost exclusively with men. Because Native American women appear to have avoided alcohol problems much more consistently than their men, while yet subject to many of the same conditions which have been blamed for promoting excessive drinking, they could serve as controls on research about Native American alcohol use. Furthermore, if we knew more about the dynamics behind the discrepancy in sex ratios of Native American problem drinkers, it might shed light on the phenomenon in other cultures. More Native American women are affected by alcohol indirectly than directly. Thus, information about how these women cope with the effects of men's drinking is even more urgently needed than studies of their own use of alcohol.

In general, more documentation of the variety of drinking behavior among subgroups of Native Americans would give depth to a portrayal of Native American alcohol use. Logically, such studies should precede any generalizations about Native Americans as a whole, much less comparisons of Native Americans with the balance of the population.

In addition to expanding subject matter coverage, Native American alcohol studies could profit from methodological improvements, as well. In addition to more comparable data on different groups, we need follow-up studies to obtain data on the same group over time. Viewed as a whole, the literature so far reads like a series of uncoordinated pilot projects, using a bewildering array of approaches whose broader usefulness remains unknown. Interesting methods are tried here and there on small samples, but never adequately tested for general applicability. The emphasis on new approaches should be weighed against the desirability of testing the established ones. It is time to supplement individualism with cooperation, in order to obtain some cumulative results.

Part of the problem is the scale of the studies which have been undertaken. A single investigator, with short-term or no research support, can do little more than pick at the edges of the problem. Although such studies have made valuable contributions, they should be supplemented by large-scale, long-term work, which in turn would require a greater and more stable commitment on the part of research sponsors. Longitudinal data is immensely important. Prospective studies are of course the best, but the available historical data could be more extensively used than it has been in the past.

We need better methods for estimating the extent of alcohol problems among Native Americans. As things now stand, the assumption that drinking problems are more prevalent among Native Americans than among the general population has an inadequate empirical base. We do not know whether alcohol problems are diminishing or increasing among Native Americans. As in the general population, the absence of appropriate direct measures forces us to infer problem drinking rates from rates of other occurrences we assume to be related, such as arrests, suicides, homicides, accidents and incidence of liver cirrhosis. The results of this approach are often disappointing, but they are particularly so in the case of Native Americans, where conditions peculiar to them make us question the comparability of the statistics. Furthermore, the logic of the assumed association is not always explicit, much less convincing, and is especially shaky across cultures. At the heart of the matter is the question discussed at length in Leland (1976a) of whether or not problem drinking is the same entity, empirically discoverable (and countable) in all groups, or rather a culture-specific complex which must be analyzed in its own terms for each group. The answer is far from obvious, and the answer probably lies somewhere in between.

Westermeyer (1976b) suggests a novel indirect method for assessing the extent of problem drinking which deserves a broader-scale trial:

counting events instead of cases. Without some such methodological
innovation, we might seriously consider suspending this whole indirect
approach to alcohol epidemiology until we find ways to improve methods
for obtaining the data we seek.

Failing that, at least we might want to focus more attention on
accidents and cirrhosis, two of the five most commonly used indicators
of alcohol problems. These rank among the highest as causes of Native
American deaths (first and fourth), and have a relatively more straightforward association with excessive drinking than suicide, homicide and
arrests, which have been emphasized so far. Accidents provide the
additional advantage of offering intervention methods which are simpler
than trying to change individual behavior directly.

We also might want to change our emphasis from the <u>extent</u> of the
association between alcohol and this whole panorama of misfortunes to
the <u>nature</u> of the associations; the latter might give us greater insight
into the former.

In the meantime, someone soon is going to take a national survey
approach to the question of how much problem drinking occurs among
Native Americans. Such data inevitably will be demanded by Congress to
justify the large-scale continuation of the Native American treatment
programs. The attendant structured questionnaires, large random samples
and possibly ethnocentric assumptions may antagonize many anthropologists
and most Native Americans. However, both will have to live with the
findings of such a survey, so they had better maximize its accuracy,
appropriateness, and usefulness for Native Americans by participating in
the planning and execution.

The research on physiological aspects of Native American responses
to alcohol, such as metabolism rates and flushing, is in particular need
of larger, more homogeneous samples and better controls over variability
introduced by differences in methods and in individual subjects' characteristics. These studies also need more anthropological input to help
avoid some of the errors resulting from lack of appreciation for the
genetic and cultural diversity encompassed under the label Native
American; that label has marred many of these studies so far.

There remain many opportunities for those who dislike large-scale
quantified studies to continue to contribute to our knowledge of Native
American drinking. Above all, they can find ways to get information
about drinking practices, beliefs and motives in a more objective fashion
than simply asking (whether by questionnaire or less formally). Questionnaires are, in many circumstances, a last resort with Native American
people. In particular, it is useless to ask them why they drink, for
even if they know, many will not tell. More ingenious methods are needed
for obtaining data in such situations. One possibility would be structured observation in both natural and experimental settings--such as in
Tracey and Nathan's (1976) investigations of drinking motives.

The Native American treatment projects would seem to present opportunities for some modest but fundamental controlled comparisons of inter-

vention strategies. To put first things first, what treatment methods are used in Indian programs? What has become of disulfiram in Native American programs? In research, silence rarely means "no news is good news." It more often indicates that what appeared likely at first to be a solution turned out not to be, and the previous proponents have quietly gone on to more promising things. Which treatment methods seem to work best with whom? (The shotgun approaches so commonly used in these Native American programs make it difficult, but not impossible, to answer that question.)

The Native American treatment programs have not been organized as laboratories to accumulate such data. For one thing, their staff members have been too busy with the everyday pressures of treatment to take on simultaneously the unfamiliar task of research. And Native Americans are generally tired of being studied by non-Native Americans. However, this may change soon; as Native Americans become ever more organized, articulate and powerful (hence less defensive) in alcohol matters, they may want to accept and even seek helpful data from all possible sources.

Such a change in Native American receptiveness to research by non-Native Americans would increase the urgent need for highly-trained Native American people. Their special knowledge and experience would make them a likely source of eventual insight on alcohol use by Native Americans. Inclusion of more Native American students in research projects could begin to provide the needed skills and motivation. The growing corps of Native American health professionals could be encouraged to cooperate in alcohol research and to organize their own. Programs to assist Native Americans in making films, such as John Adair's with Navajos (Worth and Adair 1970*), could produce materials with great potential value in alcohol prevention, education and treatment programs, and also as artifacts in themselves, as clues to culture-specific points of view about alcohol use.

Pressures from Congress, as well as the natural inclinations of the Indian Health Service (IHS), are bound to lead to more careful evaluation of Native American treatment programs; devising appropriate methods presents a very difficult problem. The social science community could help. Few scholars would probably want to evaluate programs in groups they work with, for obvious political reasons, but they could participate at a level once removed. Comparisons among Native American treatment programs could help provide a sensible evaluation methodology.

Many of the weaknesses in the literature on Native American alcohol use set forth above could be minimized and even eliminated by better communication among researchers. As mentioned earlier, communication is inhibited by the multiplicity of disciplines involved, and the consequent profusion of professional journals one must scour for results. A journal devoted to the subject would be ideal. Conferences specializing in the topic, as well as regular reviews of this rather diffuse body of literature would help. And this bibliography is an important contribution to improving communication.

Joy H. Leland

PREFACE

General consensus among a wide variety of observers, coupled with substantial medical, criminal justice, and behavioral science data support the contention that alcohol use and abuse is widespread among the native peoples of North America. The literature encompasses the pronouncements of federal and state employees, the reports of private agencies, and comments of Native Americans themselves regarding Native American alcohol use. Because of the apparent prevalence of alcohol abuse and the often startling statistical expressions of the consequences of such use and abuse, many researchers have attempted to explain why this particular group of people appears to be so catastrophically affected by alcohol.

The bibliographies on Native American alcohol use that have been compiled, perhaps with the exception of Mail and McDonald (1977) and Popham and Yawney (1967), have not been widely available. Limited distribution of reports and bibliographies, such as Skirrow (1971), Street, Wood and Chowenhill (1976), and Attneave and Kelso (1977), has handicapped researchers. Reviews of the literature--such as Brod (1975); MacAndrew and Edgerton (1969)--usually have a more limited focus, albeit wider distribution, or deal with the problem largely from a historical perspective. This bibliography attempts to pull together, from as many sources as possible, the many diverse comments and research reports on the use and abuse of alcohol by Native Americans of North America. It grew out of the work of Victoria Sears, a Native American graduate student, who was completing her Master of Social Work degree at the University of Washington. Sears compiled a list of publications on Native American alcohol abuse and was encouraged by faculty members and alcoholism program personnel to pursue and expand her work. Ernest Turner, Director of the Seattle Indian Alcoholism Program, recommended that she consult with Patricia Mail, of the Indian Health Service, who was also known to have an interest in the alcohol literature. Mail recommended that Sears continue the work and suggested that the bibliography include annotations. Sears was unable to follow through on the project; however, she did assist with the library work and deserves credit for initiating the project--see Mail and Sears (1976).

Mail continued working with the bibliography, getting considerable assistance and encouragement from Dr. Joy Leland, Desert Research Institute, University of Nevada at Reno. Leland shared her extensive collection of unpublished materials and provided advice and motivation. If Mail and McDonald labored to bring forth this volume, the midwife was certainly Leland.

Mail initiated a fortuitous collaboration when she responded to a notice placed by McDonald in the "Cooperation Column" of the October, 1976, Anthropology Newsletter. McDonald, a social science librarian with training in anthropology, was interested in developing bibliographies on a variety of topics dealing with Native Americans, including alcohol use and abuse. McDonald had bibliographic experience, Mail had experience with the literature; the result is this volume.

Finally there is the contribution of Sandra Norris. In 1976 she was librarian for the Student Association for the Study of Hallucinogens, Inc. (STASH), a drug information clearinghouse in Madison, Wisconsin. Norris contacted Mail on the recommendation of Dr. Dwight B. Heath. Norris was interested in knowing if the ongoing research included information on Native American drug use which might be shared with STASH. When STASH closed its library, Norris volunteered to locate some of the alcohol literature which had thus far eluded Mail and McDonald. Norris located nearly all of the legal inclusions, such as the many discussions of the Joseph Drybones case (entries 0064, 0124, 0511, 0565). In addition, she identified some of the more obscure articles in old Indian school journals and newsletters, and tracked down some of the more elusive published materials.

Compilation and Scope of the Bibliography

To compile this bibliography we consulted standard indexes such as the Social Science Index, Public Affairs Information Service, Sociological Abstracts, Psychological Abstracts, Social Science Citation Index, Dissertation Abstracts, Abstracts for Social Workers, Index Medicus, Classified Abstract Archives of Alcohol Literature, as well as numerous bibliography monographs. In addition, we conducted computer searches using ERIC, MEDLINE, and the National Clearinghouse for Alcohol Information. We checked citations from bibliographies of articles abstracted against the growing list of citations already completed, and reviewed material not included to determine whether it contained alcohol information pertinent to the bibliography.

We set January 1, 1977, as the cutoff date for inclusion and tried to annotate everything available at that time. We believe that the bibliography is fairly comprehensive from 1900 to 1975. Coverage of 1976 and 1977 is less complete. We would appreciate receiving references to any works which we have overlooked--so that we may include them in a revised edition of the bibliography. We have included a number of unpublished reports. Recognizing that reference to unpublished materials can be frustrating when such documents are not readily available for review, we have arranged with Rutgers University Center for Alcohol Studies to serve as a repository for this material; copies of unpublished papers which we have deposited there have been marked with two asterisks (**) in the bibliography. Requests for such papers should be directed to:

> Center for Alcohol Studies
> Rutgers University/Smithers Hall
> New Brunswick, NJ 08903

Where we were unable to obtain a copy of an unpublished paper, we provide the published abstract (if it was available)--for whatever value its contents may hold. We have not judged the quality of the works cited. We included a work if it contained references to native North American alcohol use or abuse. While some citations are historical, we decided not to duplicate MacAndrew and Edgerton's (1969) survey of drinking behavior--see also Leland (1976a).

Organization of the Bibliography

We have arranged entries alphabetically by author, and numbered in sequence, in four digits. However, in a few cases, an "A" or "B" is followed by three numbers, for example "A671", "B588". The alphanumeric entry designates citations brought to our attention after the four digit numbers had been assigned. The three numbers in the alphanumeric entry determine the filing sequence in this manner: A671 follows 0671 and precedes 0672.

Order numbers are given for all dissertations available from University Microfilms. We have included Superintendent of Document (SuDoc) numbers (if they were readily available) for United States documents. For unpublished material we have tried to give the reader some idea of the length of the work. Where possible, we give the author's profession or discipline in order to provide perspective on the author's focus and qualifications and to illustrate the great variety of people who discuss alcohol use and abuse among the indigenous people of North America.

All errors are, of course, the sole responsibility of the authors. We wish to thank the following individuals whose assistance, support, and cooperation significantly helped us: Garrick A. Bailey, University of Tulsa; Donald N. Brown, Oklahoma State University; Patrick J. Dubbs, San Diego State University; Edward C. Durgin, University of Oregon; John A. Ewing, University of North Carolina at Chapel Hill; Frances N. Ferguson, Ormond Beach, Florida; Darleen Fitzpatrick, Everett Community College; Morris A. Forslund, University of Wyoming; Herbert B. Fowler, University of Oregon; Dwight B. Heath, Brown University; Wolfgang G. Jilek, University of British Columbia; Ben Morgan Jones, University of Oklahoma; Lorraine V. Klerman, Brandeis University; Robert F. Kraus, University of Washington; Suzanne Meadow, University of Kentucky; Gifford S. Nickerson, North Carolina State University; Martin D. Topper, Southern Methodist University; Katherine M. Weist, University of Montana; Joseph Westermeyer, University of Minnesota; John Murray, Kansas State University; Robert Kruh, Kansas State University; Bernard Albaugh USPHS/IHS, Oklahoma; James M. Andre and Ina C. Palmer, USPHS/IHS, Albuquerque; Tom Bonifield, USPHS/IHS, Seattle; Harry C. Bell and Terry Bellicha, National Institue of Alcoholism and Alcohol Abuse; Olga Cokinos, USPHS/IHS, Rockville; Morris E. Dyer and Stanley C. Ghachu, USPHS/IHS, Zuni; Joyce Hulm, USPHS/IHS, Rapid City; Naomi Kalajan, USPHS/IHS, Phoenix; Elmer G. Renegar, USPHS/IHS, Gallup; Karl Reinhard and Nadine H. Rund, USPHS/IHS, Tucson; Angie Walth, USPHS/IHS, Aberdeen; W. E. Winn, USPHS/IHS, Anchorage; Ruth Alterman, Association on American Indian Affairs; Ruth Brock, Alcohol and Drug Problems Association of North America; Marilyn Brown, Social and Environmental Research Associates; Richard D. Bushnell, Washington/Alaska Blue Cross; H. W. Finkler, Indian and Northern Affairs, Ottawa; Edward F. Helmick, Alaska Native Health Board; V. William Harris, Centers for Youth Development and Achievement; J. Z. Kramer, Commissioned Officers Association of the USPHS; Joe M. Keck, Cortez Community Mission, Inc.; League of Women Voters, Minneapolis, Dallas, Minnesota; Margaret M. Mangold, Family Service Association of America; Agnes Marshall Harmon, Social Research Group; Philip A. May, Navajo Health Authority; Susan McGreevy, Kansas City Museum; Michael

Nolin, Navajo Health Systems Agency; Ernest J. Turner, Seattle Indian Alcoholism Program; Betty J. Bachman, Arizona; George Abrams, New York; Veronica Evaneshko, Arizona; Nancy Gerein, British Columbia; Marilyn L. Krause, Arizona; Joan Hampson, Washington; William F. Sears, Colorado; Kathleen Schweitzberger, Stanford University Libraries; Jerry Holtz, Teachers College Library, Columbia University.

Partial support for the project was provided by the National Institute of Alcoholism and Alcohol Abuse Grant #1 R03 AA03348-01 MSM and by the Bureau of General Research, Kansas State University. Ellen Taylor, Interlibrary Loan Librarian at Kansas State University Library obtained a great deal of the material cited. Jeri McDonald, Joshua McDonald and Kyle McDonald encouraged us and gave willingly of their time so that we could complete this work, while Ursula Chachere, Pat Mail's long suffering housemate, patiently tolerated a flood of papers, books and index cards for several years. Special support and encouragement was also provided by Ernest and Pat Turner. Mary Ann Draye, University of Washington School of Nursing, provided access to the Health Sciences Library there. Cecily Young typed the manuscript.

We welcome correspondence from anyone who identifies errors of commission or omission so that corrections may be made in any future editions.

All opinions expressed are those of the authors and do not reflect official positions or policies of the agencies or institutions with which the authors are associated.

Native American Alcohol Use: A Review
of the Literature

Introduction

The earliest accounts of Native American alcohol use appeared in the historical literature on conquest and settlement. These descriptions launched the firewater myth that Native Americans are constitutionally unable to handle liquor. However, two facts belie this persistent folk wisdom, even in these early sources: When they were first introduced to liquor, Native Americans did not act in the stereotyped way, which suggests they learned such drunken comportment from frontiersmen; and even after the stereotyped behavior became common, they exhibited selective restraint over their drunken behavior (MacAndrew and Edgerton 1969: 113, 156).[1]

The first modern contributions to the literature on Native American drinking appear primarily in anthropological studies, where discussions on alcohol use are incidental to some other focus, usually an overall view of life in the tribe described. Such materials classified in the Human Relations Area Files have formed the basis for a number of cross-cultural comparisons of drinking practices,[2] such as Horton's (1943) landmark study of the relationship between anxiety and drinking.

Between 1945 and the late 1960s several anthropologists singled out Native American alcohol use as a major focus of some pioneering studies.[3] Most of the monographs of the past ten years have included anthropologists on the team, or have been written solely by them.[4] In addition, valuable collections of recent alcohol research which include material on North American Indians have been edited by anthropologists.[5] Two of the shortest published items by an anthropologist (Lurie 1972, 1971) may turn out to be among the most important, as discussed below in the section on Explanations for Native American Drinking Behavior.

Among the unpublished items, about two-thirds of the thirty-two Ph.D. dissertations included in this bibliography were written by anthropolgists. The balance are thinly scattered among the disciplines of education, geography, health sciences, history, humanistic studies, psychology, sociology and social work. The dissertations by anthropologists include clusters at a few universities where prominent scholars have inspired an interest in research on Native American drinking among their students. John J. Honigmann at the University of North Carolina at Chapel Hill was responsible for one of these. His untimely death in 1977 was a great loss for all anthropologists, particularly the small group of specialists in Native American drinking. We hope his collaborator and wife, Irma Honigmann, will remain active in the field.[6]

Although anthropology has dominated the literature on Native American drinking so far, since the 1960s other disciplines have become active and this trend has intensified since 1970.[7] For example, a recent body of work by Westermeyer, a psychiatrist with training in anthropology, qualifies as a major contribution; he has published a series of articles which cover the principal topics of interest in the field: a concise debunking of myths and review of the literature (1974a); variability in Native American drinking styles (1972b); a challenge to the notion that Native Americans do not become "alcoholics" (1972a); treatment facility use patterns of Native Americans, both for a Native American facility (1974c) and for a general population facility (Westermeyer and Lang 1975); cross-cultural guidelines for clinical studies (1974b) and treatment of alcohol problems (1976a); the association between alcohol and violent death (Westermeyer and Brantner 1972); and methods for simplifying the problem of assessing the extent of problem drinking to produce data more easily comparable among groups.[8]

Most of the bibliographic entries refer to the United States; about thirteen per cent deal with native peoples of Canada. The importance of the Canadian contributions is greater than this proportion would suggest, however. For example, the bibliography on culture and alcohol use (Popham and Yawney 1967) include materials on Native Americans which have encouraged early attempts at synthesis. A Canadian group (Fenna, Mix, Schaefer and Gilbert 1971) initiated the recent studies comparing metabolism rates between Native Americans and other ethnic groups; and more recent Canadian work by Reed, Kalant, Gibbins, Kapur and Rankin (1976) has considerably refined the earlier approaches to this subject. Important work has come from the Addiction Research Foundation of Ontario, the Canadian Department of Northern Affairs and National Resources, the Canadian Department of Indian and Northern Affairs, and the National Museum of Canada, as well as several Canadian universities (British Columbia and St. Paul, for example). The Canadians have not only made important direct contributions to this literature, but also have helped many U.S. researchers, such as Honigmann and some of his students, to work in their country.

Since the contributions before 1970 have been given detailed treatment by Leland (1976a) and others, we concentrate here on the more recent items concerning: the association between Native American drinking and other misfortunes; alcohol use in subpopulations of Native Americans; a debunking of myths about alcohol use by Native Americans; treatment of problem drinkers; and explanations for Native American drinking behavior. Much of the information which follows is from Leland (1977) and was prepared for the Third Special Report to Congress on Alcohol and Health of the National Institute on Alcohol Abuse and Alcoholism (NIAAA). NIAAA has generously granted permission to present most of that same material here, so that it will be available to more people.

The Associations between Native American Problem Drinking and other Misfortunes

The indicators used for assessing the extent of problem drinking among Native Americans are by necessity mostly indirect, and not very satisfactory (see Levy and Kunitz 1974, 1971a). For the most part, trends and the relative prevalence of alcohol problems in this group have been inferred from the relative incidence of other misfortunes with which they are assumed to be associated, principally suicide, accidents, homicide, crime, and cirrhosis.

Suicide and Suicide Rates

The seriousness of Native American alcohol problems often is argued and illustrated in terms of the apparent close association in this group between drinking and violence, particularly suicide. At least thirty-six items[9] on this subject have appeared in recent years, most of them since 1967.

Recent word from the Indian Health Service (USHEW 1977:a*) indicates that the suicide rate among U.S. Native Americans is nearly twice the national average--about twenty-two[10] per 100,000 population, as opposed to approximately eleven per 100,000 for the nation as a whole. Furthermore, suicides among Native Americans are increasing,[11] and at a faster rate than in the general population; the ratio was 1:1 in 1968; in 1974 it was 1:8. Currently suicide is the tenth leading cause of death among Native Americans and ranks even higher among young Native American adults.

Frederick (1973) claims that over seventy-five per cent of all Native American suicides are alcohol-related, a rate said to be two or three times higher than in the general population.[12]

The literature on Native American suicides presents a far more varied picture than is suggested by such summary statistics.

The Native American suicide rates reported here vary among groups from about eight per 100,000 population to over 120 per 100,000 (see Table 1); that is, from considerably less than the national average to over ten times as high. Suicide attempt rates, not covered in the table but presented in a number of the reports, also vary greatly among tribes.

Shore (1975:86) comments:

> High suicide rates among Indian tribes with a relatively small population base have received widespread publicity and have been generalized to include all American Indians. On the other hand, examples of lower suicide rates from larger tribes have received little or no emphasis. Incomplete epidemiological statistics, a misunderstanding of the reported high rates for the small tribes, and articles in national news magazines have portrayed the stereotype of "the suicidal Indian." This stereotype is misleading and self-defeating for suicide prevention programs. Major misconceptions and their consequences are: first, an assumption that all American Indians have identical health problems and

---

* Citations in this literature review marked with an asterisk appear at the end.

Table 1. Reported Suicide Death Rates for Indians

Group	Rates per 100,000 pop.	Time Period	Trend	Reference
Oglala Sioux Pine Ridge Res.	0	1966-1967	0	Mindell & Stuart 1969:29
Chippewa	6	1940-1964	?	Paredes 1966*, Cit. Westermeyer & Brantner 1972
Quinalt Res.	0	1965-1969	0	Patterson 1969, Cit. Havighurst 1971:176
Navajo Res.	8	1954-1969	-	Levy and Kunitz 1974:100
Hopi	8	1956-1965	-	Levy and Kunitz 1971b:112
Hopi	10*	"Contemporary"	-	Levy and Kunitz 1974:102
E. Pueblos	10*	1954-1962	↑	Levy 1972*:597
All Native Americans	11	1959-1966	0	Havighurst 1971:174, 177
Navajo	13	10/68-4/71	0	Miller & Schoenfeld 1971:191
Northwest tribes (without Ft. Hall)	14	1969-1971	0	Shore 1975:89
Papago 1/	18	1969-1971	0	Conrad & Kahn, 1974*:70
Apache	21	1953-1962	-	Levy & Kunitz 1974:101-102
All Native Americans 24 res. states	22	1971	↑	Frederick 1973:6
All Native Americans 24 res. states	23	1967	↑	Ogden et al. 1970
Aberdeen Area, IHS	26	1968	½↑	Burnap 1972:Table 6
NW (with Ft. Hall)	28	1969	0	Shore 1972*:67, 1972:96
NW (with Ft. Hall)	28	1969-1971	0	Shore 1975:89
Papago 1/	30	1967-1971	0	Conrad & Kahn 1974*:70
Cheyenne	48	1960-1968	0	Barter & Weist 1970, Cit. Shore 1972*:92
Ft. Hall	69	1960-1969	↑↓	Havighurst 1971:176, Cit. Watson 1969
Ft. Hall	83	1960-1966	↑↓	Havighurst 1971:176, Cit. Dizmang 1968
Ft. Hall	98	1961-1968	0	Shore et al. 1972:1086
Ft. Hall	122	1969-1971	0	Shore 1975:89

-4-

Table 1. (continued)

Group	Rates per 100,000 pop.	Time Period	Trend	Reference
All Native Americans**	Sl H#	?	0	Reznick & Dizmang 1971:883
Various tribes	vary	?	?	May & Dizmang 1974:22
Mohave	?	1950's?	?	Devereux 1961, Cit. Bynum 1972:369
Cheyenne	0***	1966?	?	Curlee 1969:35
Cheyenne	H##	1966	epidemic	Dizmang 1967:8
Great Plains	H	?	0	May 1973*, Cit. May & Dizmang 1974:23
Blackfeet	47%H	?	0	Pambrun 1970:42
Ft. Hall (ages 15-24)	H	1961-1968	0	Dizmang et al. 1974*:45
Eskimo	doubled	1965	↑	Kraus 1972:69; Kraus 1973; and Bloom 1974*, Cit. Shore 1975:87

* Range 0-22. Levy 1972:605
** Some tribes 5-10 times higher
*** 15 attempts

#Sl H = slightly higher
H = higher

0 indicates stability
↑ indicates upward
↓ indicates downward
? indicates unknown

1/ The rate for 1969-71 is 30, but if averaged over a longer period (1967-71) including two years without any suicides, the rate is 18.

-5-

subsequently the same suicide pattern and rates; second,
a failure to recognize the importance of tribal differences;
and third, a danger that public health personnel will not
individualize their approach in developing tribal
programs for suicide prevention and crisis intervention.

Shore is referring to the wide swings in annual rates which can be produced in a small sample by a few cases, or by even a single one. For example, in 1969-1971 there were ten suicides reported among the Papago, yielding an annual rate of thirty per 100,000, nearly three times the national average. However, in the preceding two years there had been no suicides; if the average is calculated over the five-year period (1967-1971), the rate is only eighteen per 100,000--about one and one-half times the national rate (Conrad and Kahn 1974:70). The use of three-year centered averages only partially smooths out the yearly fluctuations, even for all Native Americans in the U.S. combined (see footnote 11); in individual tribes, the instability arising from the small numbers of cases is of course even more pronounced.

Westermeyer (personal communication) suggests the use of "person years" of exposure to potential suicide rather than the arbitrary "Rates per 100,000 population" (as in Table 1), which become meaningless for small populations. The number of suicides per 300,0C "person years" could result from studying 300,000 persons for one year or 15,000 people for twenty. We could have confidence in the data from studies based on a large number of "person years", disregard the rest, or at most include them to show the range of suicide rates in small populations.

Year to year variations within groups may be more than an artifact of small sample size, however; Shore (1975:91) notes that incidents tend to occur in clusters, among families or high-risk groups; in other words, suicide tends to be contagious among Native Americans as well as among the general population.

Even though Native American suicide rates may be high, remember that we are talking about small absolute numbers--1971 was the first year that the total number of reported Native American suicide deaths exceeded one hundred (Frederick 1973:6). The number in the general population was over 22,000 that year. Furthermore, Native American suicide rates may be inflated, in comparison to the general population; their suicide deaths and attempts probably are more reliably reported, because a high proportion of Native Americans receive medical service from a single entity, the Indian Health Service--which keeps careful records.

Nevertheless, when all such possible sources of distortion are taken into account, there remains convincing evidence that suicide rates are much higher among some Native American groups than in the population at large. Research in Canada indicates a similar state of affairs in that country (see, for example, Butler 1966; Cutler and Morrison 1971; Stanbury 1975; Termansen and Ryan 1970).

Suicide Victims

Despite the variability in suicide rates among tribes, Native Americans exhibit remarkable similarities in the age of the victims. While in the general population suicide rates tend to increase with age (Frederick 1973:7), in tribe after tribe of Native Americans we find that suicide is prevalent among young people, and starts to taper off after the cohort of ages twenty-four to thirty-four. The Native American population contains a high proportion of young people--the very age which is at greatest risk for suicide in that group.[13]

On the other hand, Native Americans follow general population patterns by exhibiting great sex differences in the incidence of suicide deaths and attempts. <u>Completed</u> suicides are far more common among males than females, both in the general population (an average of seventy-four per cent males for the period 1959-1966) and, even more so, among Native Americans (eighty-three per cent males for the same period) according to Ogden, Spector and Hill (1970:76).[14] Although many reports mention the prevalence of male suicides, they rarely quantify sex ratios, which would allow comparisons among groups and with the population at large.

In the case of suicide <u>attempts,</u> the sex differences run in the opposite direction from suicide deaths, both for Native Americans and for the general population--far more females than males make unsuccessful suicide gestures. Females make seventy per cent of the suicide attempts among Native Americans; the rates for all races are similar, according to Frederick (1973:4). Many of the reports quantify sex ratios for attempts (though not for deaths), and these figures vary widely among tribes. The ratio of suicide deaths to attempts also differs from tribe to tribe.

Suicide Trends

A majority of the Native American suicide studies cover only short periods of time, and thus shed no light on trends over time in the groups reported upon.

Cultural roots and precedents for self-destructive behavior are claimed for a few tribes (see Barter and Weist 1970; Dizmang 1967, 1968; Levy and Kunitz 1974). Levy and Kunitz have supplemented their own data with historical records and shown that Navajo, Apache and Hopi suicide rates appear to have remained stable for long periods of time. Their work underscores the importance of incorporating whatever longitudinal data can be found. Such evidence of historical precedents for suicide patterns led Shore (1975:91) to remark:

> ...long-standing cultural and historical influences that possibly affect a suicide pattern in specific tribes may be far more resistant to change than we have previously acknowledged.

If this is true, the implications for prevention programs are great.

Other scholars[15] contend that suicide is a recent development among

Native Americans. Unfortunately, the literature so far does not clearly indicate whether suicide is a new Native American pattern, or an old one which happens to have been recently recognized. In any case, the answer probably will be different for different tribes.

The few statements we have on short-term trends within groups show no consistent pattern. Havighurst (1971:176) points to recent sharp fluctuations at Fort Hall and Quinault Reservations. Krause (1973; 1972: 69) and Bloom (1974*, cited in Shore 1975:87) report a sharp increase in Eskimo suicide rates since 1965. Burnap (1972:3, and Table 7) shows that rates are stable in half the Aberdeen area groups, and sharply rising in the other half.

The remainder of the reports are silent on trends. Thus, the literature on Native American suicide neither confirms nor denies the reported upward trend in suicide death rates for all Native Americans combined (Frederick 1973).

Most important, for our purposes here, is to explore the role of alcohol in Native American suicides. Nearly all the suicide reports specifically point to a connection between drinking and suicide; and even the exceptions do not deny an association--they simply do not mention one. However, the extent of the relationship and its postulated nature vary greatly among the reports.

Very few of the reports quantify their estimates of the degree of association between suicide and alcohol among Native Americans; those who do are shown in Table 2. The estimates vary from forty-seven per cent to ninety-four per cent for suicide deaths, and from thirty-one per cent to fifty-six per cent for attempts. Part of this variation no doubt reflects real differences among tribes. However, much of it seems to come from different conceptions of what alcohol-associated means. To some this phrase (or various similar ones) may mean simply intoxication at the time of the act; for others it is used only to refer to frequent, chronic problem drinking; some are concerned only about alcohol use by the victims; others may include companions, or family. The nature of the hypothesized relationship varies from "co-occur," to "contributing" to strong implications of causation. However, one of the few controlled attempts to test the relationship produced negative results. Levy and Kunitz (1974:103) say:

> That Navajos tend to commit acts of aggression while drunk is a common observation. That it is the effects of ethanol that cause such acts has been accepted as fact by virtually all students of the Navajo. However, steadily increased use of alcohol does not appear to have appreciably influenced homicide and suicide rates.

The degree and nature of the association between Native American suicide and alcohol cannot be assumed; it must be demonstrated--one of the many facets of the subject where more research is needed.

Much of the literature on Native American suicide is devoted to explanations of the phenomenon, particularly of its prevalence among

Table 2. Association between Alcohol and Suicide

Group	Deaths	Attempts	Reference
Papago	80%	41%	Conrad & Kahn 1974*:70
All Native Americans*	75-80%		Frederick 1973:6
Ft. Hall	94%	44%	Shore et al. 1972:1089
Ft. Hall (under 25)	**		Dizmang et al. 1974:45*
Navajo	47%		Shore 1975:88
Navajo (pre 1945)	71%	0	Shore 1975:89
Navajo		74%M, 16%F	Miller and Schoenfeld 1971:191
Aberdeen Area, IHS		34%	Burnap 1972:Table 3
NW with Ft. Hall		55%	Shore 1972*:94
NW without Ft. Hall		31%	Shore 1972*

* reservation states
** mentioned only incidentally

young males. The discussion centers primarily on social and cultural factors, and parallels so closely the speculations covering the causes for high rates of problem drinking that, to avoid repetition, the topic will be incorporated into that portion of this chapter.

Alcohol and Accidental Death

Although accidents are the leading cause of death among Native Americans (USHEW 1977a*), and the logic of the relationship between accidents and alcohol is more straightforward than that of the lower-ranking suicide (tenth), it is curious that accidental death has been the central focus of far fewer reports.[16] Native American accident rates (and hence absolute numbers) are much higher than suicide rates (157.1[17] versus 21.8[18] per 100,000 population in 1971). The ratio of Native American to total population rates also are higher for accidental death (2.9:1) than for suicide (1.7:1)--1971 figures--see U.S. Congress, Senate (1974:50).

There is wide variation among Native American groups in the incidence of accidental death, the ratio to rates in non-Native American comparison groups, trends, the degree of alcohol involvement reported, and the postulated explanations for this epidemiological phenomenon. The reports are primarily devoted to documenting the extent of accidental deaths and demonstrating the high association with alcohol use. The fact that rates have remained stable since 1955 (U.S. Congress, Senate 1974:50) is mildly encouraging, but then matters could hardly get worse. Alcohol associated accidents are also reported to be a serious problem among Canadian native peoples--see Badcock (1976); Bienvenue and Latif (1974); Cutler and Morrison (1971); Hanlon (1972); Schmitt, Hole and Barclay (1966); Stanbury (1975); Termansen and Ryan (1970). The overall picture of Native American accidental death seems, if anything, more alarming than the suicide situation, and yet the literature contains much less discussion of possible solutions. Relationships between alcohol and accidental deaths among Native Americans clearly deserve more attention than they have so far received.

Alcohol and Homicide

Native American homicide is another form of violent death which has received less attention[19] than suicide, despite the fact that as of 1971 it ranked higher (ninth versus tenth), the rates were slightly higher (20.6 versus 18.7 per 100,000), and the rates compare even more unfavorably with those of the total population (2.4 times as great versus 1.7 times for suicide). The 1955-1971 rate of increase (thirty-seven per cent versus ninety-nine per cent) was lower for homicide than for suicide, however (U.S. Congress, Senate 1974:50).

As in the case of suicide, Native American homicide tends to occur at an earlier age than among non-Native Americans. The average age of the killer is almost twenty years younger for Native Americans than among the general population, a fact which is disturbing not only for its poignancy, but for its future implications, given the relative youth of the Native American population.

The literature on Native American homicide gives the impression, based on both anecdotal and statistical evidence, that alcohol involvement tends to be more pronounced in homicides than in suicides, but the sample is too small to serve as a basis for firm generalizations. For homicide there is less agreement than for suicide as to the nature of the relationship to alcohol. The prevalence of homicide among Native Americans and its apparent association with alcohol abuse indicates a need for more research. Among the Navajo, greatly increased use of alcohol was not found to be associated with an increase in homicides by Levy, Kunitz and Everett (1969).

Alcohol and Crime

This brings us to the more general and controversial topic of Native American crime rates and the role of alcohol. Stewart (1964) made the first extensive comparison between Native American and total population arrests. His results probably have been relied upon more than anyone else's to demonstrate the extent of problem drinking among Native Americans. Stewart (1964:65) found that:

> Throughout the nation, on Indian reservations and in urban centers, Indians have been arrested and convicted for illegal acts while under the influence of liquor at rates several times higher than have individuals of other minority groups. Furthermore, Indians have a crime rate for non-alcohol connected crimes higher than the national average and higher than any other minority group in the nation.

These results disturbed Stewart (1964:65):

> As an anthropologist who has studied the American Indian for thirty years, the conclusions expressed above come as a surprise and shock, and will be surprising to many others. Since the last of the Indian Wars about the turn of the century, the Indians have been thought of as a peaceful, inoffensive, weak people with some strange customs...Indians have been called lazy, dirty, and drunken by white Americans convinced of their own innate superiority, but the adjectives lawless, illegal, criminal or crooked have seldom if ever been used to characterize them.
>
> The fact that the relative rate of crime of Indians has not been generally acknowledged may be only a result of their absolutely small proportion of the nation.

The main challenge to Stewart's conclusions has been the charge of differential arrests, variously attributed to Native American visibility (their distinctive appearance and the relatively raucous nature of their intoxication), or to outright discrimination by the police and/or the courts.[20] The latter charge has been challenged in a number of studies which either convincingly deny discrimination (Stauss, Jensen and Harris 1977), or go further to allege the opposite--that the police and judges go easy on Native Americans.[21]

Bienvenue and Latif (1974:114) argue that in the absence of control over such variables as social class and neighborhood, the data are not adequate for assessing the discretionary role of the legal system in the high arrest and incarceration rates for Native Americans. Discrimination both in favor of and against Native Americans may tend to cancel each other out. More important, however, it seems impossible that discrimination could be severe enough to account for the degree of over-representation of Native Americans in the crime statistics. This over-representation is confirmed in studies of Native American groups where specific controls for bias have been employed--see Graves (1970:38). Native Americans are considerably over-represented in federal prisons, where they comprise 2.2 per cent of the inmates, yet they represent only one per cent of the country's population. In state prisons Native Americans are only slightly over-represented (1.2 per cent of inmates versus one per cent of the country's population), however.

Native Americans have consistently been arrested at approximately three times the Black rate and ten times the White rate,[22] according to age-adjusted figures[23] for 1950-1968 (Reasons 1972:320). These ratios have been fairly stable for that period, but represent an apparent increase over von Hentig's (1945:77) 1936-1940 ratio of 3.5 Native American arrests to every one in the general population. Despite a number of reports showing that in particular Native American groups, most arrests are for minor offenses,[24] this does not appear to be the case for Native Americans as a whole.[25]

For drinking-related offenses, the disparity between Native American and general population rates is even greater--about eight times the Black rate and over twenty times the White rate in the U.S.[26] Canadian native peoples also have been reported to be over-represented in alcohol associated arrests--see Bennett (1963); P. Brown (1952); D. G. Smith (1975); and a high proportion of arrested Canadian native people have been reported as drinking at the time an offense was committed (Finkler 1975; Honigmann and Honigmann 1970). These disproportionate rates of drinking-related arrests are one of the principal statistics cited to show that Native Americans have a greater drinking problem than the rest of the population--see Jensen, Stauss and Harris (1975). If we agree that alcohol-associated arrests are a drinking problem, the conclusion is inescapable.

The reservations where sale of liquor has been legalized (eighty-six reservations on April 27, 1977, by the BIA Division of Law Enforcement) provide a relatively untapped natural laboratory for studying some of the relationships between alcohol and arrests among Native Americans. May (1975:132) reports on a large Great Plains tribe which legalized the sale of liquor on the reservation[27] for a very short period in 1970. During the two months, arrests in the border town decreased considerably, as expected. However, contrary to expectations, arrests for intoxication on the reservation did not rise commensurately; in fact, arrests for intoxication by reservation police were lower than average during the period. Although May warns that no firm conclusions can be drawn from these tantalizing data, they certainly suggest the desirability of testing the hypothesis that alcohol legalization is associated with lower incidence of trouble with the law, especially the non-Native American legal system of the border county.[28] On the other hand, Levy and Kunitz (1974:180) seem to suggest that on-reservation sale of liquor contributes to the higher rates of cirrhosis among Apache as compared to the nearby Navajo, where tribal prohibition still is in force. A detailed comparison of the experiences of the tribes which have legalized liquor sales would certainly seem to be in order.

Despite the complications involved in interpreting Native American arrest figures, it seems to follow that Native American drinking and arrests are linked. Even if Native American drinking is more visible than other people's; even if Native Americans are discriminated against; even if they do not try as hard to avoid arrest;[29] even if tribal prohibition creates conditions which encourage arrests in nearby towns (see Riffenburgh 1964:42) and the effects of earlier national prohibition for Native Americans continue through the persistence of rapid drinking (said to have developed in response);[30] even if multiple arrests of a few individuals unduly affect the arrest statistics (for example, Littman 1970:1770); even if one compensates for all manner of conditions peculiar to Native Americans which could distort the results--it is hard to see how these could account for a drinking-related arrest differential of 20 to 1. In any case, whatever the explanations, we must face the fact that Native Americans experience more arrests related to drinking than other people do.

We also must acknowledge, however, that alcohol alone cannot account for the high Native American crime rates nationwide, because even the non-drinking related offense ratios are over four times higher for Native Americans than for Whites (but about the same as for Blacks). Since the Native American population is growing as a proportion of the total, if present rates continue or increase, Native American crime is bound to become more noticeable and troublesome over time.

Alcohol and Cirrhosis

Cirrhosis of the liver is generally acknowledged to be related to excessive alcohol consumption (Kunitz, Levy and Everett 1969:673). As of 1971, cirrhosis was the fourth ranking cause of death among Native Americans (up from eleventh in 1955[31]); it occurred nearly three times as often among Native Americans (46/100,000) as in the general population, and has increased by 185 per cent since 1955 (U.S. Congress, Senate 1974: 50).

Despite the prominence of cirrhosis among Native American health problems, and its high association with alcohol abuse in any population, the subject has not received extensive treatment in the literature on Native American drinking, and is not invoked as an indicator of the extent of Native American problems as often as the figures would seem to justify. Although a high incidence of cirrhosis has been mentioned in a few reports covering various Native American groups,[32] the subject has received detailed treatment only for California Native Americans of mixed tribal background (Day 1976*) and for three southwestern tribes (Kunitz, Levy and Everett 1969; Kunitz, Levy and Odoroff 1971; Levy and Kunitz, 1974; 1969). Among the California groups, Native American cirrhosis death rates were twice that of the comparison groups, both by sex and for both sexes combined. Rates were highest in rural counties. Among the Southwest tribes, the Navajo cirrhosis rates were slightly lower than the national age-adjusted rates, while the Apache and especially the Hopi rates greatly exceeded those for the general population. However, the small absolute numbers of Apache and Hopi cases dictate caution; these findings should be confirmed over longer periods before they can be considered established.

The cirrhosis rate rankings among the three tribes are surprising because the Navajo and Apache are noted for public drunkenness, while the Hopi have the opposite reputation. To explain their puzzling results, Levy and Kunitz (1974:106-107, 180; 1971a:232; 1969:16-17) propose a series of relationships between persisting aboriginal cultural patterns, present day drinking style, and relative accessibility of liquor supply. However, until we have firmer evidence that the cirrhosis rate for the Apache and Hopi is <u>consistently</u> higher than for the Navajos, explanations really are premature.

There are said to be three times as many male as female drinkers among Native Americans (USNCAI 1973), although the literature indicates that this varies greatly among tribes. However, there are some indications that the Native American women who do drink may be even more vulnerable to cirrhosis than men. For example, the death rate in observed cirrhosis cases was twice as high among Navajo females (twenty-eight per cent) as among males (fourteen per cent), according to the figures of Kunitz, Levy and Odoroff (1971:714); the Indian Health Service (NCAI 1973:5) reports a sex ratio in deaths from cirrhosis of only .78 males to every female. These differences might be accounted for by any number of conditions, and certainly merit more investigation.

A number of works discuss a variety of other misfortunes associated with alcohol use by Native Americans.[33]

Alcohol Use in Subpopulations of Native Americans

Youth

The effects of parental alcoholism on youth have been treated in a number of recent studies.[34] Most of these enumerate problems experienced by the children and use anecdotal evidence to establish their association with alcohol. Child abuse and neglect, removal of children to foster homes, poor school attendance and educational achievement, delinquency, high drop-out rates, early drinking by children themselves, and poor health (physical and mental) are among the most frequently cited effects.

However, in some of the studies which have attempted to test the association more formally, the results are not always clear-cut. For example, in a Pueblo village Kaufman (1973) found no association between the incidence of parental alcohol abuse and glue sniffing among children. Honigmann and Honigmann (1970:198) found, contrary to their expectations, that high parental expenditures for alcohol were not associated with poor adaptation to school by their children.

Although one can hardly doubt that family alcohol abuse affects Native American children, clear and unequivocal demonstrations of the nature and the degree of these effects have proved to be as elusive for youth as for adults. Recent studies[35] suggest, with varying amounts of conviction and supporting evidence, high (but varying) rates of drinking accompanied by associated problems among Native American youth.

Among the recent indications of the very early appearance of problem drinking among Native American children is a case of delirium tremens reported in a nine-year-old Native American boy (Sherwin and Meade 1975:1211); in every aspect except age of the patient, the example was a classic case, according to the authors. Of course a single case proves nothing, but the frightening possibility exists that other examples have simply been overlooked because no one expected to find delerium tremens in a child so young.

Native American infants have figured prominently in the early reports of the Fetal Alcohol Syndrome--patterned abnormalities in children born to alcoholic mothers.[36] Photographs of Native American subjects appeared in several of the earliest reports; one of these (Jones, Smith and Hanson 1976:130) reported that a Native American presented the most striking degree of postnatal growth deficiency encountered to date. Although there is legitimate cause for alarm in these reports, they should not be interpreted as reliable evidence of high rates of alcohol abuse among Native American mothers. Clinical impressions are generally poor bases for epidemiological inference and the samples of some of these early reports are subject to bias. They were drawn from public hospitals, where low-income people (which includes most Native Americans) are undoubtedly over-represented in the population. Nevertheless, these reports should not be ignored and can help detect problems of alcohol abuse among other Native Americans at an early stage--when the chances of helping both the infant and the mother are at their best. As for the alcohol-associated behavior of women, as indicated in the introduction, there is not enough material in the literature so far to warrant a separate review section here.

Speculation about the causes of drinking problems among Native American children receives more attention than attempts to demonstrate relationships formally. One study of special interest, by a Native American (Boatman 1968:10), reports that among Native American student subjects, drinking levels and attitudes are not correlated with status deprivation, but are associated with anomia, which he defines as:

> ...the individual's feelings regarding the indifference of community leaders to his needs, hopelessness regarding accomplishing positive goals because of the unpredictability of society, the feeling that one's personal goals are becoming ever more unobtainable, and the feeling that one is really unable to count on one's associates for social and psychological support...

Among the suggested solutions to the problem of alcohol abuse by Native American youth, the possibilities of preventive education are most frequently emphasized, particularly approaches which incorporate Native American self-determination[37] and traditional Native American values--see Pinto 1973; Werden 1974a, 1974b.

The possibilities for research on alcohol and Native American youth hardly have been scratched. Given the fact that a high proportion of Native Americans are young and apparently are launching their drinking careers very early, research on their use of alcohol would appear to be a high priority.

City Dwellers

The number of studies of Native Americans in urban settings has increased as the proportion of off-reservation dwellers has grown (to nearly half according to the 1970 census).[38] Most of these reports mention alcohol use, but in general they do not provide a very clear picture of the relationship between Native American drinking and adjustment to urban life. There is a general consensus that urban Native Americans do a lot of excessive drinking.[39] But is there more of this in the city than on the reservations?

Graves (1970) seems to imply as much, but he did not attempt to compare incidence of drunkenness on and off the reservation. Kunitz, Levy and Odoroff (1971:711) found more cirhosis among Hopis in town than on the reservation, but the numbers involved were small. Among the Navajo, where tribal prohibition still is in force, more cirrhosis was found near border towns than in more isolated areas of the reservation; but data were insufficient for comparisons between Navajo on and off the reservation (Kunitz, Levy and Odoroff 1971:711). Thus the data suggest, but do not demonstrate, that there is more alcohol abuse in towns than on the reservation. Ablon (1964:298) acknowledges that city stress often does exacerbate alcohol problems of Native Americans, but her results are not quantified:

> Such domestic problems as the drinking and violence common to many Indian families do not appear to be peculiar results of the shift from rural to urban life, but rather characteristic features of reservation family and social disorganization which are carried to the city and <u>intensified</u> by new pressures and the departure from the stability of immediate family and community (emphasis supplied).

On the other hand, Garbarino (1971:195) reports that there is less problem drinking in the city than in the town, according to one Native American.

Since we do not know if Native American alcohol abuse is worse in the city than on the reservations, we do not have the answer to a related question of interest. If it should be established that there is more excessive drinking in the city, is city life or some other factor the cause? For example, perhaps the reservations simply export (eject) their alcohol abusers. Kunitz, Levy and Odoroff (1971:717) and Ablon (1965:364) suggest this may be the case.

Alcohol abuse is often used as a principal indicator of Native American maladjustment to city life. The association between socioeconomic factors and excessive drinking is a prominent theme in the literature.[40] The postulated nature of the relationships between these and other factors are complex and will be discussed below.

Studies of urban Native Americans agree on the importance as orientation centers of Native American bars and drinking groups in urban Native American social organization.[41] Most of the reports also mention that by no means all the people who use these centers get into trouble over drinking. Many Native American bars are in the skid row areas of towns and cities. Siegal, Peterson and Chambers report (1975*) that minority group members, including Native Americans, tend to be overrepresented in these areas in terms of their proportion of the general population. Minority group members also tend to be younger and less deteriorated than the average skid row inhabitants. In addition, the skid row social environment may be one of the most accepting that Native Americans encounter in the city.[42] Furthermore, skid row is usually the cheapest place to live. Even though there are good reasons for

Native Americans to congregate on skid row, it hardly seems an ideal environment for Native Americans in the city. The possibility of providing the services now offered by Native American bars in alternate settings would seem to present an attractive opportunity for intervention and for controlled research evaluating the efficacy of such an approach.

Debunking Some Myths

The recent published literature has explicitly debunked a number of myths about Native American drinking. The classic fire-water myth, that Native Americans are racially prone to an inability to handle liquor, has been effectively attacked by MacAndrew and Edgerton (1969),[43] though the recent searches for alcohol-pertinent physiological differences in Native Americans (discussed later) provide potential, and so-far unwarranted, impetus for its revival.

The assumption that alcoholism is the major problem among Native American people has been challenged for example, by Westermeyer (1974b: 30):

> ...urgent political and economic issues may be ignored. This is especially true because much of what is done regarding alcoholism is done at the individual level, ignoring important social, cultural, and intercultural problems.
>
> It is accurate to state that alcoholism is often associated with a variety of social problems in some Indian communities today, but the relationship between alcohol and these problems is not a clearly causal one...

Although there are undoubtedly severe alcohol problems within the group, this assertion (coordinated with, but perhaps not necessarily caused by, the federal interest in Native American drinking) has almost become doctrine, without the sort of empirical base that such a status should require. This is not to say that measures should not be taken to combat problem drinking; but they should not be allowed to overshadow other urgent problems. Research on some Canadian natives also challenges for various groups the notion that alcohol use differs much from or is more of a problem among them than in the dominant society--see Blouw, Petrinka and Hildes (1973); Buckley (1968); Honigmann (1971b); Jilek-Aall (1974); Roy (1969); Williamson (1974).

It often has been argued that Native American people rarely qualify for the label "alcoholic" as used in the dominant society,[44] even though they do have many problems with alcohol. Westermeyer challenged this notion by comparing Chippewa and majority people who were hospitalized for alcohol-related problems. He found:

> In comparing these two samples...there appears to be little validity in distinguishing between majority alcoholism as one thing (i.e., "psychotic") and

Indian alcoholism as another (i.e., "social").
A similar proportion of both groups have withdrawal symptoms in the hospital. Sex ratios of
the groups do not differ significantly. Psychiatric evaluations and hepatic size and function
are similar. Except for Chippewa females, age
distributions are alike. It appears, then, that
several important variables operate independent
of ethnicity in alcoholism (1972a:326).

Leland (1976a) found that evidence in the literature was insufficient to show whether Native Americans in general can be considered somehow immune to alcoholism as manifested in the general population. Given the celebrated difficulties in defining a majority group alcoholic, which are compounded in a cross-cultural context, perhaps the wiser course would be to define Native American drinking problems in their own terms, and forget the labels.

By documenting differences in drinking attitudes and behavior among and/or within Native American tribes, Levy and Kunitz (1974) and Leland (1975) have helped debunk the myth that Native American drinking is a monolithic phenomenon universally characterized by high rates of alcohol problems.

Treatment of Native American Problem Drinkers

Some of the early efforts to deal with Native American alcohol abuse as a distinct problem appear in reports from the University of Utah School of Alcohol Studies.[45] In the absence of other models, many early programs emphasized an Alcoholics Anonymous (AA) format for treating problem drinking. Several authors have reported that the AA approach does not appeal to Native Americans.[46] Objections include AA's public discussions of personal problems, dominant society religious overtones, exclusion of non-alcoholics, efforts to influence other people's behavior and, above all, the requirement for abstinence--the latter perhaps a reaction to over-supervision by the dominant society in many matters. However, it appears that AA has been successful with Native Americans when it has been "Nativized" (probably to a point where it would be unrecognizable to other AAs)--Jilek and Jilek-Aall (1972:59); Leland (1976a:119); Littman (1967:73); Steinbring (1971*).

Western psychiatric approaches also have frequently been called inadequate for dealing with Native American problem drinking.[47] Kinzie, Shore and Pattison (1972:203*) seem to feel their "outsider's" psychiatric consultation service was helpful to Native Americans, but many of the obstacles they encountered would not have occurred in a program run by Native Americans--though other problems would have. Even Western general practitioners come in for criticism; in one case (Snyderman 1949), Native Americans are reported to have accused a White doctor of inducing a fatal case of alcoholism by prescribing whiskey as a tonic.

Lack of understanding and discrimination (conscious and unconscious)

by White staff have often been cited as interfering with treatment of
Native American drinkers. Hendrie and Hanson (1972) report on a program where White staff attitudes resulted in poorer care for Native
Americans than for other patients. Schoenfeld and Miller (1973:33)
also report negative staff reaction to Navajo alcoholics. Leon (1965)
describes a vicious circle of maladaptive interaction between BIA staff
and Native American clients.

The literature contains only a few reports of non-Native American
programs which have helped Native Americans. Hoffman and Noem (1975b)
say the Native Americans treated in an integrated program improved as
much as control patients. Kaufman, Brickner, Varner and Mashburn (1972)
report a decrease in Native American use of tranquilizers by educating
patients and Indian Health Service[48] staff on the ill effects; the
implication seems to be that a similar approach might be effective with
alcohol.[49] Christianity, particularly of the fundamentalist type, has
been one dominant-society[50] approach said[51] to deal effectively with
Native American problem drinking. However, the number of reports is
small enough to suggest that such cures tend to be short-lived (Dozier
1966:84), though there are exceptions in individual cases.

Disulfiram (a drug which causes disagreeable symptoms if alcohol
is drunk) is another dominant-society approach to alcohol abuse which
has been used in treating Native Americans.[52] The early reports were
enthusiastic. It seems that the drug was effective in counteracting
peer pressure to drink. Refusal to accept a drink by a person known to
be "on the pill" is not considered an affront, as it would be from
people who are not. An update of these evaluations would be a useful
addition to the literature.

In reaction to the apparent inadequacies of the usual Western
methods for dealing with Native American alcohol problems, the need to
adapt intervention approaches to Native American cultures has been a
recurrent theme.[53] This adaptation has been achieved to varying degrees
in different programs. Policies have been flexible enough to allow, for
example, incorporation of traditional native healing methods and practitioners.[54] A number of nativistic revitalization movements have been
found helpful in dealing with Native American problem drinkers.[55] There
are a number of historical precedents for the use of nativistic movements to control alcohol, for example the famous case of Handsome Lake
(Wallace 1959). The favorable reports on the use of traditional methods
have so far been mainly impressionistic. Joe (in Crankshaw 1976) calls
for a controlled comparison of patients who have been treated by native,
as opposed to Western methods. The Native American treatment programs
potentially are a good laboratory for research on alcohol intervention;
however, the programs probably cannot be used for this purpose until
Native American people themselves see the value and initiate the investigations.[56]

To avoid the paternalism that has characterized some programs, many
authors have urged that Native Americans be allowed to develop and run
their own alcohol programs[57] and most reports indicate that this has
happened. For one thing, the paraprofessional alcohol counselors and the

administrators of these programs almost always have been Native Americans[58]--usually recovered alcoholics.[59]

Early training programs were run primarily by Whites but Native Americans eventually contributed considerably to the programs for training alcohol counselors and administrators. The all-Native American program at Santa Cruz seems to have been well received, but so far this has not been documented in the literature. Technical assistance for the treatment programs has been provided by Native American organizations (Robinson 1974:11), as has the evaluation process (Morris and Ebrahimi 1974).

Finally, the flexible policies governing Native American alcohol programs have allowed many innovations in services, not only to the drinker, but also to those his drinking affects--see Leland 1979*; DHEW 1976b:3*. These services include substitute activities, transportation, emergency aid to families, and a wide range of assistance which in other contexts has proved helpful with the problems created by Native American drinking (Kelly and Cramer 1966). This practical and rather indirect approach may reflect the often-reported[60] Native American attitude that alcohol abuse is a social problem, rather than a disease.

In fact, Native Americans have managed to obtain a remarkable degree of autonomy over their alcohol treatment programs. The logic of having Native Americans run their own programs usually is assumed to be self-evident. However, a few studies explicitly justify the practice, citing positive benefits. For example, in some areas where Native American programs are available, a higher proportion of Native American than problem drinkers of other races appear to have entered treatment; thirty-eight per cent of total admissions were Native American in an Oklahoma program (Gregory 1975). Kline and Roberts (1973), Manning (1963), and Robinson (1974) also argue convincingly for Native American autonomy in the alcohol programs.

Will Native American self-determination survive the transfer of alcohol treatment programs from NIAAA to IHS (discussed in Leland 1979*) which began in 1978? NIAAA may have let Native Americans begin assuming control partly out of necessity,[61] in the absence of precedents for treating Native American drinking problems; IHS is not likely to be as flexible. For example, one can scarcely imagine an IHS physician listening with any receptiveness to the Apache idea of using cardinal tail feathers as a cure for drinking (Opler 1969). The notion should not be dismissed out of hand, however, because traditional healing methods are sometimes effective with certain Native Americans; we have evidence as well that treatments of <u>all</u> kinds seem to help (Towle 1975).

The transfer of Native American alcohol programs from NIAAA to the IHS has been approved and even suggested by many Native American people--see U.S. American Indian Policy Review Commission (1976); Fairbanks (1973); Region X Indian Alcohol Programs (n.d.*); U.S. Congress, Senate (1974:92-93).

Alcohol programs initiated for urban Native Americans[62] perhaps helped to provide the impetus for general health services to urban Native Americans, in the Indian Care Improvement Act of 1976.[63]

A principal defect of the treatment literature is the dearth of evaluations. However, even under the NIAAA there has been a strong movement to develop adequate techniques for evaluating Native American programs. This effort should continue under the statistics-oriented IHS. Evaluation has been inhibited primarily by not knowing how to carry it out properly. For example, Miller, Helmick, Berg, Nutting and Shorr (1974a) did not even attempt to evaluate outcome, but simply judged the efficiency with which delivery of such services as assigning patients to treatment, and record-keeping functioned; other evaluation problems are described in Rattray (1970).

However, despite the difficulties, there have been some evaluations. Wilson and Shore (1975:257-258) report a forty-four per cent improvement rate for Northwest region programs, which compared favorably with other treatment programs in the area, especially since the selection process favored the most difficult patients at the onset. These authors also are among those who have recommended interdisciplinary evaluation teams to prevent erroneous conclusions.

Shore and von Fumetti (1972) evaluated three tribally sponsored rehabilitation programs (Utah, Nevada and New Mexico). Great variation in the results achieved were reported. As long as evaluation techniques are evolving, it is especially helpful to have the same investigators evaluate several programs, so that criteria and other sources of variability can be controlled.

Efforts to evaluate the Native American alcohol programs adequately will no doubt accelerate under the IHS. The NIAAA pilot evaluations results were mixed (Towle 1974; DHEW 1976a*). Perhaps because of the emphasis on individual counseling, the per client cost of Native American programs[64] was relatively high; however, the per project cost was low, compared to the six other categories of treatment programs funded by NIAAA, possibly because tribes often provided facilities at little or no cost. The proportion of female clients[65] was slightly higher than the average for the other programs, which might mean more problem drinking among Native American women, or simply more willingness to seek treatment. Clients were younger in the Native American programs than in the others, which could reflect a Native American tendency to develop serious problems at a younger age, or merely the relative youth of the Native American population. Improvement after treatment was marked for Native American clients, but less than for the clients of the other programs.

Although evaluations of the Native American programs were not as favorable as the average for the other NIAAA programs, this is no cause for alarm.[66] It is very hard to work out evaluation criteria and techniques that are appropriate across subcultures (Westermeyer 1976a). In the meantime, it would seem more appropriate to compare Native American projects with each other, rather than with dominant-society efforts.

One suggested[67] treatment approach which does not appear to have

been tried so far is to mobilize wives in the fight against drinking--
there are indications that women sometimes can influence their husbands'
drinking habits. Identification of coping styles which work and dissemination of this knowledge might be a promising approach (Leland 1978*).

The controversial dominant-society innovation of teaching controlled
drinking might be welcomed by many Native American men, since abstinence
is so disruptive to their social life. This method does not seem to have
been tried so far. Such behavior modification techniques require more
training than the Native American staffs probably have the background to
absorb. The use of reservation bars for teaching the moderate use of
alcohol has been tried on some reservations, though not by alcohol treatment programs (Littman 1970:1784; Schusky 1975). J. A. Price (1975:25)
also has suggested teaching moderate drinking to Native Americans--and
not necessarily to those with drinking problems.

Calls for Native American prevention programs date back to the 1960s
(Association of American Indian Affairs 1964), and continue today (U.S.
American Indian Policy Review Commission 1976; Dyer 1969). Prevention
has so far taken a back seat to treatment nationwide, and it probably
does so in Native American programs as well. A dearth of materials and
tested techniques appropriate for Native Americans no doubt contributes
to the problem.

There have been suggestions (Heidenrich 1976; Leland 1976a) that
people involved in Native American alcohol programs, whether Native
American or not, are not well acquainted with the literature on the
subject. The same probably can be said of many of the researchers in
the field; any of them who want to be better acquainted with it will be
greatly aided by this annotated bibliography.

Explanations for Native American Drinking Behavior

Why do Native Americans drink? The question makes two improper
assumptions: (1) that <u>all</u> Native Americans drink (too much by implication), and (2) that such a question is answerable. The first assumption
is belied by the few studies which have looked at the range of drinking
behavior within (Graves 1970; Leland 1975) and among (Levy and Kunitz
1974) Native American groups. Many Native American people either drink
responsibly or do not drink at all--a fact which is forgotten as we
concentrate on the admittedly high proportion of Native American people
who do exhibit drinking problems. The second assumption is proved
false by our inability to explain why problem drinking occurs in <u>any</u>
particular group.

According to Brod (1975:1387):

> . . .Indians seem to use the answer to evaluate the
> attitudes of the psychiatrist; non-Indians seem to use
> the question as a substitute for "doing something"
> about a situation over which they feel diffuse guilt. . .

Whatever the reasons for asking, the question reflects deep and troubled puzzlement, not only of laymen, but of professionals, as well. Although more adequate knowledge about how Native Americans drink would logically seem to precede an attempt to answer why, perplexed preoccupation with the causes for alcohol abuse by Native Americans makes up a major segment of the literature on Native American drinking. The proposed explanations emphasize physical, social and cultural factors in varying degrees and in diverse combinations.

Physical

Several recent works on Native American drinking have focused on physical factors and the possibility of racial differences in biological sensitivity to alcohol. The underlying rationale is that apparent variations in drinking behavior among races could result from differences in brain alcohol concentration, which could be produced by biological factors--perhaps inherited, perhaps acquired.

Fenna, Mix, Schaefer and Gilbert (1971) report experiments in which a group of Canadian Natives and Eskimo[68] metabolized alcohol more slowly than Whites. Native Americans who were heavy drinkers exhibited greater adaptation to alcohol (as expressed in rate of blood alcohol clearance) than similarly classified Whites. Nevertheless, the Native Americans who were heavy drinkers metabolized alcohol more slowly than even the light-drinking Whites.[69] In addition to drinking experience, differences in diet, which also could influence metabolism rates, were taken into account, leaving the possibility of genetic factors as the cause.

Lieber (1972) called attention to methodological and other problems with the Fenna et al. (1971) study and suggested that it be repeated with more adequate controls over environmental factors and prior drug intake by the subjects. He raised the possibility of a mechanism by which (assumed) higher alcoholism rates among Native Americans might be attributable to their greater capacity for metabolic adaptation of the microsomal enzymes that appear to participate in alcohol oxidation. Bennion and Li (1976:12) pointed out that this hypothesis could be directly tested, and it probably will be soon. Ewing, Rouse and Pellizarri (1974) found no significant differences in rate of alcohol metabolism (or of absorption) between Oriental and Occidental subjects. The alcohol response of Orientals is considered by some people to be potentially pertinent. Because American Indians are thought to have come to this hemisphere from Asia, in a series of migrations across the Bering Straits, they are classified with Orientals in the anthropometric racial category "Mongoloid", and believed to share to varying degrees in Oriental gene pools. However, the connections are at best remote and, above all, conclusions about Native Americans obviously should be based on studies of Native Americans. Nevertheless, since the studies of Orientals have been cited so extensively in this new literature, I include them here.

In 1976 three more reports on Native American rates of alcohol metabolism all contradicted the earlier one by Fenna et al. (1971). Bennion and Li (1976:9) found no significant difference in alcohol metabolism rates per unit of body weight between full-blood Native Americans of mixed tribes and Whites in Arizona; they suggested that the contrary Canadian results might be accounted for by their use of inadequately matched subjects (hospitalized Native Americans versus healthy Whites) and by use of an indirect method (Breathalyzer) of measuring blood alcohol levels.

The great variability they found among individuals[70] also may play a role in the apparent contradictions between studies. Bennion and Li (1976) did confirm one finding by Fenna et al. (1971), that drinking experience apparently increases metabolism rates. However, in this study the differences were statistically significant only within the Native American group, not within the White one--again perhaps a problem of inadequately matched controls.

The other two pertinent recent studies reported results which not only contradict, but point in the opposite direction of, the findings of Fenna et al. (1971), although the findings were consistent with the idea of racial differences in alcohol response. A Canadian report by Reed, Kalant, Gibbons, Kapur and Rankin (1976) stated that the Ojibwa metabolized alcohol faster than comparison groups of Chinese and Caucasians, but this result may have been influenced by the Ojibwas' higher habitual consumption rates. The other study, by Zeiner, Paredes and Cowden (1976*) also claimed faster rates for Native Americans (Tarahumara) than for Caucasians, but did not report the actual rates, either for metabolism or habitual comsumption.

Cross-racial comparisons of physiological responses to alcohol have paralleled the metabolism studies discussed above. Wolff (1973, 1972*) reported differences among racial groups in various indicators of facial flushing. "Mongoloids" (Crees, plus Orientals of several countries of origin and degree of hybridization) exhibited more pronounced responses in less time and on less alcohol than White control groups. The short time between ingestion and rise in blood alcohol levels was interpreted as evidence that group differences are not related to variations in alcohol metabolism rates, but rather that alcohol has a direct effect on the vasomotor system. Wolff says (1973:198):

> Since cutaneous vasodilation after alcohol ingestion is probably the result of central vasomotor depression, population differences in flushing response may reflect a genetic variation in autonomic nervous system sensitivity.

Wolff reported that inexperienced Native American drinkers flushed more than experienced ones, in apparent contrast to the findings in some of the metabolism studies, that response increased with experience. On the other hand, in nondrinking Whites, alcohol produced little flushing.

Ewing, Rouse and Pellizzari (1974) also found that Oriental subjects[71] exhibited more facial flushing and associated reactions to alcohol than did Occidental controls. Moreover, these responses occurred in Orientals (full-blood and hybrids) at blood alcohol levels that had little effect on Occidentals. As possible explanations for the observed response variability, Ewing et al. (1974:209) list differences (1) in autonomic reactivity (as surmised by Wolff 1972*), (2) in levels of acetaldehyde, (3) or in some other physiologic factor. Although they seem to lean toward alternative two, they acknowledge that no specific causes have yet been demonstrated, but suggest the possibility that low rates of alcohol abuse among Oriental people may have physiological rather than cultural origins.

Zeiner, Paredes and Cowden (1976*), however, report experimental results indicating that Tarahumara did not display facial flushing, whereas Caucasian controls did so.

Thus, the results of the cross-racial comparisons of these physiological responses to alcohol are about as mixed as those concerning metabolism rates, discussed earlier. Obviously the final word is not yet in, or even in sight.

The conflicting results in these various reports no doubt reflect some great individual differences within the groups studied (see Johnston 1966*). For one thing, non-specialists are unlikely to appreciate the diversity of genes, culture and history which are subsumed under the label "Native American" (succinctly suggested in Reed, Kalant, Gibbins, Kapur and Rankin 1976). Furthermore, people whose genetic and social heritages are not necessarily homogeneous probably were included within each of the control categories, such as "Orientals", "Mongoloids" and "Caucasians." Hanna (1976) documents the fact that even in isolated groups, genetic differences between nearby villages of the same population may be greater than those between villages and other more distant, unrelated populations.

Just as every human looks detectably different from every other individual, so is each one biochemically unique (von Wartburg 1976:146*). Biomedical advances are beginning to allow detection, and hence characterization of such differences among individuals, and of sets of such differences between races. The studies described above are some of the first efforts to apply these new approaches to alcohol-related problems.

However, even at this beginning stage of the work, it already is apparent that wide variation may be exhibited, both among and within populations, in whole sets of factors which either are known to, or could, influence biological responses to alcohol. Many of these characteristics could have either hereditary or environmental (or both) antecedents. The pertinent variables include body size, shape and proportion of fat to lean muscle; alcohol dehydrogenase type;[72] drinking style, including habitual level of alcohol consumption and hence adaptation to the drug, as well as related influences: social access; degree and nature of racial mixture; personality; placebo effect (i.e., general responsiveness to stimuli versus a particular response to alcohol); age; diet; general condition and health; and even internal architecture, such as intestine length and surface configuration, as discussed in Hanna (1976). Above all, those who would explain Native American drinking on the basis of hereditary factors have to remember to demonstrate that the trait is a sex-linked one, since the incidence of problem drinking appears to be much lower among Native American women than Native American men, as is also true in the dominant U.S. society (Cahalan 1970*). The possibility of a sex-linked trait is plausible, as discussed in Jones and Jones (1976*:576-577) and Paredes (1976*:106). In the studies covered here, however, this variable has not always been included. Three studies did not have female subjects.[73] Bennion and Li (1976*) did use female subjects in both the Native American and White groups, but did not present separate analyses by sex in their original report. Wolff (1973) found no significant sex differences in facial flushing. Only Ewing and associates (Ewing, Rouse, Mueller and Mills 1976*; Ewing, Rouse and Pellizzari 1974) found and reported sex differences, a fact perhaps attributable to the participation of Beatrice Rouse on the research team.

In addition to controlling for differences in the characteristics of subjects, such as those just outlined, we also must clearly specify and reduce the methodological sources of variability: route of alcohol administration (intravenous vs. oral), initial dose size, duration of peak value, time of day (in case of diurnal variations in response), and choice of racial indicators. Studies must control for the variables just mentioned, and perhaps for a number of others not yet known to play a role, before we can be sure whether there are consistent, measurable physical differences in response to alcohol between Native Americans and other races. Even then, the relative contributions of nature versus nurture will have to be demonstrated.

Perhaps more important, plausible connections must be shown between the observed physical differences and the dependent variable of interest --Native American problem drinking. Westermeyer (1974b:30) says:

> ...the logic of such physiologic studies has been poorly worked out so far. For example, the observation that Orientals respond to alcohol in a physiologically different manner from Whites has been used to explain why Orientals have less alcoholism, but the same argument for the same reasons has been used to explain why Indians (a group quite similar to Orientals in numerous hereditary characteristics) have presumably more alcoholism. And it is a long step from merely demonstrating physiological differences to explaining what role, if any, they might play in the etiology of alcoholism.

It is easy to understand that people who are sensitive to alcohol would avoid it and the attendant unpleasant sensations. It is harder to imagine how alcohol-sensitive people could stand to drink enough to become problem drinkers. The postulated explanations perhaps give humans more credit for logic in their alcohol-related behavior than history would seem to justify. Wolff (1973:198) is well aware of the problems:

> The relevance of these findings for the problems of alcoholism remains obscure. Although Chinese and American Indians share the alcohol flushing response, the incidence of alcoholism in the two groups differs

> radically... One must draw the obvious conclusion
> that the incidence of alcoholism is determined by
> more complex factors than group variations in vasomotor
> sensitivity to alcohol. Such a biological variation
> could, however, exercise its effect through inter-
> action with sociocultural force. Conceivably, the
> prevalence of the highly visible flushing response
> will inhibit Mongoloid groups from drinking as long as
> their social structure is intact and exercises sanctions
> against intoxication. When the social cohesion of a
> culture is destroyed as it has been in the case of the
> American Indians, a greater susceptibility to alcohol
> intoxication may act as one of several predisposing
> factors for alcoholism. However, the findings of this
> report do not permit conclusions about the relation
> between biological variation in vasomotor sensitivity
> to alcohol and the incidence of alcoholism.

Ewing, Rouse, Mueller, and Mills (1976:160*) also acknowledge the contradictions, and propose the following explanation:

> Elsewhere we have suggested that ethnic groups who
> suffer major subjective discomfort on drinking may
> be significantly protected from the hazard of be-
> coming alcoholic (Ewing, Rouse and Pellizzari 1974).
> However, individual members of groups that are sub-
> ject to alcohol sensitivity might, under physiologic
> needs or social pressures, continue drinking to the
> point of developing alcoholic loss of control.

Although this particular study is not concerned with racial comparisons, the demonstration by Ewing, Rouse, Muelller, and Mills (1976*) that social factors, such as context and the pre-drinking state of subjects, have great influence on the effects of alcohol on humans also seems pertinent here, if it finally is established that Native Americans are highly sensitive to alcohol. The celebrated Native American peer pressure to drink and the pleasures of their institutionalized drinking groups (Leland 1976a:58, 76) might offset the discomfort. In fact, in all alcohol abusers, regardless of race, the pleasant mood-alterations pro-duced by the drug offset its unpleasant effects; perhaps the only dif-ference between such people and those who may be alcohol-sensitive is the threshold level for discomfort.

Von Wartburg's comments (1976*:147) seem to summarize current thinking on these physiological studies and their possible implications for Native American drinking:

> It is clear that biologic factors will never prove
> to be all-important, that is, to the exclusion of
> man's culture and social relations. Nevertheless,
> it is conceivable that people with different racial
> backgrounds have adapted over the centuries to
> differential biologic responses to alcohol by an
> adequate incorporation of alcohol consumption in a
> corresponding sociocultural context. An attempt

to search for correlations between biologic data and cultural, epidemiologic, and demographic data should be made.

However, explanations are premature until we have established the existence of the phenomenon being explained--that is, until significantly different physiological responses to alcohol by Native Americans have been adequately demonstrated.

The studies of biological responses to alcohol have generated more publicity than one would normally expect, given the restricted scope and relative inconclusiveness of the findings so far. To understand the degree of popular attention which has focused on what would normally seem to be esoteric studies, one must appreciate that: (1) the average American believes in the basic assumption of the Firewater Myth--that Native Americans suffer from hereditary, physical predispositions to alcohol problems; (2) some Native Americans apparently long for an explanation which would remove the matter from voluntary control (see for example, Akewesasne Notes 1971*:41), but combine it with a simultaneous resistance to racial explanations, which could contribute to discrimination; and (3) some social anthropologists resist[74] the idea of explaining Native American drinking behavior in physiological, genetic terms. They see such a development as a step backward, which could legitimatize the Firewater Myth they have fought against for so long.

What is the value of information about racial differences in responses to problem drinking among Native Americans? For one thing, such data could form the basis for persuasive arguments in favor of moderate drinking or abstinence in both prevention and treatment programs. Perhaps more important, these physiological differences could be measured and monitored, and thus could prove useful in behavior modification programs designed to discourage alcohol use. First, however, careful research to discover and learn the nature of such racial differences, if any, must be continued.

Social Deprivation

Various social conditions, past and present, to which Native Americans have been subjected frequently are blamed for their problem drinking. Some people trace these deprivations to the miseries resulting from political oppression, such as war and forced migration.[75] Others, such as Littman (1970); Stewart (1964); Toler (1966) reach back only as far as discriminatory prohibition,[76] which they say created an incentive to flaunt the unfair law by drinking; prevented Native Americans from learning "the proper, everday, family, self-regulated use of alcohol" (Stewart 1964:66); and encouraged the development and subsequent institutionalization of a dangerous drinking style, characterized by such behavior as rapid gulping, in the face of possible detection and arrest.

Still others[77] emphasize current (if long-standing) social conditions, such as unemployment, low income, inferior education, institutionalized oppression in boarding schools and at the hands of the BIA, discrimination, poor health, inadequate diet, substandard housing, inadequate recreational substitutes, isolation, relocation and many other misfortunes. In a number of studies the implicated deprivations are not clearly specified; when they are, the list often is so long as to defy measurement and testing. Most often, the association between alcohol and the various lacks which Native Americans suffer is merely asserted, rather than demonstrated. Exceptions to this include Maynard (1969), who showed that unemployed males had the highest mean drinking score in a Sioux group.

In a more explicit subcase of deprivation explanations, Graves (1970, 1967)[78] demonstrated the central role of economic deprivation in the adjustment of two different Native American groups--one urban and one rural. In the rural group, he found rates of drinking and intensity of feelings of deprivation higher among those who had adopted majority society goals if they had an unsatisfactory job, than if they were steadily employed, but were unrelated to the kind of job held among those who were not committed to dominant group values.

In the urban migrant group, on the other hand, all the subjects were said to be committed to dominant group goals, and all the indicators of failure in that realm were correlated with indicators of alcohol abuse and feelings of relative deprivation. The migrants who had better training for city jobs had far fewer arrests for drunkenness than the less adequately trained. Graves explains these results:

> When goals are strongly held for which society provides inadequate means of attainment, the resulting means-goals "disjunction" produces pressures for engaging in alternative, often nonapproved adaptations, of which excessive drinking is one common form (Graves 1970:42).

He proposes a theory which synthesizes two major intellectual traditions:

> One embodies theories of psychopathology, which treat drunkenness as one of many "neurotic" responses to conditions of psychic stress. Critical elements in these theories are such things as conflicts between competing but mutually incompatible goals, or the disjunctions that result from unfulfilled aspirations. The other is made up of socialization theories, which treat drunkenness as learned behavior. Critical elements are the social modes provided, and the pattern of social reinforcements and punishments by which behavior is social [sic] modified and directed. These two bodies of theory are complementary: each explains exactly what the other leaves out. Disjunction-conflict theories of psychopathology provide powerful psychological motives for drinking; social learning theories account for the channeling of these motives into specific behavior form. Their synthesis results in a true socialpsychological or "field" theory of urban Indian drunkenness (Graves 1970:39-40).

Graves claims that this framework makes it possible to explain Native American alcohol abuse "without recourse to the fact that our subjects are Indian" (1970:51), an unusual stance for an anthropologist. He concludes that better jobs would help greatly to diminish alcohol abuse among Navajo migrants to Denver.

Graves' explanatory model is applicable to other groups, as well as Native Americans; it accounts for individual differences; and it focuses on measurable dimensions (Jessor and Bruun 1970*:275). This theory of frustrated goals (called anomie) also is implicit or explicit in the explanations for Native American problem drinking offered by a number of other authors.[79]

Some authors have questioned the explanations of Native American alcohol abuse which rely on the notion of frustrated material goals, because they believed their Native American subjects had no such goals (Dosman 1972; Honigmann 1965:213; Hamer 1965:294). Reports[80] that Native Americans with more money drink more than those with less money are also potentially in conflict with this variety of deprivation explanation, as is the idea that alcohol use symbolizes economic success to some Native Americans (Lemert 1958:99).

In reviewing objections to anomie as an explanation for deviance in general and for Native American alcohol abuse in particular, Levy and Kunitz (1974:13)[81] stress: (1) the lack of evidence to support the assumption on which anomie explanations of heavy drinking are based--that is, that a drinking response is necessarily a retreat; (2) that anomie theory seems ill-suited for explaining differences in drinking behavior among groups, while cultural predisposition seems more obviously implicated; (3) that the product of anomie, that is stress, has not always been measured independently of the drinking behavior that it is said to engender.

Lurie (1971:313) points to the main trouble with anomie theory as an explanation for Native American alcohol abuse--the unwarranted assumption that all Native Americans are eager to become like White men:

> . . .It is pertinent to ask in the case of Indian drinking whether we know which success goals are being thwarted. . .
>
> As Indian people struggle for a workable cultural and social pluralism, adapting contemporary American economic necessities and some of the amenities to their own systems of values, their strivings seem to be frequently misunderstood. Although at the present time, Indian spokesmen are gaining a wider hearing, their insistence that they want to be Indians still tends either to be dismissed by "practical" whites as being as unrealistic as trying to bring back the buffalo, or encouraged by "sympathetic" whites as envisioning an actual return to the kind of Indian life depicted in museums. When Indian people begin to bring off what they evidently have in mind, improvement of their

material welfare on their own terms, their success is interpreted as fulfilling the highly individualistic aspirations of middle-class white society and as a stepping stone to total absorption into it.

The rationale for another variant of the deprivation explanation for Native American alcohol abuse holds that people with a stake in society will be less likely to engage in prohibited behavior than those who have no such stake. Honigmann and Honigmann (1970), studying a modern integrated Arctic town, used steady employment and residence in a modern home as indicators of a stake in society--that is in majority society. They found that the greater a person's stake in society, the more he avoided trouble with the law over alcohol, even though he might spend more money on liquor than many others who did get into trouble.

Ferguson (1976b) allowed for the possibility of stake in the dominant and/or the traditional Native American society, or neither society; this seems to be a useful expansion of the framework used by Honigmann and Honigmann (1970). Success in an alcohol treatment program for a group of Navajo arrested for drunkenness was measured by staff evaluations and by the number of arrests at follow-up studies. They found a significant relationship between stake in society and success in treatment. Those who had a stake only in the traditional Native American society had a high success rate (seventy-two per cent). Those who had no stake in either society had a low success rate (twenty-three per cent). Those with a stake in the dominant society only, did just as poorly (twenty-three per cent success). Most surprising, those who did the best of all were people who had a stake in both societies--a seventy-four per cent success rate. Rather than suffering from conflict of values and loyalties, these people became what McFee (1968*) has called "the 150% man." This finding has many important implications within and beyond Native American alcohol studies, since it contradicts the common assumption that one must lose the old culture to the extent that one gains the new one. The people with a stake in both societies had competencies and satisfactions from both.

One serious problem with the stake theory explanation is that it does not account for who develops what kind of stake, or how one does it. Apparently obtaining a stake in society happens by chance. The fact that some Native Americans can harmoniously incorporate both cultures into their lives does not prove that pressures to integrate into, and identify with the dominant society, play no role in the development of alcohol abuse by Native Americans who are in the process of adapting themselves to the majority society.[82]

For example, Ferguson (1968b) found that Navajo problem drinkers who were more integrated into the majority group manifested a different and less treatable form of alcohol abuse than those who were less so. (Note, however, that Ferguson 1976b, discussed earlier, offers a more explicit and refined explanation in the form of stake theory.)

Lowered self-esteem is a prominent theme in studies[83] which stress acculturation into the dominant society as an explanation for Native

American alcohol abuse. Males are said to be more prone than females to this problem, which usually is attributed to difficulties Native American men find in living up to a masculine image of competence under the social conditions that obtain (for example, when they are unemployed).

Acculturation as an explanatory device has been criticized in the literature on Native American drinking on several grounds. Lantis[84] (1968*), for example, found acculturation too broad--a global concept with limited explanatory value, saying that increasing sophistication in the social sciences leads to more specific hypotheses. Lemert (1956a) points out that the Mohave, who had many of the usual problems associated with acculturation, did not use alcohol in adapting to these problems (Devereux 1948).

Although Levy and Kunitz (1974:184) found that the pattern of alcohol use depended on the degree of acculturation ("To be like a white man means, in part, drinking like one"), according to their results, acculturation functions as the independent, rather than the dependent, variable:

> Who does and who does not become acculturated depends on where they are located in the traditional Navajo stratification system. Poorer people, in Navajo terms, have more incentive to adopt white ways than those who are wealthier (Levy and Kunitz 1974:186).

Levy and Kunitz (1974:104-106) argue that the simultaneous increases in both drinking and acculturation among the Hopi is fortuitous, because the rates of deviant drinking were similar in people originally from modern villages and in those from less modern ones. The rates were higher in off-reservation towns, but they attributed this to tendencies for traditional villages to expel their deviants, rather than to acculturation stress in these towns. Furthermore, among four groups of Navajo, rankings according to level of preoccupation with alcohol did not correspond to the rankings based on levels of acculturation (Levy and Kunitz 1974:149); Navajo who hold traditional religious beliefs, have little education and a low income receive higher "preoccupation with alcohol" scores than those who are Christians, have eight years of school and a higher income.

Graves (1967) demonstrated that the concept of acculturation, alone, could not explain why acculturating Native Americans drink no more than those who are unacculturated, whereas acculturated Spanish drink more than unacculturated Spanish. He attributes the differences to varying social controls. Among the acculturated Spanish and Native Americans, the degree of social control is similar--the traditional amounts for the Native Americans have increased while those of the Spaniards have decreased. On the other hand, among the unacculturated, the Spanish have stronger social controls from family, church and other social groups traceable to their traditional sedentary agricultural culture, while the Native Americans in question (Utes) have less, because of their independence--legacy of their aboriginal status as hunters and gatherers. Thus, Graves (1970) is explicitly demonstrating the operation of cultural factors as well as the social variables which he emphasized so much more in his study of urban Native Americans.

If deprivations are to be invoked to explain the high rates of Native American alcohol abuse, at a minimum the following must be demonstrated: that Native Americans lack the thing in question more than other people who are not famed for their drunken excesses (Blacks, for example, as Littman 1970:1770 points out); that the degree of deprivation covaries in a regular fashion with the amount of problem drinking in the group; and that there is a plausible mechanism by which the effect of the deprivation produces a response of alcohol abuse. Anything less is mere opinion. Very few of the studies to date meet these criteria. Presumably it is easier to eliminate deprivations, especially economic ones, than to manipulate cultural values and customs. Thus explanations of Native American alcohol abuse based on these theories provide relatively explicit opportunities for intervention.

Cultural Explanations

A number of quantified cross-cultural[85] studies have been made which include North American natives in their samples and have explanations of Native American drinking. These contain cultural explanations for drunkenness, but unlike many of the studies discussed later, they attempt to account more explicitly for the psychological[86] mechanism by which the cultural trait affects the behavior as expressed in the individual. The proposed explanations for cultural variations in drinking include demonstrations of associations between frequency of drunkenness and: anxiety[87] (positive, with subsistence anxiety according to Horton 1943); of power fantasies in men (positive, see McClelland, Davis, Kalin, and Wenner 1972*; Boyatzis 1976*); strong social controls over drinking (negative, see Field 1962; McClelland, Davis, Kalin, and Wenner 1972*); and general consumption level (Whitehead and Harvey 1974). Schaefer (1976*) reports support for the works cited above, and also finds a strong positive association between (1) extreme drunkenness, fear of spirits, and (2) weak family structure.

Probably the most prominent of all these cross-cultural studies of drinking has been the work of Bacon, Barry and a variety of associates.[88] These studies are best known for their demonstration of correlations between drunkenness and conflict over dependency needs.[89] The rationale for this explanation is as follows. As children develop into adults they gradually substitute the pleasures of self-reliance for the pleasures of dependency. These two opposing adaptations to life are punished and rewarded in varying combinations over time and over the life cycle in different societies. For their members this creates varying degrees of conflict between the two adaptations. Alcohol reduces this conflict and allows the expression of both. However, because of alcohol's pharmacological effect of disinhibition, drinking tends to release the one which is dominant in the person. Some conflict over dependency occurs in all people in all societies. This accounts for the universal appeal of alcohol and for the presence of substitutes (for example, gambling and tobacco among North American natives) where alcohol and other drugs were not used aboriginally (Barry 1976*:260).

The heaviest, least controlled drinking is most likely to develop where punishment of dependency and reward for self-reliance are strongest, as they tend to be in food-gathering rather than food-producing societies (Barry 1976*:260). Food-gathering societies tend to be characterized by informal social organization, which in turn is found to be associated with insobriety (Bacon 1976*; Bacon, Barry and Child 1965; Field 1962; Horton 1943; McClelland, Davis, Kalin, and Wenner 1972*). Barry says:

> ...many North American Indian tribes had character-
> istics of child training and adult behavior which
> are related to high frequency of drunkenness. The
> absence of drinking aboriginally might have developed
> during their long history, or by selective survival
> of nondrinking societies, as the only effective
> means of restraint. This hypothesis is supported by
> the destructive effect of liquor when introduced to
> these people by the Western European intruders
> (1976*:259).

Loss of traditional culture (or deculturation) is the simplest form in which culture serves as an explanation for Native American alcohol abuse.[90] Usually it is implied or explicitly claimed that to the degree the old culture is destroyed, a vacuum remains, into which alcohol promptly flows. This seems to be at logical odds with the assumption, discussed earlier in the context of acculturation, that the old culture only disappears to the degree that the new one pushes it out--in which case there would be no void for alcohol to fill. Drinking, particularly in a group, often is said to serve as a substitute for various aboriginal cultural forms; these include the search for ecstasy (Carpenter 1959; Dailey 1968; Hamer 1969; Lemert 1954a) in its various forms, such as the vision quest (Ackerman 1971), for the guardian spirit complex (Hamer 1969), for gambling (Adler and Coleman 1969), for shamanism (Ferguson 1971*), for the war party (Dizmang 1967; Freeman 1969; Hurt and Brown 1965) and its attendant customary boasting of male exploits (Hurt and Brown 1965), celebration of return (Freilich 1958*) and other forms of male expressiveness (Dozier 1966; Mohatt 1972), as well as for other, now defunct, types of institutionalized social interaction (Curley 1967; duToit 1964). Some authors say that intoxication substitutes for euphoria achieved by other means, which was highly valued in precontact society (Dailey 1968; Rattray 1970; Mohatt 1972).

Codere (1956*) traces the development of the Rum Feast from the aboriginal potlatch,[91] and points out the possibility of other precedents in aboriginal culture for modern Native American drinking patterns. Honigmann (1971a) and Lemert (1954b) also alert us to antecedents for modern drinking behavior in elements of traditional culture.

The persistence of traditional patterns, such as sharing, are often said[92] to be maladaptive in attaining majority society goals and to contribute to excessive drinking by Native Americans. Others emphasize the positive function of alcohol in adapting traditional values to modern life. For example, Waddell (1975:9) says that among the Papago alcohol

is used to:
> ...maintain a system of social credit and egalitarian economics and to provide for a means whereby individuals can attain personal power in an otherwise egalitarian system.

Drinking is said to provide a way to discharge hostility,[93] the implications being either that such emotions were suppressed in aboriginal society or that traditional avenues for their expression are no longer available. Liquor use sometimes is a mark of prestige in a way that provides continuity with the old culture (Lemert 1958:99).

There are many problems with these functional[94] explanations. One seeming contradiction in the Native American alcohol literature is the case where a modern tradition of steel working serves as an effective functional substitute for the forms of aboriginal life, yet heavy drinking is prevalent among the males (Freilich 1958*). More troublesome, knowledge of the traditions for which modern intoxication is a substitute seems useful for creating sympathetic understanding, but less so as a guide for intervention.

Lemert objects to social disintegration theories as over-simplified, emphasizing the complexity of the antecedents:
> Cultural conservatism, political consciousness, anomie, reaction to crisis, and patterning, as affected by diffusion, interclan rivalry, stereotypes and the system of social control, all operate significantly in the inebriate drinking of the Northwest Coast Indians...the difference in social control systems [should be] factored into so-called "shame" or "guilt" inculcating cultures [and] may be a crucial variable...
> (Lemert 1956a:312).

Lemert's[95] explanations for Native American drinking concentrate on the functions served by drinking, and the role of social control[96] in determining the degree of drunken excess in Native American groups.

The theme has been further summarized by Levy and Kunitz (1974:24):
> We maintain that drinking behavior is mainly a reflection of traditional forms of social organization and cultural values instead of a reflection of social disorganization.

They (1974:106) based these conclusions primarily on the fact that rates for suicide, homicide and public drunkenness scale according to levels of sociocultural integration among the Navajo, Apache, and Hopi. (Although cirrhosis did not scale in this fashion, they attribute this to the protective effects of binge drinking by the Navajo and Apache versus suspected steady drinking by the Hopi, inferred from their high cirrhosis rates. As mentioned earlier, the absolute numbers were too small to inspire much confidence in this result without further confirmation over a longer period.) The authors also were impressed by the stability of the rates and patterns of suicide and homicide over long periods, thus indicating that neither increased acculturation nor increased alcohol use have been major factors influencing such deviance.

Their preference for social organization over deprivation theories (especially anomie) is based on the following rationale (Levy and Kunitz 1974:181):

> We have suggested that different societies develop different types of personality. Hunting-and-gathering societies depend for their survival on individual prowess, competitiveness, and aggressiveness. Social control of individual aggressiveness and self-assertion are relatively weak, with the result that individuals tend to seek immediate gratification and to become emotionally labile. To the extent that insobriety facilitates aggression and promotes feelings of personal strength and omnipotence, we would expect such peoples to be fond of drinking because the experience would strengthen the image of the self rather than weaken it. The lack of social controls upon excessive acting out behavior would allow drinking despite the recognition of many untoward effects.

Thus, their theory combines the social organization explanations (of Field and Lemert) and the power explanations (of McClelland).

Although the personality attributes claimed by Levy and Kunitz may be true of some hunters and gatherers (such as the famed buffalo hunters), in others (such as in the Great Basin societies), cooperation seems more emphasized than competition. The conclusions of Levy and Kunitz suggest that intervention must occur at the level of changing perceptions and values--a soberingly difficult prospect, though perhaps no more so than other approaches to intervention.

Liquor was almost totally absent from aboriginal America (Driver 1955), with the exception of a few tribes. This fact has been invoked by Dozier (1966) to explain the prevalence of Native American alcohol abuse. Stewart (1964) asserted that prohibition robbed Native Americans of the opportunity to learn the controlled use of liquor or to develop effective social controls governing its use. If this were true, the few tribes which did have alcohol aboriginally might be expected to control drinking better than those which did not. Bacon (1976*:27) reports the association does hold, worldwide, between aboriginal use and integration of drinking customs into cultural traditions. However, Levy and Kunitz (1974) report high rates of alcohol-associated problems among the Apache, one of the tribes which did have alcohol before conquest; their report seems to belie such an association. But the aboriginal use of alcohol in a ritual context may be irrelevant to the secular use which produces current problems.

Absence of aboriginal experience with alcohol seems inadequate as an explanation for the behavior of the minority of Native Americans whose drinking offends the majority group. Despite prohibition, many people within all Native American groups have learned controlled drinking during the century or more they have been using alcohol. Furthermore, such an explanation does not take into account the fact that Native American groups have had plenty of time to learn and institutionalize a number of drinking styles during this period. Is it self-evident that it is harder or takes longer to learn a proper than an improper drinking style?

MacAndrew and Edgerton (1969),[97] relying heavily on illustrations from the Native American alcohol literature, make an excellent case for their conclusion that, when a person drinks, he comports himself in a manner which he has learned.[98] The evidence they present that Native Americans' initial reactions to alcohol were not characterized by the crazed behavior of the drunken Native American stereotype is the most powerful argument to date against the Firewater Myth that Native Americans are unable to control their drinking and racially prone to bizarre reactions to alcohol. Rather, the Native Americans learned such behavior from raucous frontiersmen,[99] who provided them with their first supplies and their models for drinking. MacAndrew and Edgerton say (1969:171):

> It is our contention, then, that if we are ever to understand drunken comportment, we must focus on the shared understandings of the nature of drunkenness that obtain among men living together in societies. It is our further contention that in those societies in which drunken changes-for-the-worse occur, these changes must be viewed in terms of the increased (though variously defined and never unlimited) freedom that these societies accord to their members when they are drunk.

They conclude (1969:173):

> The moral, then, is this. Since societies, like individuals, get the sorts of drunken comportment they allow, they deserve what they get.

The implications of this explanation for Native American alcohol use are profound. It suggests that attacks on the problem should include strategies for interrupting the learning cycle and encouraging controls from within. That is, assistance to individuals should be supplemented with measures aimed at communities--a difficult challenge, but not an impossible one.[100] MacAndrew and Edgerton do not attempt to explain differences in drunken comportment among and within tribes--perhaps these depended on which frontiersmen were the model. A more serious problem with their theory is its failure to account for the persistence of many elements of this frontier style of alcohol use in present-day Native American drinking patterns. The models have been gone a long time.[101]

However, a complementary explanation could account for the mysterious persistence, over generations and even centuries, of this seemingly dysfunctional pattern; it views Native American drinking as a political act, a gesture of banding together in symbolic resistance to the White oppressors. Far from a retreatist response to social deprivations, it is a positive, ingenious, organized, institutionalized protest. Far from reflecting an absence of group norms for handling liquor, it is patterned by rules which are sufficiently elaborated to suggest the status of ritual. Far from representing dysfunctional deviance, it effectively promotes Native Americanism by maintaining group solidarity with a dramatic, flamboyant way for one Native American to tell another one (and any White observers) that he is with the Native Americans, not with the Whites. Far from irrational, this behavior complex is calculated and aimed at a perfectly plausible motive--to draw attention to the persistence of Native Americans as a recognizable cultural group and thus help put the lie to centuries of predictions that the race will disappear. Far from reflecting a lack of integration of alcohol into the culture, as the general alcohol literature often suggests,[102] the drunkenness which characterizes Native American drinking[103] actually is initmately and intricately woven into the current culture, both reservation and urban.

Lurie (1972, 1971) has been the principal proponent of this position. Her statements have not received the attention they deserve.[104] Elements of the symbolic resistance proposition also are apparent in the works of many other authors,[105] in the form of evidence supporting the notion, though it is not always specifically offered for this purpose, let alone claimed to support it. However, there is one fatal flaw in this otherwise very adaptive device. If you swallow enough alcohol it can hurt you, and those around you, no matter what the motive is for drinking it. Brod (1975:1386-1387) comments:

> Our medical training inclines us to associate "disorder" with a behavior pattern having serious personal and social consequences, yet we can conceive of nonpathological frame of reference despite severe and even tragic consequences. Consider, for instance, our nonjudgmental attitude toward the highway carnage over a holiday weekend. Severe consequences do not make risky behavior abnormal, ipso facto.

It is at once paradoxical and poignant to think that Native Americans may have chosen to express their Native Americanism by means of outlandish drunken comportment (Lurie 1971) which can be traced to White models (MacAndrew and Edgerton 1969) that epitomize the beginning of White exploitation of their race. If Native Americans were more aware of the roots of the pattern of drinking to get spectacularly drunk, they might be more motivated to control their drinking. Given the widespread use of liquor by the dominant society, a case certainly could be made that the best way for Native Americans to distinguish themselves from Whites would be to leave liquor alone.

NOTES

[1] This work provides access to early accounts through such secondary sources as Dailey (1968); Vachon (1968).

[2] North American Indian tribes also were included in the HRAF samples used by Field (1962); Bacon, Barry and Child (1965); and Schaefer (1976). Bales (1946) refers to a few of the HRAF materials on Indians briefly and indirectly (by relying on Horton's citations) in illustrating his anecdotal account of cultural differences in rates of alcoholism.

[3] For example, Honigmann and Honigmann (1945); Hallowell (1946); Devereux (1948); Heath (1952) and Geertz (1951)--unpublished but noteworthy Harvard undergraduate papers; Berreman (1956); Hawthorne et al. (1957); Lemert (1954a, 1958); Carpenter (1959); Clairmont (1962, 1963); Stewart (1964); Hurt (1961); Hurt and Brown (1965); du Toit (1964); Hamer (1965); Dozier (1966); and Dailey (1964; 1968). Maynard was a member of the Indian Health Service Task Force on Alcoholism (IHS 1977), which set the stage for the government's declaration of Native American drinking as a high priority research and action topic. Maynard (1969) and Medicine (1969) contributed to the Pine Ridge Research Bulletins (1968 - 1969); the latter was among the first Native American contributors to this literature (see also Manning 1963; Dozier 1966).

[4] For example, Jessor, Graves, Hanson and Jessor (1968); MacAndrew and Edgerton (1969); Honigmann and Honigmann (1970); Levy and Kunitz (1974); Leland (1976a).

[5] Everett, Waddell and Heath (1976*); Waddell and Everett (n.d.*).

[6] Omer Stewart, Theodore Graves, Craig MacAndrew, Robert Edgerton, Jerrold Levy and Stephen Kunitz have inspired a number of people to study Native American drinking. We can expect more studies from Dwight Heath's graduate program providing social sciences research training on alcohol at Brown University; from Westermeyer at the University of Minnesota; Jilek at British Columbia; Waddell at Purdue University.

[7] Psychology: Whittaker (1962, 1963); Henderson (1965, 1967); Jessor et al. (1968). Sociology: Curley (1967); Kunitz et al. (1969, 1971). Social Work: Littman (1965, 1970); Savard (1968a). Physicians: Reichenbach (1967*); Sievers (1968); Szuter et al. (1965); Kuttner and Lorincz (1967, 1970).

[8] These works demonstrate that physicians can learn cross-cultural sensitivity; Shore (1972*, 1974, 1975) also comes to mind.

[9] Among these are several reviews of varying comprehensiveness:

Bynum (1972); May and Dizmang (1974); Resnick and Dizmang (1971); Shore (1975).

[10] 24 Reservation States, age-adjusted, 1974 three-year centered average.

[11] The 1955-1971 rate of increase was ninety-nine per cent (U.S. Congress, Senate 1954:50). Yearly rates (per 100,000 population) are:

1974	21.8	1966	15.2
1973	22.9	1965	12.9
1972	20.6	1964	15.8
1971	21.8	1963	15.6
1970	17.9	1962	16.8
1969	16.8	1961	16.7
1968	17.5	1960	16.8
1967	16.2	1959	17.0

[12] IHS had no data on this association, and I have been unable to find the basis for this statement in the literature.

[13] As a result, the Native American rates actually are understated relative to the general population, when crude death rates are used. Age-adjusted rates, which widen the differences between the Native Americans and the general populations, should be used. This practice of course adds to the difficulty of making comparisons among studies. Further uncontrolled variability among groups is introduced by the use of different methods and different time periods in the various reports.

[14] The proportion of male deaths has been decreasing in both groups in recent years, however (Ogden et al. 1970:76).

[15] Including many contemporary Indians, according to May and Dizmang (1974:45); also Blakeslee (1955:34).

[16] The topic is the main subject of Brown et al. (1970); Hackenberg and Gallagher (1972); Jepson (1973); Kane and Kane (1972); Schmitt, Hole and Barclay (1966); Wills (1969). Accidents are included with reports on other forms of death in Cutler and Morrison (1971); Hanlon (1972); Hill and Spector (1971*); Porvaznik (1972); Westermeyer and Brantner (1972).

[17] U.S. Congress, Senate (1974:50).

[18] DHEW (1977a*).

[19] This topic is the main focus of Baker (1959); Bloom (1974*); Levy, Kunitz and Everett (1969). It is considered, together with a variety of other types of death, in Baker (1959); Cutler and Morrison (1971); Hill

and Spector (1971*); Levy and Kunitz (1969, 1974); Paredes (1966*); Westermeyer and Brantner (1977).

[20] See Brody (1971:17); Clairmont (1962:10); Deloria (1970:344); Hayner (1942:603); Heath (1952:47); Levy and Kunitz (1971a:226, 1974:164); Littman (1970:1770); Riffenberg (1964:42); Shepardson and Hammond (1964*: 1046); Stewart (1964, citing a South Dakota report); Stratton (1973); U.S. Commission on Civil Rights (1973).

[21] See L. Boyer (1964c:218); Gregory (1975); von Hentig (1945:75); Lemert (1954a:356, 1958:102-103); Luebben (1964a, 1964b).

[22] The ratios of Native Americans to White and Black arrests vary greatly among tribes.

[23] This adjustment may account for some of the differences between the figures of Reasons (1972) and Stewart (1964) for the years where they overlap.

[24] See Bienvenue and Latif (1974:110); Graves (1970:39); Levy and Kunitz (1974:109); May (1975:131).

[25] In 1968, Native Americans had higher rates than Whites in all the categories presented, calculated from Reasons (1972:323, Table 4): robbery 7.8, homicide 6.8, assault 6.1, auto theft 6.1, rape 5.2, burglary 3.5, larceny 3.4. The Native Americans had higher rates than Blacks only for auto thefts.

[26] The ratio is sometimes reported to be even higher for Native American females than for males. See Bienvenue and Latif (1974:107); von Hentig (1945:76).

[27] In two settlements which were accessible to most of the reservation population.

[28] Much earlier, Lunger (1956:562) also had claimed there were "few problems yet from legalized sale of liquor to Indians" in Arizona.

[29] See Lemert (1954a:356); Littman (1967:69); Hawthorne et al. (1957:11).

[30] See Curley (1967:118); Devereux (1948:209); Ferguson (1970:901); Hawthorne et al. (1957:11); May (1975:133).

[31] Hill and Spector (1971*:238).

[32] Hill and Spector (1971*:239, 243); Reichenbach (1967*:84); Savard

(1968b:914, 1965:4); Sievers (1968:77); IHS Task Force on Alcoholism (1977).

[33] For example, see index entries under Aggression, Alcoholism Complications, Allergic Reactions to Alcohol, Child Neglect, Delerium Tremens, Delinquency, Deviance, Gambling, Health Problems, Homicide, Illegitimacy, Incest, Interpersonal Relationships, Mental Disorders, Mental Illness, Mortality, Overdose, Pneumonia, Poisoning, Promiscuity, Prostitution, Violence. Canadian reports with material on this topic include Ben-Dor (1966); Hawthorne et al. (1957, 1958); McKinnon and Neufeldt (1974); Murphy (1972); Oswalt (1966); Wacko (1974).

[34] See Ackerman (1971); Atcheson (1972); Byler (1974); Ervin (1969); Hoffman and Noem (1975b:165); Holloway (1965*); Littman (1970); Parmee (1968); Pinto (1973).

[35] See Cockerham (1975); Forslund and Meyers (1974); Freeman (1968); Harvey (1976); Holloway (1966, 1965*, 1964*); Maynard (1968); de Montigny (1969); Pinto (1973); Porter et al. (1973); Saslow and Harrover (1968); Schoenfeld and Miller (1973); Swanson et al. (1971); Topper (1974); Stauss, Jenson and Harris (1977); Wilson (1968).

[36] See Jones, Smith and Hanson (1976); Jones and Smith (1973); Jones, Smith, Ulleland, and Streissguth (1973); Smith, Jones and Hanson (1976); Streissguth (1976); Schaefer (1962).

[37] As far back as 1956, Lunger was calling for more Native American involvement in efforts to counter alcohol abuse by New Mexico Native American youngsters.

[38] U.S. Bureau of the Census (1973*:1).

[39] See Bienvenue and Latif (1974); Gardner (1969); Graves (1970); Hurt (1961); Jessor et al. (1968); Kuttner and Lorincz (1970); Nagler (1970); Price (1968).

[40] See Graves (1974, 1971, 1970, 1967a, 1967*); Graves and van Arsdale (1965*); Jessor and Bruun (1970*); Jessor et al. (1968); Kuttner and Lorincz (1970).

[41] See Ablon (1964); Bittker (1973); Garbarino (1971); Gardner (1969); Hurt (1961); Kuttner and Lorincz (1967); Nagata (1971*); Waddell (1975); Weightman (1972); White (1970).

[42] See a very interesting discussion of this point in Dosman (1972).

[43] Also discussed in Leland (1976a).

[44] See quotations in Leland (1976a:4-9) from Anonymous Citation in (0520); Officer (1963); Berreman (1956); Chance (1966); Devereux (1948); Dozier (1966); Freeman (1968); Hamer (1965); Heath (1964); Honigmann and Honigmann (1945); Lemert (1958, 1954a, 1954b); Littman (1970); Rohner and Rohner (1970); Sanchez (1967); Szuter et al. (1965); Wagner, cited in Fahy and Muschenheim (1965); and Werner (1963).

[45] Anonymous (1964*, 1963a, 1963b, n.d.); Bowman (1967); Manning (1963); Martinez (1966); Werner (1963).

[46] See Anonymous (1968); Dozier (1966:83); Leland (1976a:73); Price (1975:24); Shore and von Fumetti (1972:1451).

[47] See Dozier (1966:82); Hutchison (1975:186); except in collaboration with native healers, Jilek (1974:17); Westermeyer (1976b:451).

[48] Because of the scarcity of Native American Medical professionals which PL 94-437 is designed to correct, I assume that this effort, as most IHS programs still do, involved primarily Anglo staff.

[49] The scarcity of reports about Native Americans in integrated programs probably results from the fact that most Native Americans have been treated in Native American programs; it does not necessarily indicate that success in this situation is impossible. But Native American people (and others) are strongly opposed to non-Native American programs.

[50] Actually, many of the nativistic movements have been influenced by Christianity, but in these reports, Christianity in its pure, rather than assimilated, form is meant.

[51] See Gardner (1969); Hippler (1973, 1974); Hurt (1960).

[52] Ferguson (1968b, 1970); Henderson (1965); Rattray (1970); Savard 1965, 1968b); Szuter et al. (1965).

[53] See Anonymous (1974b); Bittker (1973:177); Hippler (1974:54); Hutchison (1975:186); Jilek (1972, 1974); Jilek and Jilek-Aall (1972); Kline et al. (1973:731); Shore and von Fumetti (1972:1454); Topper (1975:4); Torrey (1970:456ff); and (on a more general level, not restricted to alcohol) Wallace (1959).

[54] Jilek (1974); Jilek and Jilek-Aall (1972); Jilek and Todd (1974); Levitan and Hetrick (1971); Torrey (1970).

[55] Plains Gourd Dance: Howard (1976). Salish Winter Ceremonials: Jilek (1974); Jilek and Jilek-Aall (1972); Jilek and Todd (1974). Lakota Yuwipi healing ritual: Kemnitzer (1976). Native Treatment of

Ojibwa Wiitiko psychosis, some symptoms of which occur when the victim is drunk: Parker (1960). Peyote rituals of the Native American Church: Aberle (1966); Albaugh and Anderson (1974); Bergman (1971); La Barre (1941); Littman (1965); Roy (1973, 1969); see also Dozier (1966:72-73).

[56] Some of the Anglo-run programs have incorporated research; see Ferguson (1970, 1968b); Henderson (1967); Savard (1965, 1968b); Shore et al. (1973). However, I saw only one suggestion for using a control group in DHEW (1977b*).

[57] See U.S. American Indian Policy Review Commission Task Force #11 (1976); Archibald (1971*:494); Association of American Indian Affairs (1974:13); Barter and Barter (1974:42); Bloom (1970:66); Blumenthal (1975:257); Gregory (1975); Jilek (1974); Leon (1965:727, 1968:235); Nowak (1972:6); Price (1975:24); Robinson (1974:13); Shore (1974:66); Shore and von Fumetti (1972:1451); Westermeyer (1974b:36, 1974c).

[58] According to official reports, Robinson (1974:13); DHEW (1977b*); Rattray (1970); Meeks (1974:24); and many other non-official reports. Native paraprofessionals seem to be used frequently in Canada, too; see Bennett (1973); Blumenthal (1975); Cull and Hardy (1974); Jilek (1974); Meeks (1974); Provincial Native Action Council (1974).

[59] See Gregory (1975); Price (1975:25); Robinson (1974:13); Schoenfeld and Miller (1973:33). The appropriateness of this practice usually has been taken for granted, for both Native American and dominant society programs, although no controlled comparisons have demonstrated its superiority so far.

[60] See Dozier (1966:83); Kinzie, Shore, and Pattison (1972*:204); Shore (1974:62); Stage and Keast (1966:76); Termansen and Ryan (1970:126); Topper (1975:3).

[61] However, the official descriptions make the self-determination policy sound more deliberate than accidental, for example, Chafetz (1973*). A detailed history of the development of the Native American alcohol programs would be a welcome addition to the literature (Robinson 1974 provides a brief summary).

[62] See section on urban Native Americans; also Barter and Barter (1974).

[63] See Public Law 94-437, Sec. 3, September 30, 1976.

[64] Sixty per cent of clients, forty-eight per cent of staff time. Native Americans' aversion to hurry may be a factor in the results of these three indicators, too.

[65] Shore and von Fumetti (1972) reported females responded better than males to treatment in some programs.

[66] All of the 166 programs will be brought under evaluation in early 1977 (DHEW 1976a*, Figure 1).

[67] See Graves (1970); Lavallee (1967); Leland (1975, 1978*); Medicine (1969).

[68] Tribal composition was not specified in the original report, but has since been published by Gilbert in the Canadian Medical Association Journal (Personal Communication, J. Schaefer); most of the subjects were of tribes in the MacKenzie Basin and east.

[69] The authors acknowledge that the apparently greater adaptation by Native Americans may have been an artifact of differences between their customary intake and that of the Whites. That is, among the heavy drinkers, Native Americans may have normally consumed more than the Whites.

[70] Their sample was comprised of fourteen Navajo and Apache; five Sioux, Omaha, Kickapoo; five Pima, Papago; three Hopi, Acoma; three Eastern Woodlands.

[71] As mentioned earlier, no Native Americans were included in this study, but findings concerning Orientals are again assumed to be pertinent to American Indians. Brod (1975:1388) reminds us that this should not be accepted as doctrine: "The task of evaluating Wolff's assumption that all Native Americans are Mongoloid--or even that Eastern Cree are--belongs to our colleagues in physical anthropology."

[72] The rate-limiting step in the hepatic metabolism of ethanol is its oxidation to acetaldehyde, catalyzed by alcohol dehydrogenase. In human liver there are multiple molecular forms (isoenzymes) of alcohol dehydrogenase (Bennion and Li 1976:10). The atypical enzyme form is highly prevalent in Mongolian people, who therefore may attain higher levels of circulating acetaldehyde and more often experience aversive effects after consuming alcohol (von Wartburg 1976:146*).

[73] Fenna et al. (1971); Reed et al. (1976); Zeiner, Paredes, and Dowden (1976*).

[74] Hood (1972:1-22) chose the title, "Dirty Words", for his paper on genetic differences in responses to alcohol, explaining that he has learned by sad experience that "even to mention genetic differences between groups of people is considered a bad thing by many. . . . What we must come to recognize, and soon, is that genetic differences cannot necessarily be classified as better or worse."

[75] See Berreman (1964); Brod (1975); Codere (1955); Curley (1967); Dozier (1966); Hamer (1965); Pierre (1971).

[76] On the other hand, Heath's (1964) report that repeal of prohibition brought little change in Navajo drinking styles does not necessarily contradict these findings; it could mean the prohibition-induced pattern had become so customary that it persisted afterward, or it could mean the patterns are the product of the culture itself, rather than of introduced or imposed factors such as prohibition (discussed later).

[77] See Ablon (1965); Boatman (1968); Dailey (1964); Dozier (1966); Fairbanks (n.d.); Hamer (1965); Hayes (1975); Hurt (1961); Kehoe (1970); Kemnitzer (1972); Kuttner and Lorincz (1970); Lal (1969a, 1969b); Maynard and Twiss (1970); McNair (1969); Meeks (1974); Minnis (1963); Nurge (1970); Price (1975); Savishinsky (1970, 1971); Savishinsky and Frimmer (1973); du Toit (1964); Whittaker (1963, 1966).

[78] See also Graves (1971); Graves and Van Arsdale (1965*); Jessor and Brunn (1970*); Jessor et al. (1968).

[79] Berreman (1964); Boatman (1968), who incidentally found in favor of anomic versus social deprivation; Chance (1966); Clairmont (1962, 1963); Durgin (1974); Ferguson (1968b); Helm (1961); Honigmann and Honigmann (1945); James (1961); Maynard (1969); Norick (1970); Price (1975); Topper (1974); and Vallee (1968*).

[80] See Hayner (1942); Honigmann and Honigmann (1970); Kuttner and Lorincz (1967); Whittaker (1963); note, however, that these heavy consumers are not necessarily problem drinkers.

[81] See also Kunitz, Levy and Euler (1972*) and the various other articles by Levy, Kunitz and associates cited in the annotated bibliography.

[82] As suggested by Ablon (1971); Boag (1970); Fairbanks (n.d.); Foulks and Katz (1973); Hallowell (1950); Maynard (1969); Hurt and Brown (1965); Kemnitzer (1972); Savishinsky (1971); Whittaker (1963, 1966).

[83] See Ackerman (1971); R. M. Boyer (1964); Hurt and Brown (1965); Lechnyr, cited by Brod (1975:1390); Lubart (1969a); Medicine (1969); Mohatt (1972).

[84] See also Dosman (1972).

[85] Based on ethnographic materials in the Human Relations Area Files.

[86] Psychological elements and mechanisms are important parts of many of the explanations of Native American alcohol abuse, in such works as Ferguson (1976a); Graves (1967*, 1970, 1974); Leighton (1968*); Lemert (1958); Levy and Kunitz (1969, 1971a & b, 1974); MacAndrew and Edgerton (1969). However, in all these cases, the psychological aspect seems subordinate to either the social deprivation or the cultural explanations the authors propose; that is, they screen social or cultural factors, past and present, through an individual's personal psychology, treating it as an intervening, rather than an independent, variable. We have, therefore, not included a separate category of psychological explanations here. Distinctive personality profiles for alcoholic Native Americans have not been identified (Kline et al. 1973); Hoffman and Jackson (1973). One of the few items in the literature which seems to stress psychological proneness appears in the official newsletter of the Association of American Indian Physicians (see Clarke 1975a, 1975b). Some authors (for example, Dosman 1972:81; Graves 1974) have specifically denied that the culture of poverty, which assumes certain personality attributes as characteristic and perpetuative, is an adequate explanation of Native American drinking. A frequent criticism of psychologically oriented studies is expressed by Lemert (1956a:314): "Generally the tenet that alcoholics are working out some kind of unresolved needs or reinstating conflict of their early family lives is non-discriminating because it can be applied to too many other kinds of deviant behavior and indeed even to much normal behavior."

[87] Lemert expresses this objection to the pervasive anxiety theme: "while anxiety can give rise to drunkenness...it can also give rise to other forms of behavior: gambling, sexual misbehavior, religious ritual, and mental disease. The choices and alternatives in the process of cultural change and in the selective economy of personal growth cannot be explained at the level of the anxiety itself" (Lemert 1956a:313). This is a modification of his earlier (1954a) acceptance of Horton's anxiety theory. Others who have included anxiety in their formulations are Berreman (1956); Honigmann and Honigmann (1945). Laughlin (n.d.*), however, says anxiety is only part of the picture.

[88] See Bacon (1974*, 1976*); Bacon, Barry and Child (1965); Bacon, Barry, Child and Snyder (1965); and Barry (1976*).

[89] Among others emphasizing this explanation is Parker (1964*).

[90] See Bennett (1963); Berreman (1956); L. Boyer (1964c); Dozier (1966); Fairbanks (n.d.); Hamer (1965); Hurt and Brown (1965); Lubart (1969a); Maynard (1969); Mohatt (1972); du Toit (1964); Whittaker (1963, 1966).

[91] See also Lemert (1958).

[92] See Ablon (1965); Reifel (1963); Savishinsky (1971); IHS Task Force on Alcoholism (1977).

[93] See Balikci (1968); Hallowell (1955); Lemert (1958); C. Lewis (1970); Medicine (1969); Mohatt (1972); Savishinsky (1971); Slotkin (1953); Whittaker (1963).

[94] Bales (1946) provides a cross-cultural functional scheme, including Hopi, Zuni and East Coast Native Americans in its illustrations, in a way which implies they should have low rates of alcoholism.

[95] See Lemert (1954a, 1954b, 1956a, 1956b, 1958); Codere (1955); Mangin (1955*).

[96] Among others who have used this explanatory framework are Balikci (1968); Ferguson (1968b); Hurt and Brown (1965); C. Lewis (1970); Medicine (1969); Slotkin (1953); Swanson (1971).

[97] See reviews by Lemert (1970*); Lurie (1970*).

[98] An important element of learning is acknowledged by many other authors, including Berreman (1956:505); Curley (1967:130); Graves (1970: 52); Honigmann and Honigmann (1965:73); Lemert (1956a); Levy and Kunitz (1974:24); Lurie (1970*); Kuttner and Lorincz (1967); Wacko (1973); Westermeyer (1972b). However, Holloway (1966) points out that formal educational programs have not succeeded in motivating Native American youth.

[99] See the bibliography of MacAndrew and Edgerton (1969) for coverage of historical materials on Native American alcohol use which has not been covered here.

[100] See also Price (1975).

[101] Though in some places it is claimed they persist, for example on and near the Navajo reservation, according to Levy and Kunitz (1974).

[102] See Bacon (1976*:28).

[103] As a folk category alternative to White drinking and abstinence, see Lurie (1972); Westermeyer (1972b).

[104] Deloria (1970*:10-11) used Lurie's preliminary formulation to illustrate the absurdity of claiming that Native Americans suffer from an identity crisis; Lurie had not intended to take such a position, but was talking about a symbolic affirmation of Native Americanism.

[105] See Brod (1975:1389); Brody (1971:45-52); Browning (1971); Dosman (1972:79); Dozier (1966:77-78); Geyer (1963*); Graves (1970:52); Heath (1964:132); Helm and Lurie (1961); Honigmann (1970, 1971a:256);

James (1961:731, 736, 744); Jilek-Aall (1974:359); Jilek and Todd (1974); Kemnitzer (1972:139); Laughlin, cited in Lemert (1956a:311); Lemert (1958: 99, 1956a:313, 1954a:372); C. Lewis (1970); Littman (1970:1781); McNickle (1968:223); Nagler (1975); New York Center for Migrant Studies (n.d.); Rattray (1970); Robbins (1973); Robertson (1970); Snyder (1971*:237); Waddell (1975:14); Westermeyer (1974:31).

REFERENCES

(which do not appear in the
annotated bibliography)

Akwesasne Notes
 1971 "I believe in Apartheid", says Spokeswoman [Kahn-Tineta Horn].
 Akwesasne Notes 3(5):41.

Anonymous
 1964 American Indian Workshop Sessions (Section VIII). Notes from
 the Small Group Discussions. In *Lectures and Reports, 1964 Manual
 Supplement*. Salt Lake City: University of Utah, School of Alcohol
 Studies.

Anonymous
 1974a A Paper on Native Alcoholism Programs. Provincial Native
 Action Committee. February 22. Edmonton, Alberta, Canada. Unpublished. (Eric Shirt, Coordinator.)

Archibald, C., Jr.
 1971 The Mainstream--Where Indians Drown. *HSMHA Health Reports*
 86(1):489-494.

Bacon, Margaret K.
 1974 The Dependency-Conflict Hypothesis and the Frequency of
 Drunkenness; Further Evidence from a Cross-Cultural Stu'
 Quarterly Journal of Studies on Alcohol 35:863-876.
 1976 Cross-cultural Studies of Drinking: Integrated Drinking and
 Sex Differences in the Use of Alcoholic Beverages. In *Cross-
 Cultural Approaches to the Study of Alcohol*. M. Everett,
 J. Waddell and D. Heath (eds.). pp. 28-33. The Hague: Mouton.

Bahr, H. M., B. A. Chadwick and R. C. Day (eds.)
 1972 *Native Americans Today: Sociological Perspectives*. New York:
 Harper and Row.

Barry, Herbert, III
 1976 Cross-Cultural Evidence that Dependency Conflict Motivates
 Drunkenness. In *Cross-Cultural Approaches to the Study of
 Alcohol*. M. Everett, J. Waddell and D. Heath (eds.). pp. 249-263.
 The Hague: Mouton.

Bennion, L. J. and T. Li
 1976 Technical Report NAPS Document 02715. National Auxiliary
 Publications Service, c/o Microfilms Publications, 440 Park Avenue,
 N.Y.

Bloom, J. D.
 1974 Changing Patterns of Eskimo Homicide. Paper presented at the
 annual meeting, American Psychiatric Association, Detroit, May.

Boyatzis, R. E.
1976 Drinking as a Manifestation of Power Concerns. In *Cross-Cultural Approaches to the Study of Alcohol*. M. Everett, J. Waddell and D. Heath (eds.). pp. 265-288. The Hague: Mouton.

Brush, S. G.
1974 Should the History of Science be Rated X? *Science* 183:1164-1171.

Cahalan, D.
1970 *Problem Drinkers: A National Survey*. San Francisco: Jossey-Bass.

Chafetz, M. E.
1973 New Federal Legislation on Alcoholism: Opportunities and Problems. *American Journal of Public Health* 63(3):206-208.

Codere, Helen
1956 The Amiable Side of Kwakiutl Life: The Potlatch and the Play Potlatch. *American Anthropologist* 58:334-351, 497.

Conrad, R. D. and M. W. Kahn
1974 An Epidemiological Study of Suicide and Attempted Suicide among the Papago Indians. *American Journal of Psychiatry* 131(1):69-72.

Day, N.
1976 *Measures of Alcohol Relative Mortality and Morbidity in California*. Berkeley: California, Office of Alcoholism, Report #3.

Deloria, Vine, Jr.
1970 *We Talk, You Listen*. New York: Macmillan.

Dizmang, L. H., J. Watson, P. A. May and J. Bopp
1974 Adolescent Suicide on the Indian Reservation. *American Journal of Orthopsychiatry* 44(1):43-49.

Everett, M. W., J. O. Waddell and D. B. Heath
1976 *Cross-Cultural Approaches to the Study of Alcohol*. The Hague: Mouton.

Ewing, J. A., Beatrice A. Rouse, Robert A. Mueller and Kenneth C. Mills
1976 Alcohol as a Euphoriant Drug: Searching for a Neurochemical Basis. *Annals of the New York Academy of Sciences* 273:159-166.

Ferguson, Frances N.
1971 Eskimos in a Satellite Society. In *Native Peoples*. J. L. Elliott, ed. Scarborough: Prentice-Hall of Canada.

Freilich, Maurice
1958 Cultural Persistence among the Modern Iroquois. *Anthropos* 53:473-483.

Geyer, G. A.
   1963 Why the Indian Loses Out. Chicago Daily News, January 29.

Graves, T. D.
   1967 Psychological Acculturation in a Tri-Ethnic Community. *Southwestern Journal of Anthropology* 23:337-350.

Graves, T. D. and M. Van Arsdale
   1965 Perceived Opportunities, Expectations and the Decision to Remain on Relocation: The Case of the Navajo Indian Migrant to Denver, Colorado. *Human Organization* 23:300-307.

Heath, Dwight B.
   1976 Anthropological Perspective on Alcohol: An Historical Review. In *Cross-Cultural Approaches to the Study of Alcohol*. M. Everett, J. Waddell and D. Heath (eds.). pp. 42-101. The Hague: Mouton.

Hellon, C. P.
   1970 Mental Illness and Acculturation in the Canadian Aboriginal. *Canadian Psychiatric Association Journal* 15:(2):135-272.

Hill, C. A. and M. I. Spector
   1971 Natality and Mortality of American Indians Compared to United States Whites and Non-Whites. *Health Services Reports* 86(3):229-246.

Holloway, R.
   1964 *Student Drinking*. Winnipeg: Alcohol Education Service.
   1965 *Home Influence on Student Drinking*. Winnipeg: Alcohol Education Service.

Jessor, R. (and Reply by K. Bruun)
   1970 Correspondence. The Tri-Ethnic Study and the Problem of Culture. *Quarterly Journal of Studies on Alcohol* 29:272-277.

Johnston, F.
   1966 The Population Approach to Human Variation. *Annals of the New York Academy of Sciences* 134(2):507-515.

Jones, B. M. and M. K. Jones
   1976 Alcohol Effects in Women during the Menstrual Cycle. *Annals of the New York Academy of Sciences* 273:576-587.

Kinzie, J. D., J. H. Shore and E. M. Pattison
   1972 Anatomy of Psychiatric Consultation to Rural Indians. *Community Mental Health Journal* 8:196-207.

Kunitz, S. J., J. E. Levy and R. Euler
   1972 Drinking and Deviant Drinking among Indians in Two Arizona Communities. *National Clearinghouse for Alcohol Information Report*. 47p.

Lantis, M.
   1968 Environmental Stresses on Human Behavior. *Archives of Environmental Health* 17:578.

Laughlin, W. S.
n.d. Alcohol in Primitive and Ancient Societies. Unpublished. Cited (p. 311) in Alcoholism: Theory, Problems and Challenge: III. Alcoholism and the Sociocultural Situation. E. M. Lemert. *Quarterly Journal of Studies on Alcohol* 17:306-317.

Lechnyr, R. J.
1970 A Theory of the Effects of Identification in Alcoholism among Hopi Indian Males. Window Rock, Arizona: Indian Health Service, USPHS.

Leighton, Alexander H.
1968 Introduction--The Mental Health of the American Indian. *American Journal of Psychiatry* 125(2):217-218.

Leland, Joy
1978 Women and Alcohol in an Indian Settlement. *Medical Anthropology* 2(4):85-119.
1979 Alcohol, Anthropologists and Native Americans. *Human Organization* 38:94-99.

Lemert, E. M.
1970 Review of Drunken Comportment: A Social Explanation. *Quarterly Journal of Studies on Alcohol* 29:268-269.

Levy, Jerrold E.
1972 Navaho Suicide. In *The Emergent Native Americans*. Deward E. Walker, Jr., ed. pp. 594-613. Boston: Little, Brown.

Lurie, N. O.
1970 Review of Drunken Comportment: A Social Explanation. *American Anthropologist* 72:963-964.

Mail, Patricia and Victoria Sears.
1976 *Alcohol Use among Native Americans: A Selective, Annotated Bibliography*. Sacramento: State of California, Office of Alcoholism.

Mangin, W.
1955 Review of Alcohol and the Northwest Coast Indians. *American Anthropologist* 57:1303-1305.

May, P. A.
1973 Suicide and Suicide Attempts on the Pine Ridge Reservation. Pine Ridge, S.D.: Unpublished paper for the U.S. Public Health Service, Community Mental Health Program.

Maynard, E.
1968 Juvenile Offenses and Offenders on the Pine Ridge Reservation. *Pine Ridge Research Bulletin* 4:9-24.

McClelland, D., W. Davis, R. Kalin and E. Wanner
1972 *The Drinking Man*. New York: Free Press.

McFee, M.
   1968 The 150% Man, a Product of Blackfeet Acculturation. *American Anthropologist* 70(6):1096-1103. (Also in *Native Americans Today.* H. Bahr et al., eds. pp. 303-312. New York: Harper and Row, 1972.

Nagata, S.
   1971 The Reservation Community and the Urban Community: Hopi Indians of Moenkopi. In *The American Indian in Urban Society.* J. O. Waddell and O. M. Watson, eds. pp. 114-159. Boston: Little, Brown.

Paredes, Alfonso
   1976 Future Plans and Goals in Research: The Oklahoma Center for Alcohol and Drug-Related Studies. *Annals of the New York Academy of Sciences* 273:103-109.

Paredes, J. A.
   1966 The Land and the People. Bemidji, Minnesota: Upper Mississippi Research Project. Cited in Violent Death and Alcohol Use among the Chippewa in Minnesota. J. Westermeyer and J. Brantner. *Minnesota Medicine* 55:749-752.

Parker, S.
   1964 Ethnic Identity and Acculturation in Two Eskimo Villages. *American Anthropologist* 66:325-340.

Region X Indian Alcohol Programs
   n.d. Region X Indian Alcohol Programs Transfer Plan. Seattle: Unpublished report prepared for the USPHS Indian Health Service.

Reichenbach, D. D.
   1967 Autopsy Incidence of Disease among Southwestern American Indians. *American Medical Association Archives of Pathology* 84:81-86.

Schaefer, James M.
   1976 Drunkenness and Cultural Stress: A Holocultural Test. In *Cross-Cultural Approaches to the Study of Alcohol.* M. Everett, J. Waddell and D. Heath, eds. pp. 287-321. The Hague: Mouton.

Seixas, F. A. and S. Eggleston
   1976 Work in Progress on Alcoholism. *Annals of the New York Academy of Sciences* 273:1-3.

Shepardson, M. and B. Hammond
   1964 Charge and Persistence in an Isolated Navaho Community. *American Anthropology* 5:1029-1049.

Shore, J. H.
   1972 Suicide Patterns among Major Northwest Indian Tribes. *Transcultural Psychiatric Research Review* 9(1):67-68.

Siegal, H. A., D. M. Petersen and C. D. Chambers
1975 Emerging Skid Row--Ethnographic and Social Notes on a Changing Scene. *Journal of Drug Issues* 5:160-166.

Snyder, P. A.
1971 The Social Environment of the Urban Indian. In *The American Indian in Urban Society*. J. O. Waddell and O. M. Watson, eds. pp. 206-243. Boston: Little, Brown.

Steinbring, J.
1971 Acculturational Phenomena among the Lake Winnipeg Ojibwa of Canada. *Proceedings of the International Congress of Americanists* 3:179-188.

Tracey, D. A. and P. E. Nathan
1976 Behavioral Analysis of Chronic Alcoholism in Four Women. *Journal of Consulting and Clinical Psychology* 44(5):832-842.

University of Utah School of Alcohol Studies
1963-67 *Lectures and Reports*. Salt Lake City: University of Utah School of Alcohol Studies.

U.S. Bureau of the Census
1973 *Census of Population: 1970. Subject Reports. Final Report PC(2)-IF. American Indians*. Washington, D.C.: U.S. Government Printing Office.

U.S. Congress. House of Representatives. Committee on Interior and Insular Affairs, Subcommittee on Indian Affairs
1975 *Hearing on HR2525 and Related Bills to Implement the Federal Responsibility for the Care and Education of the Indian People by Improving the Services and Facilities of Federal Indian Health Programs and Encouraging Maximum Participation of Indians in Such Programs, and for Other Purposes*. 94th Congress, 1st Session, May 23, 24, August 5, September 25, 25. Washington, D.C.: U.S. Government Printing Office.

U.S. Department of Health, Education and Welfare. Indian Health Service
1969 *Suicide among the American Indian*. Washington, D.C.: U.S. Government Printing Office, DHEW Publication No. PHS 1903.
1976a An Overview of Seven NIAAA Alcoholism Treatment Programs for Fiscal Year 1976. Program Analysis and Evaluation Branch, NIAAA, September. Unpublished.
1976b An Evaluative Report on American Indian Alcoholism Projects. Unpublished Draft, May.
1977a Personal Communication, Mozart Spector, Program Analysis and Statistics Branch, Office of Program Planning and Evaluation, Health Services and Mental Health Administration, Public Health Service, March 28.
1977b Recent NIAAA Projects Relevant to Indians of the U.S. (excluding Alaskans). Computer Printout. Scientific Project Analysis and Retrieval System (SPARS), March 1.

Vallee, F. G.
    1968 Stresses of Change and Mental Health among the Canadian Eskimos.
    Archives of Environmental Health 17:565-570.

Waddell, J. O. and M. W. Everett (eds.)
    1979 *Drinking Behavior among Southwestern Indians.* Tucson: University of Arizona Press.

Waddell, J. O. and O. M. Watson (eds.)
    1971 *The American Indian in Urban Society.* Boston: Little, Brown.

Wartburg, J. P. von
    1976 Biologic Aspects of Alcohol: An Introduction. *Annals of the New York Academy of Sciences* 273:146-150.

Wolff, P. H.
    1972 Ethnic Difference in Alcohol Sensitivity. *Science* 175:449-450.

Worth, S. and J. Adair
    1970 Navajo Film Makers. *American Anthropologist* 72(1):9-34.

Zeiner, Arthur R., Alfonso Paredes and Lawrence Cowden
    1976 Physiologic Responses to Ethanol among the Tarahumara. *Annals of the New York Academy of Sciences* 273:151-158.

TULAPAI TO TOKAY:
AN ANNOTATED BIBLIOGRAPHY

0001　　Aberle, David F.
　　　　　1966　*The Peyote Religion among the Navaho.*　Chicago:
　　　　　Aldine.

　　　　　The author notes that the Peyote ethical code advocates
　　　　　avoidance of alcohol. The insistence on abstinence,
　　　　　along with the importance of hard work, and care for
　　　　　one's family are important tenets of the Peyote religion.

0002　　Ablon, Joan
　　　　　1964　Relocated American Indians in the San Francisco
　　　　　Bay Area: Social Interaction and Indian Identity.
　　　　　Human Organization 23:296-304.

　　　　　Presents a discussion of Native American relocatees
　　　　　and their reactions, social interactions, and affiliations.
　　　　　Three characteristic attitudes towards Anglos were
　　　　　identified: suspicion, potential dependency, and fear
　　　　　of Anglo rejection. Socializing was often conducted
　　　　　in taverns and "Indian bars"; however, urban pow-wows
　　　　　were usually free from the drinking which characterized
　　　　　reservation dances. Drinking did not seem to be a
　　　　　result of relocation, but simply a behavior transferred
　　　　　from the reservation to the city.

0003　　Ablon, Joan
　　　　　1965　American Indian Relocation: Problems of Dependency
　　　　　and Management in the City.　*Phylon* 26:362-371.

　　　　　Problems faced by Native Americans in urban environments
　　　　　results from the historic usurpation of decision-making
　　　　　power by the Federal government. The author contends
　　　　　that heavy drinking and familial disorganization are
　　　　　not the result of urban living, but rather are charac-
　　　　　teristics which Native Americans bring from the reservation
　　　　　to the city.

0004　　Ablon, Joan
　　　　　1971　Cultural Conflict in Urban Indians.　*Mental Hygiene*
　　　　　55:199-205.

　　　　　Describes the problems which relocated Native Americans
　　　　　must often face, and notes that it is necessary for
　　　　　community agencies to recognize the unique cultural
　　　　　characteristics which Native Americans bring to the
　　　　　city. Excessive drinking may result as a means of
　　　　　withdrawing from situations which are not understood
　　　　　and are painful for the Native American.

0005   Abrams, George H.J.
          1976 *The Seneca People*. Phoenix: Indian Tribal Series.

          Notes that the consumption of alcohol was prohibited
          in the first written Seneca constitution (1833). The
          constitution stipulated that any leader who imbibed
          alcohol would be deposed.

0006   Ackerman, Lillian A.
          1971 Marital Instability and Juvenile Delinquency
          among the Nez Perces. *American Anthropologist*
          73(3):595-603.

          Stress has resulted in a series of responses incon-
          gruous with aboriginal Nez Perce culture. The author
          hypothesizes that excessive alcohol use may be a
          substitute for vision quests, or may be related to
          despair over lack of status. Many parents are alcoholic,
          child neglect is not uncommon, and accidents are frequent.
          Traditional male roles have been demolished and males
          consider wages to be personal property to be used for
          gambling and drinking.

0007   Adams, Alexander B.
          1971 *Geronimo*. G.P. Putnam's Sons.

          Includes a discussion on the making of liquor and
          the effect of alcoholic beverages upon Native Americans.
          The importance of tiswin as a native beverage and the
          place of the mescal cactus as a source of food and
          liquor are considered. The use of alcohol to demoralize
          the Apache is mentioned.

0008   Adler, Nathan and Daniel Goleman
          1969 Gambling and Alcoholism: Symptom Substitution
          and Functional Equivalents. *Quarterly Journal of
          Studies on Alcohol* 30(3):733-736.

          The dynamics of gambling and alcoholism are viewed
          as functional equivalents. The Native American penchant
          for gambling prior to reservation incarceration is
          noted. It is observed that when Native Americans lost
          their autonomy alcoholism increased and the prestigious
          social role of gambler all but disappeared. Thus,
          alcoholism is postulated as a response to the loss
          of an important cultural phenomenon, gambling.

0009**   Alaska. Native Health Board
          1973 Evaluation of Alcoholism Treatment Services in
          the State of Alaska: a Description of Service Agency
          Operations and Evaluation of the Health System Operation
          Unpublished report by the Alaska Native Health Board,
          117p.

This report attempts to determine the degree to which
service agencies in Alaska are responding to clients
with drinking problems. Evaluators examined (1) the
information gathering process upon which case assessment is made, (2) treatment plans, (3) treatment plan
follow-up, and (4) evaluation of treatment plans.

0010**   Alaska. Native Health Board
1974 A System to Improve Care for the Alaska Problem
Drinker. Unpublished report by the Alaska Native
Health Board, 44 p.

A brief description of the "staging" concept used for
assessment and treatment planning. This report reflects
an attempt to divide alcoholism into stages of severity
in the physical, social, and economic realms. The four
basic steps applied to problem solving are (1) information
gathering, (2) assessment, (3) treatment planning, and
(4) treatment and follow-up.

0011**   Alaska. Native Health Board
1975 Risk Analysis: a Concept and Its Application to
Alcoholism and Mental Health. A report prepared
by the Alaska Native Health Board under contract
HSM 76-72-328, 12p.

Describes a project which attempts to design a model
which will predict whether a patient, given treatment
for alcoholism, will improve, deteriorate, or exhibit
no change at all. It is assumed that the application
of a reliable tool which would identify the risk rate
of specific populations would enable preventive services
to be focused on the individuals most likely to benefit.
Discusses the "staging" concept of determining risk.

0012**   Albaugh, Bernard J.
1973 Ethnic Therapy with American Indian Alcoholics
as an Antidote to Anomie. A paper presented at
the 8th joint meeting of the Professional Associations of the U.S. Public Health Service, 5p.

Work with the Cheyenne and Arapaho suggests that
successful alcohol treatment and rehabilitation might
be achieved through programs designed around common
Plains Indian cultural values. The author describes
a program which included (1) support from the Native
American Church, (2) counseling with traditional
ceremonial chiefs, and (3) the assistance of other
members of the tribe through charitable works.

0013   Albaugh, Bernard J.
        1975 Alcoholism and Substance Sniffing. A paper presented at the 10th joint meeting of the Professional Associations of the U.S. Public Health Service.

        Alcoholism and substance sniffing are mutually reinforcing roles that grow from the same type of psycho-social milieu. Research indicates that a significant relationship exists between (1) the presence of an alcoholic in the immediate family and sniffing, (2) chronic sniffing and future alcoholism, and (3) role confusion and ego function of the sniffer and alcoholic.

0014   Albaugh, Bernard J.
        1976 Fetal Alcohol Syndrome. A paper presented at the 11th joint meeting of the Professional Association of the U.S. Public Health Service.

        Reviews the history and developmental progress of three probable cases of Fetal Alcohol Syndrome. Chronic alcoholism during the prenatal period resulted in neonates who exhibited problems of respiratory adaptation, nutritional adaptation, and growth deficiency. Older children also exhibited physical and psychological developmental delay. The evidence reinforces reported correlations between heavy maternal drinking and congenital malformation and developmental retardation in infants.

0015   Albaugh, Bernard J. and P. Anderson
        1974 Peyote in the Treatment of Alcoholism among American Indians. *American Journal of Psychiatry* 131(11):1247-1250.

        Participation in the ceremonies of the Native American Church provide an important component in an ethnically oriented alcoholism treatment program for Southern Cheyenne and Arapaho patients. The Peyote religion offers specific advantages to Native Americans which other forms of alcohol treatment cannot: (1) it is uniquely pan-Indian; (2) it has a strict no drinking rule prior to meetings; (3) the ceremony is structured and provides a role for each participant; (4) participants are encouraged to express their problems; and (5) the meetings are conducted by men held in high regard by the participants and who share a similar cultural background. Additional aspects of the Cheyenne-Arapaho treatment program are also discussed.

0016   Alday, Rudy K.
   1971 Alcoholism versus the Southwest American Indian.
   In *Selected Papers of the 22nd Annual Meeting*, pp.
   23-24. Washington, D.C.: North American Association
   of Alcoholism Programs (now known as Alcohol and Drug
   Problems Association of North America).

   The author, a Jicarilla Apache, suggests that giving
   Native Americans large sums of money for alcohol programs without providing skilled personnel and adequate
   training for staff is merely a way to assuage guilt
   on the part of Anglos for introducing alcohol to Native
   Americans. He also suggests that successful treatment
   programs must be based on Native American values rather
   than Anglo values.

0017   Allen, James R.
   1973 The Indian Adolescent: Psychosocial Tasks of
   the Plains Indian of Western Oklahoma. *American
   Journal of Orthopsychiatry* 43(3):368-375.

   Adolescence, generally viewed as a time of psychosocial
   turmoil, brings forth problems of greater complexity
   for Native Americans compared to Anglos. As a result,
   reckless drinking is a widespread problem among Native
   American adolescents.

0018**   Andre, James M.
   1970a Alcoholism: The Effects of Chronic Excessive
   Drinking. Unpublished paper presented for the
   Community Health Representative Training Program.
   Indian Health Service, Desert Willow Training Center,
   4p.

   Provides statistical data relating to Indian arrest
   rates, on-reservation reported crimes, and the percentage of Native Americans in prison. Reviews known
   facts about excessive drinking and its effects on
   economic health, social health, mental health, and
   physical health.

0019**   Andre, James M.
   1970b Alcoholism: History, Definitions, Warning Signs,
   and Psychology of Excessive Drinking. Unpublished
   paper prepared for the Community Health Representative
   Training Program. Indian Health Service, Desert
   Willow Training Center, 8p.

   Reviews the history of alcohol use, the definition of
   alcoholism, warning signs presented by the problem
   drinker, and the psychology of excessive drinking

-61-

in order to help prepare Native American paraprofessionals for work in Native American communities.

0020**   Andre, James M.
1970c   Alcoholism: Treatments and Community Resources. Unpublished paper prepared for the Community Health Representative Training Program. Indian Health Service, Desert Willow Training Center, 11p.

Reviews various treatment modalities and provides an explanation of each type along with a discussion of the attitudes which non-Native Americans hold about Native Americans and alcohol. Also considers various rehabilitation programs and investigates community resources which can be brought to bear on the drinking problem.

0021**   Andre, James M.
1970d   The History, Patterns and Problems of Indian Drinking. Unpublished paper prepared for the Community Health Representative Training Program. Indian Health Service, Desert Willow Training Center, 11p.

Provides a review of the historical influences which affected Native American drinking, an overview of the basic patterns of Native American drinking, and a review of the problems engendered by excessive Native American drinking.

0022**   Andre, James M.
1970e   A Psychiatrist Looks at General Problems in Indian Communities. Unpublished paper presented at the 6th Annual Institute on Alcoholism, 12p.

Identifies problem drinking as the most pressing health problem among Native Americans of New Mexico. Discusses problems associated with health care delivery and suggests that greater use should be made of paraprofessionals. Notes that knowledge of local tradition and increased involvement of Native Americans are important to the success of health care programs.

0023**   Andre, James M.
1971   The Many Sides to Mental Health Problems among American Indians. Unpublished paper presented at the Western Interstate Commission for Higher Education Conference on Mental Health Issues among Indians of the Southwest, 10p.

This paper addresses a number of issues, including alcohol abuse, which Native Americans will have to face if the overall emotional, social, and environmental climate of the Native American is to improve.

0024** Andre, James M.
1974a General Comments on Alcoholism. Unpublished notes for staff training, Albuquerque Area Indian Health Service, 14p.

Reviews the history of alcohol among Native Americans and discusses various definitions of alcoholism. Follows the classic Jellinek progression in listing the signs of a problem drinker. Examines the social, psychological, and physiological effects of excessive drinking. Native American drinking is attributed to a lack of cultural means of controlling drinking. Various theories regarding Native American drinking are examined and Jellinek's typologies are outlined.

0025** Andre, James M.
1974b Using Community Resources for the Alcoholic. Unpublished staff training paper prepared for the Albuquerque Area Indian Health Service, 9p.

Discusses the ways in which community resources may be used to help the alcoholic, and identifies resources within communities and tribes which may be utilized. Summarizes the treatment of alcoholism and stresses the importance of follow-up activities.

0026** Andre, James M.
1976 The Pathological Effects of Alcohol on Economic, Social, and Mental Health. Unpublished training notes prepared for the Albuquerque Area Indian Health Service, 7p.

The effects of chronic excessive drinking are outlined, and the implications for social and physical health are reviewed. Statistics reflecting the impact of alcohol on Native American communities are reviewed. Notes that 90% of crimes on reservations are alcohol-related and 40% of delinquent youths come from homes where excessive parental drinking occurs.

0027** Andre, James M. and Stanley Ghachu
n.d. Characteristics of Completed Suicides in an American Community of the Southwest. Unpublished paper prepared for the Albuquerque Area Indian Health Service, 12p.

Examines the characteristics of nine completed suicides which occurred during a 3½ year period at Zuni. Twelve characteristics which were thought to be indicative of suicide-prone individuals were identified. Previous data indicates that alcohol had been involved in 78% of all suicides and 83% of suicide attempts. In seven of the nine cases reported there was a history of excessive drinking.

0028** Andre, James M. and Stanley Ghachu
1975 Suicidal Occurrences in an American Indian Community. Unpublished paper presented at the 10th joint meeting of the Professional Associations of the U.S. Public Health Service.

Summarizes the results of a 3½ year study of suicide among Pueblo Indians. The study revealed significant differences in suicide among Pueblo Indians compared to Native Americans nationwide. Differences in age groupings, male/female ratios, alcohol consumption, marital status, and arrest records were found.

0029** Anonymous
n.d. A.A. Comes of Age among the Navajo People. Unpublished presentation, New Mexico Commission on Alcoholism, 2p.

Discusses the effectiveness of A.A. in combating alcoholism among the Navajos.

0030 Anonymous
1832 *Laws of the Colonial and State Governments Relating to Indians and Indian Affairs, 1633-1831 Inclusive.* Washington City: Thompson and Homans.

Provides a collection of early laws which prohibited Native Americans from purchasing or possessing liquor. Laws aimed at the following groups are included: Narragansett (1801), Moravian Indians (1810), the Indians of Pennsylvania (1721), Ohio (1809), and Indiana (1807).

0031 Anonymous
1911 Keeping the Indian Sober. *Harper's Weekly* 55:23.

A description of the role played by the Special Officers of the Indian Service in preventing the sale of intoxicants to Native Americans.

0032 Anonymous
1913a Indians Hear Strong Address by Anti-Saloon Worker. *Carlisle Arrow* 10(17):2.

Remarks by Dr. Homer Tope, Superintendent of the Philadelphia Anti-Saloon League, in support of the school's vigorous and consistent warfare against liquor are reported.

0033 Anonymous
1913b Sent to Jail for Furnishing Booze to Carlisle Students. *Carlisle Arrow* 9(37):1.

Reports on the arrest and conviction of two "colored youths" who were caught giving liquor to Native American students. The two were fined and sentenced to terms in the Cumberland County jail. The federal judge was thanked for helping to stamp out intemperance.

0034 Anonymous
1915a The Cause of Total Abstinence. *Carlisle Arrow* 11(30):2-3.

A collection of maxims and anecdotes illustrating how various people have achieved and maintained abstinence; designed to show Native American youth the proper direction in life.

0035 Anonymous
1915b Sale of Liquor to Oneidas Must Stop. *Carlisle Arrow* 11(26):1.

Article notes that saloon keepers in Green Bay and DePere, Wisconsin have been selling liquor to Oneida Indians and calls for a stop of such sales.

0036 Anonymous
1916 What Indian Students Think of Alcohol: Extracts from Indian School Children's Essays on Alcohol and My Future. *The Red Man* 9(2):61-66.

A collection of excerpts on alcohol written by students in the third through ninth grades at Haskell Institute and Chilocco Indian School. There is an emphasis on the evil and deleterious effects of alcohol.

0037 Anonymous
1938 The Liquor Question as it Affects Indians. *Indians at Work* 5(11):22-26.

Discusses the advantages and disadvantages of prohibition among Native Americans. Notes that after 1933 some tribes, especially those in Oklahoma, were removed from the constraints of prohibition.

0038 Anonymous
1939 Drink and the Indians. *Indians at Work* 7(2): 6-8.

Examines the problems of enforcing prohibition on Indian reservations, especially in Alaska. The success of Special Officer William E. "Pussyfoot" Johnson in catching violators of the liquor laws is noted.

0039 Anonymous
1954 Alcohol and the Indian. *América Indígena* 14(4): 286-288.

Comments on the deleterious effects of liquor upon Native Americans. Postulates lack of entertainment as one cause of alcohol abuse. Suggests that the development of regional theater, based on indigenous folklore, would provide a constructive alternative to drinking.

0040 Anonymous
1955 Constitutional Law - Equal Protection of the Laws Prohibition of Sale of Intoxicating Liquor to Indians. *New York University Law Review* 30(7):1444-1447.

Reviews state laws regulating Native American affairs, including liquor prohibition. Considers state versus Federal authority. Concludes that Constitutional power does not justify racial classification for the prohibition of alcohol.

0041 Anonymous
1956 The Liquor Problem Among the Indians of the Southwest. *Indian Affairs* 18:3-4.

Drinking is reported to be a problem in many tribal groups, and home and tribal authority are breaking down as contempt for tradition grows. Reservation prohibition contributes to surreptitious drinking. Factionalism between religious groups contributes to problem drinking. Control over liquor distribution will continue to be a problem. Calls for early education.

0042   Anonymous
        1963a   Indian Workshop Report: Colville. *Lectures
                & Reports, 1963 Manual Supplement.* Salt Lake City:
                University of Utah School of Alcohol Studies, 1p.

        Discusses the initiation of A.A. on the Colville
        Reservation in Washington State.

0043   Anonymous
        1963b   Indian Workshop Report: Halona Navajo. *Lectures
                & Reports, 1963 Manual Supplement.* Salt Lake City:
                University of Utah School of Alcohol Studies, 1p.

        Represents a brief report of a workshop in which the
        problems of a specific district on the Navajo Reservation
        are examined. Alcohol abuse is reflected in high
        arrest rates; however, it is also felt that there is
        insufficient police coverage to adequately handle the
        problem.

0044   Anonymous
        1963c   Indian Workshop Report: Rosebud Sioux. *Lectures
                & Reports, 1963 Manual Supplement.* Salt Lake City:
                University of Utah School of Alcohol Studies, 1p.

        Very briefly reports on alcohol problems on the Rosebud
        Reservation as reflected in arrests statistics and
        discusses attempts to establish A.A. in Indian communities.

0045   Anonymous
        1968   Juvenile Offenses and Offenders on the Pine
                Ridge Reservation. *Pine Ridge Research Bulletin*
                6:9-24.

        Examines 300 Native Americans between the ages of 5
        and 17 to determine the frequency of juvenile crime
        on reservations. The report indicates that 85% of
        all arrests were for DWI or liquor violations associated with disorderly conduct.

0046   Anonymous
        1969   Felt Needs, Dependency and Community Development.
                Pine Ridge Research Bulletin 7:1-10.

        Represents a study conducted among the Oglala Sioux
        to identify situations which the community perceives
        as major problems. Alcohol abuse was consistently
        tagged as a problem. However, mixed bloods were more
        concerned about drinking than full bloods, and Anglos
        seemed to view Native American alcoholism as a greater
        problem than the Native Americans themselves.

A046**   Anonymous
                 1970 Progress Report: January-September, 1970.
                 Unpublished report circulated by the Indian
                 Development District of Arizona, 12p.

                 Describes the first nine months of operation of
                 the Southwest Indian Youth Center, which offers a
                 rehabilitation program designed for delinquent Native
                 American youth. Many of the program participants
                 were sent to the Center for drinking and alcohol
                 related offenses.

0047**   Anonymous
                 1973 An Alcoholism Education Plan for Local Community
                 Use. Unpublished paper prepared for the Western
                 Region Indian Alcoholism Training Center, 6p.

                 Identifies seven target groups in Native American
                 communities for whom alcohol eduation should be
                 tailored: (1) tribal leaders, (2) Native American
                 youth, (3) law enforcement personnel, (4) community
                 service agency personnel, (5) the alcoholic and his
                 family, (6) the paraprofessional counselor, and (7)
                 young parents. The methodology and materials required
                 for such educational programs are outlined.

0048   Anonymous
                 1974a Alcoholism Under Attack. *Akwesasne Notes*
                 6(1):29.

                 Reviews some of the programs directed at controlling
                 Native American alcohol abuse. Discusses problems
                 associated with programs which originate in the dominant
                 culture. Suggests that a revitalization of native
                 traditions is needed to effectively combat problem
                 drinking. Indicates that Anglo psychiatrists cannot
                 effectively bridge the cultural gap without parapro-
                 fessional assistance from Native Americans.

0049   Anonymous
                 1974b Federal Authority Over Indian Affairs. *Indian
                 Law Reporter* 1(1):10-16.

                 Discusses a case on the Wind River Reservation in
                 Wyoming in which the Arapaho and Shoshone tribes, after
                 allowing liquor sales within the reservation in 1953,
                 attempted to levy a tribal tax on a liquor store which
                 had been operating on land not under tribal juris-
                 diction but within reservation boundaries. The courts
                 determined that tribal licensing laws do not apply to
                 businesses in a non-Indian community, even if that
                 community is within the reservation boundaries.

0050   Anonymous
         1974c Halfway House, Poston, Arizona. *Smoke Signals*
         19(6):16-18.

         Describes how a community-based, peer-group oriented
         facility was established to provide food, shelter, and
         a non-drinking environment for recovering alcoholics.

0051   Anonymous
         1975 A Report from Pine Ridge. Conditions on the
            Oglala Sioux Reservation. *Civil Rights Digest*
            7:28-38.

         Reports the findings of a commission appointed by the
         Secretary of the Interior to examine events on the Pine
         Ridge Reservation. Indicates that alcohol and drug
         abuse is a major concern in every community on the
         reservation, and that such cases clog the judicial
         system while more serious offenses go unpunished.

0052**   Anonymous
         1976a National Indian Board of Alcohol and Drug
            Abuse Position Paper. Unpublished position paper
            prepared for the National Congress of American
            Indians, 9p.

         Examines the magnitude and reasons for alcohol and
         drug abuse among Native Americans. Recommends total
         abstinence as the only cure for alcoholism and drug
         abuse. Suggests that Native Americans should put
         forth a united front in combatting the problem.

0053   Anonymous
         1976b State Jurisdiction: Liquor Licenses. *Indian
            Law Reporter* 3:i-1, i-5.

         Examines an opinion by the Associate Solicitor, Indian
         Affairs, Department of the Interior which states that
         a tribal member may operate a liquor dealership without
         complying with the licensing or state monopoly require-
         ments of state law.

0054**   Anonymous
         1977 Drug Use among Young People at Indian Heritage
            School. Unpublished paper. Indian Heritage School,
            52p.

         Reports the results of a survey on drug use (including
         alcohol) administered to 52 students in grades 7-12.
         The results are compared to a "national sample" of
         undetermined origin, and a "Native American sample,"
         again of undetermined origin.

0055**   Archibald, Charles W., Jr.
          1973 Alcoholism - Where There's a Will, There's a Way.
          Unpublished paper presented at the 8th joint meeting
          of the Professional Associations of the U.S. Public
          Health Service, 10p.

          Alcoholism still poses a treatment problem, as medical
          team members typically limit their responsibility
          to restoration of the physical health of alcoholics,
          ignoring the emotional and social aspects of treatment.
          Suggests that if alcoholism is a disease it should be
          treated using the medical-legal model used with TB;
          that is, involuntary treatment, isolation from temp-
          tation, physical restoration, and chemotherapy with
          Antabuse if necessary. When the "will" has been
          strengthened the patient can continue on an outpatient
          basis with help in internalizing a new life style.

0056   Arizona. Commission of Indian Affairs
          1963 Reservation Survey: Health. Unpublished report,
          Arizona Commission of Indian Affairs, 65p.

          Represents a series of questionnaires administered by
          the Commission on various Arizona reservations in order
          to identify health problems. Each questionnaire
          asked the respondent to rank health problems and needs
          on his reservation. In many cases excessive drinking
          was ranked as the number one health problem. The
          Colorado River, Hualapai, Navajo, and Ak-Chin
          reservations reported that excessive drinking was
          their chief problem.

0057   Arizona. Commission of Indian Affairs
          1964 Reservation Survey: Health. Unpublished report,
          Arizona Commission of Indian Affairs, 17p.

          In 1964 the Ak-Chin, Camp Verde, Colorado River, and
          Navajo reservations reported excessive drinking as
          their number one health problem.

0058   Arizona. Commission of Indian Affairs
          1965 Reservation Survey: Health. Unpublished report,
          Arizona Commission of Indian Affairs, 17p.

          In 1965 only one reservation, Ak-Chin, indicated that
          excessive drinking was their primary health problem.

0059   Arizona. Commission of Indian Affairs
          1966 Reservation Survey: Health. Unpublished report,
          Arizona Commission of Indian Affairs, 17p.

Reservations which indicated that excessive drinking was their number one health problem in 1966 included: Camp Verde, Colorado River, Hualapai, and Navajo.

0060 Arthaud, Bradley
1970 Cause of Death in 339 Alaskan Natives as Determined by Autopsy. *Archives of Pathology* 90:433-438.

Compares a study of 339 Alaskan Native autopsies over a 10-year period to an earlier study of 103 Alaskan Native autopsies. Prematurity and tuberculosis decreased significantly as causes of death. Cirrhosis from all causes is reported at 10.2%, slightly less than the 12.8% reported for southwestern Native Americans. It is possible that other causes of death, such as pneumonia, are precipitated by alcohol abuse; however, this is not evident in autopsies.

0061 Association of American Indian Affairs, Inc.
1964 Proceedings of the Third National Conference on Indian Health. New York: Association of American Indian Affairs, Inc., 41p. (mimeographed).

A transcript of the discussion on the place of alcoholism in the field of mental health. Alcohol abuse is considered both a psychiatric disorder and a contributor to psychiatric disorders.

0062 Association of American Indian Affairs, Inc.
1974 Federal Policy and American Indian Health Needs: the Role of Consumers in a National Health Program. Report of the Sixth National Conference on Indian Health. New York: Association of American Indian Affairs, Inc., 30p. (mimeographed).

Notes that alcohol and mental illness are priority problems, and that increased education of aides and community members can help to overcome these problems. The role and importance of Native American health boards is also mentioned, and it is suggested that in the area of mental health no one can be as effective as local people.

0063 Atcheson, J.D.
1972 Problems of Mental Health in the Canadian Arctic. *Canada's Mental Health* 20(1):10-17.

Types of mental illnesses observed are described and some causative factors suggested. Alcohol abuse is noted as contributing to child neglect and deprivation.

A063   Attneave, Carolyn L. and Dianne R. Kelso
                1977 *American Indian Annotated Bibliography of Mental
                Health*. Vol. 1. Seattle: University of Washington,
                Department of Psychology.

                A survey of the literature which deals with Native
                American Mental Health. Of the articles reviewed,
                250 are annotated and another 250 are listed. Several
                indexes are furnished, including subject index, author
                index, geographic index, and tribal index. Annotations
                are accompanied by editorial comments. Papers which
                discuss alcohol abuse and use are included.

0064   Auburn, F.M.
                1970 Regina vs. Drybones. *Law Quarterly Review*
                86:306-309.

                Reviews the case of Joseph Drybones, who was arrested
                for intoxication in Yellowknife, Northwest Territories
                in 1967. Since it was felt that Drybones was dealt
                with more severely because he was an Indian, an appeal
                was made to the Supreme Court alleging that Drybones's
                civil rights under the 1960 Canadian Bill of Rights
                had been violated. The court found that no individual
                should be treated more harshly under the law than
                another, regardless of race, class, religion.

0065   Bacon, Margaret K., Herbert Barry III and Irvin L. Child
                1965 A Cross-Cultural Study of Drinking: II. Relations
                    to Other Features of Culture. *Quarterly Journal of
                    Studies on Alcohol*, Supplement #3:29-48.

                The second of a five part study, this section deals
                with the evaluation of three measures of alcohol
                consumption: frequency of ceremonial drinking,
                general consumption, and frequency of drunkenness.
                Attempts are made to correlate alcohol consumption
                with cultural variables, particularly child rearing
                practices. Native American societies (see #0066)
                are included in the sample of 110 preliterate societies.

0066   Bacon, Margaret K., Herbert Barry III, Irvin L. Child
            and Charles R. Snyder
                1965 A Cross-Cultural Study of Drinking: V. Detailed
                    Definitions and Data. *Quarterly Journal of Studies
                    on Alcohol*, Supplement #3:78-111.

                This portion of the five part study summarizes the
                variables used in the research; defines each variable
                in detail; explains the rating methodology; and presents

the raw data for 49 of the variables which were applied to 139 societies. Many Native American groups are listed, including: Apaches, Navajo, Papago, Arapaho, Cheyenne, Comanche, Crow, Hopi, Klamath, Sioux, Winnebago, and Zuni.

0067   Badcock, William T.
        1976 Problems of Native Offenders in the Correctional System. *Canadian Journal of Criminology and Correction* 18:281-289.

Native Americans are disproportionately represented in both the federal and provincial prisons in Saskatchewan and Ontario. A leading cause of imprisonment is violation of the Liquor Act.

0068   Badt, Milton B.
        1946 I Cut His Throat. *The Nevada State Bar Journal* 11(1):23-26.

Comments by an individual who served as an attorney for the Western Shoshone supporting Native Americans' civil rights, but who was unable to support legalization of Native American alcohol consumption.

0069   Bailey, Pearce
        1922 A Contribution to the Mental Pathology of Races in the United States. *Archives of Neurology and Psychiatry* 7:183-201.

A report which presents the hypothesis that certain communities and races display wide distribution and variation of nervous and mental diseases. Native Americans are typed as falling below the overall average for alcoholism.

0070   Baker, James L.
        1959 Indians, Alcohol and Homicide. *Journal of Social Therapy* 5:270-275.

Represents a review of common characteristics exhibited in a group of 36 Native Americans incarcerated in the federal penitentiary at Leavenworth, Kansas, all of whom were convicted of homicide while acutely intoxicated.

0071   Bales, Robert Freed
        1946 Cultural Differences in Rates of Alcoholism. *Quarterly Journal of Studies on Alcohol* 6(4):480-499.

Discusses three general factors which the author
believes provide insight into cultural differences
in rates of alcoholism, and cites four attitudes
which a culture may hold and which contribute to
drinking behavior. Various Native American groups
are cited as examples.

0072   Bales, Robert Freed
1959 Cultural Differences in Rates of Alcoholism.
In *Drinking and Intoxication: Selected Readings
in Social Attitudes and Controls*. Raymond G.
McCarthy ed. Pp. 263-277. New Haven: Yale Center
of Alcohol Studies. (Originally published in
Quarterly Journal of Studies on Alcohol 6:480-499.)

See citation #0071 for abstract.

0073   Balikci, Asen
1963 *Vunta Kutchin Social Change: A Study of the
People of Old Crow, Yukon Territory*. Ottawa:
Northern Co-ordination and Research Centre, Department of Northern Affairs and National Resources,
Publication #63-3.

Very briefly (p. 138-140) describes the manufacture
of homebrew and associated drinking behavior. Indicates that drinking serves as a mechanism for dissolving social inhibitions and facilitating
interpersonal contact.

0074   Balikci, Asen
1968 Bad Friends. *Human Organization* 27(3):191-199.

Describes the social atomism which exists among the
Vunta Kutchin Indians of the Yukon Territory.
Indicates that latent tensions are readily apparent
and more easily verbalized when an individual is
under the influence of alcohol. Drinking behavior
is described and it is noted that excessive drinking
creates new tensions and intensifies social atomism.
The weakness of the formal integrative social structure
brings social conflict to the fore and exacerbates
problem drinking.

0075   Banfill, B.J.
1966 *With the Indians of the Pacific*. Toronto:
The Ryerson Press.

Chapter 12 (p. 121-127) represents the recollections
of a nurse who spent time with the "Tokawaka" Indians.
She notes that it was her duty to report intoxicated

Native Americans; that moonshine was sold to Native Americans by an Anglo bootlegger; and that the Anglo escaped legal sanctions while the Native Americans were often arrested for drinking. The author also indicates that individuals who were intoxicated were not condemned by the community, but rather were perceived as victims of alcohol.

0076   Barnouw, Victor
       1950 Acculturation and Personality among the Wisconsin Chippewa. *American Anthropological Association Memoirs* #72.

       Woven into an examination of the Chippewa are various notes regarding the utilization of alcohol, its dissemination by traders, and reactions of Europeans to Chippewa drinking.

0077   Barnouw, Victor
       1963 *Culture and Personality*. Homewood, Illinois: The Dorsey Press.

       The effect of alcohol upon cultural values is noted, and specific examples, such as Benedict's observation regarding the Zuni's aversion to alcohol, are presented.

0078   Barrow, Mark V., Jerry D. Niswander and Robert Fortuine
       1972 *Health and Disease of American Indians North of Mexico: a Bibliography, 1800-1969*. Gainesville: University of Florida Press.

       Includes a section on "alcoholism and addiction."

0079   Barter, Eloise R. and James T. Barter
       1974 Urban Indians and Mental Health Problems. *Psychiatric Annals* 4(11):37-43.

       Suggests that urban Native Americans have been very successful in the development and operation of alcoholism programs, but that alcoholism masks other mental health problems.

0080   Barter, James T. and Katherine M. Weist
       1970 Historical and Contemporary Patterns of Northern Cheyenne Suicide. Unpublished paper presented at the 126th meeting of the American Psychiatric Association.

       Drinking appears to help males establish close relationships in an unstable social environment, and drinking activities are perceived as an alternative way of sustaining meaningful relationships. However, suicides are also associated with excessive drinking. The Cheyenne, in fact, blame the prevalence of drinking and the mishandling of the tribal fetish for an increase in suicide.

0081   Basso, Keith H.
       1966   The Gift of Changing Woman. *U.S. Bureau of American Ethnology Bulletin* 196:113-173 (SUDOCS #SI 2.3:196).

       Provides a detailed description of the ceremonial given when a girl comes of age. Included is a discussion of the role of Apache beer, tulapai, in the ceremony.

0082   Basso, Keith H.
       1970a   *The Cibecue Apache*. New York: Holt, Rinehart, and Winston.

       Briefly touches on the use and attitude toward alcohol among the Cibecue Apache, and notes that abuse of alcohol by medicine men can have a detrimental effect on an entire community.

0083   Basso, Keith H.
       1970b   To Give up on Words: Silence in Western Apache Culture. *Southwestern Journal of Anthropology* 26(3):213-230.

       Drinking creates culturally inappropriate behavior which is often handled with silence, a culturally sanctioned mechanism.

A083   Bearss, Edwin C.
       1968   The Arkansas Whiskey War: a Fort Smith Case Study. *Journal of the West* 7:143-172.

       Fort Smith was established to maintain peace between the Cherokees and the Osage, to survey the boundaries of the Choctaw Nation, and to keep Anglos from encroaching upon Native American land. However, the post was also established to prevent the introduction of ardent spirits into Indian Territory. Details the problems and politics involved in enforcing the laws prohibiting the sale of liquor to Native Americans.

0084   Beede, Laurence Ivan
       1968   Teen-age Indian Drinking in Seattle and King County. MA Thesis, University of Washington, 83p.

A statistical survey of youths arrested in Seattle for delinquent behavior and drinking charges. Anglos, Blacks, and Native Americans are examined. Drinking behavior, especially among Native Americans, is correlated with socioeconomic status. Social position is believed to have a greater influence on drinking behavior than ethnic identity.

0085   Beigel, Allan, E. James Hunter, John S. Tamerin, Edwin H. Chapin and Mary J. Lowery
1974 Planning for the Development of Comprehensive Community Alcoholism Services: I. The Prevalence Survey. *American Journal of Psychiatry* 131(10): 1112-1116.

A method for obtaining useful prevalence data in a brief period and at a modest cost is suggested. Application of the survey method is discussed as it was used by the Pima County Alcoholism Task Force of Tucson, Arizona. The Pima County facility serves Anglos, Native Americans, Blacks, and Mexican-Americans.

0086   Beigel, Allan, Thomas R. McCabe, John S. Tamerin, Mary J. Lowery, Edwin H. Chapin and E. James Hunter
1974 Planning for the Development of Comprehensive Community Alcoholism Services: II. Assessing Community Awareness and Attitudes. *American Journal of Psychiatry* 131(10):1116-1121.

Reports on the development of an effective community education and treatment program for alcoholism. The program was tested by the Pima County Alcoholism Task Force of Tucson, Arizona, which serves a population composed of Anglos, Native Americans, Blacks, and Mexican-Americans.

0087   Beiser, Morton
1974 Indian Mental Health. *Psychiatric Annals* 4(11):6-8.

Notes that alcoholism is one of the primary mental health problems among Native Americans.

0088   Belmont, Francois Vachon de
1951 History of Brandy in Canada. *Mid-America* 33:42-63.

Translation of observations made during the 17th century regarding Iroquoian drinking in New France. Reports on the behavior of intoxicated Native Americans, the introduction of brandy to Native Americans, and comments on the evils of drinking.

0089   Ben-Dor, Shmuel
1966 *Makkovik: Eskimos and Settlers in a Labrador Community. A Contrastive Study in Adaptation.* St. Johns: Institute of Social and Economic Research, Memorial University of Newfoundland (Newfoundland Social and Economic Studies #4).

Describes drinking behavior among both the Eskimo and settlers. Ideal Eskimo behavior condemns the drinking of even local beer and brew; however, Eskimos drink regularly. Drinking is associated with major disturbances of the peace among Eskimos, but proceeds without incident among the settlers. The majority of Eskimo drinking leads to violence, even though Eskimo fear violence. Reasons given for drinking are complex. It is noted that a regular drinker will not gain social status.

0090   Benedict, Ruth
1950 *Patterns of Culture.* New York: New American Library.

Discusses the use and abuse of alcohol among the Pueblo Indians of New Mexico. Observes that many Southwestern peoples seek visions by fasting, torture, and by the ingestion of drugs and alcohol. The Pueblos, however, do not seek such experiences and place great store upon sobriety. Notes that Zuni elders prohibited the use of alcohol in the village.

0091   Benge, William B.
1960 Law and Order on Indian Reservations. *Federal Bar Journal* 20(3):223-229.

Examines the application of state and federal laws to Indian reservations. The use of an undercover agent to expose a bootlegger is cited in one case.

0092**   Bennett, Bob
1963 Programs That Can Be Developed at the Reservation Level. Unpublished report presented to the University of Utah School of Alcohol Studies, 8p.

Discusses the roles and responsibilities of Native Americans living on reservations, and examines the direct and indirect involvement of alcohol in the disintegration of social structure among Native Americans.

0093   Bennett, Michael C.
            1973 The Indian Counsellor Project - Help for the
            Accused. *Canadian Journal of Criminology and
            Corrections* 15:1-6.

            A survey of Native Americans in federal and provincial
            prisons on Vancouver Island revealed that 15% of the
            prison population were Native Americans, while only
            2% of Vancouver Island's population were Native
            Americans. Many Native American arrests are associated
            with alcohol. The Indian Counsellor Program was
            established by the John Howard Society in order to
            assist Native American inmates.

0094   Bennion, Lynn J. and Ting-Kai Li
            1976 Alcohol Metabolism in American Indians and
            Whites. *New England Journal of Medicine* 294(1):
            9-13.

            Examines racial differences in alcohol tolerance
            using 30 Native American and Anglo volunteers. While
            it was found that heavy drinkers among both the Native
            Americans and Anglos metabolize alcohol more rapidly,
            there was no difference between the metabolic rates
            of the two populations. The results refute the claim
            that Native American drinking can be explained on
            the basis of racial differences in alcohol metabolism.

0095** Berg, Lawrence, Edward Helmick, Sheldon Miller, Paul
        Nutting and Gregory Schorr
            1973a Health Workers Opinions about Mental Illness
            in Alaska. A Component Report of the Evaluation
            of Alcoholism Treatment Services in the State of
            Alaska, prepared for the Alaska Native Health
            Board. Unpublished report, Indian Health Service,
            Office of Research and Development, 6p.

            As part of a larger study a survey was conducted among
            the medical staff of 12 hospitals, 20 alcoholism
            centers, and 280 community health aides in order to
            identify attitudes towards mental illness. Alcoholism
            agencies scored highest on treatment orientation and
            paternalistic attitudes towards clients, but lower
            on attitudes of protectiveness towards the families
            of drinkers. Health aides appeared to perceive
            drinkers as a threat to society.

0096** Berg, Lawrence, Edward Helmick, Sheldon Miller, Paul
        Nutting and Gregory Schorr
            1973b Opinions about Mental Illness of Health Workers
            in Alaska. Washington: Unpublished paper

presented at the 9th joint meeting of the Professional Associations of the U.S. Public Health Service.

The authors attempt to identify attitudes towards mental health by discipline (i.e. M.D., R.N., social workers, alcohol counselors, and paraprofessional aides). Results of the study indicate that a positive correlation exists between the amount of training an individual receives and the attitude that mental illness is a treatable disease, while an inverse correlation was found to exist between scores on the authoritarian scale and amount of training.

0097   Berg, Lawrence, Eugene Galvez, R. Marcus, Juan Joe Cipriano and Linda Lejero
1975 Developing criteria for the Primary Prevention of Alcohol. Unpublished paper presented at the 10th joint meeting of the Professional Associations of the U.S. Public Health Service.

Reports on a mechanism for assessing the degree of severity of physical, social, economic, academic, and self-concept problems among Papago Indian adolescents. Primary emphasis of the program is the prevention of alcohol abuse.

0098   Berg, Lawrence, Gregory Schorr and Paul A. Nutting
1975 Guidelines for Developing Clinical Criteria for the Ambulatory Care of Alcoholism. Unpublished paper presented at the 10th joint meeting of the Professional Associations of the U.S. Public Health Service.

Provides explicit guidelines for negotiating specific standards of acceptable care, mechanisms for monitoring efficiency of the care system, and evaluating effectiveness of treatment standards.

0099   Bergman, Robert L.
1971 Navajo Peyote Use: Its Apparent Safety. *American Journal of Psychiatry* 128(6):695-699.

Notes that the Native American Church advocates strict abstinence from alcohol. Describes the effects of mixing peyote and alcohol. Indicates that the Peyotists have had greater success in resolving drinking problems than any other agency on the Navajo Reservation.

0100   Bergman, Robert L., Morton Beiser, Carl A. Hammerschlag and Syd Beane

1976 *The American Indian: Cultural Issues in Contemporary Psychiatry*. Philadelphia: Smith, Kline & French Laboratories (includes tape).

A discussion regarding working with Native American patients which touches on the role of the aged, the Native American perception of psychopathology, traditional Native American medicine, collaboration with Western medical personnel, and the place of the family in psychiatric intervention. Alcohol abuse is attributed to crisis resolution, and is viewed as an important problem facing the Native American community.

0101   Berreman, Gerald D.
1956 Drinking Patterns of the Aleuts. *Quarterly Journal of Studies on Alcohol* 17:503-514.

Indicates that early Aleut exposure to alcohol came from Russian fur traders and it is likely that drinking behavior is patterned after White models. The author supports the theory that the drinking response is due to levels of stress within the society.

0102   Berreman, Gerald D.
1964 Aleut Reference Group Alienation, Mobility, and Acculturation. *American Anthropologist* 66(2): 231-250. (Reprinted in *The Emergent Native Americans*, Deward E. Walker, Jr., ed. Boston: Little, Brown, p. 532-549.)

Berreman views alcohol consumption among the Aleuts as accommodation by individuals seeking refuge from stress and apathy engendered by the conflict of cultural values and the inability to obtain Anglo goals and recognition.

0103   Bestor, Frank H., and Julia A. Ball
1973 *The People Speak - Will You Listen? Report of the Washington State Governor's Indian Affairs Task Force, Urban and Landless Tribes Committee*. Olympia: State of Washington (also located under Washington [State]. Urban Indian Committee).

Reviews the efforts which were necessary in order to obtain health services for urban Native Americans, including the founding of the Seattle Indian Health Board, the Seattle Indian Alcohol program, and the restoration of the Cushman Indian Hospital for Native Americans. Alcohol is noted as a major health problem.

0104   Bestor, Frank H., William R. Jeffries and Roberta Minnis
        1971 *Are You Listening Neighbor? Report of the Washington State Governor's Indian Affairs Task Force.* Olympia: State of Washington. (Also located under Washington [State]. Indian Affairs Task Force.)

        Details Native American history, politics, economics, and health problems within the State of Washington. The effects of alcohol abuse are frequently pointed out; however, it is made clear that alcoholism is not universal among Native Americans, and that there are counter influences to abusive drinking, such as the Indian Shaker Church, and other religious movements.

0105** Bethesda Research Institute
        1976 Indian Alcoholism: a National Demonstration Project. Unpublished draft of a proposal for a five state demonstration project, Bethesda Research Institute, 127p.

        A complex proposal requesting 9 million dollars to develop comprehensive alcoholism services for Native Americans in the states of Arizona, California, Kansas, New Mexico, and Oklahoma. Considerable discussion is devoted to outlining the proposed identification, evaluation, education, prevention, and treatment programs.

0106   Bienvenue, Rita M. and A.H. Latif
        1974 Arrests, Disposition and Recidivism: a Comparison of Indians and Whites. *Canadian Journal of Criminology and Corrections* 16(2):105-116.

        41.3% of Native American male arrests involve alcohol, while 77.9% of Native American female arrests in Winnipeg, Manitoba, involve alcohol. Native Americans tend to receive lighter sentences than non-Native Americans, but display higher rates of recidivism.

0107   Bittker, Thomas
        1973 Dilemmas of Mental Health Service Delivery to Off-Reservation Indians. *Anthropological Quarterly* 46:172-182.

        The off-reservation Native American has been conspicuously ignored by contemporary health service delivery systems. This is particularly apparent in the paucity of programs and treatment facilities available to those individuals with alcohol abuse problems. The author explores some of the reasons for this situation and makes suggestions for dealing with the mental health problems of off-reservation Native Americans.

0108** Bittker, Thomas E., and Richard J. Metzner
        1973 Barriers in the Relationships of Physicians
            and Alcoholic Patients in Transcultural Settings.
            Unpublished paper presented at the 8th joint meeting
            of the Professional Associations of the U.S. Public
            Health Service.

        Identifies four barriers to the development of success-
        ful therapeutic relationships between alcoholic patients
        and physicians: (1) the physician's fear of the
        patient's excessive dependency; (2) the patient's
        perception of the physician as guilt-provoking and
        authoritative; (3) conflicting world views; and (4)
        inability to share feelings and perceptions across
        cultures. To assist in overcoming these barriers
        videotape sessions adapting Kagan's Interpersonal
        Process Recall Technique were implemented.

0109   Blakeslee, Clement
        1955 Some Observations on the Indians of Crow Creek
            Reservation, South Dakota. *Plains Anthropologist*
            5:31-35.

        Describes a "feast-famine" economy in which much
        eating and drinking takes place during the two weeks
        after subsistence checks arrive, while sobriety and
        scarcity characterize the two weeks before the arrival
        of checks. Older men frowned on drunkenness; however,
        their opposition to drinking was passive. Anglos
        seemed to be more concerned about Native American
        drinking than Native Americans themselves.

0110   Blanchard, Joseph D., Evelyn L. Blanchard and Samuel Roll
        1976 A Psychological Autopsy of an Indian Adolescent
            Suicide with Implications for Community Services.
            Suicide and Life Threatening Behavior 6(1):3-10.

        Notes that suicide was accomplished by the ingestion
        of an overdose of drugs while the boy was intoxicated,
        and that alcohol abuse was extant in the boy's family.

0111   Blauvett, Hiram
        1928 First Prohibition Officer: Chief Oratam.
            Mentor 16:52-53.

        Chief Oratam, Sachem of the Achkinheshacky Indians,
        a tribe of the Lenni Lenape or Delawares was instru-
        mental in developing a treaty between Peter Stuyvesant's
        colonists of the New Netherlands and the Indians; it
        prohibited the sale or trade of liquor to the Indians.

0112   Blevans, Stephen A.
            1967 A Critical Review of the Anthropological
            Literature on Drinking, Drunkenness, and Alcoholism.
            MA Thesis, University of Washington, 119p.

            A review of anthropological literature which roughly
            categorizes and identifies major themes and theories.
            Various authors' approaches are compared and con-
            trasted.

0113   Bloom, Joseph D.
            1970 Socio-cultural Aspects of Alcoholism. *Alaska
            Medicine* 12(3):65-67.

            The author advocates a broadly based preventive program
            in order to deal with Native American drinking problems.
            He suggests that a preventive program must support
            those endeavors which strengthen the economy, cohesive-
            ness, pride, and sense of control within the native
            community. Efforts at local control and administration
            must be encouraged, and the entire socio-cultural
            milieu must be examined and considered in the design
            of treatment, rehabilitation, and preventive programs.

0114   Bloom, Joseph D.
            1975 Patterns of Eskimo Homicide. *Bulletin of the
            American Academy of Psychiatry and Law* 3(3):165-174.

            Alcohol figures prominently in episodes of violence
            among the Eskimo, and rampant drinking associated
            with psychopathology is emerging in high school
            populations.

0115   Blouw, R., A. Petrinka, and J.A. Hildes
            1973 Health of Indians on the Hudson's Bay Railway.
            Canadian Journal of Public Health 64(1):58-62.

            Alcoholism and the problems so often associated with
            it were not noted to any great degree among the
            130 Cree and Cree-Metis living between Gillam and
            Churchill.

0116   Blumenthal, L.M.
            1975 Providing an Integrated Alcohol and Drug Related
            System of Services to a Large, Sparsely Populated
            Area. In *Proceedings of the 31st International
            Congress on Alcoholism and Drug Dependence,* Vol. 2.
            Pp. 256-258. Bangkok, Thailand: International
            Council on Alcohol and Addictions.

Discusses the staffing patterns, locations, and
programs of the Alberta (Canada) Alcoholism and
Drug Abuse Commission which serves a large Native
American population.

0117   Boag, Thomas J.
       1970 Mental Health of Native Peoples of the Arctic.
       Canadian Psychiatric Association Journal 15(2):
       115-120.

       A review and discussion of arctic psychopathologies,
       focusing on the stereotypes and misunderstanding
       which have developed as a result of incomplete data.
       Alcoholism in particular is regarded as the current
       major problem, and is attributed to stress induced
       by cultural discontinuity and rapid change.

0118   Boatman, John F.
       1968 Drinking among Indian Teenagers. MS Thesis,
       University of Wisconsin, Milwaukee.

       Attempts to determine the relationship between drinking
       levels, anomie, and status deprivation among Native
       American adolescents. Concludes that there exists
       a positive relationship between anomie and drinking
       levels; however, no such relationship exists between
       status deprivation and drinking levels.

0119** Bock, George E. and Robert L. Bergman
       1967 Indians and Alcohol. Unpublished paper pre-
       sented at a seminar on Indian Health, University
       of Arizona, 17p.

       A review of the historical circumstances and attitudes
       of Native Americans and non-Native Americans which
       contribute to alcohol abuse. Experiences on the Navajo
       Reservation serve to illustrate key points. Reviews
       attempts to deal with the problem, including A.A.
       programs and the Gallup Community Treatment Program.
       The importance of paraprofessionals is stressed and
       the role of the Native American Church is noted.

0120   Bock, Philip K.
       1966 The Micmac Indians of Restigouche: History
       and Contemporary Description. *National Museum of
       Canada Bulletin* #213:79-83.

       When first introduced to liquor the Micmacs refused
       it, but later became ardent consumers of alcohol and
       occasionally served as middlemen in the brandy trade.
       Beer, wine, distilled liquor and home brew are all

consumed. Drinking serves a variety of social
and personal functions which are briefly discussed.

A120** Bollinger, Henry E., Jr. and Vesta Starkey
1965 A Survey of Problem Drinking on the Mescalero
Apache Indian Reservation. Unpublished report
for the U.S. Public Health Service, Division of
Indian Health, Albuquerque Area Office, 9p.

The Mescalero Apaches repealed restrictions on the
sale of alcohol in 1964. The authors undertook a
survey designed to assess the extent of drinking
among the Mescalero Apache in order to plan for
preventive and curative programs. Hospital records,
arrest data, and interviews with tribal judges
revealed that 114 tribal members were problem drinkers
and that they accounted for 30% of all arrests. The
survey also indicated that 50% of all deaths during
the study period were due to alcohol.

0121   Bolyai, John Zoltan
1974 The Seattle Diphtheria Epidemic 1972-1973 and
its Relationship to Diphtheria among North American
Native Americans. MPH Thesis, School of Public
Health, University of Washington, 69p.

A report on the Seattle diphtheria epidemic of 1972-
1973 which occurred mainly among adult male inhabitants of Seattle's Skid Road, and predominantly
among Native Americans, 98% of whom were identified
as alcoholic.

0122   Bourke, John G.
1894 Distillation by Early American Indians. *American
Anthropologist* 7:297-299.

Discussion of Apache production of fermented beverages.
Suggests that tiswin was a sacred intoxicant rather
than simply a secular beverage. A Cherokee sour-mash
corn gruel is also mentioned, as is a liquor made
from the maguey.

0123** Bowechop, Sandra
1970 The Drunken Indian. Senior Thesis, School of
Social Work, University of Washington, 21p.

A review of factors contributing to the stereotype
of the "drunken Indian." The importance of recognizing
cultural differences in the counseling situation is
highlighted.

0124   Bowker, W.F.
         1970   The Canadian Bill of Rights - s.94(b) Indian Act -
            Irreconcilable Conflict - Equality Before the Law -
            Regina vs. Drybones. *Alberta Law Review* 8:409-418.

         Review of the conflicting assertions contained in the
         Canadian Bill of Rights and sections of the Indian
         Act. Regina vs. Drybones and Regina vs. Gonzales are
         both cited in the discussion. The issue of Native
         American prohibition is addressed and it is suggested
         that protective legislation is not discriminatory.

0125   Bowles, R.P., J.L. Hanley, B.W. Hodgins and G.A. Rawlyk
         1972   *The Indian: Assimilation, Integration or Separation?*
            Scarborough, Ontario: Prentice-Hall of Canada.

         The experiences of a reporter in a beer bar close
         to the Blackfoot Reserve south of Calgary are recounted
         and Native American drinking behavior in general is
         cursorily examined.

0126   Bowman, Norman L.
         1967   Annual Progress Report on Commission on Al-
            coholism. *Lectures and Notes, 1967 Manual Supplement.*
            Salt Lake City: University of Utah, School of Alcohol
            Studies, 3p.

         A survey of alcoholism programs on the Navajo Reser-
         vation revealed that emphasis was placed on preventive
         education, and that additional attention was needed
         in the areas of treatment and rehabilitation.

0127   Boyce, George A.
         1965a   *Alcohol and American Indian Students.*   Washington,
            D.C.:   Bureau of Indian Affairs, Branch of Education.

         A guide for both Native American students and teachers
         which discusses patterns of drinking in both Native
         American and non-Native American communities and suggests
         methods for dealing with alcohol education. Designed
         primarily as a curriculum guide for teachers and
         administrators, it may also be used as a text for
         students.

0128   Boyce, George A.
         1965b   *Alcohol and American Indian Students.*   ERIC
            Document ED 023520.

         See citation #0127 for annotation.

0129   Boyer, L. Bryce
         1964a Folk Psychiatry of the Apaches of the Mescalero
            Indian Reservation. In *Magic, Faith, and Healing*,
            Ari Kiev, ed. Pp. 384-419. New York: The Free Press.

         It is observed that Apaches manufactured alcoholic
         beverages, but that drunkenness is a fairly recent
         occurrence, coinciding with the introduction of Western
         liquors. Problems caused by excessive drinking are
         noted.

0130   Boyer, L. Bryce
         1964b Psychoanalytic Insights in Working with Ethnic
            Minorities. *Social Casework* 45(9):519-526.

         Discusses work with the Mescalero Apache and other
         Native American groups concerning alcohol problems.

0131   Boyer, L. Bryce
         1964c Psychological Problems of a Group of Apaches:
            Alcoholic Hallucinosis and Latent Homosexuality
            among Typical Men. In *The Psychoanalytic Study
            of Society*, Warner Muensterberger and Sidney Axelrad,
            eds. Vol. 3. Pp. 203-277. New York: International
            Universities Press.

         A psychoanalytic investigation into Apache socio-
         cultural and psychological orientation, with emphasis
         on drinking behavior and latent homosexual tendencies.

0132   Boyer, Ruth M.
         1964 The Matrifocal Family among the Mescalero:
            Additional Data. *American Anthropologist* 66(3):
            539-602.

         Suggests that economic-cultural factors contribute
         to male drinking behavior. The male's role as hunter-
         warrior has been destroyed, and while work is available,
         it is usually "White man's work" and is not acceptable
         to the Apache male. Enforced idleness, therefore,
         leads to participation in drinking parties.

0133   Braasch, W.F., B.J. Branton and A.J. Chesley
         1949 Survey of Medical Care among the Upper Midwest
            Indians. *Journal of the American Medical Association*
            139(4):220-226.

         Alcoholism is cited as a factor which hampers economic
         and social progress. Notes that prohibition of alcohol
         is easily circumvented and that males are the heaviest
         drinkers.

0134   Brakel, Samuel J.
              1976 American Indian Tribal Courts: Separate? 'Yes,'
                 Equal? 'Probably Not.' *American Bar Association
                 Journal* 62:1002-1006.

              Notes that prohibition is found in many tribal codes,
              but that in operation it is ineffective and sometimes
              counterproductive.

0135**   Brelsford, Gregg
              1976 Athabascan Drinking Behavior: A Preliminary
                 Ethnography. Unpublished paper presented at the
                 3rd annual meeting of the Alaskan Anthropological
                 Association, 8p.

              Drinking behavior in an unidentified Athabascan
              village which is legally dry and quite isolated
              is described. Drinking is exclusively a social
              activity. Three stages of intoxication with associ-
              ated behavior patterns are identified.

A135   Brelsford, Gregg
              1977 Athabascan Drinking Behavior: A Preliminary
                 Ethnography. *Alaska Department of Health and
                 Social Services Quarterly* 34(1):14-20.

              Social aspects of drinking behavior in a rural
              Athabascan village in Alaska are described, including
              systematic patterns of drinking, the rules and values
              which prescribe alcohol consumption, the frequency
              and duration of individual activity, the role of the
              young, and the effects of drinking on the village.
              Drinking behavior is supported by economic, social,
              and religious factors which must be acknowledged by
              alcohol rehabilitation programs.

0136   Brents, Thomas E., Clarence T. Johnson and Alfred Oftedal
              1914 Liquor Suppression Officers meet in Conference
                 in Denver. *Carlisle Arrow* 10(19):3.

              A report on the conference held for the Special
              Officers for the suppression of liquor traffic among
              Native Americans.

0137   Brod, Thomas M.
              1975 Alcoholism as a Mental Health Problem of Native
                 Americans: a Review of the Literature. *Archives
                 of General Psychiatry* 32:1385-1391.

              The labels "alcoholism" and "alcoholic" are used
              indiscriminately to the detriment of Native Americans.

-89-

The author reviews the following points: (1) severity of Native American drinking, (2) cultural predisposition to drinking, (3) individual motivation for drinking, and (4) sociocultural stresses. Native American alcohol abuse represents a behavior which is the product of historic and cultural factors screened through an individual's personal psychology.

0138 Brody, Hugh
  1971 *Indians on Skid Row*. Ottawa: Northern Science Research Group, Department of Indian Affairs and Northern Development, Publication #70-2.

  The life-style of Native Americans on the skid row of a Canadian prairie town is detailed. Notes that while drinking is a part of the life-style, it is not the total life-style.

0139 Brown, De Koven
  1910 Indian Workers for Temperance. *Colliers* 45(24): 23-24.

  A report on the dedication of the new Indian Shaker Church at Mud Bay, Washington. A major doctrine of the Church is temperance.

0140** Brown, Donald N.
  1965 A Study of Heavy Drinking at Taos Pueblo. Unpublished report on file with the Department of Anthropology, University of Arizona, 33p.

  Research at Taos Pueblo indicates the existence of three patterns of heavy drinking: (1) traditional heavy social drinking, (2) drinking partners where two to three men drink together, and (3) individual heavy drinking.

0141 Brown, Donald N.
  1967 Patterns of Heavy Drinking at Taos Pueblo, New Mexico. Unpublished paper presented at the Southwestern and Rocky Mountain Division meetings of the American Association for the Advancement of Science, 12p.

  Although Pueblo Indians are generally reported to have few problems with alcohol, statistical and social indicators suggest that alcohol abuse is a major problem. The paper outlines drinking problems, beginning with an historical overview and detailing the relationship of drinking to criminal activity and health problems.

0142   Brown, Paula
           1952 Changes in Ojibwa Social Control. *American Anthropologist* 54(1):57-70.

           Describes the changes in social control among the Red Lake Ojibwa which resulted from the introduction of Western legal proceedings. The major cases before the tribal court were for intoxication and civil disputes.

0143   Brown, R. Chris, Bale S. Gurunanjappa, Rodney T. Hawk and Delphine Bitsuie
           1970 The Epidemiology of Accidents among the Navajo Indians. *Public Health Reports* 85(10):881-888.

           Accidents are a leading cause of death among Native Americans, and alcohol is the chief contributor to accidents.

0144** Brown, Reynold W.
           1969 An Indian Alcoholism Education Program. Unpublished report to the Ute Tribe Alcoholism Program, 7p.

           Describes the developmental background, curriculum outline, and staff participation in an alcohol education program.

0145   Browning, Randell
           1971 The Drinking History of a Nootka Indian. MA Thesis, University of Washington, 105p.

           Attempts to examine Native American drinking by analyzing the drinking history of an individual Nootka male, Alex Thomas. Suggests that Native American drinking is qualitatively different from non-Native American drinking. Drinking for Thomas was a social process reinforced by self-identity and an urge for recognition by both Native Americans and Anglos.

0146   Bruman, Henry John
           1941 Aboriginal Drink Areas of New Spain. Ph.D. Dissertation, University of California, Berkeley, 243p. Not available from University Microfilms.

           A detailed investigation of the cultivation and harvesting of materials used by Native Americans in the manufacture of alcoholic beverages. The major portion of the study focuses on Mexico and Central America; however, Bruman does examine the

Northwest Cactus Region (saguaro and pitahaya fruit), and the Tesguino Region (maize beer) inhabited by the Pima, Papago, and Apaches.

0147   Bryde, John F.
1971 *Modern Indian Psychology*. Vermillion, South Dakota: Institute of Indian Studies, University of South Dakota.

An extensive discussion of Native American values, personality development, and self-concept. Notes that the introduction of alcohol coincided with the fur trade and mentions that alcohol resulted in internal fighting among the Sioux. The consequences associated with Native American alcohol abuse are noted.

0148   Buckley, Patricia Lorraine
1968 A Cross-Cultural Study of Drinking Patterns in Three Ethnic Groups, Coast Salish Indians of the Mission Reserve, Immigrant Italians and Anglo-Saxons of East Vancouver. MA Thesis, University of British Columbia, 115p.

An examination of drinking patterns observed among Coast Salish Indians, Anglo-Saxon residents of Vancouver, British Columbia, and Italian immigrants. Five hypotheses are tested regarding attitudes towards drinking, reasons for drinking, settings and time of day of drinking, and cultural perspectives regarding alcohol use. Suggests a high degree of similarity between Anglo and Native American patterns and a difference between Anglo and Italian patterns.

0149** Buehlman, John
1976 Which Way the Morrow. Unpublished report of research project on the Yankton Sioux Reservation, 41p.

A report on alcohol use and abuse on the Yankton Sioux Reservation. Cultural deprivation, racism, and detrimental drinking styles complicate alcohol abuse. Solutions to the problem will have to include the following "needs": cultural identification and appreciation, individual and group dynamics, comprehensive treatment, staff training, education of youth and the elderly, prevention, and continuous assessment.

0150   Burck, Charles G.
1976 Changing Habits of American Drinking. *Fortune* 94(4):156-166.

The myth of the "drunken Indian" is examined and it is noted that Native Americans learned drinking behavior from Anglo trappers, traders, and settlers. Native Americans simply adopted those patterns which suited their purposes.

0151** Burnap, Donald W.
1972 Suicide and Suicide Gestures. Unpublished report prepared for the Aberdeen Area Indian Health Service, 8p.

Indicates that 34.1% of all suicide attempts by Native Americans in the Aberdeen area were alcohol related.

0152 Burns, M., J.M. Daily and H. Moskowitz
1974 *Drinking Practices and Problems of Urban American Indians in Los Angeles*. Available from the National Technical Information Service, PB 251 727/4GI. 410p.

Survey report of the drinking practices and associated problems of 552 urban Native Americans in the Los Angeles area. Drinking was rated using the Quantity-Frequency-Variability Index. One-third of the respondents were judged to be heavy drinkers, while another 18% were defined as moderate drinkers. Drinking was identified as a major health problem among urban Native Americans by the respondents themselves, although few of those surveyed identified themselves as alcoholic or alcohol abusers.

0153** Burns, Thomas
1974 Mental Health Guidelines for Treatment of Patients with Alcohol Related Problems and for Preventive Programs. Unpublished report, Phoenix Area Office, Indian Health Service, 21p.

Proposed guidelines for working with Native American problem drinkers. Discusses diagnosis, treatment, prevention, and consultation.

0154 Bushnell, John H.
1970 Lives in Profile: a Longitudinal Study of Contemporary Hupa Men from Young Adulthood to the Middle Years. *Transactions of the New York Academy of Sciences* 32(7):787-801.

Biographical sketches of five Hupa males, detailing their lives over a 20 year period (1948-1968). Three of the men demonstrated a history of problems with alcohol. The "alcoholism syndrome" is noted as a chronic problem for many families.

0155   Butler, G.C.
            1966 Incidence of Suicide among the Ethnic Groups
            of the Northwest Territories and Yukon Territory.
            Medical Services Journal 21:252-256.

            Notes that alcohol is related to a large percentage
            of attempted and completed suicides.

0156   Butterfass, Theodore O.
            1929 The Liquor Traffic among the Indians of New
            York State in the Colonial Period. MA Thesis,
            Columbia University, 114p.

            Examines the political impact of the liquor trade
            among the Iroquois on the development of colonial
            America. Notes that alcohol played an important
            part in attempts by the English, French, and Dutch
            to solicit favor with the Iroquois. Also discusses
            early attempts to prohibit the liquor trade among
            the Indians.

0157   Byler, William
            1974 Indian Children and Foster Care. In *Indian
            Child Welfare Program. Hearings Before the U.S.
            Senate Interior & Insular Affairs Committee,
            Subcommittee on Indian Affairs, 93rd Congress
            2nd Session* (SUDOCS #Y4. In8/13:In2/33).

            In citing the enormous impact which child removal
            has on people it is noted that alcohol abuse is
            one of the most frequently mentioned grounds for
            removing children from Native American parental control.
            Indicates that the same standard is not applied to
            the children of Anglo alcoholics.

0158   Byler, William
            1977 Removing Children: the Destruction of American
            Indian Families. *Civil Rights Digest* 9(4):18-27.

            Notes that alcohol abuse is frequently used as an
            excuse to remove Native American children from
            parents. Indicates that the standard is applied
            unevenly, as alcohol abuse is rarely used as grounds
            for removing non-Native American children from parental
            custody.

0159   Bynum, Jack
            1972 Suicide and the American Indian: an Analysis
            of Recent Trends. In *Native Americans Today:
            Sociological Perspectives*, H.M. Bahr, B.A. Chadwick
            and R.C. Day eds. Pp. 367-377. New York: Harper
            & Row.

Notes that intoxication is frequently associated with suicide attempts and completions. Suicide and alcoholism are viewed as symptoms of cultural deterioration.

0160   Carpenter, Edmund S.
       1959   Alcohol in the Iroquois Dream Quest. *American Journal of Psychiatry* 116(8):148-151.

       The role of alcohol from the 17th century to the present is described. The transition of alcohol from a substance which assisted in dream seeking to a substance which helped release tension and aggression, and finally to a substance defined as evil by the prophet Handsome Lake is discussed.

0161   Castetter, Edward F. and Willis H. Bell
       1937   The Aboriginal Utilization of the Tall Cacti in the American Southwest. *University of New Mexico Bulletin* [Biological Series] 5(1).

       Mentions that the Pima and Papago manufacture a wine from the fruit of the "pitahaya" or saguaro cactus.

0162   Castetter, Edward F., Willis H. Bell and Alvin R. Grove
       1938   The Early Utilization and the Distribution of the Agave in the American Southwest. *University of New Mexico Bulletin* [Biological Series] 5(4).

       Notes that the agave was used by the Apache, Pima, and Papago to manufacture alcoholic beverages.

0163   Chance, Norman A.
       1960   Culture Change and Integration: an Eskimo Example. *American Anthropologist* 62:1028-1044.

       A study of adjustment by Eskimos in Kaktovik, Alaska, to acculturation. Unlike many other Eskimo villages, norms regarding drinking, interpersonal relations and religious beliefs have been retained. Peer pressure helps to control drinking and the village council imposed a ban on the consumption of alcohol.

0164   Chance, Norman A.
       1966   *The Eskimo of North Alaska*. New York: Holt, Rinehart, and Winston.

       Liquor was initially introduced to the North Alaska coast in 1867; it disrupted and demoralized village life. Lack of native controls are evident; however, no solutions are suggested.

0165   Chapman, Arthur
        1915 War on Bootlegging among Indians. *Carlisle Arrow* 11(37):4-5.

        Reports on federal efforts to suppress liquor traffic among Native Americans.

0166   Cherrington, Ernest Hurst
        1925 *Standard Encyclopedia of the Alcohol Problem*. Westerville, Ohio: American Issue Publishing Co.

        Pages 3-42 provide an historical review of Native American alcohol use.

0167   Child, Irvin L., Margaret K. Bacon and Herbert Barry III
        1965 A Cross-Cultural Study of Drinking: I. Descriptive Measurements of Drinking Customs. *Quarterly Journal of Studies on Alcohol, Supplement* #3:1-28.

        The first of a five part series, this paper examines the methodological problems associated with rating the importance of alcohol and drinking behavior cross-culturally. Various Native American groups are mentioned in the paper.

0168   Child, Irvin L., Herbert Barry III and Margaret K. Bacon
        1965 A Cross-Cultural Study of Drinking: III. Sex Differences. *Quarterly Journal of Studies on Alcohol, Supplement* #3:49-61.

        Attempts to identify differences in the drinking patterns of males and females in 113 societies. Numerous Native American groups are included in the sample.

0169** Chinn, Dick
        1970 University of Nevada: Alcohol Studies. Unpublished paper, University of Nevada Alcohol Studies Program, 8p.

        Examines the history, organization, and goals of the Nevada Inter-Tribal Alcoholism Program.

0170   Chittenden, Hiram Martin
        1954 *The American Fur Trade of the Far West*. Stanford, California: Academic Reprints. [Also published by Frances P. Harper (New York) 1902 and Barnes and Noble, (New York) 1935.]

        Notes the relationship between Native Americans, alcohol, and the fur trade. Examines the impact of alcohol on

Native Americans, the fur trade, and later Native American-Anglo relations.

0171   Clairmont, Donald H.J.
       1962 *Notes on the Drinking Behavior of the Eskimos and Indians in the Aklavik Area: A Preliminary Report*. Ottawa: Department of Northern Affairs and National Resources, Northern Coordination and Research Centre, Publication #62-4.

       A descriptive account of drinking behavior at Aklavik and Inuvik. Community attitudes toward drinking are reviewed and it is noted that assimilation of Anglo values without the means to achieve dominant cultural goals is a major factor contributing to alcohol abuse.

0172   Clairmont, Donald H.J.
       1963 *Deviance among Indians and Eskimos in Aklavik, N.W.T.* Ottawa: Department of Northern Affairs and National Resources, Northern Coordination Research Centre, Publication #63-9.

       Describes alcohol use in Aklavik, Inuvik, and the surrounding bush. Home brew is still manufactured; however, commercial liquor is available and is more popular. Binge drinking is frequent and group drinking is the norm. Drinking patterns and attitudes towards drinking are examined, and it is suggested that means-goal disjunction is a major factor contributing to drinking.

0173   Clark, Norman H.
       1965 *The Dry Years: Prohibition and Social Change in Washington*. Seattle: University of Washington Press.

       Reviews the history of prohibition in the State of Washington, and notes that prohibition was first applied to Native Americans. Indicates that drunkenness brought about the "fall" of Native Americans from which they have never recovered. Provides some observations regarding the devastation alcohol brought to the Native Americans of Washington State.

0174   Clarke, Frank
       1975a Thoughts on Indian Alcoholism. *Association of American Indian Physicians Newsletter* 3(2):3, part 1.

       Discusses the effects of alcohol, the definition of alcoholism, the motivation for drinking, and whether Native Americans are more prone to alcoholism than other groups.

0175   Clarke, Frank
        1975b Thoughts on Indian Alcoholism. *Association of
        American Indian Physicians Newsletter* 3(2):3, part 2.

        The author considers whether there is anything
        physiologically different about Native Americans;
        whether Native Americans are psychologically prone
        to pathological drinking; and various treatment
        methods.

0176   Cockerham, William C.
        1975 Drinking Attitudes and Practices among Wind
        River Reservation Indian Youth. *Journal of Studies
        on Alcohol* 36:321-326.

        Represents a study of drinking attitudes expressed
        by 7th and 8th grade Native American students,
        mostly Shoshone and Arapaho, as elicited by a survey
        questionnaire administered to 144 students. There
        were some differences between male and female points
        of view; nevertheless, despite the possibility of
        getting into trouble for illegal drinking, the
        adolescents expressed very positive attitudes towards
        alcohol consumption.

0177   Cockerham, William C.
        1977 Patterns of Alcohol and Multiple Drug Use
        among Rural White and American Indian Adolescents.
        The International Journal of Addictions 12(2-3):
        271-295.

        Attempts to determine (1) whether those adolescents
        who use alcohol are more likely than those who don't
        to use other drugs, and (2) whether differences in
        the use of multiple drugs exists between Anglo and
        Native American adolescents. Suggests that there is
        a greater prevalence of alcohol, marijuana, and hard
        drug use among rural Native American adolescents than
        among rural Anglo adolescents. Findings also indicate
        that users of one drug, be it alcohol, marijuana, or
        hard drugs, are more likely to use another drug when
        compared to non-drug users.

0178   Codere, Helen
        1955 Review of *Alcohol and the Northwest Coast
        Indians*. *American Anthropologist* 57:1303-1305.

        Discusses the strengths and weaknesses of Lemert's
        study. Criticizes Lemert for failing to examine the
        relationship between Native American drinking patterns
        and the drinking patterns of the Anglos with whom the

Native Americans associate. Suggests the drinking patterns exhibited by the Northwest Coast Indians may very well have been learned from Anglos.

0179   Coffey, T.G.
       1966a Problem Drinking among American Indians. *Alcoholism Treatment Digest*, release #82:12-15.

       A cursory review of Native American alcohol use from the inception of Native American prohibition in 1832 to the 1953 termination of prohibition. Discusses various socio-cultural and psychological theories regarding Native American drinking.

0180   Coffey, T.G.
       1966b Problem Drinking among American Indians. *Oregon Review on Alcoholism*, #8.

       A brief analysis of treatment literature, including a discussion of past programs and suggestions for future programs.

0181   Cohen, Fay G.
       1973 Indian Patrol in Minneapolis: Social Control and Social Change in an Urban Context. *Law and Society Review* 7(4):779-786.

       A description of the Indian Patrol of Minneapolis sponsored by the American Indian Movement (AIM). Patrollers watch police activity and arrange for drunks to be taken home. All members of the Patrol perceived arrest of intoxicated Native Americans as a form of discrimination, while local police viewed such arrests as protective custody.

0182   Cohen, Felix S.
       1971 *Handbook of Federal Indian Law*. Albuquerque: University of New Mexico Press. (Originally published by the U.S. Government Printing Office, 1942 SUDOCS #I 48.6:In2.)

       A compendium and discussion of federal laws and regulations governing Native American affairs. The chapter on liquor laws (chapter 17, p. 352-357) includes an historical overview of the topic, a review of federal powers relating to alcohol and Native Americans, enumeration of existing prohibitions, and the localities where prohibition is enforced. In short the chapter summarizes the principal regulations regarding Native Americans and alcohol.

0183   Cohen, Warren H. and Philip J. Mause
                1968 The Indian: the Forgotten American. *Harvard
                 Law Review* 81(1):1818-1858.

           A consideration of the problems facing Native
           Americans from a legal and institutional perspective.
           Federal policy has vacillated between attempted
           assimilation of Native Americans and protection
           of their cultural identity. Issues which demonstrate
           the ambiguities of federal paternalism and tribal
           sovereignty include economics, religion, and pro-
           hibition. It is noted that reservation prohibition
           has not only been ineffective in preventing access
           to alcohol, but may, in fact, contribute to the
           problem. Repeal of reservation prohibition might
           facilitate a change to more responsible drinking
           patterns and increase tribal revenues.

0184   Collins, Thomas William
                1971 The Northern Ute Economic Development Program:
                 Social and Cultural Dimensions. Ph.D. Dissertation,
                 University of Colorado, 196p. U.M. Order #71-25813.

           Three socio-economic groups are identified and their
           characteristics outlined. The drinking behavior of
           each group is related to political power, level of
           acculturation, and peer relations. It is also
           observed that the use of alcohol aids in the emphasis
           of Native American identity and serves as a rejection
           of the core values of the dominant society.

0185**   Colorado, Joseph
                1977 Development of a Model Native Alcoholism
                 Program. Unpublished paper presented at the
                 1st annual Native American Alcoholism Conference,
                 University of California, Berkeley, 5p.

           Description of an Alaskan Native detox program.
           It is estimated that 60%-90% of Alaskan Native
           youth and adults suffer from serious alcohol problems.
           The problems faced by detox and drop-in centers are
           enumerated and the characteristics of successful
           programs are proposed as the basis for a model
           program.

0186   Colton, Harold S.
                1934 A Brief Survey of Hopi Common Law. *Museum
                 Notes* 7(6):21-24. (*Plateau* is current title.)

           Observations concerning Hopi attitudes and traditional
           law enforcement. Notes that Hopis on the reservation
           do not drink alcoholic beverages.

0187 Conrad, Rex Dwayne
  1972 Suicide among the Papago Indians. MA Thesis, University of Arizona, 79p.

  A review of Native American suicide literature and major theories regarding suicide. Examines the relationship between suicide and alcohol abuse. Notes that alcohol was involved in 8 of 10 successful suicides. Also investigates excessive alcohol use as it relates to tribal traditions and present cultural stresses.

0189 Conrad, Rex Dwayne
  1974 An Epidemiological Study of Suicide and Attempted Suicide among the Papago Indians. *American Journal of Psychiatry* 131:69-72.

  Alcohol was involved in 8 out of 10 successful suicides and 14 out of 34 unsuccessful suicides. Risk factors include sex (males), heavy drinking, age (20-29), unemployment, residence, and interpersonal relations.

0190 Coult, Allan Donald
  1962 Conflict and Stability in a Hualapai Community. Ph.D. Dissertation, University of California, Berkeley, 260p. Not available from University Microfilms.

  The most important off-reservation establishments are taverns, and drinking is manifest in most activities. Alcoholic beverages constitute a major expense for Hualapai households. Males tend to drink more than females, and it is estimated that 50% of all adult males are alcoholics. Various drinking patterns are described.

A190 Covington, James W.
  1953 The Indian Liquor Trade at Peoria, 1864. *Journal of the Illinois State Historical Society* 46:142-150.

  Treaties were negotiated with those Native American tribes which inhabited what is now Illinois; they stipulated that the tribes were to move west of the Mississippi River; however, no time limit was set for completion of the removal. As a result, the time between initial Anglo settlement and Native American removal was one of turmoil, much of which was caused by the sale of alcohol. Provides several letters describing the liquor trade among Native Americans in Peoria and along the Illinois River.

0191   Crahan, M.E.
        1968 God's Flesh and Other Precolumbian Phantastica.
        Masterkey 42(3):96-103.

        Reviews the ceremonial and secular use of alcoholic
        beverages by Native Americans. Drinking behavior
        among the Native Americans of the southwestern United
        States is also discussed.

0192   Crankshaw, Libbet
        1976 Reports of Meetings, Medical Anthropology
        Roundtables at San Francisco: Health and the
        Family. *Medical Anthropology Newsletter* 7(3):5-7.

        Reports on remarks made by Jennie Joe regarding a
        new treatment approach to alcoholism utilized on
        the Navajo reservation. Ms. Joe described the involve-
        ment of the traditional medicine man with the alcoholic
        client as an alternative treatment modality. This new
        approach attempts to develop strong family support
        for the alcoholic.

0193   Cull, John G. and Richard E. Hardy
        1974 *Organization and Administration of Drug Abuse
        Treatment Programs.* Springfield, Illinois:
        Charles C. Thomas.

        Chapter 12 describes the organization, administration,
        financing, educational programs, rehabilitation
        programs, and research projects of the Alcoholism
        Commission of Saskatchewan. Notes that close contact
        is maintained with the Native Alcohol Council, and
        indicates that Native American paraprofessionals
        are utilized in outreach services.

0194   Curlee, Wilson V.
        1969 Suicide and Self-destructive Behavior on the
        Cheyenne River Reservation. In *Suicide among the
        American Indians.* Washington, D.C.: National
        Institute of Mental Health, Indian Health Service,
        Public Health Service Publication #1903 (SUDOCS
        #FS 2.22:Su 3/2).

        Notes that alcohol abuse among Native Americans
        contributes significantly to self-destructive behavior.

0195   Curley, Richard T.
        1967 Drinking Patterns of the Mescalero Apache.
        Quarterly Journal of Studies on Alcohol 28:116-131.

A lack of responsibility among men and women, dependency on the government for employment, and lack of satisfactory role models for Apache youth contribute to destructive drinking behavior. The author describes Apache drinking patterns as "blitz drinking," or drinking with the object of getting drunk as rapidly as possible. However, drinking is an important group activity and provides an opportunity for sociability in a culture where there is little else to do.

0196   Cutler, Ron E. and N. Morrison
1971 *Sudden Death: a Study of Characteristics of Victims and Events Leading to Sudden Death in British Columbia with Primary Emphasis on Apparent Alcohol Involvement and Indian Sudden Death.* Vancouver: The Alcoholism Foundation of British Columbia.

The sudden death rate of Native Americans was four times that of non-Native Americans, while suicide was three times as great and homicide 30 times as great. 71% of Native Americans had been drinking shortly before their deaths. Factors contributing to Native American alcohol use are examined and discussed.

0197   Dailey, R.C.
1964 Alcohol and the Indians of Ontario: Past and Present. Unpublished paper prepared for the Addiction Research Foundation, substudy 1-20-64, 54p.

Reviews the history of alcohol and its relationship to the Iroquoian and Algonkian Indians of Ontario. Three stages of drinking behavior through time are identified. The legal aspects of Native American drinking are considered, and the psychological impact of discriminatory laws is noted. Drinking patterns on contemporary reserves are described. Suggests that the alcohol problem is viewed as one of economics rather than health.

0198   Dailey, R.C.
1966 Alcohol and the North American Indian: Implication for the Management of Problems. Unpublished paper presented to the 17th annual meeting of the North American Association of Alcoholism Programs, 10p. [substudy 2-20-66, Addiction Research Foundation].

Examines the differences in drinking attitudes between Native Americans and non-Native Americans. Alcohol use by Native Americans is divided into three phases:

accommodation, deprivation, recreation. Dailey suggests that the "Zeta" type be applied to Native American alcoholism to denote drinking that is periodic, explosive, and community-wide. Suggests ways in which Native American alcoholism may be approached.

0199   Dailey, R.C.
         1968 The Role of Alcohol among North American Indian Tribes as Reported in the *Jesuit Relations*. *Anthropologica* 10:45-57.

An analysis of the *Jesuit Relations* reveals European attitudes toward Native American drinking behavior. The author also examines Iroquoian culture for parallel behavior that was present prior to the introduction of alcohol in order to illustrate the hypothesis that while alcohol was new, many of the actions observed relative to its consumption were extant in the Iroquoian culture.

0200   Dann, Jeffrey L.
         1967 A Study of an Indian Tavern on Skid Road. MA Thesis, University of Washington, 142p.

Represents a preliminary tavern ethnography which examines bar behavior and the skid road environment. The urban tavern is seen as a place in which newly arrived Indians can obtain information about the city, thereby facilitating the process of urbanization.

0201   Davis, Edward H.
         1920 The Papago Ceremony of Vikita. *Indian Notes and Monographs* 3(4):158-178.

Notes that many Papagos became intoxicated on tiswin during the Vikita ceremony.

0202   Davis, Laurence
         1959 Criminal Jurisdiction over Indian Country in Arizona. *Arizona Law Review* 1(1):62-101.

Discusses jurisdictional questions regarding Native Americans, particularly in regard to the sale of liquor. On August 15, 1953, Congress granted the states jurisdiction over the sale of liquor to tribal Native Americans. Where state and tribal liquor regulations differed, the state had final authority.

0203   Davis, Robert E.
         1976 The Primary Prevention of Alcohol Problems. *Alcohol Health and Research World* Spring 1976:10-12.

Examines strategies for primary prevention of problem drinking; reports on the comprehensive community approach used to control spree drinking among Eskimos in Labrador in which sales of alcohol were restricted to taverns, orders for alcoholic beverages had to be placed three weeks in advance, and laws were enacted regulating public drinking.

0204   Deardorff, Merle H.
          1951   The Religion of Handsome Lake: Its Origins and Development. *U.S. Bureau of American Ethnology Bulletin* 149:77-107 (SUDOCS #SI 2.3:149).

          Notes the influence of alcohol on the development of the Handsome Lake religion.

0205   Deloria, Vine, Jr.
          1969   *Custer Died for Your Sins: an Indian Manifesto.* New York: Macmillan.

          Circumstances contributing to the abuse of alcohol among Native Americans are briefly noted.

0206   Deloria, Vine, Jr.
          1970   The Urban Scene and the American Indian. In *Indian Voices: the First Convocation of American Indian Scholars.* San Francisco: The Indian Historian Press. Pp. 333-353.

          Public drinking among Native Americans is considered as it relates to the stereotype of the drunken Indian. Indicates that Indian Centers have had to deal with the social problems, including alcohol, of urban Native Americans because the federal government won't recognize urban Native Americans.

0207   Deloria, Vine, Jr., and Kirke Kickingbird
          1973   *Treaties and Agreements of the Indian Tribes of the Pacific Northwest.* Washington, D.C.: The Institute for the Development of Indian Law.

          Reproduces the treaties and agreements which were executed between the Native Americans of the Pacific Northwest and the federal government. In many of the treaties the use of alcohol or "ardent spirits" was prohibited on the reservation, and harsh penalties were provided for both consumers and providers of alcoholic beverages.

0208   deMontigny, Lionel H.
          1969   Attitude of Low Expectancy. *Indian Health* 2(3):1-3 [publication of Billings Area Indian Health Service].

Because so little is expected of Native American children in terms of achievement, the children live up to (or down to) the expectations, thereby producing a self-fulfilling prophecy. This situation colors the life of Native Americans and contributes to problems with alcohol.

0209 Denison, B. Webster
1950 *Alaska Today*. Caldwell, Idaho: Caxton Printers.

Pages 256-274 provide a description of conditions affecting the Alaskan Native and the attitudes of non-Natives. Problems stemming from the excessive consumption of alcohol are briefly noted and the work of missionaries for the advancement of temperance is mentioned. It is suggested that less liquor and more work will make Alaskan Natives as progressive as Whites.

0210 Densmore, Frances
1929 Papago Music. *U.S. Bureau of American Ethnology Bulletin* #90 (SUDOCS #SI 2.3:90).

In this extensive report on the music of the Papago Indians of the Sonoran desert, the songs which accompany the Rain Ceremony (also known as the Wine Feast) are noted and analyzed. Legends which accompany the wine songs are abstracted and the manufacture of wine described. Densmore notes that the ceremony is also reported as the tiswin ceremony.

0211 Devereux, George
1948 The Function of Alcohol in Mojave Society. *Quarterly Journal of Studies on Alcohol* 9:207-251.

The historical, sociocultural, and unconscious aspects of Mohave alcoholism are described and discussed. Indicates that drinking has been integrated with Mohave culture and psychology. The absence of a high level of anxiety and the preservation of certain basic cultural attitudes serve to explain why the intoxicated Mohave is not aggressively antisocial, and why Mohave society has withstood the ravages of alcoholism observed in other tribes.

0212 Devereux, George
1961 Mohave Ethnopsychiatry and Suicide: the Psychiatric Knowledge and the Psychic Disturbances of an Indian Tribe. *U.S. Bureau of American Ethnology Bulletin* #175 (SUDOCS #SI 2.3:175).

Provides an in-depth analysis of Mohave behavior interpreted psychologically and psychiatrically. The use of alcohol relative to observed disturbances is noted and a special discussion of the functions of alcohol is appended. The issue is raised as to whether all Mohave heavy drinking is truly alcoholic, or merely provides an excuse for other behaviors.

0213   Dickman, Phil
        1969 Thoughts on Relocation. *Musk-Ox* #6:21-31.

Discusses the problems, including alcohol problems, engendered by the relocation of Chippewas from Camp 10 to Dene Village in the community of Churchill.

0214   Diethelm, Oskar
        1955 *Etiology of Chronic Alcoholism.* Springfield, Illinois: Charles C. Thomas.

Observation on an Apache reservation leads to the assumption that the Native American is no more susceptible to alcohol than other inhabitants of the United States. Indicates that drinking behavior depends upon social, rather than racial factors.

0215   Dizmang, Larry H.
        1967 Suicide among the Cheyenne Indians. *Bulletin of Suicidology* 1967:8-11.

Discusses the relationship between alcoholism and violent crime and the decline of self-esteem.

0216   Dizmang, Larry H.
        1968 Observations on Suicidal Behavior among the Shoshone-Bannock Indians. In *Indian Education: Hearings before U.S. Senate Special Subcommittee on Indian Education of the Committee on Labor and Public Welfare*, 90th Congress, 1st and 2nd sessions, Pp. 2351-2355 (SUDOCS #Y4.L11/2:In 2/2).

Reports that alcohol was often involved in suicides and that many males who attempted and/or completed suicide had prior arrest records for intoxication. Indicates that suicide is clearly associated with excessive alcohol consumption.

0217   Dizmang, Larry H.
        1974 Adolescent Suicide on an Indian Reservation. *American Journal of Orthopsychiatry* 44(1):43-49.

The background of ten Native American youths who committed suicide before the age of 25 are compared with a control group from the same tribe. Results indicate that alcohol and inhalant abuse are associated with suicides.

0218   Dodson, John W.
            1972 Socioeconomic Aspects of Drinking Patterns on the Wind River Reservation. MA Thesis, University of Utah.

         An investigation of certain sociocultural variables on the Wind River Reservation, Wyoming, is undertaken in an effort to explain drinking patterns among the Shoshone and Arapaho residents. Drinking patterns are divided into two types, public drinking and controlled drinking. The differential occurrence of these patterns is explained by economic conditions extant on the reservation.

0219   Donnelly, Joseph Peter
            1940 The Liquor Traffic among the Aborigines of the New Northwest 1800-1860. Ph.D. Dissertation, St. Louis University, 323p. U.M. Order #00-00480.

         Explores the introduction of alcoholic beverages among Native Americans and describes the trade in liquor between Whites and Native Americans which resulted.

0220   Dosman, E.J.
            1972 *Indians: the Urban Dilemma*. Toronto: McClelland and Stewart.

         In a chapter entitled "The Logic of Skid Row" (p. 68-83) Dosman notes that alcoholism is so rampant among Native Americans that it had to be eliminated as a criminal offense in order to keep the courts from becoming hopelessly clogged. Native American drinking is not held to be a response to the stresses of life, but rather a means which enables indigents to live outside the norms of the larger society.

0221   Dozier, Edward P.
            1964 American Indian Alcoholism. Unpublished paper prepared for the University of Utah School of Alcohol Studies, 15p. (For published version, see #0222.)

         Presents the sociocultural background of Native American drinking and delineates some typical drinking patterns. Three approaches to the control of drinking are noted and four activities in which Native Americans could become directly involved and which would reduce drinking are discussed.

0222   Dozier, Edward P.
1966   Problem Drinking among American Indians: the Role of Sociocultural Deprivation. *Quarterly Journal of Studies on Alcohol* 27:72-87.

Eliminating the "racial tendency to drunkenness" argument, the author examines the unique historical, social, and cultural circumstances contributing to excessive use of alcohol and criminality rates among Native Americans. The function of alcohol in Native American communities is discussed, and some solutions to the problem of alcohol abuse are examined.

0223   Drilling, Vern
1970a   Problems with Alcohol among Urban Indians in Minneapolis. ERIC document ED 043 434, 50p.

Historically it is believed that Native Americans have problems with alcohol which are disproportionate when compared with persons from other cultures. One of the purposes of this paper was to identify individual and cultural differences in the use of alcohol which might exist between Native Americans, Anglos, and Blacks in Minneapolis. It is suggested that current treatment facilities are unsuccessful in working with Native Americans; the creation of a special Native American recovery program is recommended.

0224   Drilling, Vern
1970b   Problems with Alcohol among Urban Indians in Minneapolis. Paper prepared for the Office of Community Programs, University of Minnesota, 48p.

This is the same paper, with minor differences, as citation #0223.

0225   Driver, Harold E.
1955   Alcoholic Beverages in Native North America. *Proceedings of the Indiana Academy of Science* 64:50-51.

Only one-fourth of all native peoples manufactured and drank alcoholic beverages, and these were almost exclusively confined to the southwest U.S., Mexico, and Central America. Distillation was a European import which spread rapidly after its introduction.

0226   Driver, Harold E.
        1969 *Indians of North America*. Chicago: University
           of Chicago Press.

           Chapter 7 examines Native American use of narcotics
           and stimulants, including alcohol. Discusses attitudes
           toward alcohol by groups such as the Native American
           Church, and briefly mentions drunkenness as a factor
           in Native American-Anglo relations.

0227   Driver, Harold E. and William C. Massey
        1957 Comparative Studies of North American Indians:
           Narcotics and Stimulants. *Transactions of the
           American Philosophical Society* 47(2):260-275.

           Review of the cultivation, manufacture and use of
           narcotic and stimulant drugs, including alcohol.
           Alcoholic beverages were produced mainly from the
           agave (maguey), dasylirion (sotol), other cacti,
           maize, mesquite, and screwbean. Alcohol played
           both a sacred and secular role depending upon the
           tribe involved.

0228   Drucker, Philip
        1958 The Native Brotherhoods: Modern Intertribal
           Organizations on the Northwest Coast. *U.S. Bureau
           of American Ethnology Bulletin* #168 (SUDOCS #SI
           2.3:168).

           Examines the history of native brotherhood movements
           in Alaska and British Columbia. Investigates the
           attitude of the movements toward liquor. Most Native
           Americans in both Alaska and British Columbia regard
           liquor as a problem; however, British Columbia
           brotherhood members favor removal of discriminatory
           restrictions on the sale of liquor, while members of
           the Alaska brotherhoods oppose removal of such
           restrictions.

0229   Dubbs, Patrick James
        1975 The Urban Adaptation Patterns of Alaska Eskimos
           in Anchorage, Alaska. Ph.D. Dissertation, Michigan
           State University, 257p. U.M. Order #76-05548.

           Notes that consumption of alcohol is a frequent
           response to stress by Eskimos. Identifies a three-
           fold drinking pattern: (1) chronic-continuous,
           (2) episodic, and (3) variable-social. Reports
           that the social pattern represents the typical drinking
           behavior.

0230   Duncan, Earle
        1973 Alcohol and the Indian. In *Indians without
        Tipis*, D.B. Sealey and V.J. Kirkness eds. Pp.
        217-224. Vancouver: William Clare.

        Answers a series of general questions about Native
        American drinking in an effort to dispell the myths
        surrounding the topic. Estimates that 6%-10% of Native
        Americans are alcoholic, but that many hide the fact
        as a result of the stigma attached to alcoholism.

0231   Durgin, Edward C.
        1974 Brewing and Boozing: a Study of Drinking
        Patterns among the Hare Indians. Ph.D. Dissertation,
        University of Oregon, 169p. U.M. Order #75-03870.

        Provides an account of the drinking behavior of the
        Hare Indians of Fort Good Hope, Northwest Territories,
        Canada. Examines the sociocultural contexts of
        drinking, the patterns of drinking in the community,
        and the methods of social control and governmental
        controls excercised over drinking behavior. Theorizes
        that drinking is encouraged by a means-goal dis-
        junction due to high unemployment, White domination,
        and rapid social change.

0232   duToit, Brian M.
        1964 Substitution: a Process in Culture Change.
        Human Organization 23:16-23.

        Represents a study of a Klamath community in which
        excessive drinking was defined as deviant; however,
        beginning in the late 1940s the rate of alcohol
        consumption increased so that what was once deviant
        behavior became the modal behavior. Drunkenness
        became culturally acceptable, and drinking parties
        replaced lost social institutions.

0233   Dyer, Dorothy T.
        1969 Human Problem in an Indian Culture. *Family
        Coordinator* 18:322-325.

        A report on a course in Family and Human Development
        which was taught to tribal employees, Headstart
        teachers, and other agency personnel on the Standing
        Rock Sioux Reservation. Alcohol was among the key
        reservation problems identified and discussed.

0234** Dyer, Morris E.
        1974 Inhalation of Volatile Hydrocarbons: Its Effects
        and Its Relationship to Alcoholism and Drug Abuse.

Unpublished paper prepared by the Department of
Health Education, Public Health Service Indian
Hospital, Zuni, New Mexico, 32p.

Suggests that solvent sniffing serves as a substitute
for alcohol among teenagers below the age of 14-15.
Reports that solvent sniffing peaks at about age 14
and alcohol abuse begins to predominate around age 15.

0235**   Dyer, Morris E.
1976 Workshop Report. Unpublished report presented
at the Indian Health Service Multi-area Health
Education Training Course, 10p.

Identifies a pattern of alcohol abuse and solvent
sniffing in which many individuals switch from
solvents to alcohol in their mid-teens. Reports
on programs which attempt to reduce the use of
alcohol and solvents.

0236   Eddy, R.
1887 *Alcohol in History: an Account of Intemperance
in All Ages.* New York: The National Temperance
Society and Publication House.

Observes that Native Americans knew nothing of
"intoxicating drinks" until the arrival of Europeans.
Describes the effects of liquor on Native Americans
and examines attempts to control Native American
drinking. Suggests that growing intemperance among
Native Americans is not their "fault."

0237**   Educational Research Associates
1975 A Study of the Incidence and Patterns of Drug
and Alcohol Use in Hoopa Community Young Adults.
Unpublished report prepared by Educational Research
Associates, 15p.

Survey of drug and alcohol use among 173 young adults,
ages 14-27, in the Hupa area (125 of the 173 were
Native Americans). No difference between Native
American and White alcohol use was observed. Themes
relating to drug and alcohol use in Hupa society
are discussed.

0238   Edwards, E. Daniel
1970a Indian Alcoholism and Treatment. In *Syllabus
on Individual Counseling.* Salt Lake City: University
of Utah, Western Regional Indian Alcoholism Training
Center.

An overview of the sociocultural elements which are
believed to contribute to and underlie Native American
alcoholism. Dependency and hostility are major
features of Native American drinking. Identifies
keys to the counseling of Native American clients.

0239   Edwards, E. Daniel
1970b Motivation and Counseling for the Indian
Alcoholic. In *Syllabus on Individual Counseling*.
Salt Lake City: University of Utah, Western
Regional Indian Alcoholism Training Center.

Reviews some of the stereotypes associated with Native
American drinking and suggests methods of reaching the
alcoholic.

0240**   Edwards, E. Daniel and Margie E. Edwards
1976 American Indians and Culture - Federal Policies,
Implications for Social Work Practice. Unpublished
paper, University of Utah, School of Social Work.

Notes that alcoholism is a major health problem and
indicates that non-Native Americans' reluctance to
treat the alcoholic Native American is a major barrier
to treatment.

0241   Eggleston, Elizabeth
1976 Urban Indians in Criminal Courts. *University of Western Australia Law Review* 12(3):368-404.

Examines the relationship of Native Americans to
various aspects of the legal system, including bail,
legal representation, juries and sentencing.
Discusses whether alcoholism should be considered
a criminal or health problem.

0242**   Ehn, Shirley E. and Jay C. Whitecrow
n.d. Formal Theatre as a Native American Drug
Prevention/Alternative Program. Unpublished
paper prepared by the Tulsa Indian Council on
Alcoholism and Drug Abuse, 7p.

Suggests that a group activity which engenders a
feeling of community is needed in order to overcome
alcohol and drug abuse among Native American youth.
Describes an attempt to provide such an activity by
initiating an All-Indian Theatre.

0243   Eidlin, Harold
1970 *Delinquency Prevention Reporter*. Washington, D.C.:
U.S. Department of Health Education and Welfare
(SUDOCS #HE 17.810, before June 1970, HE 17.22).

Describes a federally supported program in Arizona which helps Native American youth face problems associated with delinquency, truancy, alcoholism, and suicide.

0244   Embry, C.B.
        1956 *America's Concentration Camps: The Facts about Our Indian Reservations Today.* New York: D. McKay.

Suggests that alcohol abuse may be an escape from adverse conditions on reservations. Refutes the argument that Native Americans are genetically prone to alcoholism. Argues that loss of autonomy, self-esteem, and culture are the contributing factors in Native American alcohol abuse.

0245** Erickson, Gerald
        1971 Mental Health Needs and Resources in a Northern Community. Unpublished paper prepared for the Psychological Service Centre, University of Manitoba, School of Social Work, 55p.

A report which attempts to delineate perceptions of care givers and mental health resources available to the northern Canadian community of La Pas, Manitoba. Alcoholism was reported as a major problem by all those surveyed (teachers, physicians, social workers, nurses). A proposed design for mental health services is appended, as is the survey instrument.

0246   Ervin, Alexander M.
        1968 *New Northern Townsmen in Inuvik.* Ottawa: Northern Science Research Group, MacKenzie Delta Research Project Vol. 5.

Discusses heavy drinking among Native Americans, Eskimo and Metis in Inuvik. Describes drinking behavior and outlines the social and economic cost of alcohol abuse.

0247   Ervin, Alexander M.
        1969 Conflicting Styles of Life in a Northern Canadian Town. *Arctic* 22(2):90-105.

Indicates that alcohol abuse represents a problem among the residents of the town of Inuvik. Fights, juvenile delinquency, family instability, and malnutrition among children result from alcohol abuse.

0248**   Escalante, Fernando
n.d. Group Pressure and Excessive Drinking among Indians: an Indian's Perspective. Unpublished paper prepared for the Committee for Economic Opportunity, Alcohol Program, Tucson, Arizona, 32p.

Suggests that alcohol abuse among Native Americans may be the result of historical Native American-Anglo relationships. Indicates that drinking is a learned and valued means of engaging in social life and often serves to forge a common bond which joins all Native American groups. Examples are drawn from the Navajo, Apache, Mohave, Sioux, Forest Potawatomi, Papago, Yaqui, and Northwest Coast tribes.

0249**   Everett, Michael W.
n.d. Theory and Practice in the Ethnography of Problem Drinking. Unpublished paper, 13p.

Discusses the use of anthropological methods for the cross-cultural investigation of alcohol use and abuse.

0250   Everett, Michael W.
1970 Pathology in White Mountain Apache Culture: a Preliminary Analysis. *Western Canadian Journal of Anthropology* 2(1):180-203.

Drinking is not considered by the White Mountain Apache to be pathological; however, drinking plays an important role in pathologies such as suicide, homicide, and criminal assaults.

0251   Everett, Michael W.
1971 White Mountain Apache Medical Decision Making. *Anthropological Papers of the University of Arizona* 21:135-150.

Apathy, self-directed aggression, social factionalism, and alcohol abuse are means by which Apaches avoid direct conflict. Notes that alcohol is viewed by some Apaches as a cause of disease.

0252**   Everett, Michael W.
1972a American Indian "Social Pathology": a Re-examination. Unpublished paper, 48p.

Notes that alcohol is frequently involved in homicides and suicides, and that some suicides may actually be accidents resulting from intoxication.

0253**   Everett, Michael W.
         1972b Drinking and Trouble: the Apachean Experience.
         Unpublished paper, 36p.

         A discussion of the "drinking-bad talking-fighting"
         pattern of behavior. Apaches do not perceive drinking,
         fighting, suicide, and homicide as pathological, but
         rather as coping behavior in a transitional culture.
         Also examines Apache drinking taxonomy, the definition
         of appropriate drinking situations, and attributes of
         various types of liquor.

0254**   Everett, Michael W.
         1972c Verbal Conflict and Physical Violence: the Role
         of Alcohol in Apache Problem Solving Strategies.
         Unpublished paper, 36p.

         Examines the relationship between alcohol use and
         interpersonal conflict. Attempts to construct an
         ethnography of drinking which will (1) specify the
         situational and decision-making parameters of problem
         drinking and (2) assess the causal role of drinking
         in conflict processes.

0255**   Everett, Michael W.
         1972d White Mountain Apache Inter-Generational Problem
         Drinking. Unpublished paper presented at the
         71st annual meeting of the American Anthropological
         Association, 9p.

         Outlines Apache problem drinking among both adults
         and teenagers. Adults believe that drinking is bad,
         yet continue to drink. However, adolescents believe
         that drinking promotes group camaraderie and that
         conflict arises from adult criticism and confrontation.
         Understanding Native American perception of drinking
         is vital for community awareness, educational, thera-
         peutic and rehabilitative programs.

0256**   Everett, Michael W., Carla J. Baha, Edwin DeClay,
         Marilyn Endfield and Karen Selby
         1973a Anthropological Expertise and the "Realities"
         of White Mountain Apache Adolescent Drinking.
         Unpublished paper presented at the 32nd annual
         meeting of the Society for Applied Anthropology, 43p.

         Examines the use of anthropology in designing an
         alcohol prevention program. Reviews a program
         designed to fit the needs and perceptions of a
         specific community. Discusses the use of an anthro-
         pologist on health teams.

0257**   Everett, Michael W., Carla J. Baha, Edwin DeClay,
         Marilyn Endfield and Karen Selby
            1973b Parents, Children, and Friends: Intergenera-
               tional Drinking among the White Mountain Apache.
               Unpublished paper, 11p.

            Attempts to (1) describe teenage drinking practices
            and (2) link these to adult drinking behavior through
            socialization variables. Finds that parent-child
            relations do not adequately explain Apache adolescent
            drinking unless coupled with peer group perspective.

0258**   Everett, Michael W., Marilyn R. Endfield and Justina Cruz
            1973 Cowboys, Indians, and "Alcoholism": White Mountain
               Apache Solutions to Problem Drinking. Unpublished
               paper presented at the 72nd annual meeting of the
               American Anthropological Association.

            Investigates problems faced by the White Mountain
            Apache Tribal Alcoholism Program. Drinking was
            traditional behavior aboriginally and rules of
            conduct still exist. Problem drinking is an Anglo
            construct which does not fit into traditional Apache
            definitions.

0259   Ewing, John A., Beatrice A. Rouse and E.D. Pellizzari
            1974 Alcohol Sensitivity and Ethnic Background.
               American Journal of Psychiatry 131(2):206-210.

            Examines racial differences in alcohol metabolism.
            Orientals (including Native Americans) are shown
            to be more sensitive to alcohol than "Occidentals."
            Suggests that physiological differences may exist
            and that differences in cultural drinking patterns
            may have physiological foundations.

0260   Fahy, Agnes and Carl Muschenheim
            1965 Third National Conference on American Indian
               Health. *Journal of the American Medical Association*
               194:1093-1096.

            A debate was conducted as to whether alcoholism was
            causative of mental illness or symptomatic of other
            conditions. Some conferees indicated that alcohol
            was a safety valve which prevented more serious
            psychiatric problems.

0261 Fairbanks, Robert A.
            1973 The Cheyenne-Arapaho and Alcoholism: Does the
               Tribe have a Legal Right to a Medical Remedy?
               American Indian Law Review 1:55-77.

Briefly reviews the history of the Cheyenne and Arapaho tribes and the factors that have created a very high rate of alcohol abuse among the two groups. Examines federal treaties, statutes, and moral obligations of the dominant society to discover prerogatives for designing and funding a comprehensive alcoholism program which addresses the basic etiologies of the problem. Sees the program as a joint responsibility of the Bureau of Indian Affairs and the Indian Health Service.

0262**   Fairbanks, Rulon R.
n.d. Summary of Marriage and Family Counseling Concepts. Unpublished paper prepared for the University of Utah, Western Region Indian Alcoholism Training Center, 18p.

Includes a section entitled "Stresses on the American Indian Family that Cause Problem Drinking and Alcoholism."

0263   Farber, William O.
1958 Report: Off-Reservation Law Enforcement in South Dakota. In *Indian Problems of Law and Order. Program and Proceedings, 3rd annual Conference on Indian Affairs.* Pp. 1-15. Vermillion, South Dakota: Institute of Indian Studies, University of South Dakota.

Discrimination in handling intoxicated Native Americans is noted.

0264   Farber, William O., Philip A. Odeen and Robert A. Tschetter
1957 *Indians, Law Enforcement, and Local Government.* Vermillion, South Dakota: Governmental Research Bureau, University of South Dakota, Report #37.

Alcohol abuse is the overwhelming law enforcement problem among Native Americans. Native American drinking is classified as both alcoholic and non-alcoholic. Alcohol abuse is attributed to despondency, and a desire to achieve a feeling of equality relative to non-Native Americans. Treatment such as Native American A.A. chapters, legalizing liquor sales to Native Americans, and Native American treatment centers is suggested.

0265   Farris, John J. and Ben Morgan Jones
1977 Ethanol Metabolism and Memory Impairment in American Indians and Caucasians. *Alcohol Technical Reports* 6(1):1-4.

Seventeen full-blooded male Native Americans from various tribes demonstrated a significantly faster rate of alcohol metabolism than did a group of seventeen male Caucasians of similar age, education, weight, and drinking history. However, no significant difference in memory decrement was observed.

0266   Fenna, D., L. Mix, O. Schaefer and J.A.L. Gilbert
        1971 Ethanol Metabolism in Various Racial Groups.
        Canadian Medical Association Journal 105:472-475.

The authors attempt to check out casual reports from medical and law enforcement observers--which had been unverified--that Eskimos and Native Americans take longer to sober up after a drinking episode than Anglos. This apparent difference was investigated by administering ethanol to selected subjects and determining their blood alcohol concentrations by use of a Breathalyser. Concentrations fell significantly faster in Anglos. Neither previous experience with alcohol nor general diet appeared to account for the difference, leaving the possibility of genetic factors as the cause. However, the total sample size was 64 so results should be interpreted with caution.

0267   Fenton, William N.
        1941 Iroquois Suicide: a Study in the Stability of a Culture Pattern. *U.S. Bureau of American Ethnology Bulletin #128* (SUDOCS #SI 2.3:128).

Alcohol and drunkenness figure in a few of the suicides investigated, but not the majority.

0268   Feraca, Stephen E.
        1969 Peyotism. *Pine Ridge Research Bulletin* 10:34-45.

Sioux who do not belong to the Native American Church associate the taking of peyote with alcoholism and heroin use. However, the Native American Church discourages drinking, and many view the Church as a solution to alcoholism.

0269** Ferguson, Frances N.
        1965 Gallup Research Project: Community Treatment Plan for Navaho Problem Drinkers. Unpublished paper presented at the 1st annual Institute on Alcohol Studies, Western New Mexico University in conjunction with the New Mexico Commission on Alcoholism, 14p.

-119-

Describes the programs of the Gallup Treatment Plan. Suggests that Native American problem drinkers are people who have no idea about how to proceed in the present day world.

0270**   Ferguson, Frances N.
          1966 The Peer Group and Navaho Problem Drinking. Unpublished paper presented at the 1st annual meeting of the Southern Anthropological Society, 14p.

          Describes a Navajo drinking group in Gallup, New Mexico. Examines Navajo drinking from a functional and dysfunctional perspective. Discusses the Gallup Treatment Project and speculates as to why the project is able to succeed.

0271   Ferguson, Frances N.
          1967 The Navaho Drinker as an Individual: Implications of the National Institute of Mental Health Gallup Treatment Program. *Lectures and Notes, 1967 Manual Supplement*. Salt Lake City: University of Utah, School of Alcohol Studies.

          Identifies characteristics of the Navajo peer drinking group, and examines individual differences within the group.

0272   Ferguson, Frances N.
          1968a Community Treatment Plan for Navajo Problem Drinkers. Unpublished report, McKinley County Family Consultation Service, Gallup, New Mexico, 226p.

          Presents a summary of a four year project which funded a clinic for Navajo problem drinkers in Gallup, New Mexico. Of the 121 clients enrolled, 21% continued to maintain sobriety at the close of the project, and many others showed marked improvement.

0273   Ferguson, Frances N.
          1968b Navajo Drinking: Some Tentative Hypotheses. *Human Organization* 27:159-167.

          Provides a description of an 18 month treatment program in Gallup, New Mexico, which centers around the use of Antabuse and individual therapy. The author postulates two types of excessive drinkers. Successful treatment tended to be with older, less acculturated individuals who did not have unrealistic aspirations regarding the dominant culture. Level

of acculturation is postulated as directly related
to success or failure in the program.

0274   Ferguson, Frances N.
1970 A Treatment Program for Navajo Alcoholics:
Results after Four Years. *Quarterly Journal of
Studies on Alcohol* 31:898-919.

A description of an experimental, long term treatment
program for Navajo Indians who had been frequently
arrested and jailed for drunkenness. Program components include disulfiram therapy, counseling (in
Navajo and English), education, employment, and
welfare assistance. Characteristics of those
individuals having the greatest success in the
program included: (1) a high arrest rate, (2) older,
(3) less education, and (4) less facility with English.

0275   Ferguson, Frances N.
1972 A Stake in Society: its Relevance to Response
by Navajo Alcoholics in a Treatment Program. Ph.D.
Dissertation, University of North Carolina, 192p.
U.M. Order #73-16471.

Analyzes 110 Navajo male alcoholics in a demonstration
project in Gallup, New Mexico, and attempts to test
the hypothesis developed by John and Irma Honigmann
that success in treatment is related to having a
stake in society. The study concludes that older
Navajo men with a stake in traditional Navajo society
did succeed in an alcohol treatment program; however,
Navajos with a stake in contemporary Western society
did not do well in treatment. Various other variables
are examined.

0276   Ferguson, Frances N.
1975 Change from Without and Within: Navajo Indians'
Response to an Alcoholism Treatment Program in
Terms of Social Stake. In *Atti del XL Congresso
Internazionale degli Americanisti*, Roma-Genova 1972,
Vol. 2, pp. 557-563. Genoa: Tilgher.

Describes a treatment program in Gallup, New Mexico,
for Navajo problem drinkers. Summarizes results which
appear in the author's dissertation (see annotation
above).

0277   Ferguson, Frances N.
1976a Similarities and Differences among a Heavily
Arrested Group of Navajo Indian Drinkers in a Southwestern American Town. In *Cross-Cultural Approaches*

to the *Study of Alcohol*, Michael W. Everett, Jack O. Waddell and Dwight B. Heath, eds. Pp. 161-171. The Hague: Mouton.

Provides yet another analysis of the data collected during the Gallup Treatment Program. Discusses the similarities and differences of the people who participated in the project. Notes that the sociability of drinking was a primary factor in the use of alcohol. The data indicate a great variety in the characteristics of heavily arrested drinkers; suggests that additional research regarding these differences is needed.

0278   Ferguson, Frances N.
1976b Stake Theory as an Explanatory Device in Navajo Alcoholism Treatment Response. *Human Organization* 35:65-78.

Examines stake theory as it applies to 110 Navajo males undergoing treatment for alcoholism or problem drinking. Having a stake in society was divided into four categories: none, traditional, modern, and both. The success or failure of patients in each of the four operationally defined categories is analyzed. Most successful in treatment programs were Navajos with a stake in both traditional and modern society.

0279   Fey, H.E.
1955 Ira Hayes, Our Accuser. *Christian Century* 72:166-167.

An editorial written on the occasion of Ira Hayes's death. Hayes was the Pima Indian who helped raise the U.S. flag on Iwo Jima, became alcoholic and died pauper stricken. The editorial focused attention on the problem of alcohol abuse among Native Americans.

0280   Field, Peter B.
1962 A New Cross-Cultural Study of Drunkenness. In *Society, Culture and Drinking*, D.J. Pittman and C.R. Snyder eds. Pp. 48-74. New York: John Wiley.

The author postulates that the degree of looseness in social organization affects the level of drunkenness. Therefore, the high rate of insobriety found in hunting-gathering societies stems not from Horton's postulated "subsistence anxiety," but rather from the informal nature of such cultures.

0281   Finkler, Harold W.
          1975 *Inuit and the Administration of Criminal Justice in the Northwest Territories: the Case of Frobisher Bay.* Ottawa: Department of Indian and Northern Affairs.

          The history of Inuit relations with alcohol is traced and the criminogenic role of alcohol is examined. Notes that alcohol is a factor in 80% of all convictions of Inuit.

A281   Finney, Frank F.
          1956 The Osage Indians and the Liquor Problem before Oklahoma Statehood. *Chronicles of Oklahoma* 34: 456-464.

          Details the use of alcohol by the Osage and describes the effects of alcohol on the tribe. Notes that while the Osage resided in Kansas they were reduced to a "pitiable plight" by alcohol. However, after settling in Indian Territory in what is now Oklahoma the Osage seemed to renounce alcohol until the Oklahoma land rush of 1889, after which alcohol again caused problems for the tribe.

0282   Fisher, Karen
          1977 Papago Harvest. *Arizona Highways* 53(6):2-5.

          A brief article on the manufacture of saguaro wine and other foodstuffs made from the fruit of the saguaro cactus.

0283   Fitzpatrick, Darlene
          1968 The "Shake": the Indian Shaker Church Curing Ritual among the Yakima. MA Thesis, University of Washington, 95p.

          Notes that Indian Shakers do not perceive drinking as a psychological disorder, so in conducting a "shake" over a drinking member of the religion, the drinking rather than the cause of the drinking is treated. The Shaker religion is viewed as a psychotherapeutic treatment which can help problem drinkers.

0284** Fitzpatrick, Darlene
          1976 Indian Shaker Temperance. Unpublished manuscript, 42p.

          Analyzes the Shaker religion among the Yakima as a mechanism for the control of excessive drinking.

Shaker perceptions of alcohol are compared to the role of drinking in Yakima society.

0285   Flannery, Regina
        1932 The Position of Women among the Mescalero Apache. *Primitive Man* 5(1):26-32.

        Notes that the manufacture of tiswin, an alcoholic beverage, is exclusively the task of women, although the recipe is known to men.

0286   Fogleman, Billye Y. Sherman
        1972 Adaptive Mechanisms of the North American Indian to an Urban Setting. Ph.D. Dissertation, Southern Methodist University, 298p. U.M. Order #72-27286.

        Notes that bars serve as social centers as well as drinking places for Native Americans in Dallas, Texas. Drinking behavior is one of five persistent gossip themes used to denigrate Native American leaders; however, alcohol abuse is not considered a problem among the Native Americans of Dallas.

0287   Folsom, R.D.
        1974 American Indians Imprisoned in the Oklahoma Penitentiary: a Punishment More Primitive than Torture. *American Indian Law Review* 2(1):85-109.

        Four percent of Oklahoma's population is Native American, but eight percent of the prisoners in the state penal institutions are Native American. Alcohol figures prominently in arrests and most criminal activity is directly related to alcohol.

0288** Fontana, Bernard L.
        1973 Suicide at San Xavier. Unpublished paper presented at the Indian Suicide and Alcoholism Workshop, Phoenix, Arizona, 13p.

        Recent circumstances on the San Xavier Indian Reservation have contributed to a loss of community control over decision making. The result is a marked increase in suicides and deaths due to alcohol.

0289** Forslund, Morris A.
        n.d. Drinking Problems of Native American and White Youth. Unpublished paper, University of Wyoming, Department of Sociology, 12p.

        Report of a study which compares drinking among Shoshone and Arapaho adolescents with drinking among

Anglo adolescents. Significant differences between
Native Americans and Anglos were found for all
variables. The data suggest that Native American
adolescents have more problems with alcohol than
Anglo adolescents.

0290   Forslund, Morris A.
1974a Drug Use, Delinquency and Alcohol Use among
Indian and Anglo Youth in Wyoming. ERIC document,
ED 100 597, 64p.

Part one of the report's three sections presents a
general review of the literature relevant to understanding the drug problem in the United States. Part
two presents a summary of data obtained in an investigation into the nature and magnitude of the delinquency
problem among the youth of the Wind River Reservation.
Part three provides data on the similarities and
differences in drug and alcohol use of Native American
and Anglo youth.

0291**   Forslund, Morris A.
1974b Indian and Non-Indian Delinquency: a Self
Report Study of Wind River Reservation Area Youth.
Unpublished paper, University of Wyoming, Department
of Sociology, 57p.

Findings did not indicate a greater involvement of
Native Americans than Anglos in illegal drinking.

0292   Forslund, Morris A. and Virginia A. Cranston
1975 A Self-Report Comparison of Indian and Anglo
Delinquency in Wyoming. *Criminology* 13(2):193-198.

Notes that more Anglos than Native Americans had
consumed alcohol when adults were not present; however,
Native American females drank more than Anglo females.

0293   Forslund, Morris A. and Ralph Meyers
1974 Delinquency among Wind River Indian Reservation
Youth. *Criminology* 12(1):97-106.

A high percentage of the charges lodged against
adolescents on the Wind River Reservation were for
alcohol related offenses.

0294**   Foster, Ashley
1972 A Study of Attitudes toward Health and Preventive
Health Care. Unpublished paper presented at the
seventh joint meeting of the Clinical Society and
the Commissioned Officers Association of the U.S.
Public Health Service.

Report of a study which examines the perception of Native American adolescents regarding health and health problems. Most of the people surveyed considered themselves to be in good health and indicated that alcohol and drugs were serious problems only for other people.

0295**   Foster, Kenneth W.
          1975 Etiology of Indian Drinking. Unpublished paper prepared for partial course fulfillment. University of California, Berkeley, School of Public Health, 21p.

The author suggests that an association exists between the loosely structured Native American societies and the flamboyant style of drinking which is representative of most Native Americans. Reviews major theories and concludes that anomie, social disintegration, and anxiety theories lead to dead ends.

0296   Foulks, Edward F. and Solomon Katz
          1973 The Mental Health of Alaskan Natives. *Acta Psychiatrica Scandinavica* 49:91-96.

Observes that alcohol is a contributing factor in a major portion of the mental disorders among the Athabascans and Aleuts. Mental disorders in general and alcoholism were seen to be related to increases in population, cash economy, and Westernization.

0297   Franciscan Fathers
          1910 *An Ethnologic Dictionary of the Navaho Language*. St. Michaels, Arizona: The Franciscan Fathers. (Reprinted 1968 by the Franciscan Fathers.)

Descriptive material is provided which mentions traditional alcoholic beverages. Indicates that drunkenness is lightly regarded unless it is carried on habitually or precipitates feuds.

0298**   Francisco, Geraldine and Arlene Smith
          1975 Project Shoshonwua: an Adolescent Directed Program for the Prevention of Alcohol and Drug Use on the Papago Reservation. Unpublished paper presented at the Workshop on Mental Health Programs for American Indian Youth, sponsored by the American Psychiatric Association, Portland, Oregon, 4p.

Describes a program which attempts to identify alcohol problems among teen-agers as early as possible in order to change attitudes and use patterns. Estimates that 60% of all teen-agers consistently use alcohol and/or drugs. Notes that alcohol use usually begins between the ages of 10-12.

0299 Frederick, Calvin J.
1973 *Suicide, Homicide, and Alcoholism among American Indians: Guidelines for Help.* Washington, D.C.: National Institute of Mental Health, Center for Studies of Crime and Delinquency, DHEW publication (HSM)73-9124 (SUDOCS #HE 20.3808:In2).

Provides very general guidelines for individuals working with Native Americans in the area of suicide, homicide, and alcoholism. Promotes the standard therapies for alcoholism, and suggests that additional bureaucracy be created, but does not advocate the use of native psychotherapies.

0300 Frederikson, Otto F.
1931 The Liquor Question in Kansas before Constitutional Prohibition. Ph.D. Dissertation, University of Kansas. Not available from University Microfilms.

Provides an introduction to the history of the liquor trade among Native Americans, and the attempt to institute prohibition among Native Americans by the federal government as well as Native Americans themselves. Details the introduction and effect of liquor among the Kansa, Osage, Shawnee, Delaware, Ottawa, Kickapoo, Potawatomi, Iowa, Sac, and Fox.

0301 Frederikson, Otto F.
1932 The Liquor Question among the Indian Tribes in Kansas, 1804-1881. *University of Kansas Bulletin* [Humanistic Studies] vol. 4, #4.

Examines the origin of liquor among the Native Americans of Kansas. Indicates that liquor became a problem for Native Americans with the influx of Anglos. Federal efforts to prohibit the liquor trade among Native Americans is noted. Based on author's Ph.D. Dissertation (see citation #0300).

0302 Freeman, Daniel M.A.
1968 Adolescent Crises of the Kiowa-Apache Indian Male. In *Minority Group Adolescents in the United States,* Eugene B. Brody ed. Pp. 157-204. Baltimore: Williams and Wilkins.

Alcohol had initially been used as an adjunct in the vision quest; however, it is now used more and more to withdraw from reality. Severe alcoholism is virtually universal among adolescent and adult males. Alcohol serves as an outlet for aggression, permits the creation of fantasies, and allows for exhibitionism and competition. Notes that the Peyote religion offers a possible solution to alcohol abuse.

0303   French, Laurence and Renitia Bertoluzzi
        1975 The Drunken Indian Stereotype and the Eastern Cherokees. *Appalachian Journal* 2(4):332-344.

Explores the various causes of drinking pathologies and their relevance to Native Americans in general and the Qualla Cherokees in particular. Investigates the manner in which different groups perceive drinking situations and provides some insights into the particular drinking patterns of the Qualla Cherokees.

0304   Friedman, M.
        1913 Keeping Liquor away from Indians. *Carlisle Arrow* 9(28):1.

Suggests that Native Americans lost their lands and became wards of the government because of intoxication. Calls for increased federal enforcement of prohibition among Native Americans and better education regarding the effects of alcohol use.

0305   Fry, Alan
        1970 *How a People Die*. Garden City: Doubleday.

A novel about Native Americans in British Columbia, detailing the impact of alcohol on village life. In telling about the death of a single child, the author examines attitudes and arguments on both sides of the "Indian problem," and reviews the history of Native Americans and alcohol.

0306   Fry, Alan
        1971 *Come a Long Journey*. Garden City: Doubleday.

A novel concerning the relationship between an Anglo hunter and a Native American companion in the Yukon Territory. Notes the destructive effect of alcohol on Native Americans.

0307   Fuchs, Estelle and Robert J. Havighurst
        1972 *To Live on this Earth: American Indian Education*. Garden City: Doubleday.

Chapter VI (p. 136-156) examines the effects of education on the mental health of Native American youth. Notes that suicide is closely tied to excessive alcohol consumption.

0308 Fuller, Lauren L.
1975 Alcoholic Beverage Control: Should the Remaining Reservations Repeal Prohibition under 18 U.S.C. 1161? *American Indian Law Review* 3(2):429-444.

Federal prohibition still remains in force on Indian reservations unless a tribe has exercised its option to legalize the introduction, possession, and sale of intoxicants, subject to state law and tribal requirements. Only 86 tribes, less than half, have chosen to exercise this option. This paper maintains that such prohibition must be repealed and that harsh punishment for sale and possession of alcohol must be eliminated. It is believed that alcoholism is a cultural-sociological problem and that restoration of Native American dignity, which would be demonstrated by removal of discriminatory prohibitions, would be a significant first step in solving the problem.

0309 Gabe, Ruth C., Graham H. Phelps and James A. Ruck
1968 An Exploratory Study of the Incidence of Alcohol-Related Arrests among American Indians of Onondaga County, New York. MSW Thesis, Syracuse University, 85p.

Details the extent and nature of alcohol-related arrests among Native Americans of Onondaga County, New York. It was found that Native Americans were arrested at a rate 20 times more than that of Anglos and 1½ times as often as Blacks. Alcohol was related to 73% of all Native American arrests, compared to 44% for Anglos and 35% for Blacks.

0310 Gabourie, Fred W.
1971 Justice and the Urban American Indian. *California State Bar Journal* 46(1):36-49.

Notes that 75-80% of the cases involving urban Native Americans handled by a particular law firm involve alcohol.

0311 Garbarino, Merwyn S.
1970 Seminole Girl. *Trans-action* 7:40-46.

A brief biography of a young Seminole girl which relates the conflict of a college educated Native American returning to the reservation. Alcohol is only incidentally mentioned; however the article examines conflicts resulting from acculturation; these often result in alcohol abuse among Native American young people.

0312   Garbarino, Merwyn S.
                1971 Life in the City: Chicago. In *The American
                Indian in Urban Society*, Jack O. Waddell and O.
                Michael Watson eds. Pp. 168-205. Boston: Little,
                Brown.

                The consensus among informants is that problem drinkers
                learn their drinking patterns on the reservation.
                Notes that beer and whiskey are preferred by controlled
                social drinkers, while wine is preferred by the
                problem drinker.

0313   Gardner, Richard E.
                1969 The Role of a Pan-Indian Church in Urban
                Indian Life. *Anthropology UCLA* 1(1):14-26.

                A survey of Native Americans in Los Angeles revealed
                that out of 158 households 31.6% of the respondents
                believed alcoholism to be a major problem among urban
                Native Americans. Destructive drinking was associated
                with the impersonality of the city and with a lack of
                knowledge of other resources. Native American bars
                encouraged drinking, but also served as social centers.
                Notes that a Protestant Pan-Indian church provided an
                alternative to drinking by assuming the role of
                a social center previously filled by the bars. The
                church also attempted to provide members with the
                skills needed to survive in an urban environment.

0314   Garfield, Viola E.
                1939 Tsimshian Clan and Society. *University of
                Washington Publications in Anthropology* 7(3):167-340.

                Includes observations on the Rum Feast, an outgrowth
                of the potlatch, but based on the provision of alcohol
                rather than traditional gifts. The object of the feast
                is to provide so much alcohol that the guests cannot
                drink it all, and fall into a stupor. The discussion
                indicates that alcohol found a natural place in the
                social cycle of the Tsimshian.

0315**   Gearing, Fred
                1960 Toward an Adequate Therapy for Alcoholism in
                Non-Western Cultures: an Exploratory Study of
                American Indian Drinking. Unpublished report
                on file with the University of Washington, Department
                of Anthropology, 31p.

                Attempts to identify a measurable psychological variable
                which would differentiate Native American drinking from
                non-Native American drinking. No such variable is

discovered; however, the author contends that clinical psychiatric investigations, coupled with a thorough examination of cultural influence and authority systems might yield clues to control Native American alcohol abuse.

0316** Geertz, Clifford
1951 Drought, Death, and Alcohol in Five Southwestern Cultures. Unpublished paper, 122p.

An examination of how five Southwestern cultures, Texans, Spanish-Americans, Mormons, Zuni, and Navajo, handle the internal and external stresses associated with drought and death. The function of alcohol in both highlighting and relieving stress in each of the five groups is examined.

0317** Geiogamah, Hanay
1972 *Body Indian* (a play in five scenes). Performed by the Red Earth Performing Group, Seattle, Washington.

A powerful and symbolic one-act play about urban Native Americans and drinking. Bobby Lee, who lost his leg to a train in a drinking related accident, is repeatedly maimed by his "friends" as they search his passed-out form for money with which to purchase alcohol. The ultimate maiming occurs when Lee's friends take his artificial leg to hock for wine.

A317** Giles, David K. and Philip Tsosie
1971 Program Description. Unpublished report, Southwest Indian Youth Center, 17p.

Outlines program goals of a rehabilitation program designed for Native American youth who have been convicted of drinking, sniffing glue, truancy, and other offenses (see also citation #A046).

0318 Gillin, John
1942 Acquired Drives in Culture Contact. *American Anthropologist* 44:545-554.

Discussion of factors contributing to Chippewa anxiety and problems in acculturation. Notes that status anxiety is not relieved if one follows government patterns. The prime example of government vacillation is alcohol; prohibited variously to Native Americans, then to Anglos and Native Americans, and finally to Native Americans only. Government policy seems to insist on Native Americans becoming like Anglos in all respects save status.

0319**   Golden, Sandra
            1977 Treatment of Indian Alcoholism a Dilemma?
            NIAAA Transfer to IHS. Unpublished paper presented at the 1st annual Native American Alcoholism Conference, 16p.

            Review of the specialized nature of Native American alcohol programs and the issues involved in the proposed transfer of Native American alcohol programs from the National Institute of Alcohol Abuse and Alcoholism (NIAAA) to the Indian Health Service (IHS).

0320   Goldman, Stanford M., Maurice L. Sievers, William K. Carlile and Samuel L. Cohen
            1971 Radiographic Findings in Southwestern Indians. Paper presented at the 6th joint meetings of the Clinical Society and the Commissioned Officers Association of the U.S. Public Health Service.

            Reports on a review of radiographic findings from the Phoenix Indian Medical Center over a 15 year period. Evidence indicates that clinicians must modify their usual diagnostic considerations when evaluating Southwestern Native Americans. In evaluating gastrointestinal bleeding, esophageal varices studies should be emphasized more than examination for peptic ulcer.

0321   Goldman, Stanford M., Maurice L. Sievers, William K. Carlile and Samuel L. Cohen
            1972 Roentgen Manifestations of Disease in Southwestern Indians. *Radiology* 103(2):303-306.

            A report of radiographic findings from the Phoenix Indian Medical Clinic. Notes that massive gastrointestinal bleeding is usually due to esophageal varices secondary to cirrhosis (see citation #0320).

0322   Goldstein, Sol and Phillip Trautman
            1969 Report on the Quinault Indian Consultation. In *Indian Education: Hearings before the U.S. Senate Special Subcommittee on Indian Education of the Committee on Labor and Public Welfare*. 90th Congress, 1st and 2nd Sessions. Pp. 2343-2350 (SUDOCS #Y4.L11/2:In2/2).

            Suicide and alcoholism represent major health problems among Quinault youth. Suicide was reported to be a general topic of conversation among intoxicated teenagers.

0323   Graburn, N.H.H.
        1969 *Eskimos without Igloos: Social and Economic Development in Sugluk.* Boston: Little, Brown.

        Reports on the introduction of alcohol to the Sallumiut. In 1959 the Sallumiut did not drink, even though it was legal for them to do so. However, beginning in 1960 home brew began to be manufactured and drinking began to create disruptions in family life and the town.

0324** Gracia, M.F.
        1973 Analysis of Incidence of Alcoholic Intake by Indian Population in One State of U.S.A. (Montana), in Relation to Admissions to a Psychiatric Hospital for Treatment and Hospitalization. Paper presented at the IXth International Congress of Anthropological and Ethnological Sciences, 11p.

        Examines Native American patients in the Montana State Hospital regarding acceptance of referral for alcoholism. Individuals most willing to accept treatment came from cohesive, organized tribes. The revival of Native American traditions is seen as a positive trend toward combatting alcoholism.

0325** Grant, Claude W., Kenneth A. Griffiths and Fenton E. Moss
        1971 An Evaluation of the Alcoholism Rehabilitation Center Located at Fairbanks, Alaska. Unpublished report, University of Utah, School of Social Work, 92p.

        Report of an evaluation conducted at the request of the Alaska Bureau of Indian Affairs in which the Rehabilitation Center's administration treatment program, and community relations are examined.

0326   Graves, Theodore D.
        1967 Acculturation, Access, and Alcohol in a Tri-ethnic Community. *American Anthropologist* 69: 306-321.

        Examines the differences in alcohol use and abuse among Native Americans, Chicanos, and Anglos relative to levels of acculturation and degree of access to the economic system.

0327   Graves, Theodore D.
        1970 The Personal Adjustment of Navajo Indian Migrants to Denver, Colorado. *American Anthropologist* 72: 35-54.

Native American drinking is explained in terms of structural and psychological variables which also exist in non-Native American populations. The author concludes that the high rate of Native American drinking results from the fact that Native Americans, relative to other groups, are less prepared for urban living and the accompanying stresses.

0328   Graves, Theodore D.
1971 Drinking and Drunkenness among Urban Indians. In *The American Indian in Urban Society*, Jack O. Waddell and O. Michael Watson eds. Pp. 274-311. Boston: Little, Brown.

Analysis of the structure and function of drinking among Navajo urban migrants reveals that aside from a socialization factor, the drinking also allows for release of hostility and relief from stress. Concludes that the Native Americans with the highest risk are the ones least prepared for urban living.

0329   Graves, Theodore D.
1974 Urban Indian Personality and the "Culture of Poverty." *American Ethnologist* 1(1):65-86.

Report of a study designed to test the success of Navajo urban migrants in terms of their acquisition of middle-class personality traits. It was expected that a delayed gratification orientation would provide psychological protection against drunkenness; however, just the opposite was found. The frustration of not being able to live up to middle-class expectations often caused more drinking.

0330   Green, Lillian
1914 Commissioner Sells Attends Liquor-Suppression Conference. *Carlisle Arrow* 10(19):1-2.

An interview with Commissioner Cato Sells reveals his earnest belief that liquor is retarding the development of Native Americans. A call for reforms to protect Native Americans from alcohol is made.

A330   Gregory, Dick
1975 Racial Differences in the Incidence and Prevalence of Alcohol Abuse in Oklahoma. *Alcohol Technical Reports* (Oklahoma. Department of Mental Health. Division of Alcoholism) 4:37-41.

Examines indicators of alcohol abuse, such as alcohol-related arrests, admissions to alcohol treatment facilities, and rates of morbidity and mortality related to alcoholism for Whites, Blacks and Indians in Oklahoma. Notes that Indians exhibit the greatest prevalence of alcoholism, alcohol related arrests, and are inordinately represented in the number of admissions to treatment facilities.

0331 Grinnell, George Bird
1962 *Blackfoot Lodge Tales: the Story of a Prairie People*. Lincoln: University of Nebraska Press.

Provides an historical overview of the whiskey trade between settlers and Native Americans and the effect of liquor on Native Americans.

0332 Grossman, Peter Holmes
1965 Drinking Motivation: a Cluster Analytic Study of Three Samples. Ph.D. Dissertation, University of Colorado, 196p. U.M. Order #66-02793 (also Research Report #28, Tri-Ethnic Research Project, University of Colorado).

Examines patterns of alcohol use and drinking motivation by applying a standardized list of questions to three selected populations: (1) an adult tri-ethnic community, (2) a high school student sample, and (3) a university student sample. Native Americans were included in the community and high school samples.

0333 Guidotti, Tee L.
1973 Health Care for a Rural Minority. *California Medicine* 118(4):98-104.

Problems associated with the provision of health care to Native Americans are discussed. Notes that provision of health care in rural areas poses problems distinct from those faced in more populated regions. Indicates that alcoholism has played such a major role in Native American society that it has been institutionalized as a cultural norm. Discusses lessons learned in health care delivery from the Modoc Indians of Northern California.

0334 Guillemin, J.
1975 *Urban Renegades: the Cultural Strategy of American Indians*. New York: Columbia University Press.

Chapter III (p. 126-213) examines the adaptation of Micmac Indians to contemporary communities, especially Boston. Notes that heavy drinking, particularly among males, appears to be a pan-Native American phenomenon.

-135-

Indicates that the style of alcohol consumption distinguishes Native American drinking from non-Native American drinking.

0335   Haas, Theodore
        1949 *The Indian and the Law*. Tribal Relations Pamphlets, Washington, D.C.: U.S. Bureau of Indian Affairs (SUDOCS #I20.2:T73/9/#2).

        Discussion of the popularity of alcohol as a trade item and congressional attempts to control the liquor traffic.

0336   Haas, Theodore
        1957 The Legal Aspects of Indian Affairs from 1887 to 1957. *Annals of the American Academy of Political and Social Science* 311:12-22.

        A review of significant legislation affecting Native American affairs. Notes that one of the most important and oldest laws is the one regulating the use of alcohol by Native Americans. Passed in 1802, the law authorized the president to regulate the sale and distribution of alcohol among Native Americans. Amended in 1892, it was broadened to prohibit the gift of intoxicants to Native Americans. The law was finally overturned in 1953, leaving prohibition a local option for tribal governments.

0337** Hackenberg, Robert A.
        1965 Alcoholism: Its Social and Cultural Background. Unpublished paper, 3p.

        Alcoholic behavior is defined as a recent alternative for Native Americans. A migrant, agricultural life-style is viewed as contributing to Native American alcoholism.

0338   Hackenberg, Robert A. and Mary M. Gallagher
        1972 The Costs of Cultural Change: Accidental Injury and Modernization among the Papago Indians. *Human Organization* 31:211-226.

        Suggests that an accident case rate is an acceptable index of stress resulting from modernization. Observes that both excessive drinking and a marked increase in accidental injuries are indicators of stress among the Papago.

0339   Haddad, Susan
        1972 I Can't Really Get Involved in Urban Indian Problems, Because Anytime I May Go Home. *NLADA Briefcase* 30(5):161-167.

The BIA Relocation Program sent thousands of Native Americans to the cities and then abandoned them. Many returned to the reservation; however, many remained in the urban setting, drowning themselves in alcohol. The efforts of recovered alcoholic Mike Chosa are detailed in the fight to organize Chicago Native Americans and give them a voice in their affairs.

A339   Hafen, Brent Q.
1977 *Alcohol: The Crutch That Cripples.* St. Paul: West Publishing Co.

In a chapter entitled "Incidence and Severity of the Indian Alcohol Problem" Hafen discusses the prevalence of alcohol problems among Native American people and suggests that social status and low self-esteem contribute to alcohol abuse. Indicates that the answers to the social and cultural problems which precipitate abusive drinking lie with Native American people themselves.

0340**   Haffner, Marlene
1972 Diphtheria Outbreak on the Navajo Reservation. Unpublished paper presented at the 7th joint meeting of the Clinical Society and the Commissioned Officers Association of the U.S. Public Health Service.

Describes a diphtheria outbreak on the Navajo Reservation between August, 1970 and November, 1971. Case histories of 25 patients, five of which are alcoholic, are reviewed.

0341   Hagan, William T.
1966 *Indian Police and Judges.* New Haven: Yale University Press.

Considers the problems posed by liquor to tribal law enforcement officials.

0342   Haldeman, Jack C.
1951a Problems of Alaskan Eskimos, Indians, and Aleuts. *Public Health Reports* 66(27):912-917.

Among Alaska's Native population alcohol is responsible for 8 times the number of deaths as compared to non-Anglos in the rest of the U.S.

0343   Haldeman, Jack C.
1951b Violent and Accidental Deaths as a Health Problem in Alaska. In *Science in Alaska: Proceedings*

of the *2nd Alaskan Science Conference.* Pp. 103-107. College, Alaska: Alaska Division, American Association for the Advancement of Science.

Alcoholism is held to be Alaska's major health problem. Alcoholism leads as the cause of death among non-Anglo females.

0344   Hallowell, A. Irving
1946 Some Psychological Characteristics of the Northeastern Indians. *Robert S. Peabody Foundation for Archaeology Papers* 3:195-225.

The effect of alcohol on culturally structured inhibitions is disasterous, provoking quarrels, physical violence, injuries, and homicide.

0345   Hallowell, A. Irving
1950 Values, Acculturation and Mental Health. *American Journal of Orthopsychiatry* 20:732-743 (reprinted in *The Emergent Native Americans,* Deward Walker, Jr. ed. Pp. 584-594. Boston: Little, Brown.

Drinking behavior is only mentioned in passing; however, the loss of values and the psychological impact of acculturation may well be a contributing factor in drinking behavior, especially among males.

0346   Hallowell, A. Irving
1955 *Culture and Experience.* Philadelphia: University of Pennsylvania Press.

Notes the effect of alcohol on the Native Americans of the Eastern Woodlands. Mentions that alcohol so released traditional cultural restraints that in-group homicide became a problem where it had never before existed.

0347   Halverson, Darrell R.
1966 Tuberculosis Alcoholic and His Ethnic Group: an Exploratory Study. Unpublished paper, Medical Student Research Meeting, University of Washington.

Anglo, Native American, Black, and Oriental tubercular alcoholic and non-alcoholic discharged patients were compared. Differences were found in age, education, religion, marital status, disease level, hospital treatment, and duration of illness.

0348   Hamer, John H.
       1965   Acculturation Stress and the Functions of Alcohol among the Forest Potawatomi. *Quarterly Journal of Studies on Alcohol* 26:285-302.

   Historical as well as contemporary drinking behavior in the Potawatomi community of Whitehorse is discussed. Functional aspects of drinking include: (1) providing individuals with a means of coping with an unpredictable universe, as well as an escape from anxiety; (2) permitting individuals to temporarily assume desirable status positions in a changing social structure; (3) serving as a means of categorizing groups in an acculturation situtation; and (4) providing a solvent for tensions.

0349   Hamer, John H.
       1969   Guardian Spirits: Alcohol and Cultural Defense Mechanisms. *Anthropologica* 11:215-241.

   The Forest Potawatomi guardian spirit quest and social drinking are defined as institutional outlets for the sublimation of dependency as well as providing a situationally acceptable means for releasing aggression.

0350   Hanlon, John J.
       1972   Interaction between Man and the Arctic Environment; Past, Present, and Prospective. *Archives of Environmental Health* 25:234-238.

   Culture change among the indigenous population of the Arctic is manifested in increasing number of deaths due to alcoholism, increased incidence of alcoholic psychosis, and extremely high accident rates, which are tied to alcohol.

0351   Hanna, Joel M.
       1976   Ethnic Groups, Human Variation, and Alcohol Use. In *Cross-Cultural Approaches to the Study of Alcohol*, Michael W. Everett, Jack O. Waddell and Dwight B. Heath eds. Pp. 235-242. The Hague: Mouton.

   A review of literature dealing with biological variation as it relates to the occurrence of alcoholism in different ethnic groups. It is postulated that since Native Americans tend to be smaller than Anglos and Afro-Americans they may experience proportionately greater increases in brain alcohol concentrations per drink.

0352   Hano, Arnold
        1973 Among the Navajos: What It Is Like Living
           on an Indian Reservation. *Seventeen Magazine*
           32(1):88-89, 96-97.

        Reports on life among Navajo students at the boarding
        school at Many Farms. Notes that about 10% of the
        student body drink to excess and about 62% of the
        students believe alcohol abuse to be a problem.

0353** Harkins, Arthur M. and Richard G. Woods
        1969 Barrow and Kotzebue: an Exploratory Comparison
           of Acculturation and Education in Two Large North-
           western Alaskan Villages. Unpublished report.
           University of Minnesota Training Center for Community
           Problems.

        Community problems, especially among adolescents,
        includes glue sniffing and excessive drinking.
        Drinking in both Barrow and Kotzebue follows a binge
        pattern.

0354   Harmer, Ruth Mulvey
        1956 Uprooting the Indians. *Atlantic Monthly*
           197(3):54-57.

        Contends that the BIA Relocation Program is a failure.
        Notes that alcohol is a factor in the Native American's
        inability to adjust to an urban environment.

0355   Hartocollis, Peter
        1967 A History of Alcohol Problems in Kansas:
           1854-1966. *Bulletin of the Menninger Clinic*
           31:136-153.

        In tracing the history of alcohol abuse in Kansas,
        it is noted that the initial concern regarding
        alcohol was fostered by the "occasional belligerence
        of local Indians against the White settlers" after
        the Indians had been drinking. With the creation of
        the Kansas Territory in 1854 steps were taken to
        control the sale of alcohol to Native Americans.
        Additional prohibitory laws were passed in 1861 when
        Kansas became a state.

0356   Harvey, Elinor B.
        1976 Psychiatric Consultation and Social Work at a
           Secondary School for Eskimo, Indian, and Aleut
           Students in Alaska. In *Circumpolar Health: Proceedings
           of the Third International Symposium*, Roy J. Shepard
           and S. Itoh eds. Pp. 517-525. Toronto: University
           of Toronto Press.

Findings of a psychiatric social work program at the Mt. Edgecumbe School revealed that the largest problem during a 5-year study consisted of students referred for disruptive behavior while intoxicated. The proportion of drinkers among southeast Alaskan Native Americans was high in comparison to their numbers in the total student body, indicating a differential ethnic use of alcohol. Changes in the curriculum to emphasize Native cultures and other special programs seemed to alleviate some of the problems.

0357   Hassrick, Royal B.
1947   Alcohol and Indians. *The American Indian* 4(2):19-26.

Argues for the repeal of prohibition for Native Americans. Notes that alcohol abuse is the result of social and psychological factors rather than biological differences and that prohibition is discrimination against a people held to be inferior.

0358   Hauser, S. Frederick
1942   A Study of Alcoholism in an American Indian Tribe. MA Thesis, Columbia University, 104p.

Attempts to provide an ethnographic analysis of alcohol use among the Pomo Indians of Northern California.

0359   Havard, V.
1896   Drink Plants of the North American Indian. *Torrey Botanical Club Bulletin* 23(2):33-46.

A description of plants used by Native Americans in the manufacture of beverages. Plants are divided into three categories: (1) those used in the manufacture of alcoholic beverages, (2) those resulting in stimulating, exhilarating, or intoxicating beverages other than alcohol, and (3) those furnishing palatable juices. The manufacture of alcoholic beverages is reportedly found only among southwestern Native Americans, specifically the Pimas, Maricopas, Yumas, and Apaches.

0360   Havighurst, Robert J.
1971   The Extent and Significance of Suicide among American Indians Today. *Mental Hygiene* 55(2):174-177.

Notes that suicide rates are closely related to alcoholism and other variables. Reviews studies by Dizmang (1968, 1974, citations #0216, 0217) and testimony regarding the Quinaults submitted by Patterson (1969, citation #0688) to the Special Subcommittee on Indian Education.

0361   Havighurst, Robert J. and Bernice Neugarten
        1955 *American Indian and White Children: a Socio-Psychological Investigation*. Chicago: University of Chicago Press.

        When children from six tribes (Hopi, Navajo, Papago, Sioux, Zia, and Zuni) were asked to respond to the words "fear" and "worst thing" many mentioned intoxicated individuals, and drinking appeared as a subsidiary theme in moral ideology tests.

0362   Haworth, David D.
        1968 Alcoholism Pilot Study Program at the U.S. Public Health Service Hospital, Shiprock, New Mexico. Unpublished paper presented at the third joint meeting of the Clinical Society and Commissioned Officers Association of the U.S. Public Health Service.

        Report of an alcoholic rehabilitation program which utilizes the Turquoise Lodge (New Mexico State Commission on Alcoholism facility) for inpatient detoxification, followed by counselor contacts, AA group meetings, and follow-up visits by paraprofessional workers.

0363   Hawthorne, H.B., Cyril S. Belshaw and S.M. Jamieson
        1957 The Indians of British Columbia and Alcohol. *Alcoholism Review* 2(3):10-14.

        Briefly investigates drinking behavior; provides an analysis of the effects of Native American drinking and offers possible solutions to the problem of Native American alcohol abuse.

0364   Hawthorne, H.B., Cyril S. Belshaw and S.M. Jamieson
        1958 *The Indians of British Columbia: a Study of Contemporary Social Adjustment*. Toronto: University of Toronto Press.

        Chapter 26, entitled "The Question of Liquor" examines the relationship between alcohol and Native Americans in British Columbia. Indicates that Native Americans are perceived by Anglos as heavy and unreliable drinkers. Reports that officials tend to ignore the presence of alcoholism among Native Americans; as a result, necessary treatment is not as readily available to Native Americans as it is to Anglos.

0365   Hayner, Norman S.
        1942 Variability in the Criminal Behavior of American
        Indians. *American Journal of Sociology* 47:602-613.

   Notes that discriminatory prohibition probably
   contributes to liquor problems among Native Americans
   and that prohibition is easier to enforce in those
   areas where Native Americans live apart from Anglos.

0366   Hays, Hoffman Reynolds
        1975 *Children of the Raven: the Seven Indian Nations
        of the Northwest Coast.* New York: McGraw-Hill.

   Examines the introduction of alcohol to Native Americans
   of the Northwest Coast. Suggests that heavy drinking
   resulted from Native Americans' recognition that they
   were dominated by Europeans. Notes that prohibition
   was not successful and that the psychological factors
   involved in Native American alcohol abuse have not
   yet been alleviated.

0367** Hays, Terence E.
        1968 San Carlos Apache Drinking Groups: Institu-
        tionalized Deviance as a Factor in Community
        Disorganization. Unpublished paper presented
        at the 67th annual meeting of the American
        Anthropological Association, 6p.

   Suggests that the drinking group phenomenon must
   be viewed in the context of the factions which have
   arisen in conjunction with the economic, political,
   and religious adaptations required by the dominant
   society. Indicates that group drinking provides a
   traditional setting for norm violation.

A367   Heaston, Michael D.
        1971 Whiskey Regulations and Indian Land Titles in
        New Mexico Territory 1851-1861. *Journal of the
        West* 10(3):474-483.

   Under the auspices of the War Department, trade and
   land issues were governed and regulated by a series
   of intercourse acts between Native Americans and non-
   Native Americans. The first set of regulations were
   passed in 1790 and the last in 1834. One of the
   regulated trade items was liquor, which was introduced
   into the New Mexico Territory by the Spanish, and
   which was observed to have a demoralizing and adverse
   effect upon Native Americans. Negotiations with the
   Utes, Apaches, and Navajos were designed to settle
   land disputes and prohibit the use of liquor by Native

Americans. However, failure to establish a permanent reservation for Native Americans in the New Mexico Territory and lax application of the Intercourse Act of 1834 led to numerous wars between Native Americans and Anglos.

0368 Heath, Dwight B.
  1952 Alcohol in a Navaho Community. AB Thesis, Harvard University, 94p.

  Reviews field reports of observations on the Rimrock Navajos and provides a description of drinking behavior and the characteristics of drinkers. Notes that drinking is a social act but that patterns of drinking differ significantly from that of Anglos. Attributes the lack of social controls over alcohol use to the relatively recent introduction of alcohol to the Navajos.

0369** Heath, Dwight B.
  1960 Persistence and Change in Navaho Drinking Patterns. Unpublished paper presented at the 59th annual meeting of the American Anthropological Association, 7p.

  Reviews Navajo drinking patterns from 1941 through 1960. Indicates that change in pre- and post-prohibition drinking patterns are few. Estimates that 15% of drinkers can be categorized as "heavy drinkers."

0370 Heath, Dwight B.
  1964 Prohibition and Post-Repeal Drinking Patterns among the Navajo. *Quarterly Journal of Studies on Alcohol* 25:119-135.

  Drinking patterns among the Navajo before and after prohibition (1953 for Native Americans) are reviewed in terms of who, what, where, how, and why. There has been little evidence of change in drinking patterns since 1941 despite the repeal of federal and state prohibition laws. The nature of drinking groups remains unchanged.

0371 Heath, Dwight B.
  1975 A Critical Review of Ethnographic Studies of Alcohol Use. In *Research Advances in Alcohol and Drug Problems*, R.J. Gibbins, ed. Vol. 2:1-92. New York: John Wiley.

  A review of the anthropological literature on alcohol use. Numerous references to Native American alcohol use.

0372**   Hegg, Theodore D.
         1967 Health Survey of the Muckleshoot Indians.
         Unpublished report prepared for the University
         of Washington Departments of Preventive Medicine
         and Pediatrics, 17p.

         Reports that 18.5% of all deaths are due to accidents
         reflecting the high level of alcohol involvement
         and destructive drinking habits.

0373   Heidenreich, C. Adrian
         1976 Alcohol and Drug Use and Abuse among Indian-
         Americans: a Review of Issues and Sources. *Journal
         of Drug Issues* 6(3):256-272.

         Provides a review of Native American alcohol and drug
         use for professionals who may work with Native American
         patients or communities.

0374   Heizer, Robert F.
         1974 *The Destruction of California Indians.* Santa
         Barbara: Peregrine Smith.

         Chapter 9 reviews the role of alcohol in the destruction
         of California Native Americans.

0375   Helm, June
         1961 The Lynx Point People: the Dynamics of a Northern
         Athapaskan Band. *National Museum of Canada, Bulletin*
         #176.

         Brew parties serve as the major social and recreational
         activity of the entire community. Drinking is highly
         valued and equated with having a good time. Details
         of drinking behavior are noted and social control
         mechanisms are discussed.

0376   Helm, June and Nancy O. Lurie
         1961 *The Subsistence Economy of the Dogrib Indians
         of Lac la Marte in the Mackenzie District of the
         Northwest Territories.* Ottawa: Northern Co-ordination
         and Research Centre, Department of Northern Affairs
         and National Resources, Publication #61-3.

         Very briefly discusses the manufacture of home brew
         and drinking behavior. Mentions that consumption of
         alcohol serves as the only form of recreation available
         to males and indicates that drinking represents
         defiance against Anglos.

A376　　　Helmick, Edward F., William T. McClure and Patricia
　　　　　M. Mitchell
　　　　　　　1977 A Project to Analyze Risk to Alcohol Abuse
　　　　　　　among Alaskan Native Students. In *Currents in
　　　　　　　Alcoholism*, Frank A. Seixas ed., vol. 2:367-376.
　　　　　　　New York: Grune and Stratton.

　　　　　　　Reports on an attempt to develop a tool which, when
　　　　　　　applied to a population, would enable one to predict
　　　　　　　whether members of the population would have a
　　　　　　　significant chance of developing a drinking problem.

0377**　　Helmick, Edward F., S.I. Miller, L. Berg, P. Nutting
　　　　　and G. Schorr
　　　　　　　1975a A Project to Analyze Risk to Alcohol Abuse
　　　　　　　among Alaska Natives. Paper presented at the 10th
　　　　　　　joint meeting of the Professional Associations
　　　　　　　of the U.S. Public Health Service.

　　　　　　　Attempts to identify factors which enable one to
　　　　　　　predict an individual's reaction to treatment for
　　　　　　　alcoholism. Provides a list of over 40 risk factors.

0378**　　Helmick, Edward F., S.I. Miller, L. Berg, P. Nutting
　　　　　and G. Schorr
　　　　　　　1975b A System to Improve Care for the Alaska Problem
　　　　　　　Drinker. Unpublished paper presented at the 10th
　　　　　　　joint meeting of the Professional Associations of
　　　　　　　the U.S. Public Health Service.

　　　　　　　Discusses information which is required to provide
　　　　　　　effective treatment.

0379　　　Helmick, Edward F., S.I. Miller, L. Berg, P. Nutting
　　　　　and G. Schorr
　　　　　　　1976 Demonstration of an Evaluation Scheme to Improve
　　　　　　　Care for the Alaskan Problem Drinker. *Annals of
　　　　　　　the New York Academy of Sciences* 273:646-652.

　　　　　　　Discusses the need for a method to evaluate the
　　　　　　　effectiveness of alcohol programs provided Native
　　　　　　　Americans in Alaska. Adherence to minimum standards,
　　　　　　　such as those adopted by the State of Alaska, is
　　　　　　　recommended in order to improve care provided problem
　　　　　　　drinkers.

0380**　　Henderson, Norman B.
　　　　　　　1965 Community Treatment Plan for Navaho Problem
　　　　　　　Drinkers. Unpublished paper presented at the
　　　　　　　University of Utah School of Alcohol Studies, 8p.

0381   Henderson, Norman B.
        1967 Cross-Cultural Action Research: Some Limitations,
        Advantages, and Problems. *Journal of Social
        Psychology* 73:61-70.

        Navajo Problem Drinker Treatment Program data indicates
        limitations, such as a limited sample and inconsistent
        control of variables; advantages, such as a copious
        supply of informants; and problems, such as cultural
        stereotyping, ethnocentrism.

0382** Henderson, Norman B.
        1973 Indian Problem Drinking: Stereotype or Reality?
        a Study of Navajo Problem Drinking. Unpublished
        paper presented at the 129th meeting of the American
        Psychological Association, 15p.

        Despite Native Americans' problems with alcohol, the
        author rejects the drunken Indian stereotype.

A382   Henderson, Norman B.
        1974 Navaho Rehabilitation Project: A Final Report.
        HRAFlex Book. New Haven: Human Relations Area Files.

        Describes the staff, data collection methods, client
        recruitment procedures, and social setting. A report
        on the first nine months of the Gallup Community
        Treatment Plan for Native American problem drinkers,
        designed to intervene in the multiple arrest cycle
        of Navajo alcoholics.

0383   Hendrie, Hugh C. and Diane Hanson
        1972 A Comparative Study of the Psychiatric Care of
        Indian and Metis. *American Journal of Ortho-
        psychiatry* 42:480-489.

        Research revealed that Native Americans and Metis
        with personality disorders, such as alcoholism and
        drug abuse, received fewer follow-up outpatient
        appointments and had shorter hospital stays than
        did the control group. Differences were related to
        staff attitudes regarding the potential benefit of
        outpatient therapy on "lower class" Native Americans
        and Metis. It was also reported that patients with
        alcohol and drug problems kept fewer appointments
        than the control group.

0384   Henk, Matthew L.
        1969 Treatment Programs for the Navajo Alcoholic.
        Unpublished paper presented at the 4th joint meeting
        of the Clinical Society and the Commissioned Officers
        Association of the U.S. Public Health Service.

Reports on inpatient, outpatient, and contract medical care provided Navajo alcoholics. Notes that treatment success is directly related to the amount of follow-up treatment a patient receives.

0385   Hertzberg, H.W.
       1971 *The Search for an American Indian Identity: Modern Pan-Indian Movements*. Syracuse, New York: Syracuse University Press.

       Chapter 10, "The Peyote Cult," notes that Peyotists recognize alcoholism as a major problem for Native Americans and indicates that temperance is an important tenet of the Peyote religion.

0386   Hill, Thomas Warren
       1976 "Feeling Good" and "Getting High": Alcohol Use of Urban Indians. Ph.D. Dissertation, University of Pennsylvania, 243p. U.M. Order #77-00844.

       Provides a description and analysis of the drinking patterns of Winnebago and Santee Dakota in Sioux City, Iowa. Includes a review of selected literature concerning Native American drinking, as well as a discussion of drinking norms and behavior. Concludes that the groups involved utilize multiple sets of drinking norms, some of which define heavy drinking as acceptable behavior. Offers a new model to explain drinking behavior and cautions that an understanding of Native American drinking requires a holistic paradigm which includes sociocultural, psychological, and biological variables.

0387   Hippler, Arthur E.
       1969 Fusion and Frustration: Dimensions in the Cross-Cultural Ethnopsychology of Suicide. *American Anthropologist* 71:1074-1087.

       Heavy drinking is a form of risk taking which exhibits the same dynamics associated with suicide.

0388   Hippler, Arthur E.
       1970a *From Village to Town: an Intermediate Step in the Acculturation of Alaska Eskimos*. Minneapolis: University of Minnesota Training Center for Community Programs.

       Alcohol use by Eskimos does not result in clinical symptoms associated with heavy drinking. While evidence of alcoholism among the Anglo population of Nome exists, it is, ironically, the Eskimos rather than the Anglos that are stereotyped as having a drinking problem.

0389   Hippler, Arthur E.
        1970b Patterns of Migration, Urbanization and
        Acculturation. In *Science in Alaska. Proceedings
        of the 20th Alaska Science Conference*, Eleanor C.
        Viereck ed. Pp. 99-108. College, Alaska: Alaska
        Division, American Association for the Advancement
        of Science.

        Indicates that personal pathologies, such as alcohol
        abuse, are evidence of the difficulties associated
        with acculturation. Points out that law enforcement
        officers often assume that Native Americans are drunks.

0390   Hippler, Arthur E.
        1973 Fundamentalist Christianity: an Alaskan Athabaskan
        Technique for Overcoming Alcohol Abuse. *Transcultural
        Psychiatric Research Review* 10(2):173-179.

        See Annotation #0391.

0391   Hippler, Arthur E.
        1974 An Alaskan Athabaskan Technique for Overcoming
        Alcohol Abuse. *Arctic* 27(1):53-67.

        Indicates that the methodology for overcoming alcohol
        abuse among Native Americans is dependent upon the
        existing means of social control in each society. The
        Athabaskans of interior Alaska "...tend to overcome
        alcohol abuse by adhering to fundamentalist Christianity
        which reflects their need for an external superego
        that in the past took the form of a nearly absolute
        chieftainship."

0392** Hirokawa, Theodore
        1971 Suicide and Suicide Gestures at Fort Hall.
        Unpublished communication with S.J. Kunitz, 41p.

        Indicates that a large number of suicide threats
        and attempts occur while the individual is intoxicated.
        Suggests that a broad approach to drug and alcohol
        abuse prevention would be a beneficial program.
        However, dealing with the alcohol problem might not
        solve the underlying problems which precipitated
        the suicide threat.

0393   Hirschfeld, Mervyn and Austin Smith
        1954 Alcohol Intoxication in Indians. *Journal of the
        American Medical Association* 156(14):1375.

        In the "Notes and Queries" section Hirschfeld asks
        if there is medical evidence that Native Americans
        react differently to alcohol than other races. The

response does not answer the question directly; however, it is suggested that the drinking style of Native Americans is a learned behavior.

0394   Hobart, C.W.
1976 Socio-Economic Correlates of Mortality and Morbidity among Inuit Infants. In *Circumpolar Health: Proceedings of the Third International Symposium*, Roy J. Shepard and S. Itoh eds. Pp. 452-461. Toronto: University of Toronto Press.

A study of infant mortality and morbidity indices indicates that maternal and paternal alcohol use adversely affects infant health.

0395   Hoffman, Helmut and Douglas N. Jackson
1973 Comparison of Measured Psychopathology in Indian and Non-Indian Alcoholics. *Psychological Reports* 33:793-794.

The Differential Personality Inventory was administered to 24 Chippewa and one Sioux hospitalized for the treatment of alcoholism. The comparison population was 75 Anglos matched for age, sex, and education. Native Americans scored significantly higher than Anglos on 7 of 27 clinical scales; however, there were no significant differences on scales reflecting character disorders. Results are attributed to socio-economic deprivation. It is recommended that separate norms be developed on standardized measures of psychopathology for specific ethnic groups.

0396   Hoffman, Helmut and Avis A. Noem
1975a Alcoholism and Abstinence among Relatives of American Indian Alcoholics. *Journal of Studies on Alcohol* 36:165.

A brief report of a study conducted among patients of an alcoholism treatment facility in Minnesota. Alcoholism was found to be more prevalent in the families of alcoholics than non-alcoholics, and among Native Americans than non-Native Americans. The high incidence of alcoholism in the Native American population was hypothesized as being related to (1) social frustration and poor socioeconomic conditions on the reservations, (2) stress in early life caused by absence of natural parents, and (3) exposure to heavy drinking in childhood.

A396   Hoffmann, Helmut and Avis A. Noem
         1975b Adjustment of Chippewa Indian Alcoholics to a
         Predominantly White Treatment Program. *Psychological
         Reports* 37:1284-1286.

         Investigates whether Native American alcoholics
         differ from non-Native American alcoholics and whether
         Native Americans benefit from an integrated treatment
         program. Native Americans and non-Native Americans
         admitted to a state hospital alcohol treatment unit
         over a two year period are compared on background,
         admissions, and discharge variables. Suggests that
         an integrated treatment program would benefit Native
         American alcoholics.

0397   Holloway, M.A.
         1974 Illness Perception and Knowledge among Seattle
         Urban Indians. M.S. (Nursing) Thesis, University
         of Washington, 75p.

         Results of a survey regarding perceptions of illness
         among Native Americans of Seattle reveals that the
         majority of the respondents believed alcohol to be
         the most serious health problem among Native Americans.
         Concludes that there is need for further investigation
         into the help-seeking behavior of Native American
         alcoholics.

0398   Holloway, Robert
         1966 *Drinking among Indian Youth: A Study of the
         Drinking Behavior, Attitudes and Beliefs of Indian
         and Metis Young People in Manitoba*. Winnipeg:
         Alcohol Education Service.

         Describes the drinking behavior, attitudes, and
         knowledge of alcohol among Native American and Metis
         youth in Manitoba, Canada. Comparison data between
         Native Americans and non-Native Americans are pro-
         vided. Indicates that the role of alcohol education
         is uncertain; it appears that Native Americans may
         intellectually understand educational dictums to drink
         moderately, but not be motivated by such programs.

0399   Honigmann, John
         1949 *Culture and Ethos of Kaska Society*. New Haven:
         Yale University Press, Yale University Publications
         in Anthropology, #40.

         Notes that in the last 25 years the Kaska have learned
         the process of fermentation and now manufacture their
         own wine and beer.

0400   Honigmann, John
        1962 Review of *The Subsistence Economy of the Dogrib
        Indians of Lac la Martre in the Mackenzie District
        of the Northwest Territories*. American Anthropologist
        64:658-659.

        Notes that the main events in the lives of the Dogrib
        are brew parties, religious services, and life crises.
        See citation #0376 for a full annotation of the book.

0401   Honigmann, John
        1965 Social Disintegration in Five Northern Communities.
        Canadian Review of Sociology and Anthropology 2(4):
        199-214.

        Examines social disintegration in five communities:
        Lower Post (Kaska), Attawapiskat (Cree), Great Whale
        River (Algonkian and Eskimo), Frobisher Bay (Eskimo),
        and Old Crow (Kutchin). Notes that alcohol serves
        as a major mode of recreation. Uses alcohol as an
        index of disintegration.

0402** Honigmann, John
        1968 Adaptation of Indians, Eskimos, and Persons
        of Partial Indigenous Background in a Canadian
        Northern Town. Unpublished paper presented at
        the 67th annual meeting of the American Anthro-
        pological Association, 11p.

        Reports on adaptation to town life by various ethnic
        groups in Inuvik. Notes that alcohol use leads to
        frequent trouble with the police.

0403** Honigmann, John
        1970 Formation of Mackenzie Delta Frontier Culture.
        Unpublished paper presented at the annual meeting
        of the Northeastern Anthropological Society, 10p.

        Examines the development of a "Frontier Culture,"
        a local subculture which has developed in the Inuvik
        and Mackenzie Delta area. The role of alcohol in the
        Frontier Culture is discussed and it is noted that
        members of the Frontier Culture believe that traditional
        values pertaining to the use of alcohol, gambling,
        and police are not appropriate to the frontier.

0404   Honigmann, John
        1971a Alcohol in its Cultural Context. In *Proceedings:
        First Annual Alcoholism Conference of NIAAA*, M.
        Chafetz ed. Pp. 252-257. Washington, D.C.:
        National Institute on Alcohol Abuse and Alcoholism (may

be located under: Alcoholism Conference of the
National Institute on Alcohol Abuse and Alcoholism,
SUDOCS #HE 20.2430/2:971).

Provides a review of anthropological theories regarding
heavy Native American drinking and suggests that
research also needs to focus on non-drinkers in the
same population, as well as the culture as a whole
for antecedents to drinking behavior. The need for
investigation into the symbolism of drinking rather
than the gross observation of drinking behavior is
also noted.

0405   Honigmann, John
       1971b Northern Townsmen. *Northwest Anthropological
         Research Notes* 5(1):97-122.

Examines Native American and Metis adaptation to town
living. Folklore holds that alcohol is a major problem
of native town life; however, careful investigation
failed to corroborate the myth. Drinking is primarily
a social activity and varies along a series of sociocultural indices. Differential use of alcohol is
noted for various towns and groups of Native Americans.

0406   Honigmann, John and Irma Honigmann
       1945 Drinking in an Indian-White Community. *Quarterly
         Journal of Studies on Alcohol* 5:575-619.

Represents a comparative study of Native American
and Anglo drinking in the Canadian wilderness.
Describes the preparation of brews, drinking styles,
and drunken behavior. Horton's (1943) theories are
applied and the authors find that the characteristic
drinking behavior of Native Americans and Anglos
support Horton's anxiety theorems.

0407   Honigmann, John and Irma Honigmann
       1965 How the Baffin Island Eskimo Have Learned to
         Use Alcohol. *Social Forces* 44:73-83.

Eskimos in Frobisher Bay became legally entitled to
consume alcoholic beverages in 1960; initially this
resulted in many arrests for drunkenness. In order
to control drinking a law was passed in 1962 which
limited the sale of alcohol. Public drunkenness has
since declined, and the older Eskimo have begun to
learn a drinking pattern resembling that of their
Canadian neighbors.

0408   Honigmann, John and Irma Honigmann
                1966 Urban Eskimo Learn How to Drink. *California
                    Alcoholism Review* 1:53-55.

                This article is a condensation of Honigmann and
                Honigmann (1965). See citation #0407 for annotation.

0409**   Honigmann, John and Irma Honigmann
                1968 Alcohol in a Canadian Northern Town. Unpublished
                    report, University of North Carolina, Institute
                    for Research in Social Science.

                Examines drinking behavior of non-Anglos in Fort
                Mackenzie, utilizing age, sex, ethnicity, and em-
                ployment as variables. Results are compared with
                data from Frobisher Bay and Aklavik. Drinking behavior
                is characterized as "frontier style," that is, few
                social controls apply to drinking. Notes that a
                nonconformist pattern of alcohol use is part of Native
                cultural identity. Discusses the concept of social
                stake and indicates that individuals with a stake
                in society exhibit less alcohol-related problems
                than individuals without a stake.

0410**   Honigmann, John and Irma Honigmann
                1969 Success in School: Adaptation in a New Canadian
                    Arctic Town. Unpublished manuscript, University
                    of North Carolina, Institute for Research in Social
                    Science, 85p.

                Examines the adaptation of 412 children, ages 6 to 20
                of Native American, Eskimo, and Metis background to
                formal education in Inuvik. Discusses the use of
                alcohol in a culture with a "frontier" quality.

0411   Honigmann, John and Irma Honigmann
                1970 *Arctic Townsmen: Ethnic Backgrounds and
                    Modernization*. Ottawa: Canadian Research Centre
                    for Anthropology, St. Paul University.

                Investigates the role of alcohol in Inuvik. Describes
                drinking behavior, alcohol use by ethnic group, alcohol
                as an adaptive mechanism, and the relation between
                alcohol and arrests.

0412**   Hood, William R.
                1972 Dirty Words: Genetic Differences in Response to
                    Alcohol. Unpublished paper presented at the annual
                    meeting of the American Psychological Association,
                    22p.

Examines genetic factors regarding alcohol abuse. Suggests that alcohol abuse among Native Americans is not necessarily genetic, medical, psychological, cultural, social, economic, or political, but rather a composite of all these factors. A comprehensive ecological and systems analysis approach is recommended.

0413   Horton, Donald D.
1943 The Functions of Alcohol in Primitive Societies: a Cross-Cultural Study. *Quarterly Journal of Studies on Alcohol* 4:199-320.

The major thesis of this classic study is that anxiety lies at the root of primitive drinking behavior. Alcohol is viewed as an agent of social cohesion. Contrasted with anxiety is counteranxiety, which may inhibit drunken behavior and stems from society's attitudes towards liquor; the stricter the sanctions and attitudes, the more counteranxiety. Based on this theory Horton rates 56 primitive societies as to their level of "drunkenness."

0414   Howard, James H.
1976 The Plains Gourd Dance as a Revitalization Movement. *American Ethnologist* 3:243-259.

Cites the case of one Comanche Gourd Dancer who claims that participation in the Gourd Dance helped him to achieve and maintain sobriety.

0415**   Howard-Craft, A.
1975 The Native American Male Alcoholic. Unpublished paper prepared for the Native American MPH Program, School of Public Health, University of California, Berkeley, 14p.

A review of some of the factors which make successful relocation to urban areas difficult for Native American males. Suggests some reasons why Alcoholics Anonymous groups are not always suitable as therapeutic regimen for Native Americans. Two case histories are presented and various problems are highlighted.

0416   Howay, F.W.
1942 The Introduction of Intoxicating Liquors amongst Indians of the Northwest Coast. *British Columbia Historical Review* 6(3):157-169.

Reviews the introduction of alcohol to the Native Americans of the Northwest Coast. Initially Native Americans rejected alcoholic beverages, which were not used for trade. However, in the 1790s traders began to note a desire among Native Americans for brandy, and liquor became an accepted trade item.

0417 Hoyt, Olga
   1972 *American Indians Today*. New York: Abelard-Schuman.

   A survey of contemporary Native American affairs aimed mainly at a juvenile audience. Alcohol is noted as a major problem among Native Americans. Suggests that factors contributing to alcohol problems include inadequate education, lack of employment opportunities, lack of recreational facilities, and social disorganization.

0418 Hrdlicka, Ales
   1904 Method of Preparing Tesvino among the White River Apache. *American Anthropologist* 6:190-191.

   Tulapai or tesvino is a mildly intoxicating drink manufactured by the White River Apaches. This article details the method of manufacture of the beverage.

0419 Hrdlicka, Ales
   1908 Physiological and Medical Observations among the Indians of Southwestern United States and Northern Mexico. *U.S. Bureau of American Ethnology Bulletin* #34 (SUDOCS #SI 2.3:34).

   Notes each tribe in southwestern U.S. and northern Mexico which manufactures alcoholic beverages; describes the alcoholic drinks.

A419 Hudson, Peter J.
   1934 Temperance Meetings among the Choctaws. *Chronicles of Oklahoma* 12:130-132.

   Furnishes an eyewitness account of a temperance meeting held in 1876 by the Choctaws.

0420 Huffaker, Clair
   1967 *Nobody Loves a Drunken Indian*. New York: Paperback Library.

   A novel about a fictitious Paiute Indian Reservation near Phoenix, Arizona, whose inhabitants are engaged in a fight for civil rights and the validation of original treaties. Reservation conditions are well described, and reasons behind Native American drinking are suggested.

0421   Hummer, H.R.
        1913 Insanity among the Indians. *American Journal of Insanity* 69(3):615-623.

        Alcohol abuse is ranked third as a cause of insanity. Reports a homicidal tendency among Native American alcoholics.

0422   Hurt, Wesley R.
        1960 The Yankton Dakota Church: a Nationalistic Movement of Northern Plains Indians. In *Essays in the Science of Culture in Honor of Leslie A. White*, G.L. Dole and R.L. Carneiro eds. New York: Thomas Y. Crowell.

        Notes that the Church has not been effective in combatting alcoholism among its members, and that part of the discrimination directed against Dakotas results from racism, which includes the belief that Native Americans cannot handle liquor.

0423   Hurt, Wesley R.
        1961 The Urbanization of the Yankton Sioux. *Human Organization* 20(4):226-231.

        Mention is made of the role of alcohol in Native American urbanization. Notes that social drinking is important among urban Native Americans and that informally organized "drinking clubs" provide a major focus for social activities within the Native American community.

0424   Hurt, Wesley R. and R.M. Brown
        1965 Social Drinking Patterns of the Yankton Sioux. *Human Organization* 24:222-230.

        The authors postulate a causal relationship between sociocultural organization and drinking patterns; they review the history and culture of the Yankton Sioux in order to demonstrate their hypothesis.

0425   Hussey, Hugh H.
        1976 Editorial: Indian's Intolerance to Ethanol. *Journal of the American Medical Association* 235:1596-1597.

        After a short historical overview of Native Americans' experience with alcoholic beverages and an examination of three studies of physiologic response to ethanol ingestion by Native Americans and non-Native Americans, it is suggested that Native Americans' lack of cultural exposure to and experience with alcoholic beverages accounts for their inability to handle strong (i.e. distilled) beverages.

0426   Hutchinson, C.H.
1975 The "Drunken Indian": An American Casualty. Unpublished paper presented at the 31st International Congress on Alcoholism and Drug Dependence.

Reviews changes brought about by Anglos and the introduction of alcohol. Native Americans' views regarding alcohol abuse are included.

0427   Indian Historian Press
1972- *Index to Literature on the American Indian*. San Francisco: The Indian Historian Press.

An annual index to literature on Native Americans which includes a section on alcoholism.

0428   Indian Rights Association
1904 *A Danger to Be Averted*. Philadelphia: Indian Rights Association, pamphlet #69.

Reproduces a letter sent to every member of the U.S. Senate calling for immediate action to protect the Five Civilized Tribes and other Native Americans from the liquor traffic.

0429   Jacobs, Wilbur R.
1950 *Diplomacy and Indian Gifts: Anglo-French Rivalry along the Ohio and Northwest Frontiers, 1748-63*. Palo Alto: Stanford University Press.

Examines the role of liquor in trade between Native Americans and European colonists.

0430   Jacobs, Wilbur R.
1967 *The Appalachian Indian Frontier: The Edmond Atkin Report and the Plan of 1755*. Lincoln: University of Nebraska Press. (Also located under: Atkin, Edmond.)

A reprint and annotation of Edmond Atkin's 1755 report on Indians and trade in the southeast. Mention is made of the effect of liquor on Native Americans and the role of alcohol in Native American-Anglo trade.

0431   Jacobs, Wilbur R.
1972 *Dispossessing the American Indian*. New York: Charles Scribner's and Sons.

Relations between Native Americans and Anglos on the colonial frontier, including the role of alcohol in trade, are examined.

0432   James, Bernard J.
       1961 Social-psychological Dimensions of Ojibway Acculturation. *American Anthropologist* 63: 721-746.

Examines the relationship between income, dependency on public assistance, racial prejudice, drinking, Native American self-image, and role patterns. Notes that intoxication is the most frequent cause of loss of emotional control and contributes to violence; however, drinking is also usually a social affair.

0433   Jaywardene, C.H.S.
       1975 Violence among the Eskimo. *Canadian Journal of Criminology and Corrections* 17(4):307-314.

Examines violent behavior in relation to alcohol consumption. While violence existed aboriginally, alcohol has exacerbated the problem. Notes that Eskimos are not generally violent unless intoxicated.

0434   Jensen, Gary F., Joseph H. Stauss and V. William Harris
       1975 Crime, Delinquency, and the American Indian. *Human Organization* 36:252-257.

Examines the relationship between alcohol and delinquency. Tests the cultural deviance hypothesis to determine whether youths who drink the most come from cultures where drinking is the norm. Reveals that youths with the most alcohol violations come from home situations with problems. Suggests that there is no support for the cultural deviance hypothesis. Notes that Native Americans are disproportionately represented in official crime statistics. Summarizes the nature of Native American conflicts with the law and contrasts the finding with data on urban Blacks. Presents data from three Native American boarding schools detailing adolescent rule-breaking behavior. Notes that the Native American arrest rate for alcohol related crimes is 22 times greater than that for Blacks or Anglos. Suggests that Native Americans are not arrested more often because of discriminatory practices, but rather because they have more problems with alcohol. Alcohol abuse is correlated with tribal affiliation.

0435   Jepson, William W.
        1973   Indians, Alcohol, and Violent Death. *Minnesota Medicine* 56(8):697.

        An editorial which discusses the findings of Westermeyer and Brantner (1972, citation #0936). Concludes that cross-cultural studies help call attention to the special health problems of minorities.

0436   Jessor, Richard
        1964   *Toward a Social Psychology of Excessive Alcohol Use*. University of Colorado, Institute of Behavioral Science, Publication #46.

        Provides a theoretical framework and methodological orientation for the study of deviance and excessive alcohol consumption, utilizing empirical data from an Anglo, Mexican-American, and Native American community.

0437** Jessor, Richard
        1975   Social-Psychological Research on Alcohol Use. Unpublished paper prepared for the conference, "A Review of Research in Alcoholism," sponsored by the National Academy of Sciences, 11p.

        Reviews the major themes of research in alcoholism and points out new directions for research. Notes that not all unemployed Native Americans are alcoholics and questions whether heavy drinking among Native Americans is due to lower class status, culture, limited access to economic opportunities or all of the above.

0438   Jessor, Richard, Theodore D. Graves, Robert C. Hanson and S.L. Jessor
        1968   *Society, Personality and Deviant Behavior: a Study of a Tri-Ethnic Community*. New York: Holt, Rinehart, and Winston.

        An interdisciplinary theory of deviant behavior was tested in a small, rural southwestern Colorado community, utilizing heavy drinking as an example of deviance. Describes the drinking behavior of the Anglo, Mexican-American, and Native American residents of the town.

0439   Jilek, Wolfgang G.
        1972   Psychohygienic and Therapeutic Aspects of the Salish Guardian Spirit Ceremonial. MA Thesis, University of British Columbia, 135p.

A descriptive study of the resurgence, growth, and current practice of the winter ceremonial in the Upper Stalo region of British Columbia. This revived ceremony is felt to be one of the most effective therapies available to combat alcoholism and alcohol abuse among the Coast Salish.

0440   Jilek, Wolfgang G.
        1974   Indian Healing Power: Indigenous Therapeutic
            Practices in the Pacific Northwest. *Psychiatric
            Annals* 4(11):13-21.

Promotes the idea that professionals in the field of mental health should collaborate with native practitioners to promote mental health among Native Americans. Notes the Coast Salish prohibition against alcohol and psychedelic drugs during the six month ceremonial season.

0441   Jilek, Wolfgang G. and Louise Jilek-Aall
        1972   Transcultural Psychotherapy with Salish Indians.
            Transcultural Psychiatric Research Review 9(1):58-62.

Describes steps taken to combine traditional Western and traditional Native American psychotherapeutic approaches with Native American patients in the Fraser Valley in British Columbia. Native therapeutic activities center around Native American Alcoholics Anonymous groups and the winter spirit ceremonials. Native American modifications of traditional AA meetings are noted. Suggests that Western psychiatrists must recognize the need to modify treatment to fit indigenous procedures.

0442   Jilek, Wolfgang G. and Norman Todd
        1974   Witchdoctors Succeed Where Doctors Fail:
            Psychotherapy among Coast Salish Indians.
            Canadian Psychiatric Association Journal 19(4):
            351-356.

The authors maintain that the health problems of the Coast Salish are inseparable from their sociocultural situation. Notes that a recommended therapeutic regimen is participation in the Salish winter ceremonial, as alcohol and drug use is prohibited during the six-month ceremonial season.

0443   Jilek-Aall, Louise
        1974   Psychosocial Aspects of Drinking among Coast
            Salish Indians. *Canadian Psychiatric Association
            Journal* 19(4):357-361.

Maintains that alcohol must not be viewed as a problem for all Native Americans. Defines six drinking patterns: (1) drinking to have fun, (2) drinking to gain spiritual power, (3) potlatch type drinking, (4) drinking to be like a White man, (5) drinking to spite Anglos, and (6) drinking to escape from reality. Observes that failure to deal adequately with Native American drinking is due in part to the inability of Western medicine to recognize the pathogenic role of and psychosocial relationships between Native Americans and Anglos.

0444**   Johnson, Dale and Carmen A. Johnson
    1968 Community Mental Health Planning with Western Washington Indian Villages. Unpublished report to the Olympic Center for Mental Health and Mental Retardation, Department of Institutions, 26p.

Examines the mental health problems and needs, including alcohol abuse, of Western Washington Native Americans.

0445   Jones, Dorothy M.
    1974 *The Urban Native Encounters the Social Service System.* Fairbanks: University of Alaska, Institute of Social, Economic, and Government Research, 69p.

Exploration of relationships between Native Alaskans and social service agencies. Notes that Anglos have a higher incidence of alcoholism than Native Alaskans; however, Native drinking patterns are more obvious and receive greater attention.

0446   Jones, Dorothy M.
    1976 *Aleuts in Transition: a Comparison of Two Villages.* Seattle: University of Washington Press.

Reviews Aleut history and compares adaptation to European intrusions in the villages of New Harbor and Iliaka. One of the villages has succeeded in adapting, while the other exhibits a host of sociocultural pathologies, including poverty, excessive drinking and child neglect. The role of alcohol in the two villages is described. Drinking is the predominant leisure time activity; however, it is controlled in one village and uncontrolled in the other.

0447   Jones, Kenneth L. and David W. Smith
    1973 Recognition of the Fetal Alcohol Syndrome in Early Infancy. *The Lancet* 2(7836):999-1001.

Report of the Fetal Alcohol Syndrome in three Native American children.

0448   Jones, Kenneth L., David W. Smith and James W. Hanson
              1976 The Fetal Alcohol Syndrome: Clinical Delineation.
              Annals of the New York Academy of Sciences 273:
              130-137.

          A review of the characteristics exhibited by the
          initial 11 Native American children who helped to
          define the Fetal Alcohol Syndrome.

0449   Jones, Kenneth L., David W. Smith, Christy N. Ulleland
          and Ann Pytkowicz Streissguth
              1973 Pattern of Malformation in Offspring of Chronic
              Alcoholic Mothers. *The Lancet* 1(7815):1267-1271.

          Report of eight children, three of which were Native
          Americans, born to alcoholic mothers. The children
          exhibited marked patterns of altered growth and morpho-
          genesis which is attributed to the maternal alcoholism.

0450   Jorgensen, Joseph G.
              1972 *The Sun Dance Religion: Power for the Powerless*.
              Chicago: University of Chicago Press.

          Details alcohol problems among Native Americans,
          particularly Utes. Notes that Native Americans
          are frequently jailed for intoxication, while
          obviously drunk Anglos are not arrested. The Sun
          Dance is seen as an alternative to drinking and
          participants in the ceremony practice rigorous
          temperance.

0451   Joseph, Alice, R.B. Spicer and Jane Chesky
              1949 *The Desert People*. Chicago: University of
              Chicago Press.

          Discussion of alcohol use is spread throughout this
          ethnography of the Papago. Use of alcohol in the Rain
          Ceremony is noted, and contemporary use of alcohol
          outside a ceremonial context is investigated.

0452   Joyce, Kevin
              1975 Alcohol and the Indians. *Medical Times* 103(6):
              124-137.

          A condensation of *Alcoholism: a High Priority Health
          Problem* (see citation #0878) published by the U.S.
          Indian Health Service, Task Force on Alcoholism.
          Briefly traces the origins, causes, and characteristics
          of Native American alcohol use.

0453   Kahn, Marvin W. and John L. Delk
            1973 Developing a Community Mental Health Clinic on
            an Indian Reservation. *The International Journal
            of Social Psychiatry* 19(3):299-306.

            Details the elements involved in establishing a
            mental health clinic on the Papago Reservation.
            Notes that alcohol abuse was a major problem; dis-
            cusses treatment approaches.

0454   Kahn, Marvin W., Jesse Lewis and Eugene Galvez
            1974 An Evaluation Study of a Group Therapy Procedure
            with Reservation Adolescent Indians. *Psychotherapy:
            Theory, Research and Practice* 11(3):239-242.

            Examines a mental health intervention program for
            adolescent males on the Papago Reservation. The
            youths were all delinquents with arrest records
            for drunkenness and ready to drop out of school.
            Reports on the results of the first 13 months of
            the program, which included a marked drop in arrests
            and absenteeism.

0455   Kahn, Marvin W., Cecil Williams, Eugene Galvez, Linda
            Lejero, Rex D. Conrad and George Goldstein
            1975 The Papago Psychology Service: a Community
            Mental Health Program on an American Indian
            Reservation. *American Journal of Community
            Psychology* 3(2):81-97.

            Description of a community mental health program run
            by the Papago tribe and staffed by trained Native
            American paraprofessionals. The program is aimed
            at alcoholism, suicide, and vehicular accidents and
            attempts to blend traditional and Western medical
            practices. Treatment methodology is reviewed and
            discussed.

0456   Kane, Robert L. and Rosalie A. Kane
            1972 *Federal Health Care (with Reservations)*. New
            York: Springer Publishing Company.

            Examination of the Indian Health Service's medical
            delivery system as it operates on the Navajo Reservation,
            and of Native American health problems and needs.
            Alcoholism is discussed throughout the book, especially
            in the chapter "Infection and Afflictions."

0457**   Kane, Stephen L.
            1972 A Study of Related Problems of Nevada Indians
            Resulting from the Misuse of Alcohol. Unpublished

paper prepared for the Nevada Inter-Tribal Council Alcoholism Program, 18p.

Provides an historical overview of Nevada Native Americans' contacts with alcohol and discusses the legal, economic, environmental, medical, and family problems which result from excessive drinking. Possible solutions, such as half-way houses, improved medical and counseling follow-up, and improved education, are explored.

0458** Kaplan, Bert
1962 The Social Functions of Navaho "Heavy Drinking." Unpublished paper presented at the annual meeting of the Society for Applied Anthropology, 7p.

Heavy drinking among the Navajo is seen both as an attack and a support of the Navajo value system. Drinking provides an institutionalized outlet for submerged values. Removal of heavy drinking is seen as a danger to Navajo society unless other social institutions are found to replace the outlet provided by drinking.

0459 Kaplan, Bert and Dale Johnson
1964 The Social Meaning of Navaho Psychopathology and Psychotherapy. In *Magic, Faith and Healing*, Ari Kiev, ed. Pp. 203-229. New York: Free Press.

Three major categories of mental illness are identified and described: (1) mother craziness, (2) ghost sickness, and (3) crazy violence. The latter is often associated with alcohol-induced intoxication. Evidence suggests that "crazy violence" is a major hysterical disorder, and that alcohol is an excuse or trigger rather than the actual cause of the disorder.

0460 Kaufman, Arthur
1973 Gasoline Sniffing among Children in a Pueblo Indian Village. *Pediatrics* 51:1060-1064.

Gasoline was found to be a major form of drug abuse among children in a Pueblo village. No significant relationship between alcohol and gasoline sniffing was found.

0461 Kaufman, Arthur, Philip W. Brickner, Richard Varner and William Mashburn
1972 Tranquilizer Control. *Journal of the American Medical Association* 221:1504-1506.

Report of a comprehensive program aimed at reducing the distribution of tranquilizing drugs at the Public Health Service Indian Hospital at Rapid City, South Dakota. Native Americans' problems with alcohol were emphasized in order to illustrate the abuse potential of tranquilizers.

0462   Kealear, Charles A.
        1914 Arapaho Indians Drunk at Dance. *Carlisle Arrow* 10(23):1-2.

An account of a meeting among the Arapaho which was to be a festive occasion, but was ruined when 10 to 12 young males appeared on the scene intoxicated. Calls for prohibition among Native Americans.

0463   Kehoe, Alice B.
        1970 The Dakotas in Saskatchewan. In *The Modern Sioux*, Ethel Nurge, ed. Pp. 148-172. Lincoln: University of Nebraska Press.

Notes that prohibition still exists on Native American reserves in Canada; however, it is legal for Native Americans to purchase liquor in adjacent towns. Indicates that a large proportion of welfare funds are spent on alcohol. Suggests that drunkenness will not be alleviated until the underlying socioeconomic causes are ameliorated.

0464   Kelbert, M. and L. Hale
        1954 The Introduction of Alcohol into Iroquois Society. Toronto: Addiction Research Foundation, substudy 1-K&H-65, 37p.

The role of liquor, as observed by fur traders, missionaries, and other early travellers, is discussed as it affected the Iroquois. Drinking patterns, drinking behavior, and attitudes towards alcohol are examined.

0465   Kelly, Roger E. and John O. Cramer
        1966 *American Indians in Small Cities: A Survey of Urban Acculturation in Two Northern Arizona Communities.* Flagstaff: Northern Arizona University, Department of Rehabilitation, Rehabilitation Monographs #1.

Investigates assimilation of self-relocated Navajos in Winslow and Flagstaff, Arizona. Drinking is a major source of recreation and informants indicated that drinking was a problem in the urban setting.

0466   Kemnitzer, Luis S.
            1972 The Structure of Country Drinking Parties on
               the Pine Ridge Reservation, South Dakota. *Plains
               Anthropologist* 17:134-142.

            Provides a brief description of contemporary life
            on the Pine Ridge Reservation. Recounts the intro-
            duction of alcohol to the Sioux. Analyzes country
            drinking parties and attempts to relate the parties
            to other aspects of reservation culture. Suggests
            that drinking parties may serve as a means of conflict
            resolution and are, therefore, a "...positive con-
            tribution to Oglala social and cultural life..."

0467   Kemnitzer, Luis S.
            1973 Adjustment and Value Conflict in Urbanizing
               Dakota Indians Measured by the Q-Sort Technique.
               American Anthropologist 75:687-707.

            As part of a larger study of Native American migration
            to the San Francisco Bay Area, a Q-sort test was
            devised in order to identify and measure value conflict.
            Problems, such as alcohol abuse, faced by migrants
            are illustrated by case studies. Suggests that
            alcohol may be an escape from conflict.

0468   Kemnitzer, Luis S.
            1976 Structure, Content, and Cultural Meaning of
               Yuwipi: a Modern Lakota Healing Ritual. *American
               Ethnologist* 3:261-280.

            An analysis of a contemporary healing ritual as
            practiced by the Oglala Sioux of the Pine Ridge
            Reservation. Briefly mentions the condition of
            "ablapsi" which can result from having one thing
            in mind all the time. Alcoholics are thought to
            suffer from "ablapsi."

0469**   Keneally, Henry J., Jr.
            1966 The First Step: Identification of the Drinking
               Problem in the Indian Community. Unpublished paper
               presented at the University of Utah, School of Alcohol
               Studies, 7p.

            Suggests that the first step in solving alcohol abuse
            in Native American communities should be a survey
            designed to determine the nature of the problem.
            Only after this has been accomplished can projects
            be designed to deal with the situation.

0470   Kester, F.E.
            1963 Alaska's Population as Seen through Its Death
            Rates. In *Science in Alaska. Proceedings of the
            13th Alaskan Science Conference*, George Dahlgren,
            Jr., ed. Pp. 194-209. College, Alaska: Alaska
            Division, American Association for the Advancement
            of Science.

            Suggests that alcohol probably plays a role in many
            violent deaths, especially among Natives.

0471**   Kilen, Allan G.
            1970 *Annual Evaluation of the Inter-Tribal Council
            of Nevada, Inc. Alcoholism Program: from February
            1969 to January 1970*. Reno: Inter-Tribal Council
            of Nevada, Inc.

            Reports on the progress of the Inter-Tribal Council's
            alcoholism program. Reviews the history of the agency,
            staffing, treatment methodologies, rehabilitation
            and educational approaches utilized by the program.

0472**   Kim, Yong C.
            1970 Ecology of Chronic Alcoholics: Psycho-Social
            Point of View. Unpublished report, Alcoholism
            Commission of Saskatchewan.

            Provides data on 499 alcoholics who registered for
            treatment at the Regina Alcoholism Rehabilitation
            Centre. Of the total 17% were treaty Native Americans
            and 3% were Metis.

0473   Kim, Yong C.
            1972 *A Study of Alcohol Consumption and Alcoholism
            among Saskatchewan Indians: Social and Cultural
            Variables*. Regina: Alcoholism Commission of
            Saskatchewan, Research Division.

            Reviews the anthropological literature regarding
            motivations for drinking, attitudes toward drinking
            and drunkenness and relates the findings of the
            review to the results of a study of alcohol use
            among 100 Saskatchewan Native Americans.

0474   Kleinfeld, Judith and Joseph D. Bloom
            1973 *A Long Way from Home*. Fairbanks: Center for
            Northern Educational Research and Institute for Social,
            Economic, and Government Research, Report #38.

            Reports on the problems of regional high schools,
            Urban Boarding Home programs, and public boarding

schools particularly as they affect Eskimo students.
Notes that severe drinking often seriously disrupts
the educational process. Recommends the establishment
of village high schools.

0475   Kleinfeld, Judith and Joseph D. Bloom
        1977 Boarding School: Effects on the Mental Health
        of Eskimo Adolescents. *American Journal of Psychiatry*
        143:411-417.

   Examined 132 Eskimo adolescents from four boarding
   schools in order to determine the effect of boarding
   schools on Eskimo mental health. Indicates that
   alcohol was a serious problem, as heavy drinking was
   a popular form of entertainment. Violent drinking
   and anti-Anglo militancy assumed peer group norms
   in one of the schools.

0476   Kline, James A. and Arthur C. Roberts
        1973 A Residential Alcoholism Treatment Program for
        American Indians. *Quarterly Journal of Studies
        on Alcohol* 34:860-868.

   A description of the Mendocino State Hospital (California) Indian Alcoholism Program, its stengths and
   some of the barriers and problems encountered in its
   implementation.

0477   Kline, James A., Vitali V. Rozynko, Garry Flint and
        A.C. Roberts
        1973 Personality Characteristics of Male Native
        American Alcoholic Patients. *International Journal
        of Addictions* 8:729-732.

   Examines the personality characteristics of male
   Native American alcoholics and attempts to identify
   a constellation of character traits. Notes that
   alcohol abuse may serve a variety of functions, and
   suggests multi-modality treatment programs.

0478   Kluckhohn, Clyde
        1944 Navaho Witchcraft. *Papers of the Peabody
        Museum of American Archaeology and Ethnology*,
        vol. 22#2.

   Notes that both witchcraft and alcohol are suitable
   methods of dealing with aggression. Alcohol is seen
   as an adjustment mechanism which provides release
   from traditional cultural constraints.

0479**   Knight, Mary
         1967 The Muckleshoot Reservation: a Contemporary
         Review. Unpublished paper prepared for the Depart-
         ment of Anthropology, University of Washington, 25p.

         Notes that drinking is a major recreational outlet,
         but is not held to be a major problem. Rather drinking
         is felt to be symptomatic of socio-economic problems.
         The Shaker religion provides an alternative to
         recreational drinking among the Muckleshoot.

0480**   Knisley, E.R.
         1972 Native Alaskan, Eskimos, and Aleuts, and Their
         Drinking Habits. Unpublished paper presented at
         the 30th International Congress on Alcoholism and
         Drug Dependency.

         Indicates that Alaskan Natives react to urban life
         and enforced idleness by drinking. Examines drinking
         behavior and the impact of modernization among Alaskan
         Natives.

0481   Koolage, William W., Jr.
         1971 Adaptation of Chipewyan Indians and Other Persons
         of Native Background in Churchill, Manitoba. Ph.D.
         Dissertation, University of North Carolina, 229p.
         U.M. Order #71-20978.

         An analysis of Chipewyan and other Native peoples'
         adaptation to a Eurocanadian town, with particular
         attention to the role of alcohol in adaptation.

0482   Krause, Marilyn L.
         1969 A Study of Drinking on a Plateau Indian Reser-
         vation. MA Thesis, University of Washington, 138p.

         An ethnology of "normal" drinking by members of the
         Yakima tribe. Case study material helps to define
         patterns of drinking which are contrasted to the
         usual assumptions of social disorganization and pathology.
         The public drinking which leads observers to label
         Native American drinking as deviant, in fact reflects
         a continuation of traditional institutions. The drinking
         simply provides an excuse to engage in intense sociali-
         zation.

0483   Krause, Robert F.
         1972 Changing Patterns of Suicidal Behavior in North
         Alaskan Eskimo. *Transcultural Psychiatric Research
         Review* 9(1):69-71.

Indicates that contemporary Eskimo suicide patterns differ markedly from traditional patterns and are often associated with alcohol intoxication.

0484** Krause, Robert F.
1973 Eskimo Suicide. Unpublished paper presented at the 129th meeting of the American Psychiatric Association, 13p.

Points out that traditional Eskimo suicide was performed by the elderly, while contemporary suicide is greatest among Eskimo ages 15-25. Indicates that alcohol is frequently involved in suicides.

0485** Krutz, Gordon V.
1966 Monthly Report for January, February, March and April, 1966...Alcoholism and the Reno-Sparks Indian Colony. Unpublished memorandum submitted to the Phoenix Indian Health Service Area Health Educator, 7p.

Report of a survey to determine the extent of problem drinking in the Reno-Sparks Indian Colony. Describes the setting, and discusses drinking behavior. Provides a tentative proposal to assist problem drinkers.

0486 Kunitz, Stephen Joshua
1970 Navajo Drinking Patterns. Ph.D. Dissertation, Yale University, 340p. U.M. Order #70-26174.

A consideration of Navajo style of drinking as "normal" activity for most young men; Navajo drinking data (medical, legal, and social) are contrasted with Hopi and White Mountain Apache data to ascertain differences in cultural influences on drinking behavior. Levels of acculturation, social integration, and past histories are contrasted in a discussion of drinking styles. Various methodologies for collecting data are discussed.

A486 Kunitz, Stephen Joshua
1977 Underdevelopment and Social Services on the Navajo Reservation. *Human Organization* 36(4):398-405.

Examines the relationship of social services to economic underdevelopment on the Navajo Reservation. Notes that nearly all Federal monies spent on the reservation are devoted to the provision of human services (i.e. education, health, alcoholism rehabilitation). No matter the etiology of alcoholism, homicide, and suicide from reservation to reservation, human service workers tend to impose uniform interpretations on these problems which may or may not be adequate. Cautions against promotion of the "disease concept" of alcoholism. Suggests that alcohol abuse must be seen in the larger context of Navajo society.

0487   Kunitz, Stephen Joshua and Jerrold E. Levy
         1974 Changing Ideas of Alcohol Use among Navajo Indians. *Quarterly Journal of Studies on Alcohol* 35:243-259.

There appears to be a growing acceptance of the idea that heavy drinking is maladaptive, deviant behavior and a sign of disease in the individual Navajo drinker. The history of Navajo drinking and the role of the "style of drinking" are discussed as a background to this new label of the heavy drinker as "sick." The influence of paraprofessionals in changing the definitions of deviant behavior is also examined.

0488   Kunitz, Stephen Joshua, Jerrold E. Levy and Michael W. Everett
         1969 Alcoholic Cirrhosis among the Navaho. *Quarterly Journal of Studies on Alcohol* 30:672-685.

A report on an attempt to assess the prevalence of drinking or the extent of alcoholism in contemporary Navajo populations from a review of medical diagnoses of cirrhosis. An increase in cirrhosis was observed between the more isolated, traditional areas of the reservation and those areas of the reservation adjacent to liquor supplies, such as Gallup and Shiprock. However, the Navajo were not found to have a greater prevalence of cirrhosis than other populations, and in fact had lower mortality rates from cirrhosis than the nation as a whole.

0489   Kunitz, Stephen Joshua, Jerrold E. Levy and Charles L. Odoroff
         1971 The Epidemiology of Alcoholic Cirrhosis in Two Southwestern Indian Tribes. *Quarterly Journal of Studies on Alcohol* 32:706-720.

Liver cirrhosis death rates among the Hopi are over four times higher than the national average; however, among the Navajo the age-adjusted rate is slightly less than in the general U.S. population. Contrasted drinking patterns rather than acculturation type stresses are suggested as a possible explanation for the differential cirrhosis rates.

0490   Kunstadter, Peter
        1961 Culture Change, Social Structure and Health
        Behavior: a Quantitative Study of Clinic Use among
        the Apaches of the Mescalero Reservation. Ph.D.
        Dissertation, University of Michigan, 815p. U.M.
        Order #61-02766.

        Discusses contemporary patterns of alcohol abuse, and
        briefly reviews drinking behavior in an historical
        context.

0491   Kupferer, H.J. and J.A. Humphrey
        1975 Fatal Indian Violence in North-Carolina.
        Anthropological Quarterly 48:236-244.

        Notes that violence among both the Eastern Cherokee
        and Lumbee tribes is associated with drinking.

0492   Kuttner, Robert E. and Albert B. Lorincz
        1967 Alcoholism and Addiction in Urbanized Sioux
        Indians. *Mental Hygiene* 51:530-542.

        A study in Omaha, Nebraska, of various Native American
        groups, all members of the Siouan language family
        (Omaha, Ponca, Winnebago, and Sioux [Dakota]). In
        the manner of skid road cultures the drinking group
        served to raise money for the purchase of alcohol,
        and solitary drinking was a rare event. The authors
        advance the thesis that drinking behavior was due to
        inadequate family training rather than feelings of
        group inferiority, acculturative stress, frustration
        of ambition, or other usually assumed "causes" of
        Native American drinking behavior.

0493   Kuttner, Robert E. and Albert B. Lorincz
        1970 Promiscuity and Prostitution in Urbanized Indian
        Communities. *Mental Hygiene* 54(1):79-91.

        Prostitution remains an enduring Native American problem,
        particularly in industrialized urban areas. Native
        American prostitution was not found to be a commercial
        venture, but rather an activity geared to provide a
        bare sustenance level of support. Emphasizes the
        close relation between prostitution and alcoholism
        and indicates that alcoholism and poverty must be
        confronted if solutions to prostitution are to be
        found.

0494   LaBarre, Weston
        1938 Native American Beers. *American Anthropologist*
        40:124-135.

A survey of the beers and wines of both North and South
America which constituted the undistilled liquor
of the native inhabitants of the New World. The
various native names for the beverages are furnished,
and there is a discussion of the methods of preparation
and use of fermented beverages within various cultures.

0495   LaBarre, Weston
        1941 A Cultist Drug-Addiction in an Indian Alcoholic.
        Bulletin of the Menninger Clinic 5:40-46.

        Reports on the case history of an alcoholic Osage
        Indian who became involved with peyote.

0496   LaBarre, Weston
        1969 The Peyote Cult. New York: Schocken Books.

        Notes that conflicting beliefs regarding peyote and
        alcohol exist. Some insist that adherence to the
        peyote religion (Native American Church) reduces
        alcohol consumption and abuse. However, others
        contend that alcohol is used in conjunction with
        peyote. LaBarre indicates that in tribes north of
        Mexico the trend is to avoid alcohol if one is
        following the Peyote Road.

0497** LaBuff, Stephen
        n.d. An Alternative. Salem, Oregon: Chemawa
        Alcoholism Education Program, 24p.

        An illustrated pamphlet which explains the alcoholism
        intervention and education program at the Chemawa
        Indian School.

0498   Lagasse, Jean H.
        1959 The People of Indian Ancestry in Manitoba.
        Winnipeg: Canada. Department of Agriculture.

        A social and economic study of Native Americans in
        Manitoba. Discusses alcohol use and related legis-
        lation, as well as drinking patterns. Recommends
        that Native Americans be placed under the same
        liquor legislation which applies to non-Native Americans.

0499** Laing, A.
        n.d. The Indian People and the Indian Act. Unpublished
        paper presented to the Ryerson Men's Club, Vancouver,
        British Columbia, 10p.

        Notes that the prohibition of liquor among Native
        Americans stemmed from the belief that Native Americans

should be protected from that which harmed them. Suggests that prohibition should be abolished and that Native Americans should be treated as responsible citizens.

0500   Lal, Ravindra
       1969a   From Duck Lake to Camp 10: Old Fashioned Relocation. *Musk-Ox* 6:5-13.

       Examines the effects of relocation on the Chipewyan. Postulates a causal connection between the social disorganization resulting from relocation and excessive drinking in the new community.

0501   Lal, Ravindra
       1969b   Some Observations of the Social Life of the Chipewyans of Camp 10, Churchill and Their Implications for Community Development. *Musk-Ox* 6:14-20.

       Notes that relocation disrupted leadership, altered patterns of cooperation, and led to uncontrolled drinking.

0502   Lamoureaux, Calvin
       1914   Alcohol. *Carlisle Arrow* 10(33):1.

       An essay by a sixth grader which discusses alcohol and the results of excessive drinking.

0503   Lang, Gretchen Mary Chesley
       1974   Adaptive Strategies of Urban Indian Drinkers. Ph.D. Dissertation, University of Missouri-Columbia, 217p. U.M. Order #75-20132.

       Represents an ethnography of alcoholic Chippewa males in Minneapolis. The author attempts to describe adaptive strategies utilized by alcoholic male Chippewas. Both subsistence patterns and social relationships are examined. Concludes that the use of public facilities, work patterns, geographical mobility, and lack of success in alcoholism rehabilitation programs contributes to or forms the adaptive strategy of urban male Chippewas.

0504   Langness, Lewis L. and Lawrence Hennigh
       1964   American Indian Drinking: Alcoholism or Insobriety? Unpublished paper presented at the fifth annual Mental Health Research Meeting, 16p.

       Observes that alcoholism (i.e. addictive or compulsive drinking) is rare among Native Americans, while insobriety (extreme or frequent drunkenness) is common. Reviews various hypotheses concerning Native American drinking and suggests 12 areas which future research should focus upon.

0505** Lavallee, Mary Ann
1967 Problems That Concern Indian Women. Unpublished paper presented at the Saskatchewan Indian Women's Conference, 5p.

Encourages women to take a more active stand on issues and to participate in civic and community affairs. Alcohol use and action which women can take is specifically mentioned.

0506 Lawrence, William J.
1972 Tribal Injustice: The Red Lake Court of Indian Offenses. *North Dakota Law Review* 48(4):639-659.

Reviews the history of the Red Lake Court of Indian Offenses, established by the Bureau of Indian Affairs in 1884. The Court was allowed to rule on cases approved by the Indian Agent, including liquor violations. Suggests that one of the most serious problems lies in the Court's perception of alcohol problems as solely criminal offenses. Reservation prohibition is seen to contribute to alcoholism and alcohol-related problems and bootleg liquor interests on the tribal council seek to perpetuate the situation.

0507 League of Women Voters - Dallas
1974 *The American Indian in an Urban Community: Dallas*. Dallas: The League of Women Voters.

A pamphlet which describes the problems, including excessive drinking, faced by Native Americans attempting to adapt to an urban environment.

0508 League of Women Voters - Minneapolis
1968 *Indians in Minneapolis*. Minneapolis: The League of Women Voters and the University of Minnesota, Training Center for Community Programs.

A survey of the problems confronting Native Americans in Minneapolis, and a review of the agencies which provide programs for Native Americans. Discusses programs for Native American alcoholics, such as Alcoholics Anonymous, and a half-way house operated by the City.

0509   League of Women Voters - Minnesota
            1974 *Indians in Minnesota*. St. Paul: League of
            Women Voters of Minnesota.

            A comprehensive overview of contemporary Native
            Americans, primarily Chippewa and Sioux, in Minnesota.
            Notes that alcoholism affects every Native American
            in the state whether he drinks or not. Indicates that
            Native Americans exhibit more alcohol-related problems
            than the general population.

A509   Leatham, Raymond Claude
            1975 A Study of the Relationship between Self-Concept
            Variables and Different Lengths of Sobriety for Male
            American Indian Alcoholics and Male American Indian
            Non-Alcoholics. Ed.D. Dissertation, University of
            South Dakota. U.M. Order #76-24514.

            Report of a study which sought to determine whether
            varying lengths of sobriety affected the self-concept
            of Native American alcoholics. Eighty subjects were
            involved. Alcoholic subjects were drawn from treatment
            centers throughout South Dakota, while the non-alcoholic
            control group was drawn from Sioux City, Iowa. Data
            derived from the application of the Tennessee self-
            concept scale indicates that length of sobriety is
            related to self-concept, and that achievement and
            maintenance of sobriety tends to be accompanied by
            reduced levels of psychological disturbance and increased
            levels of self esteem.

0510   Lechnyr, Ronald Joseph
            1973 Powerlessness, Self-Esteem, and Empathy: a
            Study of the Impact of Training on Indian Para-
            professionals. D.S.W. Dissertation, University
            of Utah, 234p. U.M. Order #73-21207.

            A trend study of Native American and non-Native
            American alcohol counselors in their 1st, 7th, and
            12th months of training at the Western Regional
            Indian Alcohol Training Center. Three variables
            were examined: powerlessness, self-esteem, and
            empathy. A total of 141 Native Americans from 52
            tribes and 20 states were represented in the sample.

0511   Leigh, L.H.
            1970 The Indian Act, the Supremacy of Parliament,
            and the Equal Protection of the Laws. *McGill Law
            Journal* 16:389-398.

A discussion of the issues raised by the case of Regina vs. Drybones, which pointed out the contradictions between the Indian Act and the Canadian Bill of Rights.

0512** Leighton, Alexander H. and Donald A. Kennedy
1957 Pilot Study of Cultural Items in Medical Diagnosis: a Field Report. Unpublished report to the U.S. Public Health Service, Division of Indian Health, 37p.

Examines problems encountered in the cross-cultural practice of medicine. Drinking was defined as a psychiatric problem of major proportions.

0513 Leighton, Alexander H. and Dorothea C. Leighton
1945 The Navaho Door. Cambridge: Harvard University Press.

An examination of Navajo health and recommendations to the Indian Health Service for improvement of health care delivery. Two observations are made regarding alcohol. First, Navajos are not accustomed to saving money and often spend it immediately on alcohol, gambling, or tobacco. Second, control of the liquor traffic seems to be the major concern of the Tribal Police.

0514** Leland, Joy
1971 Anthropologists Can Handle Alcohol. Unpublished paper presented at the annual meeting of the Southwestern Anthropological Association, 34p.

Examines the use of Jellinek's postulated diagnostic symptoms of alcohol addiction. Suggests that additional research is needed in order to determine whether or not Native American drinking represents alcoholism or merely a different style of drinking.

0515 Leland, Joy
1972 Alcohol Addiction among American Indians. MA Thesis, University of Nevada, Reno.

A preliminary version of Leland 1976a (see citation #0520 for annotation).

0516 Leland, Joy
1973a Indian Alcohol Users: an Insider's View. Terminal Progress Report, National Institute of Mental Health Small Grant #1 R18 MH 22524-07, 61p.

Reports the findings of an investigation of a small
Native American colony in Nevada. Presents a folk
taxonomy of drinking styles, identifies Native
American criteria for "minimum" and "maximum" drinking
rates, and suggests practical applications for the
data with respect to education and control programs.

0517**   Leland, Joy
         1973b Alcohol Use in a Nevada Indian Group: An
         Ethnoscience Approach. Unpublished paper pre-
         sented at the 32nd annual meeting of the Society
         for Applied Anthropology, 15p.

         Report of the classification of a community's drinking
         styles by the residents of the community. The folk
         categories which were obtained permitted the com-
         putation of the percentage of the population which
         fell into the different styles of drinking. The data
         suggest that Native Americans do not drink more than
         the general population, and may in fact, have
         statistically fewer problem drinkers.

0518**   Leland, Joy
         1974 Scope of Acquaintance in a Nevada Indian Colony.
         Unpublished paper presented at the Great Basin
         Anthropological Conference, 10p.

         Analyzes the manner in which residents of a community
         identified each other. Style of drinking did not
         serve as a recognition factor.

0519   Leland, Joy
         1975 Drinking Styles in an Indian Settlement: a
         Numerical Folk Taxonomy. Ph.D. Dissertation,
         University of California, Irvine, 355p. U.M. Order
         #76-13876.

         A detailed description of the development of a union
         folk taxonomy of drinking practices in a Nevada Native
         American community. Various attitudes and perceptions
         regarding drinking behavior were examined. Results
         indicate that while the stereotype of Native American
         drinking as a monolithic phenomenon may exist in the
         minds of many individuals, it does not exist in reality.
         Five distinct styles of handling liquor were identified.

0520   Leland, Joy
         1976a *Firewater Myths: North American Indian Drinking
         and Alcohol Addiction*. New Brunswick: Rutgers
         University, Center of Alcohol Studies, Monograph #11.

Applies the World Health Organization Jellinek criteria to a number of Native American groups in an effort to determine the presence or absence of alcohol addiction among these groups. Specifically attempts to test the hypothesis that alcohol addiction is rare among Native Americans. No clear-cut evidence is found which supported or discredited the hypothesis. In addition, the author asserts that there is little agreement as to what constitutes valid indicators of alcohol addiction. As a result, analysis of the differences in the incidence of alcohol addiction among various Native American groups and between Native Americans and non-Native Americans must await the development of valid indicators of alcohol addiction.

0521** Leland, Joy
1976b Women and Alcohol in an Indian Settlement. Unpublished paper presented at the Great Basin Anthropological Conference, 9p.

Examines the drinking behavior of women in a Nevada Native American colony. Women were found to drink less than males and in ways which were less destructive. Drinking appears to be the main focus of the battle of the sexes in Native American communities. Indicates that the primary coping mechanism of Native American women is withdrawal.

0522 Leland, Joy
1977 North American Indian Drinking and Alcohol Abuse: A Critical Review of the Literature. Unpublished manuscript, for inclusion in the NIAAA third Special Report to Congress on Alcohol and Health. Rockville, Maryland: National Clearing House for Alcohol Information.

A critical review of the literature on Native American alcohol use. Examines the extent and perception of the problem by various disciplines. Investigates the physiological, sociological, and cultural explanations of Native American drinking. Suggests topics for additional research.

A522** Leland, Joy
1977a The Research Literature and Government Policy Concerning Native American Alcohol Problems. Unpublished paper presented at the 76th annual meeting of the American Anthropological Association, 16p.

Reviews government policies regarding Native American alcohol problems and the role of anthropologists in policy formulation. While anthropological concepts and perceptions are evident in policy statements, there are few anthropologists involved in policy formulation or implementation. Discusses the issues involved in the transfer of "mature" Native American alcohol programs from the NIAAA to the IHS.

0523 Lemert, Edwin M.
1954a Alcohol and the Northwest Coast Indians. *University of California Publications in Culture and Society* 2(6):304-406.

Provides observations on the drinking patterns, function of alcohol, and influences of alcohol within Northwest Coast cultures. The author agrees in part with Horton (1943) that drinking is the result of anxiety. Factors militating against drunkenness, such as the Shaker Church and winter ceremonies, are noted. Drinking now serves to help reintegrate the individual as a part of an intimate group, and thus has positive functions.

0524 Lemert, Edwin M.
1954b The Life and Death of an Indian State. *Human Organization* 13:23-27.

Describes the missionary activities of the Oblates of Mary Immaculate order among the Salish of the Gulf of Georgia. Details the manner in which the missionaries assumed the political power of the chiefs. Mentions that the priests forbade the consumption of all alcohol and that drunkenness drew fines which were used for the upkeep of the church. Lemert suggests that epidemic diseases and increased wealth rather than Anglos and alcohol precipitated the crises faced by the Northwest Coast Indians in the latter part of the 19th century. Notes that drinking became an integral part of winter ceremonies, and it is for this reason that the missionaries were so opposed to the consumption of alcohol.

0525 Lemert, Edwin M.
1956a Alcoholism: Theory, Problems, and Challenge: Alcoholism and the Sociocultural Situation. *Quarterly Journal of Studies on Alcohol* 17:306-317.

A review of various theories of alcoholism and a discussion of how these theories do or do not apply to selected cultures, including the Northwest Coast tribes, the Aleut, and the Klamath. The author argues that studies of alcoholism must be related to the sociocultural setting in which the drinking is conducted, and that for some societies alcohol consumption may not be a sign of social pathology or disintegrating culture, but rather a learned social behavior which is rewarded.

0526   Lemert, Edwin M.
         1956b On Alcohol among Northwest Coast Indians [reply to Codere's review, see citation #0178]. *American Anthropologist* 58:561-562.

         A rebuttal to Codere's review of Lemert's book (citation #0523) in which Lemert indicates that he could find no references to drinking or the whiskey feast in the writings of early Kwakiutl ethnographers.

0527   Lemert, Edwin M.
         1958 The Use of Alcohol in Three Salish Indian Tribes. *Quarterly Journal of Studies on Alcohol* 19:90-107.

         A study of drinking behavior among three Canadian Salish tribes in British Columbia. Alcohol consumption historically began with White contact, and some drinking patterns still reflect the influence of this early period. Present-day drinking resembles that of the surrounding Anglo population, but contains differentiating characteristics that are specifically Native American. The function of alcohol in Native American society differed from the accepted function in Anglo society. Among the Salish alcohol allows for the release of aggression without the imposition of cultural sanctions.

0528   Lemert, Edwin M.
         1962 Alcohol, Values, and Social Control. In *Society, Culture and Drinking Patterns*, David J. Pittman and Charles R. Snyder, eds. Pp. 553-571. New York: John Wiley.

         A consideration of the multi-faceted aspects of drinking behavior and social controls over intoxication and drunkenness. Various Native American populations are cited as examples in which weak social controls could not contain the excesses of Indians once liquor had been introduced. Other Native American groups are mentioned for self-instituted controls and functional equivalents to drinking which served to control drinking. Four models of social control are suggested and discussed.

0529   Lemert, Edwin M.
           1967 *Human Deviance, Social Problems, and Social Control.* Englewood Cliffs, N.J.: Prentice-Hall.

   Chapter 5 deals specifically with social control in relation to alcohol. Lemert specifically mentions several groups of Native Americans in sections dealing with "Ritual and Drunkenness" and "Contact and Interaction with White Society." Lemert views the absence of social control over drunkenness to be the result of the fact that drunkenness took on a reactionary significance--a means of resisting Anglo values and substantiating traditional values.

0530   Leon, Robert L.
           1965 Maladaptive Interaction between Bureau of Indian Affairs Staff and Indian Clients. *American Journal of Orthopsychiatry* 35:723-728.

   A discussion of attitudes and interaction between BIA staff and Native American clients which handicapped progress toward Native American self-determination and tribal autonomy. Alcohol use and abuse is cited as a form of passive aggression against the BIA.

0531   Leon, Robert L.
           1968 Some Implications for a Preventive Program for American Indians. *American Journal of Psychiatry* 125:232-236.

   Efforts to combat psychosocial problems, such as alcoholism, within the Native American community should focus upon involving the Native American in the determination of his own fate. Problems such as alcoholism, broken families, and neglected children can only be overcome through Native American initiated programs.

0532   Leupp, Francis E.
           1910 *The Indian and His Problem.* New York: Scribner (reprinted by Johnson Reprint, 1970).

   Makes several passing remarks concerning the "Liquor Question" among Native Americans. Very briefly mentions the effect of liquor on Native Americans and describes the Federal government's attempt to ban the sale of alcohol to Native Americans.

0533   Levi, M.C.
           1956 *Chippewa Indians of Yesterday and Today.* New York: Pageant Press.

Describes the Chippewas' experience with alcohol from its introduction to the present.

0534**   Levine, Harry Gene
         1977   The Good Creature of God and Demon Rum. Unpublished paper, University of California, Berkeley, Social Research Group, 81p.

         A study of Colonial and 19th century American thought regarding alcohol and drunkenness. Notes that all the Colonies prohibited the sale of liquor to Native Americans as the colonists believed that alcohol use by Native Americans always led to violence.

0535   Levine, Saul V., M.R. Eastwood and Quentin Rae-Grant
         1974   Psychiatric Service to Northern Indians. *Canadian Psychiatric Association Journal* 19:343-349.

         Report of a mental health project in Northern Ontario known by the name Sioux Lookout Project. Excessive drinking is one of the problems with which the project attempts to deal.

0536   Levitan, Sar A. and Barbara Hetrick
         1971   *Big Brother's Indian Programs - with Reservations.* New York: McGraw-Hill.

         Chapter three, entitled "Improving Health Care" notes that alcoholism constitutes a major health problem for Native Americans.

0537**   Levy, Jerrold E.
         n.d.   Looking at What through Whose Glasses. Unpublished paper prepared for the U.S. Public Health Service, Division of Indian Health, Navajo Area, 13p.

         Cautions that there are three "realities" for any given situation: the observer's, the observed's, and statistical indications. To illustrate the point, Levy examines the subject of alcohol and Navajo drinking behavior.

0538   Levy, Jerrold E.
         1965   Navajo Suicide. *Human Organization* 24:308-318. (Reprinted in *The Emergent Native Americans*, Deward E. Walker, Jr., ed. Pp. 594-613. Boston: Little, Brown, 1972.)

         Alcohol is thought to figure in most Navajo suicides; however, it is not possible to determine if alcohol is causal, symptomatic, or only superficially associated.

Indicates that the role of alcohol in Navajo life has not been adequately studied, but suggests that the socially disruptive use of alcohol has come to be recognized as a primary sign of anomie.

0539 Levy, Jerrold E. and Stephen Joshua Kunitz
  1969 Notes on Some White Mountain Apache Social Pathologies. *Plateau* 42:11-19.

A preliminary report which indicates that contemporary high death rates from homicide and suicide may have had pre-reservation precursors in the White Mountain Apache culture. Suggests that suicide and homicide patterns represent a continuation of tribal behavior rather than a recent response to acculturation. The only new element in behavior patterns is the presence of alcohol.

0540 Levy, Jerrold E. and Stephen Joshua Kunitz
  1971a Indian Drinking: Problems of Data Collection and Interpretation. In *Proceedings: First Annual Alcoholism Conference of NIAAA*, M. Chafetz, ed. Pp. 217-236. Washington, D.C.: National Institute on Alcohol Abuse and Alcoholism. (May be located under: Alcoholism Conference of the National Institute on Alcohol Abuse and Alcoholism, SUDOCS #HE 20.2430/2:971).

A survey of methodologies and theories applied to Native American drinking research. The authors examine the anthropological, sociological, and clinical approaches to data gathering, and the pitfalls and strengths of each method are discussed. It is suggested that Native American alcohol research be multidisciplinary and that programs should deal with the problem through the strengths of Native American society, not from the point of view of Anglo society.

0541 Levy, Jerrold E. and Stephen Joshua Kunitz
  1971b Indian Reservations, Anomie, and Social Pathologies. *Southwestern Journal of Anthropology* 27:97-128.

Examines several common theories regarding the relationship between social pathologies, such as alcoholism, suicide, and homicide, and social disorganization and anomie. Suggests that the prevalence of pathological behaviors is largely explainable in terms of persisting elements of aboriginal culture, rather than as responses to acculturation.

0542   Levy, Jerrold E. and Stephen Joshua Kunitz
            1974 *Indian Drinking: Navajo Practices and Anglo-American Theories*. New York: Wiley-Interscience.

    Provides a detailed analysis of Navajo male drinking behavior. The data were collected in such a manner as to permit cross-cultural comparison. Compares Navajo drinking patterns with those of the White Mountain Apache and Puebloan groups. The authors believe that patterns of alcohol use may be explained in terms of persisting cultural configurations established in aboriginal times and surviving to the present. They argue against cultural disintegration as a causal factor in the high level of Native American drinking. They also warn of the dangers in labelling normal Native American drinkers as "sick."

0543   Levy, Jerrold E., Stephen Joshua Kunitz and Michael W. Everett
            1969 Navajo Criminal Homicide. *Southwestern Journal of Anthropology* 25:124-152.

    An investigation of homicide among the Navajo and its relationship to alcohol and levels of acculturation.

0544** Levy, Jerrold E., James H. Shore and Donald Gordon
            1973 Suicide Prevention among Shoshone-Bannock Indians. Unpublished report submitted to the Shoshone-Bannock Tribes, supported by National Institute of Mental Health Research Grant #MH 18984-01, 18p.

    Observes that there is a clustering of alcohol deaths, cirrhosis, suicide, and homicide in small, specific subgroups of the population.

0545   Lewis, Claudia
            1970 *Indian Families of the Northwest Coast: the Impact of Change*. Chicago: University of Chicago Press.

    The impact of alcohol on a Native American community on Vancouver Island, British Columbia is discussed throughout the book. Native American drinking is seen as resulting from a number of factors, including, a lack of means of control over excessive drinking, release of aggression, and rebellion against Anglos.

0546   Lewis, Thomas H.
            1970 Notes on the Heyoka, the Teton Dakota "Contrary" Cult. *Pine Ridge Research Bulletin* 11:7-19.

Contemporary Oglala Sioux ceremonials contain remnants of the Heyoka Society. One aspect of Heyoka contrary behavior is mimicking drunken behavior and emphasizing alcohol in costume and action.

0547   Lieber, Charles S.
1972 Metabolism of Ethanol and Alcoholism: Racial and Acquired Factors. *Annals of Internal Medicine* 76:326-327.

Examines an article by Fenna, Mix, Schaefer and Gilbert (1971, see citation #0266) and suggests that a more rigid study design is required in order to obtain conclusive results.

0548   Lindquist, G.E.
1944 *The Indian in American Life*. New York: Friendship Press. (Reprinted by AMS Press, 1976.)

Four factors contributing to alcohol use among Native Americans are noted: (1) repeal of the 18th amendment, (2) the ease with which alcohol may be procured, (3) confusion regarding liquor laws, and (4) an attitude of easy-come-easy-go regarding money. Proper education by Christian agencies is seen as a solution.

0549   Littman, Gerald
1967 Einige Bemerkungen über Trinksitten unter amerikanischen Indianern in Chicago. In 27th International Congress on Alcohol and Alcoholism, Frankfurt am Main, *Internationaler Kongress Alkohol und Alkoholismus*. Hamburg: Neuland-Verlagsgesellschaft.

After a brief survey of the recent history of the Native American, the author turns to the major causes of alcoholism among Native Americans in general, but especially in the Chicago area where the author is active. Abusive drinking among Native Americans in the Chicago area is attributed to two factors: (1) basic differences in social values and (2) tensions involved in adjusting to a different culture.

0550   Littman, Gerald
1970 Alcoholism, Illness, and Social Pathology among American Indians in Transition. *American Journal of Public Health* 60:1769-1787.

Description of Native American alcoholism and related pathology among residents of Chicago. The physiological variables of Native Americans in transition, and the needs for appropriate rehabilitation and training programs are discussed. Alcoholism is seen as having its source in emotional and psychological conflicts arising in urban and Native American-Anglo confrontation situations.

0551   Llewellyn, Karl N. and E. Adamson Hoebel
        1941 *The Cheyenne Way. Conflict and Case Law in Primitive Jurisprudence.* Norman: University of Oklahoma Press.

        Examines the role of alcohol in cases of homicide. Indicates that an exception to banishment is granted if drunkenness leads to homicide.

0552   Llewellyn, Karl N. and E. Adamson Hoebel
        1973 The Cheyenne Way. Conflict and Case Law in Primitive Jurisprudence. In *Law and the American Indian*, Monroe E. Price, ed. Pp. 136-138. New York: Bobbs-Merrill.

        Indicates that the commission of homicide while one is intoxicated warrants special consideration. Suggests that drunkenness is considered a valid defense for homicide.

0553   Lobban, Mary C.
        1971 Personal View. *British Medical Journal* 1(5744):344.

        Reports personal reflections of a visit to Inuvik, Canada. Notes that in one instance five Eskimos drank themselves to death and that alcohol abuse resulted in brawls, homicides and death.

A553   Locklear, Herbert H.
        1977 American Indian Alcoholism: Program for Treatment. *Social Work* 22(3):202-207.

        Describes the planning and development of an alcoholism center for Baltimore's Native American population and assesses the results of the first year's operation. Indicates that much of the program's success stems from a recognition of the cultural conflict between Native American and non-Native American populations.

0554   Loeb, E.M.
        1943 Primitive Intoxicants. *Quarterly Journal of Studies on Alcohol* 4:387-398.

        An historical review of drinking behavior among primitive groups, including North American Indians.

A554   Lookout, F. Morris
        1975 Alcohol and the Native American. *Alcohol Technical Reports* 4(4):30-37.

        Discusses the problems of Native American alcoholism based on interviews with American Indian alcoholism project directors, Bureau of Indian Affairs personnel, and Indian health representatives. Background information is presented on organizational structures, religion, and leadership, as well as statistics on alcohol abuse. Concludes that training and education are a compelling need of Native Americans and that provision of such services would do much to attack problems rather than symptoms.

0555   Lookout, F. Morris
        1977 Alcohol Drinking and the Indian Predicament. *Alcohol Technical Reports* 6:13-16.

        An overview of alcohol use among Native Americans which stresses the heterogeneity of Native Americans.

0556   Lovrich, Frank
        1951 The Assimilation of the Indian in Rapid City. MA Thesis, University of South Dakota, 101p.

        Pages 58-59 report the results of a questionnaire which indicates that a majority of Native Americans favor repeal of laws restricting the sale of alcohol to Native Americans. Results indicate that Anglos also favor repeal of such laws.

0557   Lubart, Joseph M.
        1969a Field Study of the Problems of Adaptation of Mackenzie Delta Eskimos to Social and Economic Change. *Psychiatry* 32:447-458.

        Behavioral indications of social breakdown, such as excessive alcohol use, are discussed. Indicates that alcohol abuse is widespread, and that there appears to be a correlation between women's sexual activity and drinking behavior.

0558   Lubart, Joseph M.
        1969b *Psychodynamic Problems of Adaptation, Mackenzie Delta Eskimos: a Preliminary Study.* Ottawa: Mackenzie Delta Research Project, Publication #7.

        An attempt to ascertain basic Eskimo personality based on a study of traditional behavior and an analysis of behavior change when faced with culture change, especially while under the influence of alcohol.

0559   Luebben, Ralph A.
        1964a Anglo Law and Navaho Behavior. *Kiva* 29(3):
           60-75.

        It was found that a higher percentage of Navajos were
        arrested for offenses against the public peace (such
        as drunkenness) than Anglos. Because the more accul-
        turated Navajos were arrested more frequently than less
        acculturated individuals, the author believes that
        significant change is needed in Navajo culture before
        successful off-reservation life styles can be achieved
        by the Navajo.

0560   Luebben, Ralph A.
        1964b Prejudice and Discrimination against Navahos
           in a Mining Community. *Kiva* 30(1):1-17.

        Bar behavior, both before and after the repeal of
        prohibition, is briefly noted. Indicates that on-
        reservation drinking patterns persisted off the
        reservation also.

0561   Lumholtz, Carl Sofus
        1971 *New Trails in Mexico; an Account of One Year's
           Exploration in North-West Sonora, Mexico, and South-
           Western Arizona, 1909-1910.* Glorieta, New Mexico:
           Rio Grande Press (originally published in 1912).

        Observations by early Spanish explorers on Native
        American uses of cactus. The Papago Indians are
        reported to make an intoxicating drink from the fruit
        of the saguaro cactus. The cactus wine or *navait* is
        consumed at an annual ceremony designed to bring rain.

0562   Lunger, Harold L.
        1956 Seek Ways to Counter Indians' Drinking and
           Delinquency - Few Problems Yet from Legalized
           Sale of Liquor to Indians. *Christian Century*
           73(18):560-561.

        Represents two very brief newsnotes reporting that
        the New Mexico State Commission on Indian Affairs
        would like seven Native Americans to be trained and
        employed as police and that the Indian Service be
        granted the authority to inspect liquor establishments
        near the reservation. The second item reports that
        no increase in problems attributed to alcohol resulted
        from the legalization of the sale of alcohol to Native
        Americans.

0563   Lurie, Nancy O.
          1971 The World's Oldest On-Going Protest Demonstration:
          North American Indian Drinking Patterns. *Pacific
          Historical Review* 40:311-332.

          Lurie challenges the idea that Native Americans drink
          because of an identity crisis. Compares and contrasts
          Native American drinking with that of Blacks. Hypoth-
          esizes that Native Americans want to succeed on their
          own terms as Native Americans, while at the same time
          borrowing freely from the material aspects of Anglo
          culture. As a result, Native American drinking becomes
          an established means of asserting and validating
          Indianness. The author suggests three alternatives
          to drinking.

0564   Lurie, Nancy O.
          1972 Indian Drinking Patterns. *American Journal of
          Orthopsychiatry* 42:554.

          In a letter to the editor, Lurie reaffirms her thesis
          that Native American drinking is not the problem that
          Anglos make it out to be, but is, in fact, a functionally
          adaptive cultural pattern--expressing resistance to the
          threat posed by Anglo society to the continuation of
          Native American sociocultural distinctiveness.

0565   Lysyk, K.
          1968a Canadian Bill of Rights - Irreconcilable Conflict
          with Another Federal Enactment - Equality before the
          Law and the Liquor Provisions of the Indian Act.
          Canadian Bar Review 46:141-149.

          A discussion of the implications arising from the
          conviction of Joseph Drybones on charges of intoxi-
          cation in Yellowknife, Northwest Territories, Canada.
          At issue is the definition of equality under the law
          as set forth in the 1960 Canadian Bill of Rights versus
          the provisions of the Indian Act. Notes that most
          officials believe that the liquor provisions of the
          Indian Act should be deleted, and that Native Americans
          should be dealt with the same as other citizens under
          terms of Provincial and Territorial liquor legislation.

0566   Lysyk, K.
          1968b Human Rights and the Native People of Canada.
          Canadian Bar Review 46:695-705.

          Reviews the status of Native American rights under
          Canadian law. Notes that the case of Regina vs. Drybones
          challenges the validity of the liquor provisions of the
          Indian Act.

0567   MacAndrew, Craig and Robert Edgerton
            1969 *Drunken Comportment: a Social Explanation*.
               Chicago: Aldine.

            A strongly supported thesis that alcohol-related
            behavior is essentially a learned behavior. The
            history of Native American contact with alcohol and
            the gradual "learning" of behavior which is classified
            as "drunken Indian behavior" is detailed. That Native
            Americans learned such behavior from the rejects of
            European and Colonial society is documented.

0568   McBeth, Kate C. and Mazie Crawford
            1914 The Rise and Fall of King Alcohol in the Nez
               Perce Indian Country. *The Red Man* 6(7):259-265.

            Examines the attempt to prohibit the sale of alcohol
            on the Nez Perce Reservation in the early 1900s.
            The Nez Perce desired prohibition and included it
            in a treaty; however, in 1905 the Circuit Court of
            Appeals declared Native Americans to be citizens
            and struck down prohibition. In 1907 the Supreme
            Court upheld reservation prohibition and in 1912
            when prohibition was placed on the Lewiston County
            ballot, the Nez Perce voted to keep the county dry.

0569   McClelland, David C., William N. Davis, Eric Wanner
        and Rudolf Kalin
            1966 A Cross-Cultural Study of Folk Tale Content
               and Drinking. *Sociometry* 29:308-333.

            Examines a random cross-cultural sample in an attempt
            to identify correlations between drinking and folk
            tale themes associated with drinking. Results suggest
            that a feeling of weakness in the face of heavy demands
            leads men to dream of magical potency and seek it in
            heavy drinking. Several Native American groups were
            included in the sample.

0570   McCracken, Robert Dale
            1968 Urban Migration and the Changing Structure of
               Navajo Social Relations. Ph.D. Dissertation, University
               of Colorado, 406p. U.M. Order #68-14216.

            Informants kept diaries for 2-week periods while on the
            reservation and in Denver. A great deal of the entries
            refer to drinking and associated behavior. Notes that
            wives have a strong influence on husbands' drinking
            behavior, especially in urban environments.

0571   MacDonald, John A.
        1968 The Canadian Bill of Rights: Canadian Indians
            and the Courts. *Criminal Law Quarterly* 10:305-319.

        Discusses the Canadian Bill of Rights as it affects
        the right of Native Americans to possess and consume
        alcoholic beverages off reserves. Various cases are
        cited including that of Joseph Drybones.

0572   McDonald, Thomas
        1975 Group Psychotherapy with Native American Women.
            International Journal of Group Psychotherapy 25:
            410-420.

        Alcoholism represents one symptom of the trauma faced
        by Native Americans who migrate to urban areas. The
        article examines the case of eight Native American
        women who turned to group therapy in an attempt to
        cope with life in San Diego.

0573** McGreevy, Susan
        1975 Morning Star Lodge: An Indian Halfway House.
            Unpublished paper presented at the 74th annual
            meeting of the American Anthropological Association,
            16p.

        Examines current theories regarding Native American
        alcohol problems and reasons why current treatment
        methods are unsuccessful. Reports on the establishment
        of a Native American halfway house in Kansas City.

0574   Macgregor, Gordon
        1946 *Warriors without Weapons*. Chicago: University
            of Chicago Press.

        Examines the personality development of the Oglala
        and Brule Sioux. Mentions that reservation prohibition
        is ineffective.

0575** McGunigle, Elizabeth R.
        1973 Problem Drinking among American Indians and a
            New Look at its Cause. Unpublished paper, Colorado
            College, Southwest Studies Summer Institute, 13p.

        Reviews the history of Native American alcohol use
        and investigates major theories regarding Native
        American drinking. Suggests that Native American
        alcoholism may be due to "cerebral allergic/addictive
        response."

0576   MacKinnon, A.A. and A.H. Neufeldt
            1974 A Survey of Mental Health "North of 60."
               Canada's Mental Health 22(1):3-6.

            In an attempt to determine the mental health status
            of individuals in Canada's north country, seventeen
            communities, with large Native American and Metis
            populations, were surveyed. A moderate correlation
            between alcohol abuse and psychosomatic symptomatology
            was noted.

0577   MacKinnon, Victor S.
            1973 Booze, Religion, Indians and the Canadian Bill
               of Rights. *Public Law* 1973:295-315.

            Examines the Canadian Bill of Rights as it applies
            in the case of the Queen vs. Drybones.

0578   Macklin, June
            1975 Roundtable on Application of Anthropology to
               Health Programs. *Medical Anthropology Newsletter*
               6(2):2-3.

            A summary of discussions presented at the Roundtable
            meetings held in Mexico City. Valene Smith reported
            on a study of alcoholism among Native Americans, with
            particular attention to the relationship between hypo-
            glycemia, diet and alcoholism. There appears to be
            evidence to indicate that a shift from a nearly 100%
            protein diet to a 100% carbohydrate diet is closely
            related to alcoholism.

0579   MacLeod, William C.
            1928 *The American Indian Frontier.* New York:
               Alfred A. Knopf. (Reprinted in 1968 by Dawsons.)

            Chapter III, entitled "How the Indian Tried Prohibition
            but Drank Too Much", discusses the use of alcohol among
            both North American Indians and the Aztecs. Maintains
            that the island of Manhattan was taken from a Native
            American word meaning "the island where we all became
            intoxicated." Describes the resulting trade in liquor
            which was established between Native Americans and
            Anglos, and recounts the efforts of Native Americans,
            as well as various governments to combat the problem.

0580   McNair, Crawford N.
            1969 Drinking Patterns and Deviance in a Multi-Racial
               Community in Northern Canada. Unpublished paper
               prepared for the Alcoholism and Drug Addiction
               Research Foundation of Ontario, substudy 32-1969, 17p.

Investigates the drinking patterns of a town inhabited by loggers, construction workers, Kaska Indians, and Tahltan Indians. Local behavior is seen to deviate from the norms of the larger culture in a number of areas, especially in the excessive consumption of liquor. Notes that a negative racial identity contributes to alcohol abuse among Native Americans.

0581   McNickle, D'Arcy
1968 The Sociocultural Setting of Indian Life. *American Journal of Psychiatry* 125:219-223.

Four types of Native American student personalities are identified: conservatives, shaper-uppers, the angries, and the self-haters. Only the angry, militant, nativistic oriented students seemed to have trouble with alcohol, using it as a reaction to stress.

0582   McSwain, Romola Mae
1965 The Role of Wives in the Urban Adjustment of Navaho Migrant Families to Denver, Colorado. MA Thesis, University of Hawaii, 286p.

In attempting to define successful urban adaptation, McSwain employs two criteria: (1) the ability to obtain adequate economic resources, and (2) the ability to control drinking. The use of alcohol among Navajos is briefly discussed. Nine case studies are presented in which the two variables noted above are examined.

0583**   Mail, Patricia D.
1966 The Use and Influence of Alcohol in the San Carlos Apache: an Interim Report. Unpublished report submitted to the Phoenix Area Indian Health Service Research Advisory Committee, 49p.

Examines drinking behavior on the San Carlos Reservation in terms of village residence, age, and sex. Suggests that Native Americans will never be able to deal successfully with alcohol until it is readily and legally available on reservations.

0584   Mail, Patricia D.
1967 The Prevalence of Problem Drinking in the San Carlos Apache. MPH Thesis, Yale University, 126p.

Represents a survey of the San Carlos Apache to establish a baseline for drinking behavior. A total of 4418 people were surveyed and drinking behavior was classified into 5 categories. Males drank significantly more than females. Preventive programs for youth and more recreational facilities were deemed necessary.

0585** Mail, Patricia D.
1973a Problem Drinking among Southwestern Indians. Unpublished paper prepared for the Seattle University Symposium on Alcohol, 48p.

A review of the etiology of problem drinking among Southwestern Native Americans, especially the San Carlos Apache. Discusses various treatment methodologies employed to overcome Native American alcohol abuse.

0586** Mail, Patricia D.
1973b Firewater Antidote: An Indian Alcoholism Treatment Program. Unpublished paper prepared for the Seattle University Alcohol Studies Program, 22p.

A report on one Native American organization's development of an alcoholism program utilizing federal funding.

0587** Mail, Patricia D.
1974a Drinking in a Reservation Community. Unpublished paper prepared for the Seattle University Alcohol Studies Program, 23p.

Investigates drinking on the San Carlos Apache Reservation with respect to the scope and extent of the problem, contributing factors, and the sociocultural setting of which alcohol abuse is a part. Recommends a comprehensive program which includes medical care and counseling.

0588** Mail, Patricia D.
1974b Native American Alcohol Behavior: An Overview. Unpublished paper prepared for the Seattle University Alcohol Studies Program, 69p.

Examines alcohol use among Apaches and Papagos. The differences in the two groups' experiences are discussed and solutions to alcohol abuse are offered.

A588 Mail, Patricia D.
1978 Hippocrates was a Medicine Man: The Health Care of Native Americans in the Twentieth Century. *Annals of the American Academy of Political and Social Science* 436:40-49.

Notes that the provision of health and medical care to American Indians and Alaskan Natives has undergone major changes in the 150 years during which the Federal government has assumed responsibility for delivery of such services. Patterns of Native American health care are rapidly approaching the patterns characteristic of low income populations in the Western world; that is, they exhibit a reduction in infectious diseases and an increase in psychosocial problems. Briefly discusses alcohol problems as an acculturative response.

B588 Mail, Patricia D. and David R. McDonald
  1977 Native Americans and Alcohol: a Preliminary, Annotated Bibliography. *Behavior Science Research* 12(3):169-196.

A preliminary, annotated bibliography which provides 132 citations to published and unpublished literature on Native American alcohol use and abuse, accompanied by a brief review of methodological and theoretical issues reported in the literature.

0589 Mandelbaum, D.G.
  1965 Alcohol and Culture. *Current Anthropology* 6:281-293.

An overview of the relationship between cultural patterns and drinking patterns. Several Native American groups are cited in the paper.

0590 Mangin, William
  1962 Review of *Primitive Drinking: a Study of the Uses and Functions of Alcohol in Preliterate Societies*. *American Anthropologist* 64:857-860.

See citation #0909 for an annotation of the book under review.

0591 Mann, Marty
  1963 Various Approaches That Have Been Utilized in the Treatment and Prevention of Alcoholism. *Lectures and Notes 1963 Manual Supplement*. Salt Lake City: University of Utah, School of Alcohol Studies.

Notes that the history of the United States reinforces the myth that Native Americans cannot drink. Points out that Native Americans' problems with alcohol differ little from alcohol problems exhibited in the majority population.

0592   Manning, Leah
        1963 Step by Step Report of How an A.A. Program
        Began in a Northern Nevada Indian Reservation.
        Lectures and Notes 1963 Manual Supplement. Salt
        Lake City: University of Utah, School of Alcohol
        Studies.

        Traces the development of a Native American A.A.
        program and discusses A.A. as a treatment methodology.

0593   Manzolillo, Lola R.
        1955 The American Indian in an Urban Situation:
        Minneapolis, Minnesota. MA Thesis, University
        of Minnesota, 155p.

        Notes that excessive drinking formed the major
        recreational activity of Native Americans in the
        Minneapolis area.

0594   Margolin, Sydney G.
        1962 A Consideration of Constitutional Factors in
        Aggressivity. *Psychoanalytic Quarterly* 31:299-300.

        A brief report outlining major problems which accompany
        a high rate of alcoholism among the Ute Indians of
        Colorado.

0595** Marsden, Gillian
        1975 National Health Insurance and Community Health
        Centers: An Analysis of Implications for the Seattle
        Indian Health Board. Unpublished report, University
        of Washington, Department of Health Services,
        Technical Assistance & Continuing Education Project.

        An analysis of six major national health insurance
        bills before the 93rd Congress and their implications
        for an urban Native American clinic. Notes that
        alcoholism counseling is an important feature which
        may not be available under federal insurance programs.
        Alcohol is a major problem for urban Native Americans,
        but a problem which few national health insurance
        proposals adequately consider.

0596   Martinez, Fredrick H.
        1966 Developing a Tribal Program for Indian Alcohol
        Problems. *Lectures and Notes 1966 Manual Supplement.*
        Salt Lake City: University of Utah, School of
        Alcohol Studies.

        Description of alcohol programs developed by the New
        Mexico Commission on Alcoholism to meet the needs of

Pueblo Indians, Apaches, and Navajos. Discusses various treatment methodologies.

0597** Martinez, Fredrick H.
1968 Extent and Scope of Indian Drinking Problems. Unpublished paper presented to the University of Utah, School of Alcohol Studies, 8p.

Examines the historical, socioeconomic, cultural, and environmental factors which contribute to Native American drinking.

0598 Marx, Herbert
1972 Federal Liquor Legislation Is Hardly Justifiable as Protective of Indians - a Reply to Professor Bowker. *Saskatchewan Law Review* 37(2):101-106.

Discusses the implications of the Drybones case and considers the concept of "equal protection." Points out that the provisions of the Indian Act do not constitute "protective" legislation and that there is no evidence that protective legislation is reasonable or even necessary. Suggests that numerous agencies could better protect Native Americans from alcohol abuse through educational programs.

0599 Marx, Herbert
1973 The Canadian Bill of Rights and R.V. Drybones-- a New Outlook? *Northern Ireland Legal Quarterly* 24:74-93.

Suggests that in losing the Drybones case, the Canadian government won a decisive victory in upholding the Bill of Rights.

0600 Mason, Velma Garcia
1976 *What Life Will We Make for Our Children?* Inglewood, California: Multicultural Drug Abuse Prevention Program.

A booklet designed as a resource for Native American substance abuse training programs. Suggests that reliance upon Native value systems can help individuals deal with alcohol problems.

0601 May, Philip A.
1975 Arrests, Alcohol, and Alcohol Legalization among an American Indian Tribe. *Plains Anthropologist* 20:129-134.

Examines the contemporary and historical relationships between Native Americans, alcohol, and arrests.

0602   May, Philip A.
        1976 Alcohol Legalization and Native Americans: a
        Sociological Inquiry. Ph.D. Dissertation, University
        of Montana, 223p. U.M. Order #77-00720.

Numerous laws have been applied to Native Americans regarding the purchase, consumption and possession of alcoholic beverages. The author investigates the possibility that the various laws have influenced contemporary drinking patterns of Native Americans. The author provides a list of tribes which have legalized alcohol and compares reservations that continue prohibition with those that have legalized alcohol in an effort to determine the effect of legalization on variables such as alcoholism, alcohol-related arrests and mortality. Finds that tribes which have legalized alcohol have lower rates for alcohol-related arrests and mortality. Concludes that laws may have a significant effect on Native American drinking patterns.

A602   May, Philip A.
        1977a Alcohol Beverage Control: A Survey of Tribal
        Alcohol Statutes. *American Indian Law Review*
        5(1):217-228.

Public Law 83-277 repealed federal prohibition and enabled Native Americans to legally consume alcoholic beverages off the reservation. The law also granted individual tribes the power to maintain or repeal prohibition on their reservation. At the end of 1974, 92 out of 293 federally recognized reservations had legalized alcohol in some capacity. Reviews tribal alcohol laws.

B602   May, Philip A.
        1977b Explanation of Native American Drinking: A
        Literature Review. *Plains Anthropologist* 22(77):
        223-232.

In behavioral science literature the drinking patterns of some Native Americans have received considerable attention. Because the modal Native American drinking style has been viewed and characterized as different from the patterns of most other groups in the United States, numerous works have attempted to explain this divergence. May reviews the most common explanations of Native American drinking behavior, which can generally be classified as (1) biological, (2) psychoanalytic, (3) anomic, and (4) normative. In addition, three approaches to the study of Native American drinking are described: (1) the ethnography, (2) the social problem and (3) the integrative study.

0603   May, Philip A. and Larry H. Dizmang
1974   Suicide and the American Indian. *Psychiatric Annals* 4:22-28.

Reports that alcohol is often associated with suicides.

0604   Maynard, Eileen
1968   Negative Ethnic Image among Oglala Sioux High School Students. *Pine Ridge Research Bulletin* 6:18-25.

Reports that Native American high school students held negative images of themselves, and that part of the image included the "drunken Indian" stereotype.

0605   Maynard, Eileen
1969   Drinking as Part of an Adjustment Syndrome among the Oglala Sioux. *Pine Ridge Research Bulletin* 9:35-51.

A discussion documenting the scope of drinking problems among the Oglala Sioux using various indices, including arrest records, an acculturation scale, and other socioeconomic factors. Possible causes are identified, and an alcohol adjustment syndrome is postulated as a means of coping with intolerable stress, especially among males. Types of stress affecting the Sioux are noted, and solutions proposed. Economic problems are singled out as the most plausible on which to concentrate an attack on problem drinking.

0606   Maynard, Eileen and Gayla Twiss
1970   *That These People May Live: Conditions among the Oglala Sioux of the Pine Ridge Reservation*. Washington, D.C.: Government Printing Office, DHEW Publication #HSM 72-508 (SUDOCS #HE 20.2652:P39).

A guide to conditions among present day Oglala Sioux. The section on mental health discusses alcohol abuse. Suggests that alcohol abuse is employed as a coping mechanism and that drinking will continue until socioeconomic conditions improve.

0607   Mead, Margaret
1965   *The Changing Culture of an Indian Tribe*. New York: Capricorn Books.

An ethnographic overview of a Mississippi Valley tribe called the "Antlers." The use and abuse of alcohol is noted, especially as an index of maladjustment.

0608 Medicine, Bea
1969 The Changing Dakota Family and the Stress Therein. *Pine Ridge Research Bulletin* 9:

Examines motivations for drinking and social pressures influencing drinking behavior. Increasing independence of women exacerbates alcohol abuse among males; however, drinking is a valued male attribute associated with adult privileges and prerogatives.

0609 Meeks, Donald E.
1974 The Experience of the Addiction Research Foundation of Ontario in Organizing Alcohol Programmes. In *Alcohol and Drug Dependence, Proceedings of the 1974 Workshop of the Association of Psychiatrists in Africa.* Pp. 19-24. Lausanne: International Council on Alcohol and Addictions.

Reviews the philosophy and methodology of the Addiction Research Foundation. Discusses alcohol abuse in the Canadian Native American village of Kenora, in which heavy drinking is seen as an adaptive mechanism employed to cope with oppressive living conditions. Suggests that use of indigenous paraprofessionals is the key to village programs. Programs should not aim so much at alcoholism as at the underlying social, economic, and community problems which contribute to alcoholism.

A609 Memphis State University
1977 *Alcohol Abuse Training Relevant to Minority Populations. Handbook: Native Americans.* Arlington, Virginia: Alcoholism Research Information Center.

Furnishes guidelines for the development of education programs aimed at preventing Native American alcohol abuse.

0610 Mendelsohn, B. and W. Richards
1973 Alaskan Native Adolescents' Descriptions of Their Mental Health Problems. Unpublished paper presented at the 8th joint meeting of the Professional Associations of the U.S. Public Health Service.

Adolescent Alaskan Natives exhibit problems common to Native American youth, such as suicidal behavior, heavy drinking, and academic difficulties. This paper examines Alaskan Native adolescents' perception of their mental health, utilizing poems, drawings, autobiographies, and discussions.

0611   Mendez, Alfredo F.
       1970 Government Medical Service to the Seminole Indians. *Journal of the Florida Medical Association* 57(8):28-32.

       Notes that alcoholism is a problem for both males and females and alcoholism prevention is a high priority program.

0612   Mercer, G.W.
       1970 The Kenora Waystation. Unpublished report, Addiction Research Foundation, project G 178, 19p.

       Analysis of the impact of a "way station" which was established in Kenora, Ontario, to serve intoxicated Native Americans.

0613   Meritt, Edgar B.
       1914 Assistant Commissioner Meritt on the Suppression of the Liquor Traffic among Indians. *The Red Man* 6(7):56.

       Notes that Meritt was instrumental in obtaining appropriations from Congress to support a liquor suppression campaign. Meritt is reported as saying that "...the average Indian of this country cannot be too carefully protected from his greatest weakness and worst enemy, intoxicating liquor..."

0614   Meritt, Edgar B.
       1915 Service Employees to Promote Total Abstinence among Indians. *Carlisle Arrow* 11(39):5.

       Text of an announcement sent to the 600 Indian employees of the Bureau of Indian Affairs advising superintendents and their staffs to endorse a crusade against liquor.

A614   Merk, Frederick
       1968 *Fur Trade and Empire: George Simpson's Journal 1824-1825.* Cambridge: The Belknap Press of Harvard University. (Also located under Simpson, George, Sir.)

       Observations of a trader in the early 19th century regarding Native American reactions to liquor. Quotes Native Americans as saying that they trap only for liquor rather than other trade goods. Reports that liquor is considered an essential item in trade, especially with the plains tribes.

0615   Michal, Mary L., R. LaJeune Bradford, Paul H. Honda and Gail H. Sherman.
> 1973 *Health of the American Indian: Report of a Regional Task Force.* Washington, D.C.: U.S. Department of Health Education and Welfare Publication #HSM 73-5118 (also located under United States. Maternal and Child Health Service).

An overview of Native American health problems. Notes that cirrhosis of the liver is the 7th leading killer of Native Americans and that alcohol is related to many motor vehicle accidents.

0616   Milam, James R.
> 1974 *The Emergent Comprehensive Concept of Alcoholism.* Kirkland, Washington: Alcoholism Center Associates Press.

Classifies Native Americans as a racial group which has had short exposure to alcohol, a high genetic susceptibility to alcoholism, and a high rate of alcoholism.

0617** Miller, Maurice W. and Don Ostendorf
> n.d. Indian Mental Health Programs. Unpublished paper prepared by the Tribal Guidance Center, White Mountain Apache Reservation, 6p.

In dealing with maladaptive strategies, such as alcoholism programs should be developed at the individual, group, and community levels. Mental health programs should be culture specific and should be developed cooperatively by Native Americans and Anglos.

0618   Miller, Sheldon I. and Lawrence S. Schoenfeld
> 1971 Suicide Attempt Patterns among the Navajo Indians. *International Journal of Social Psychiatry* 17(3): 189-193.

Notes that alcohol was related to 74% of male suicides; however, only 16% of female suicides were associated with alcohol.

0619   Miller, Sheldon I., Edward Helmick, Lawrence Berg, Paul Nutting and Gregory Shorr
> 1974a Alcoholism: a Statewide Program Evaluation. *American Journal of Psychiatry* 131:210-214.

Examines alcoholism and the delivery of health care to alcoholics in Alaska. The staging concept is utilized as an assessment tool to determine the degree of impairment of the problem drinker and to assist in identifying appropriate treatment.

0620   Miller, Sheldon I., Edward Helmick, Lawrence Berg, Paul Nutting and Gregory Shorr
    1974b Evaluation of Alcoholism Treatment Services in the State of Alaska. Paper presented at the 9th joint meeting of the Professional Associations of the U.S. Public Health Service.

Reviews services provided Native Alaskan problem drinkers. Concludes that (1) many agencies do not keep adequate records; (2) clients are mostly treated without follow-up and evaluation; (3) there is little evidence of any attempt to evaluate effectiveness of treatment modalities; and (4) even in areas which exhibit all the necessary components for problem solving, there is little evidence of coordination of resources necessary to achieve treatment success.

A620   Miller, Sheldon I., Edward Helmick, Lawrence Berg, Paul Nutting and Gregory Shorr
    1975 An Evaluation of Alcoholism Treatment Services for Alaskan Natives. *Hospital and Community Psychiatry* 26(12):829-831.

Published version of entry #0620.

0621   Milligan, Donald
    1972 Selective Bibliography of Indian Resource Material from a Social Work Perspective. MSW Thesis, University of Washington, 24p.

References to literature on alcohol appear on pages 21-22.

0622** Mindell, Carl F.
    1967a Clinical Aspects of the Use of Alcohol among the Oglala Sioux. Unpublished paper presented at the Rosebud Sioux Tribal Workshop on Alcohol, 13p.

Considers the extent of alcohol abuse among the Oglala Sioux of the Pine Ridge Reservation, and examines some of the functions of alcohol within the culture. Two patterns of drinking were identified: reactive (binge) drinking and addictive drinking.

0623**   Mindell, Carl F.
        1967b Some Mental Health Issues in an American Indian Tribe. Unpublished paper presented at a Seminar on Indian Health, University of Arizona, 14p.

        Reviews the major mental health problems among the Oglala Sioux. Notes that individuals drink not only to vent hostility and aggression, but also to enjoy themselves and socialize.

0624   Mindell, Carl F.
        1968 Poverty, Mental Health and the Sioux. *Pine Ridge Research Bulletin* 6:26-34.

        In discussing indices of poverty and its effects on the Oglala Sioux, it is noted that evidence of social disorganization is reflected in, and contributed to by the high rate of alcohol consumption.

0625   Mindell, Carl F. and Paul Stuart
        1968 Suicide and Self-Destructive Behavior in the Oglala Sioux. *Pine Ridge Research Bulletin* 1:14-23.

        Aggressive feelings among the Sioux are usually expressed indirectly through gossip or avoidance, unless alcohol is involved. Suggests that paraprofessionals be trained to deal with alcohol abuse.

0626   Mindell, Carl F. and Paul Stuart
        1969 Suicide and Self-Destructive Behavior in the Oglala Sioux: Some Clinical Aspects and Community Approaches. In *Suicide among the American Indians*. Pp. 25-33. Washington, D.C.: U.S. Public Health Service publication #1903 (SUDOCS #FS 2.22:Su 3/2).

        Notes that alcohol is a factor in many suicides. Suggests that alcoholism programs utilizing paraprofessionals be established in conjunction with suicide prevention programs.

0627   Minnis, Mhyra S.
        1963 The Relationship of the Social Structure of an Indian Community to Adult and Juvenile Delinquency. *Social Forces* 41:395-403.

        Notes that Native Americans tend to be arrested for drunkenness in towns adjacent to the reservation while Anglos are allowed to go free.

0628** Mito, Bob and S. Sata Lindbergh
1971 The Dilemma of Urban Indian Health. Report prepared for the Seattle Indian Health Board under Public Health Service Grant #PHS-AM-05250, 37p.

Alcoholism is viewed as the most disastrous health problem affecting urban Native Americans in Seattle. Identifies nine reasons for alcohol abuse among Native Americans.

0629** Mjelde, Lee Ann
1976 Indian Alcoholism. Unpublished paper prepared for course AIS 230, University of Washington, 15p.

Identifies two factors which contributed to Native American alcohol abuse: (1) lack of social norms prescribing drinking behavior, and (2) Anglo greed for furs and land. Contemporary contributing factors include discrimination, identity problems, and other sociocultural problems.

0630 Mohatt, Gerald
1972 The Sacred Water: The Quest for Personal Power through Drinking among the Teton Sioux. In *The Drinking Man*, David C. McClelland, William N. Davis, Rudolf Kalin and Eric Wanner, eds. Pp. 261-275. New York: The Free Press.

Acculturation prevented young Sioux males from behaving in a manner which would result in tribal respect. Alcohol, however, represented a partial solution, as drinking enabled individuals to behave "...in ways that proved to him and others that he was indeed brave and to be respected..." Four case histories are presented.

0631 Molinari, Carol
1976 Alcoholism: Alaska's Number One Health Problem. *Alcohol Health and Research World* 1976 (summer): 2-6.

Native American alcoholism is attributed to remoteness, severe climatic variations, language differences, and disruptive social change. Notes that the construction of the Alaskan pipeline adds to Native American drinking problems.

0632 Montana. Department of Health and Environmental Sciences
1971 *The Montana State Plan for Alcohol Abuse and Alcoholism Prevention, Treatment, and Rehabilitation. Fiscal Year 1971*. Helena: Montana State Department of Health and Environmental Sciences.

Indicates that Native Americans have an excessive drinking problem, and that programs for Native Americans are coordinated through the Montana Indian Commission on Alcohol and Drug Abuse, with individual tribal programs funded by the NIAAA.

0633   Montana. Department of Health and Environmental Sciences
1972 *The Montana State Plan for Alcohol Abuse and Alcoholism Prevention, Treatment, and Rehabilitation. Fiscal Year 1973.* Helena: Montana State Department of Health and Evironmental Sciences.

Provides statistics on Native American alcoholism in Montana.

0634   Montana. Department of Health and Environmental Sciences
1973 *The Montana State Plan for Alcohol Abuse and Alcoholism Prevention, Treatment, and Rehabilitation. Fiscal Year 1974.* Helena: Montana State Department of Health and Environmental Sciences.

Provides statistics on the extent of Native American alcoholism in Montana and reviews Native American alcoholism programs regarding their sources of funding and activities.

0635   Montana. Department of Health and Environmental Sciences
1974 *The Montana State Plan for Alcohol Abuse and Alcoholism Prevention, Treatment, and Rehabilitation. Fiscal Year 1975.* Helena: Montana State Department of Health and Environmental Sciences.

Includes a section devoted to an examination of alcoholism among Montana Native Americans. Identifies priority areas, such as comprehensive planning, treatment alternatives, rehabilitation programs.

0636   Montana. State Department of Institutions.
1975 *Montana State Plan for Alcohol Abuse and Alcoholism Prevention, Treatment and Rehabilitation. Fiscal Year 1976.* Helena: Montana State Department of Institutions, Adaptive Services Division.

Notes that input from Native Americans will be sought and incorporated in planning for alcoholism programs. Indicates that Native American youth make up a high proportion of problem drinkers.

A636   Morgan, Lael
1974 *And the Land Provides: Alaskan Natives in a Year of Transition.* Garden City: Anchor Press.

A chapter entitled "Bethel: a Battle with the Bottle" recounts the experiences of an alcoholism counselor who worked with the Eskimo of Bethel, Alaska. Boredom, isolation, and custom are cited as causes of alcohol abuse. Criticizes the PHS hospital for failure to treat alcoholism as a medical problem, and suggests that social workers were ineffective because of "rigid schedules."

0637   Morris, Joan and Fred Ebrahimi
1974 American Indian Alcoholism Evaluation-Monitoring-Design Project: Final Report. Glendale, California: Tribal American Training Consultants Associated (distributed by National Technical Information Service PB-240 724/5 G1).

A detailed report of a project designed to evaluate Native American alcoholism programs and computerize record keeping systems for the programs. Six Native American programs participated in the pilot study: Anadarko, Oklahoma; Eagle Butte, South Dakota; Laguna, New Mexico; Pawnee, Oklahoma; Rosebud, South Dakota; and the residential Inter-Tribal Alcoholism Treatment Center at Sheridan, Wyoming.

0638   Morse, J.
1822 *A Report to the Secretary of War of the U.S. on Indian Affairs*. New Haven: S. Converse (reprinted 1970, A.M. Kelley and 1972, Scholarly Press).

Included in the appendices of the report are notes on trade with the Crees and Assiniboins in which liquor is exchanged for furs. Also comments on the drinking behavior of the Crees.

0639**   Mosher, James F.
1975 Liquor Legislation and Native Americans: History and Perspective. Unpublished paper on file, University of California, Berkeley, School of Law, 55p.

Reviewing the evolution of laws passed to control liquor consumption by Native Americans, it becomes obvious that the liquor laws were simply a means for Anglos to impose their morality upon Native Americans, to manipulate trade to the Anglos' advantage, and to destroy the independence and sovereignty of Native American tribes. It is also apparent that Native Americans learned, that is assumed, the drinking patterns of Anglo traders and trappers.

0640** Moss, Fenton E.
n.d. Outline of Causation of Indian Alcoholism.
Unpublished paper prepared for the Western Region
Indian Alcoholism Training Center, University of Utah,

Forty-two theories concerning the etiology of Native
American alcoholism are classified under six headings:
cultural, social, economic, biological, psychological,
and combinations of the above.

0641** Moss, Fenton E.
1967 The Reservation Alcoholism Committee. Unpublished
paper prepared for the Western Region Indian Alcoholism
Training Center, University of Utah, 4p.

Provides guidance in setting up a reservation alcoholism
committee. Suggests that the membership yield a cross-
sectional representation of the community and that the
committee have community sanction. Discusses the
purpose of such a committee, selection of a chairman,
frequency of meetings, and the necessity for minutes.

0642** Moss, Fenton E.
1968a Problems Resulting from Excessive Drinking of
the Ute Indians. Unpublished paper prepared for the
Western Region Indian Alcoholism Training Center,
University of Utah, 5p.

Documents the impact of alcohol abuse on the Ute
Indians using medical, police, and social service
reports and records. Estimates that 38% of the
adults drink to excess and that 91% of deaths in the
previous five years were related to excessive drinking.

0643 Moss, Fenton E.
1968b Proposed Alcoholism Project for the Uintah-
Ouray Indian Reservation. In *An Indian Alcoholism
Training Project*, Fenton E. Moss, Lamar Beatty, and
Ray Christensen, eds. Pp. 89-105. Salt Lake City:
University of Utah Bureau of Indian Services.

Outlines the severity of excessive drinking on the Ute
Indian Reservation, detailing the effect of alcohol
abuse in terms of health problems, child neglect,
unemployment, and time in jail. Examines a program
designed to combat the problem.

0644** Moss, Fenton E.
1970a An Alcoholism Program for Indian Communities.
Unpublished paper prepared for the Western Region
Indian Alcoholism Training Center, University of
Utah, 5p.

Defines a successful community alcoholism program as one which has (1) an established coordinating committee, (2) an educational program, (3) a broad based rehabilitation program, and (4) a research component to evaluate the effectiveness of the program. Guidelines for setting up the coordinating committee may be found in Moss (1967, citation #0641).

0645**   Moss, Fenton E.
1970b Cultural Theories on the Causation of Indian Alcoholism. Unpublished paper prepared for the Western Region Indian Alcoholism Training Center, University of Utah, 5p.

Discusses the following possible causes of Native American alcoholism: (1) defiance of prohibition, (2) lack of drinking norms, (3) cultural disruption, (4) governmental paternalism, (5) drinking celebration, (6) perpetuation of drinking practices, (7) medicinal, and (8) permissiveness.

0646**   Moss, Fenton E.
1971 Qualifications of an Indian Alcoholism Counselor. Unpublished paper prepared for the Western Region Indian Alcoholism Training Center, University of Utah, 1p.

A brief discussion of the skills required of a successful Native American alcoholism counselor.

0647**   Moss, Fenton E.
1972 The Causation of Psychological Factors Underlying Alcoholism among Indians. Unpublished paper prepared for the Western Region Indian Alcoholism Training Center, University of Utah, 4p.

A review of psychological factors contributing to Native American alcohol abuse, such as (1) poor self-image, (2) feelings of inferiority, (3) role confusion, (4) pent-up aggression, (5) inability to handle frustration, (6) escape from boredom and deprivation, and (7) lack of shame concerning intoxication.

0648**   Moss, Fenton E.
1976 American Indians and Alcoholism. Unpublished paper prepared for the Western Region Indian Alcoholism Training Center, University of Utah, 7p.

Describes drinking patterns among Native Americans and indicates that 35% of adult Native Americans abuse alcohol. Forty-two factors contributing to

Native American alcohol abuse are listed and divided into five categories.

0649 Moss, Fenton E., Lamar Beatty and Ray Christensen
  1968 *An Indian Alcoholism Training Project.* Salt Lake City: University of Utah Bureau of Indian Services.

  Project report on a series of summer workshops held in 1967 which laid the foundation for Indian community alcoholism programs and led to the creation of the Western Region Indian Alcoholism Training Center at the University of Utah.

0650** Moss, Fenton E. and Reynold W. Brown
  n.d. Historical Development of the Ute Tribal Alcoholism Program. Unpublished paper prepared for the Western Region Indian Alcoholism Training Center, University of Utah, 4p.

  A report on the individuals and events which led up to the foundation of the Ute Tribal Alcoholism Program.

0651 Muggia, Albert L.
  1970 Upper G.I. Bleeding among Navajos. Paper presented at the 5th joint meeting of the Clinical Society and Commissioned Officers Association of the U.S. Public Health Service.

  See citation #0652 for annotation.

0652 Muggia, Albert L.
  1971a Upper Gastrointestinal Bleeding among Navajo Indians. *Rocky Mountain Medical Journal* 68(9): 29-31.

  Upper gastrointestinal bleeding is a problem of sizeable proportion among Navajo patients at the Gallup Indian Medical Center. Of the 50 patients studied, 43 had a history of alcoholism. Patients who stopped drinking demonstrated remission of their esophageal varices, with complete disappearance in 9 months.

0653 Muggia, Albert L.
  1971b Disease among the Navajo Indians. *Rocky Mountain Medical Journal* 68(11):39-49.

  Cites alcoholism as the greatest single cause of mortality among Navajos and a contributing factor in other medical disorders, such as gastrointestinal bleeding, and cirrhosis of the liver.

0654   Munz, C. Stewart
         1960 How the Curricula of the Special Navajo Programs
         Meet the Needs of the Students at the Intermountain
         School in Regard to Their use of Alcoholic Beverages.
         MS Thesis,(education), Utah State University, 93p.

         Knowledge of "drinking" is identified as a functional
         need for Navajo students at the Intermountain School
         in order to adapt to the world. A survey was under-
         taken in order to assess students' attitudes and
         knowledge concerning alcohol. It was found that as
         students progress in school they increase their knowledge
         of alcohol; however, weaknesses were identified and
         curriculum changes suggested.

0655** Munz, Victor R.
         1977 Evaluation Report of Seattle Indian Alcoholism
         Program. Unpublished report, King County Division
         of Alcoholism Service, Department of Public Health,
         20p.

         Reviews the structure, goals, and objectives of the
         Seattle Indian Alcoholism Program.

0656   Murphy, Jane M.
         1972 A Cross-Cultural Comparison of Psychiatric
         Disorder: Eskimos of Alaska, Yorubas of Nigeria,
         and Nova Scotians of Canada. In *Transcultural
         Research in Mental Health*, W.P. Lebra, ed. Vol. 2.
         Pp. 213-226. Honolulu: University of Hawaii Press.

         Compares psychiatric disorders among Eskimos, Yorubans,
         and Anglos. Among the Eskimos, alcohol is cited as
         contributing to sociopathology.

0657   Nagel, Gerald S.
         1974 Economics of the Reservation. *Current History*
         67:245-249, 278-279.

         Low Native American income stems from chronic and
         widespread unemployment, caused in part by the Native
         Americans' lack of skills and a scarcity of employment
         opportunities on the reservation. Such conditions
         give rise to mental illness, chief among which is
         alcoholism.

0658   Nagler, M.
         1970 *Indians in the City. A Study of the Urbanization
         of Indians in Toronto*. Ottawa: Canadian Research
         Centre for Anthropology, Saint Paul University.

An examination of alcohol use among Native Americans in Toronto. Alcohol serves as a social agent which not only permits Native Americans to resolve, at least temporarily, their frustrations, but also serves as a source of recreation.

0659 Nagler, M.
  1975 *Natives without a Home.* Don Mills, Ontario: Longman.

Discusses patterns of deviance, including alcohol abuse, among Canadian urban Native Americans. Drinking serves as both a recreational activity and as an expression of cultural conflict.

A659 Nelson, Leonard
  1977 Alcoholism in Zuni, New Mexico. *Preventive Medicine* 6:152-166.

An investigation into the etiology and medical and social consequences of alcoholism among the Zuni Indians revealed that alcohol is a major factor in Zuni mortality, especially among the young. Because multiple causes and modifying factors have made alcoholism a major health problem among the Zuni, the author proposes that a community-based rehabilitation program be established. Since many Zuni alcoholics believe that they are "possessed," a unique feature of the rehabilitation program would be the inclusion of a medicine man on the staff.

0660 Nelson, Thurston D.
  1968 Efforts to Rehabilitate the Standing Rock Sioux. MA Thesis, North Dakota State University, 94p.

A sketchy history of Sioux and federal government relationships, particularly attempts to control and civilize the Sioux. Notes that most arrests are connected with drinking and that governmental efforts to rehabilitate the Sioux have led to degradation, impoverishment, and drunkenness.

0661 Nilsson, Joel
  1973 For Apaches Alcoholism is One Form of Suicide. *The Arizona Daily Star* May 27, 1973-June 3, 1973.

Estimates that 200 Apaches have died as a result of alcohol abuse. Notes that alcohol abuse is a severe health problem, but that tremendous peer pressure to drink exists.

0662**   New York (State). Center for Migrant Studies
           n.d.   Patterns of Drinking among a Band of Algonkian
                  Indians: Description, Etiology, and Tentative
                  Management. Unpublished report of the New York
                  State Center for Migrant Studies, 10p.

           Examines the drinking behavior of a band of Rapid
           Lake Reserve Algonkians. Factors contributing to
           alcohol abuse incude peer pressure, lack of adequate
           nondeviant role models, and an understanding of Native
           American identity in contemporary society. A
           cooperative program administered by Native Americans
           as well as government officials is needed in order
           to control the problem.

0663**   Noble, Gaile P.
           1973   Indians and Alcohol. Unpublished paper pre-
                  sented to the Faculty at the School of Social
                  Work, University of Washington, 16p.

           An examination of drinking behavior which considers
           the impact of abusive drinking and discussion of
           prevailing theories and treatment methodologies.
           Case material is drawn from the Navajo Reservation.

0664   Norick, Frank A.
           1970   Acculturation and Drinking in Alaska. *Rehabili-
                  tation Record* 11:13-17.

           Native Americans and Eskimos of Alaska drink rapidly
           until the supply of alcohol is extinguished or the
           drinker loses consciousness. Middle-class goals
           and values, inculcated by the educational system,
           conflict with the reality of village life. Excessive
           drinking represents an attempt to deal with the
           resultant stress and emotional conflict.

0665**   Noriego, Julian L., T.V. Mitchell, P.A. Zuazua, W.S.
           Goodwin and John A. Egoak
           1975   An Approach to the Suicide-Alcohol Related
                  Problems of the Supai Tribe of Northern Arizona.
                  Unpublished report, Indian Health Service Desert
                  Willow Training Center, 6p.

            Factors which contribute to alcohol abuse and suicide
            attempts among the Supai include cultural identity
            conflicts, loss of traditional heritage, prejudice,
            familial disruption, and peer pressure. Proposed
            solutions include community education programs, con-
            struction of a community center, and emphasis on
            developing programs for children.

0666**   North Puget Sound Health Council
         1977 Status Report: Health and Health Related Problems
         of Minority and Disadvantaged Peoples. Unpublished
         report, North Puget Sound Health Council, 19p.

         Indicates that leading causes of Native American
         morbidity include alcoholism and cirrhosis of the
         liver. Alcoholism is attributed to unemployment,
         low levels of education, lack of self-esteem, and
         cultural barriers.

0667   Nowak, Jean
         1972 Another First for the First Americans. *HSMHA
         World* 7(2):6-7 (published by the U.S. Health Services
         Mental Health Administration).

         A brief report on the interagency cooperation which
         helped to create the Inter-Tribal Alcoholism Treatment
         Center in Sheridan, Wyoming. Four tribes, the Crow,
         Northern Cheyenne, Shoshone, and Arapaho, combined
         resources to build the Center.

0668   Nurge, Ethel
         1970 *The Modern Sioux*. Lincoln: University of
         Nebraska Press.

         Notes in a chapter on "The Dakota Diet" that sugar
         deficient diets and an abnormal need for sugar may
         contribute to alcoholism, although later Nurge comments
         that too many sweets are consumed as part of the
         contemporary diet.

0669   Nybroten, Norman
         1964 Economy and Conditions of the Fort Hall Indian
         Reservation. University of Idaho, Bureau of Business
         and Economic Research, Report 9.

         Alcohol is noted as a problem; however, it is not felt
         to be significantly worse than for the U.S. population
         as a whole.

0670**   Officer, James E.
         1963 The Concern of the Bureau of Indian Affairs over
         Indian Alcoholism. Unpublished report presented
         to the School of Alcohol Studies, University of Utah, 7p

         Reviews the exploitation of Native Americans which
         resulted from the use of alcohol and discusses the
         Bureau of Indian Affairs' concern about the apparent
         lack of motivation among Native American communities
         to mobilize against the problem.

0671   Ogden, Michael, M.I. Spector and C.A. Hill
        1970 Suicides and Homicides among Indians. *Public Health Reports* 85:75-80.

        Notes that suicide is closely related to alcohol use. Suggests that suicide and homicide, like alcohol abuse, are symptomatic of deeper problems within the Native American community.

A671   O'Meara, James E.
        1933 The Control of Liquor Traffic among the Indians of New France and the Work of the Church in Suppressing It. MA Thesis, John Carroll University, 49p.

        Documents the use of alcoholic beverages among Native Americans; investigates the relationship between the fur trade and the introduction of liquor to Native Americans. Examines the position of the Roman Catholic Church and the attempt by the Jesuits to prohibit the use and trade of alcohol to Native Americans.

0672   Omran, A.R. and B. Loughlin
        1972 An Epidemiological Study of Accidents among the Navajo Indians. *Journal of the Egyptian Medical Association* 55:1-22.

        Presents data collected during the Navajo-Cornell Field Health Research Project on accidental injury in rural areas. Notes that drinking is associated with most of the serious accidents and some fatalities. Suggests that prohibition be repealed.

0673   Opler, Morris Edward
        1941 *An Apache Life-Way: The Economic, Social, and Religious Institutions of the Chiricahua Indians.* Chicago: University of Chicago Press.

        Pages 368-370 describe the manufacture of alcoholic beverages, particularly tiswin, a weak beer made from maize.

0674   Opler, Morris Edward
        1969 *Apache Odyssey: a Journey between Two Worlds.* New York: Holt, Rinehart, and Winston.

        Presents the biography of an Apache named Chris. Observations throughout the narrative reflect attitudes towards alcohol and drinking behavior.

0675**   Oregon. Division of Mental Health
               1976 Report on the Primary Prevention of Alcohol and
               Drug Abuse in Oregon. Unpublished report, Department
               of Human Resources. Division of Mental Health, Office
               of Programs for Alcohol and Drug Problems.

               Review of a statewide project designed to educate and
               prevent alcohol and drug abuse. One of the six
               demonstration projects was conducted on the Umatilla
               Reservation.

0676   Oregon. Indian Commission on Alcohol and Drug Abuse
               1974 *1975 State Plan*. Salem: Oregon Indian
               Commission on Alcohol and Drug Abuse.

               Reviews the problems created by alcohol abuse among
               Native Americans of Oregon. Provides an historical
               and statistical overview of alcohol abuse among Native
               Americans. Inventories existing programs and outlines
               possible solutions to the problem. Indicates that
               Native Americans and Anglos must work together, but
               that Native Americans must assume responsibility
               for program planning.

0677   Oswalt, Wendell
               1963 *Napaskiak: an Alaskan Eskimo Community*. Tucson:
               University of Arizona Press.

               Briefly mentions that adolescents in this Eskimo
               village begin to consume alcohol at about the age
               of 16. Lists village council rules concerning
               alcoholic beverages; describes the drinking behavior
               of both males and females. Indicates that drinking
               is one of the greatest problems facing the community,
               but that alcohol is one of the most satisfying forms
               of diversion for many people. Community members
               believe that the incidence of drinking is less now
               than 10 years ago.

0678   Oswalt, Wendell
               1966 *This Land Was Theirs: A Study of the North
               American Indian*. New York: John Wiley.

               Discusses the impact of alcohol on the Chippewa,
               Kuskowagamiut, Fox, Iroquois, and Natchez. Comments
               that "...one remarkable characteristic rarely reported
               for American Indians is that the Hopi as a group have
               rejected the use of alcoholic beverages."

0679**   Oxereok, Charles H.
              1976 Alcoholism and Alcohol Abuse among Alaska Natives. Testimony prepared for the American Indian Policy Review Commission hearings, 13p.

              An overview of the enormity of alcohol and alcohol abuse problems confronting the Alaskan Native. Indicates that 50% of all Alaskan Native deaths are attributable, either directly or indirectly, to alcohol. Suggests that alcohol abuse occurs as early as the 4th and 5th grades and that physicians hide the magnitude of the problem by failing to note alcohol as a contributing factor in many illnesses.

0680**   Palmer, Ina C.
              1977 Using the Case Study Method for In-Service Training on Alcoholism for Nursing Personnel. Unpublished paper presented at the 12th annual meeting of the U.S. Public Health Service Professional Associations, 7p.

              Use of the case study method encourages nurses to freely discuss attitudes and problems encountered in caring for the alcoholic patient. The case of a 29 year old Native American admitted to a Public Health Service Hospital was used in the paper.

0681   Pambrun, Audra
              1970 Suicide among the Blackfeet Indians: Brief Report. *Bulletin of Suicidology* 7:42-43.

              Excessive drinking is a contributing factor in suicide.

A681   Parish, John C.
              1922 Liquor and the Indians. *Palimpsest* 3:201-213.

              Discusses the liquor trade among Native Americans in the Mississippi Valley. Notes that the French initially encouraged the liquor trade in order to ensure that Native Americans would continue to trade with the French and not turn to the Dutch and/or English. The United States, after securing the Mississippi Valley through the Louisiana Purchase, attempted with little success to prohibit the sale of liquor to Native Americans.

0682   Parker, Seymour
              1960 The Wiitiko Psychosis in the Context of Ojibwa Personality and Culture. *American Anthropologist* 62:603-623.

Notes that the only time during which repressed rage toward the supernatural is expressed is under the influence of alcohol.

0683   Parkin, Michael
        1974 Suicide and Culture in Fairbanks: A Comparison of Three Cultural Groups in a Small City of Interior Alaska. *Psychiatry* 37:60-67.

Compares the incidence and patterns of suicide among Athabascans, Eskimos, and non-Natives in Fairbanks, Alaska. Drinking was involved in many of the suicides, particularly among Native American females.

0684** Parmee, Edward A.
        1961 Existing Factors Affecting the Program of Education for San Carlos Apaches. Unpublished paper presented to the Coordinating Council for Research in Indian Education, 7p.

Excessive adult drinking is seen to lead to the corruption of many Apache youth as the result of disrupted home life, a lowering of moral standards, and violence which accompanies alcohol abuse.

0685   Parmee, Edward A.
        1968 *Formal Education and Culture Change: A Modern Apache Indian Community and Government Education Programs*. Tucson: University of Arizona Press.

The influence of alcohol is discussed in terms of school attendance, family solidarity, and delinquent behavior. Reports that during the summer months 55% of all juvenile arrests on the reservations were for one charge, disorderly conduct, drunk.

0686   Pascarosa, Paul and Sanford Futterman
        1976 Ethnopsychedelic Therapy for Alcoholics: Observations on the Peyote Ritual of the Native American Church. *Journal of Psychedelic Drugs* 8(3):215-221.

Suggests that the use of peyote within the confines of ritual meetings may represent a useful treatment for alcoholism among Native Americans. Suggests that the spiritual support found in the Native American Church is analogous to that of Alcoholics Anonymous.

0687   Pascarosa, Paul, Sanford Futterman and Mark Halsweig
        1976 Observations of Alcoholics in the Peyote Ritual: A Pilot Study. *Annals of the New York Academy of Sciences* 273:518-524.

The addition of peyote to a structured healing ceremony has been shown to be an effective therapeutic regimen for alcoholism. The authors attempt to identify the components of the peyote ritual which benefit alcoholics.

0688   Patterson, Harold L.
       1969 Suicide among Youth on the Quinault Indian Reservation. In *Hearings before the U.S. Senate Special Subcommittee on Indian Education of the Committee on Labor and Public Welfare, 90th Congress, 1st and 2nd Sessions.* Pp. 2016-2021. (SUDOCS #Y4 .L11/2:In 2/2.)

       Reports that alcohol is associated with most suicides.

0689   Petterson, Jay R.
       1972 Education, Jurisdiction, and Inadequate Facilities as Causes of Juvenile Delinquency among Indians. *North Dakota Law Review* 48:661-694.

       The issue of differential law enforcement, especially regarding arrests for intoxication, is raised.

0690   Pierre, George
       1971 *American Indian Crisis.* San Antonio, Texas: Naylor.

       A chief of the Colville Confederated Tribes notes that Native American excessive drinking is probably similar to Anglo excessive drinking. However, he goes on to indicate that alcohol is a major problem for Native Americans, and attributes drunkenness to Anglo influence.

0691   Pincock, T.A.
       1964 Alcoholism in Tuberculosis Patients. *Canadian Medical Association Journal* 91:851-854.

       Reports that 19% of Native American patients were alcoholic compared to 15% of the Anglos. Native Americans with alcohol complications comprised 35% of the treatment population, while Anglos with alcohol complications made up 19.5% of the population. Notes that alcoholism among TB patients is considered a serious problem.

0692   Pinto, Leonard J.
       1973 Alcohol and Drug Abuse among Native American Youth on Reservations: A Growing Crisis. In *Drug Use in America: Problem in Perspective,* Appendix Vol. 1: 1157-1178. Washington, D.C.: Government Printing Office (SUDOCS #Y3M33/2:1/973).

-221-

A broad review of reservation drinking and suggestions for programs which may improve reservation environments. A series of probable causes for initial and continued drinking are examined, and Native American drinking behavior is contrasted with that of other societies.

0693 Pittman, David J.
  1975 Social and Cultural Factors in Alcohol and Drug Dependency: an International Overview. In *Proceedings of the 31st International Congress on Alcoholism and Drug Dependence*, Vol. 2:32-38. Lausanne: International Council on Alcohol and Addictions.

  Pittman classifies Native Americans as belonging to the ambivalent cultural complex in which there is a conflict between coexisting value structures and the appropriate functions of alcohol.

0694 Popham, Robert E. and Carole D. Yawney
  1967 *Culture and Alcohol Use: A Bibliography of Anthropological Studies*. Toronto: Addiction Research Foundation.

  A comprehensive review of alcohol literature from an anthropological perspective.

0695 Porter, Margaret R., Theodore A. Vieira, Gary J. Kaplan, Jack R. Heesch and Ardell B. Colyar
  1973 Drug Use in Anchorage, Alaska: A Survey of 15,634 Students in Grades 6 through 12 - 1971. *Journal of the American Medical Association* 223:657-664.

  Reports that 34.7% of the Natives reported using only alcohol or tobacco, while 43.5% reported using other drugs as well as alcohol. The percentage of Native students reporting use of drugs in addition to alcohol was the highest for any ethnic group.

0696 Porvaznik, John
  1972 Surgical Problems of the Navajo and Hopi Indians. *American Journal of Surgery* 123:545-548.

  Alcoholism is cited as the leading cause of traumatic injury producing serious morbidity and mortality. Medical and surgical problems related to acute intoxication are very common; however, problems related to chronic alcoholism are reported to be rare.

0697 Prager, Kenneth M.
  1972 Alcoholism and the American Indian. *Harvard Medical Alumnae Bulletin* 47:20-25.

Reports on alcohol use on the Cheyenne River Reservation in South Dakota. Notes that alcohol is involved in a great many violent deaths on the reservation. The success rate of the usual treatment programs is near zero. Suggests that the Public Health Service needs to develop programs which will attack the problems giving rise to alcoholism.

0698** Press, Daniel S., Douglas Sakiestewa and Roslyn D. Kane
1974 A Study of the Indian Health Service and Indian Tribal Involvement in Health. Report prepared by Urban Associates, Inc. for the Office of Special Concerns, Department of Health, Education, and Welfare, 37p.

Examines the Indian Health Service policies and programs as they influence tribal endeavors to become self-determining. Alcoholism is noted as a priority problem distinguished by the Indian Health Service's lack of support. Some efforts to confront the alcohol problem are presented and suggestions made with respect to the need for increased data and better planning.

0699 Price, John A.
1968 The Migration and Adaptation of American Indians to Los Angeles. *Human Organization* 27:168-175.

Reports that 16% of the relocatees returned to the reservation from Los Angeles because of alcohol problems. Also indicates that in 32% of survey respondents drunkenness was attributed to maladjustment to urban living.

0700 Price, John A.
1975 Applied Analysis of North American Indian Drinking Patterns. *Human Organization* 34:17-26.

Problems inherent in alcohol consumption have become extremely serious among Native Americans in North America, especially with the breakdown of traditional cultural controls and the frustration from discrimination, low economic standing, peer group pressure to drink socially, and the spread of pathological drinking patterns. Legal solutions have proved unjust and ineffective. Enhancement of existing social controls within Native American societies as a means of counteracting dysfunctional and self-destructive drinking behavior is recommended, as is Native American participation in and sponsorship of workshops regarding alcohol use and abuse.

0701 Price, Monroe E.
  1973 *Law and the American Indian*. Indianapolis: Bobbs-Merrill.

  Very briefly (p. 18, 90, 350) mentions that attempts have been made to prohibit and control the use of alcoholic beverages among Native Americans. Reviews the major court cases which deal with Native American alcohol use.

0702** Provincial Native Action Committee
  1974 Native Alcoholism Programs. Unpublished report of the Provincial Native Action Committee, Edmonton, 19p.

  Examines the provincial and federal jurisdictional problems regarding Native American alcoholism programs. Suggests that such programs be administered by the health division rather than the Indian affairs division. Outlines goals and objectives of treatment programs and notes that Native American involvement and staffing are essential to the success of alcoholism programs.

0703 Prucha, Francis Paul
  1970 *American Indian Policy in the Formative Years: the Indian Trade and Intercourse Acts, 1780-1834*. Lincoln: University of Nebraska Press.

  A systematic account of federal Indian policy with a consideration of the role of liquor in Native American-Anglo trade relations. Chapter VI, "The Crusade Against Whiskey," examines frontier trade, liquor, and the problems liquor caused Native Americans and the federal government.

0704 Query, William T. and Joy M. Query
  1972 Aggressive Responses to the Holtzman Inkblot Techniques by Indian and White Alcoholics. *Journal of Cross-Cultural Psychology* 3:413-416.

  18 hospitalized Native American alcoholics and 21 hospitalized Anglo alcoholics were examined in order to determine the presence or absence of cultural differences. The authors conclude that no differences were found utilizing behavioral and projective tests, but "...evidence suggests that non-movement-hostile fantasy substitutes for actual aggression among Indians... and may be a contributing factor to Native American alcoholism.

A704   Rachal, J. Valley, Jay R. Williams, Mary L. Brehm, Betty Cavanaugh, R. Paul Moore and William C. Eckerman
1975 A National Study of Adolescent Drinking Behavior, Attitudes and Correlates. Available through the National Technical Information Service, PB-246 002/0GI.

Reports the results of a questionnaire administered to 13,122 high school students, including 794 Native Americans, concerning drinking practices, attitudes, and problems. Reveals that the largest proportion of heavy drinkers was found among the Native American population. Notes that Native American youths tend to drink more than any other racial/ethnic group.

0705   Raspa, G.
1973 Incidence of Emotional Disorders and/or Alcoholism by Diagnosis or Clinical Impression. Unpublished paper presented at the 8th joint meeting of the Professional Associations of the U.S. Public Health Service.

A random review of 100 medical records from a total of 5317 records indicated that 17% of the records yielded a diagnosis or clinical impression of emotional disorder and/or alcoholism. The incidence of alcoholism was almost as great as that of emotional disturbance.

0706   Rattray, Richard
1970 Comprehensive Treatment Program for Indian Problem Drinkers. Iowa, Office of the Governor, State Office of Economic Opportunity, Division of Vocational Rehabilitation Education & Services, 85p.

Report of a demonstration project in two Iowa communities which included 195 Native Americans from 17 tribes. The program provided both medical and non-medical treatment and Antabuse was utilized. Attempted to demonstrate that treatment would result in increased employment, less absenteeism, high self-esteem, and a decrease in alcohol related arrests.

0707   Reagan, Albert
1930 Notes on the Indians of the Fort Apache Region. *Anthropological Papers of the American Museum of Natural History* 31(5):281-345.

Briefly discusses the method utilized in the manufacture of tiswin (also called tulapai), a beer made from corn. Indicates that the drinking of tiswin is detrimental to the tribe, leading to indolence, fighting and immoral practices. Observes that drinking lowers resistance to disease and that deaths and illness from exposure frequently follow drinking bouts.

0708 Reasons, Charles H.
  1972 Crime and the American Indian. In *Native Americans Today: Sociological Perspectives*, H.M. Bahr, B.A. Chadwick and R.C. Day, eds. Pp. 319-326. New York: Harper and Row.

Native American arrest rates exceed that of Anglos and Blacks for alcohol-related crimes. Federal paternalism and prohibition are seen as contributing to drinking problems.

0709 Reed, T. Edward, Harold Kalant, Robert J. Gibbins, Bushan M. Kapur and James G. Rankin
  1976 Alcohol and Acetaldehyde Metabolism in Caucasians, Chinese, and Amerinds. *Canadian Medical Association Journal* 115:851-855.

Ethanol was administered by mouth to 102 volunteers, including 24 Ojibwa males. Decreasing postabsorption values differed significantly among the three groups. Habitual level of alcohol consumption, proportion of body fat, and genetic factors appear to account for most of the differences.

0710 Reese, Kenneth M.
  1975 Obstacles to the Psychological Development of American Indian Children. *Family Law Quarterly* 9:573-593.

Outlines the effects of alcoholism on families and children, as observed among the Crow and Northern Cheyenne. Some solutions are proposed.

0711** Reifel, Ben
  1963 Factors Unique to Indian Reservations That Contribute to Indian Drinking. Unpublished paper presented at the School of Alcohol Studies, University of Utah, 7p.

Identifies five factors in which Anglo and Native Americans differ and which contribute to Native American alcohol abuse: (1) orientation to the present, (2) concept of time, (3) concept of savings, (4) concept of work role, (5) sharing with relatives.

0712**   Reinhard, Karl R. and Naoma I. Greenwalt
   1974 Problem-Specific, Time Loss Impact of Disease in Southwestern American Indian Communities. Unpublished paper presented at the 102nd annual meeting of the American Public Health Association, 9p.

   Illness related to alcohol abuse is examined in terms of impact and time-loss for both urban and reservation Papago Indians. The clinical care time-loss for urban residents is consistently higher than that for reservation residents.

0713**   Reinhard, Karl R., R.S. Klappenbach, E.W. Rogg, J.W. Justice and David A. Rabin
   1975 Mortality and Morbidity Related to Alcohol Consumption in a Southwestern American Indian Population. Unpublished paper, Indian Health Service, Health Programs Center, Office of Research and Development, 48p.

   A review of death certificates and automated medical records revealed that 7.9% of all deaths in a ten-year period among the Papago were alcohol-related. Increased mortality correlated with geographic accessibility to alcohol sources.

0714**   Reinhard, Karl R., Anne L. Todd, Michael A. Madden and David A. Rabin
   1976 A Search for Correlated Diabetes Mellitus and Alcoholic Liver Disease in a Southwestern American Indian Population. Unpublished paper presented at the 11th annual meeting of the U.S. Public Health Service Professional Associations, 43p.

   Clinical reports linking diabetes and alcoholic liver disease are prevalent in the Sells Service Unit of the Indian Health Service. A review of automated medical records indicates that no correlation between the two diseases exists.

0715   Resnik, H.L.P. and Larry H. Dizmang
   1971 Observations on Suicidal Behavior among American Indians. *American Journal of Psychiatry* 127: 882-887.

   Reports that the high incidence of alcoholism is a contributing factor in Native American suicide.

0716   Rhodes, Robert J. and Lewis L. Langness
                1967 American Indian Drinking and Related Health
                Problems. Unpublished paper, University of
                Washington.

                Compares Native American drinking patterns in selected
                communities with skid road drinking in order to
                determine if the "alcoholic career" is similar for
                Native Americans and Anglos.

0717**   Richards, W. and J. Shields
                1972 Psychological Study of a Multiproblem Eskimo
                Family. Unpublished paper presented at the 7th
                joint meeting of the Clinical Society and the
                Commissioned Officers Association of the U.S.
                Public Health Service.

                Of 12 family members, 7 had severe drinking or drug
                abuse problems. Examines therapy techniques employed
                to assist the family.

0718   Riffenburgh, Arthur S.
                1964 Cultural Influences and Crime among Indian-
                Americans of the Southwest. *Federal Probation*
                28(3):38-46.

                Points out that many Native Americans must drive to
                off-reservation towns to drink, and if they become
                intoxicated often are unable to return home and are,
                therefore, arrested. Frequently this results in
                negative relations between Native Americans and Anglos,
                and supports the "drunken Indian" stereotype. As a
                result, geographic isolation has a direct effect on
                the Native American arrest rate for drunkenness.
                Riffenburgh also indicates that previous and continuing
                prohibition on many reservations results in the
                establishment of taverns at the edge of reservations
                and that many of the tavern owners take advantage of
                Native Americans.

0719   Ritzenthaler, Robert and Mary Sellers
                1955 Indians in an Urban Situation. *Wisconsin
                Archaeologist* 36:147-161.

                Reports that taverns served as primary social centers
                for many Native Americans (Oneidas, Chippewas, and
                others) in Milwaukee. Drinking behavior is examined.

0720   Robbins, Richard H.
                1970 Drinking Behavior and Identity Resolution. Ph.D.
                Dissertation, University of North Carolina, Chapel
                Hill, 195p. U.M. Order #71-03592.

An analysis of Naskapi Indian adaptation to a Western wage-earning environment. The drinking behavior of the Naskapi is viewed as a part of the adaptation, a bid for new status reinforcements to replace old status roles.

0721   Robbins, Richard H.
        1973 Alcohol and the Identity Struggle: Some Effects of Economic Change on Interpersonal Relations. *American Anthropologist* 75:99-122.

Investigates the drinking behavior of male Naskapi Indians utilizing the hypothesis that "...Naskapi drinking interactions serve as a locus of interpersonal conflict which stems from recent changes in their economic life..." Robbins concludes that economic aid programs may prove detrimental rather than beneficial as they change the means of access to goods and activities necessary for identity maintenance.

0722   Robertson, G.G. and Michael Baizerman
        1969 Psychiatric Consultation on Two Indian Reservations. *Hospital and Community Psychiatry* 20(6):186-

A follow-up report on the work done by Stage and Keast (1966) which attempted to develop psychiatric services for the Crow and Northern Cheyenne of Montana. Locating treatment, referral, and aftercare facilities for alcoholics proved especially difficult.

0723   Robertson, Heather
        1970 *Reservations Are for Indians*. Toronto: James Lorimer.

A stark and grim look at life on four Canadian Indian Reserves in Manitoba. The role and effects of liquor are described. The "drink-in" is postulated as a means of maintaining identity and gaining attention and recognition from Anglos.

0724   Robinson, Doane
        1918 The War on Whiskey in the Fur Trade. *South Dakota Historical Collections* 9:169-233.

Efforts to curtail the use of liquor in order to promote the fur trade among Native Americans are reviewed in a series of letters taken from the records of the Indian Agent at Fort Pierre. The documents indicate that "...the prevention of the use of strong drink has...been considered the one thing needed to insure the prosperity of the Indian race and its advancement in civilization."

0725   Robinson, Shirley
            1974 Self-Help Programs for Indians and Alaskan
            Natives. *Alcohol Health and Research World* 1974
            (summer):11-16.

            Reviews the programs which the National Institute
            on Alcohol Abuse and Alcoholism has promoted among
            Native Americans and Alaskan Natives. Notes that
            the NIAAA is committed to developing appropriate
            alcoholism services for Native Americans and that
            the NIAAA encourages Native American involvement in
            planning and implementation of programs. Describes
            model programs.

0726   Rohner, Ronald P. and Evelyn C. Rohner
            1970 *The Kwakiutl: Indians of British Columbia*.
            New York: Holt, Rinehart, and Winston.

            Indicates that drinking is widespread and a popular
            pastime, and that individuals drink until they pass
            out. Intoxication enables people to express their
            latent anger, either verbally or through fighting.

0727   Romance, G.L.
            1971 A Too Distant Drum: An Experience in Indian
            Health Alcoholism Programming. Unpublished paper
            presented at the 6th joint Meeting of the Clinical
            Society and the Commissioned Officers Association
            of the U.S. Public Health Service.

            Recounts the author's experience in attempting to
            establish a meeting of patients, helpers, and former
            problem drinkers. Suggests that programs are doomed
            to fail unless the community itself perceives a need
            for alcoholism programs.

0728   Ross, John Alan
            1968 Political Conflict on the Colville Reservation.
            Northwest Anthropological Research Notes 2:29-91.

            Indicates that several trappers refused to let their
            men supply liquor to Native Americans because of the
            deleterious effects of the liquor trade on Native
            Americans and the resulting effects on the fur trade.

0729   Ross, W.G.
            1975 Whaling and Eskimos: Hudson Bay 1860-1915.
            National Museum of Man Publications in Ethnology
            10:119-124.

The use of alcohol is cited as a factor in the deterioration of the physical and mental health of Western Arctic Eskimos. It seems unlikely that whalers contributed in any major way to the provision of alcohol to Eskimos, as whalers did not carry enough alcohol to produce the observed deterioration from drinking. Suggests that traders and trappers may have introduced alcohol in quantity to the Arctic.

0730   Rotman, Arthur Edel
1969 Navaho Indian Problem Drinking: An Analysis of Five Life Histories. MA Thesis, San Francisco State University, 430p.

Phenomenological life experiences coupled with social relationships may precipitate uncontrolled drinking if negative encounters prevent personal gratification. A key to Navajo alcohol abuse may be found in the interrelationship of culture change to social and psychological imperatives. Alcohol is used to temporarily relieve the stress engendered by acculturation.

0731   Rousseau, Victor
1910 Pussyfoot...a Word of Warning to Illicit Whiskey Sellers in the West. *Harper's Weekly* 54:8-9, February 26.

An account of the activities of William Eugene "Pussyfoot" Johnson, a special government agent whose job was to prevent the illicit whiskey trade conducted in Indian territory.

0732   Roy, Chunilal
1969 A Preliminary Inquiry into the Nature of Mental Illness amongst the Canadian Indians of Saskatchewan. *Transcultural Psychiatric Research Review* 6:83-85.

Report on preliminary findings of the characteristics of mental disorder among the Cree Indians. No significant differences were found between Native Americans and non-Native Americans in the incidence of alcoholism.

0733   Roy, Chunilal
1973 Indian Peyotists and Alcohol. *American Journal of Psychiatry* 130:329-330.

In response to an article by Bergman (1971) Roy indicates in a letter to the editor that a strong correlation between peyote use and sobriety seemed to exist and should be investigated.

0734   Roy, Chunilal, Adjit Choudhuri and Donald Irvine
         1970 The Prevalence of Mental Disorders among
            Saskatchewan Indians. *Journal of Cross-Cultural
            Psychology* 1:383-392.

         The authors found the usual definition of alcoholism
         of little use in identifying cases of alcoholism
         among Cree and Saulteaux Indians. They report that
         all Native Americans who once drank heavily, but
         have stopped, belong to the Peyote Cult.

0735   Rude, Douglas H.
         1970 Glue and Paint Sniffing in an Indian Community.
            Unpublished paper presented at the 5th joint meeting
            of the Clinical Society and the Commissioned Officers
            Association of the U.S. Public Health Service.

         Indicates that sniffing is often combined with alcohol
         abuse.

0736   Safford, W.E.
         1917 Narcotic Plants and Stimulants of the Ancient
            Americans. In *Annual Report of the Smithsonian
            Institution, 1916.* Washington, D.C.: Government
            Printing Office (SUDOCS #SI 1.1:1916).

         Describes the ceremonial use of the "Black Drink" of
         the Carolinas and Florida. Indicates that the
         Cultachiches and Catawaba Indians are noted for
         making use of the intoxicating Black Drink.

0737   Salone, Emile
         1904 Les Sauvages du Canada et les Malades Importeés
            de France au XVIII Siecle: La Pictoe et L'Alcoolisme.
            Journal de la Societe des Americanistes 4:1-17.

         According to 17th century sources the sole purpose of
         drinking among Native Americans was to get as drunk
         as possible for as long as possible. Missionaries
         attempted to restrain the traffic in alcohol; however,
         it soon became clear that alcohol could be obtained
         from the Dutch as well as the French. The question
         was not would Native Americans drink, but rather would
         they drink Dutch or French liquor? The paper is an
         historical account of the effects of alcohol and the
         steps taken to curb the liquor trade.

0738   Saltonstall, Richard, Jr.
         1977 Drums along the Penobscot. *Blair and Ketchum's
            Country Journal* 4(8):32-39.

Alcoholism is a grave problem among Native Americans of Maine. Alcohol abuse is attributed to severe isolation, lack of cultural identity, and drinking patterns learned from Anglos.

0739 Sanchez, Paul R.
  1967 Nature of the Alcoholism Problem. *Lectures and Notes, 1967 Manual Supplement.* Salt Lake City: School of Alcohol Studies, University of Utah.

Historical evidence suggests that the root of Native American alcoholism can be found in the lack of familiarity with alcoholic beverages. Contemporary drinking experience is divided into three periods: (1) the impact period, 16th to 18th centuries, (2) the prohibition period, 1830-1950, and (3) the recreation period, 1950 to the present. The characteristic drinking pattern of each period is examined. The Native American problem drinker is a "binge drinker" with few Native Americans truly addicted to alcohol.

0740** Sanford, Nevitt
  1967 Recent Thoughts and Research Relevant to Health Education. Unpublished paper presented to the Workshop for Field Training Supervisors, School of Public Health, University of California, Berkeley, 13p.

A review of Native American alcohol use and abuse with some observations concerning the relevance of education in dealing with alcohol problems. Three groups of drinkers are identified: escapist, facilitative, and integrative. The Pueblo Indians (no tribe specified) are cited as an example of escapist drinking, while the Hopi are cited as an example of integrative abstinence in the sense that the Hopi declared their reservation dry because Anglos were known to drink.

0741 Saslow, Harry L. and May J. Harrover
  1968 Research on Psychosocial Adjustment of Indian Youth. *American Journal of Psychiatry* 125:224-231.

The school experiences of Native American children accentuate rather than resolve identity problems, with the result that Native American students exhibit increased behavioral and disciplinary problems. Indicates that the urban Native American seems to lack community stability, which precipitates abusive drinking behavior.

0742   Saum, Lewis O.
        1965 *The Fur Trader and the Indian*. Seattle: University
        of Washington Press.

        Comments on the role of liquor in the fur trade and
        recounts traders' observations concerning Native
        Americans and liquor.

0743** Savard, Robert J.
        1965 The Use of Dilsulfiram in Treatment of Alcohol
        Problems in an American Indian Population. Un-
        published paper presented at the School of Alcohol
        Studies, University of Utah.

        Discusses a preliminary study conducted at the Fort
        Defiance Indian Hospital in which dilsulfiram was
        used to help problem drinkers break the alcoholic
        cycle.

0744   Savard, Robert J.
        1968a Cultural Stress and Alcoholism: a Study of
        Their Relationships among Navajo Alcoholic Men.
        Ph.D. Dissertation, University of Minnesota, 214p.
        U.M. Order #69-1532.

        Explores the hypothesis that alcoholic Navajos are
        less able to express anger and to enter into uncon-
        strained social relationships than are non-alcoholics,
        and that alcoholic men will report that they are better
        able to express anger when intoxicated. Savard
        examines various reported reasons for drinking among
        the Navajo, as well as patterns of drinking and comments
        on the effects of prohibition on the reservation.

0745   Savard, Robert J.
        1968b Effects of Disulfiram Therapy on Relationships
        within the Navajo Drinking Group. *Quarterly Journal
        of Studies on Alcohol* 29:909-916.

        A report on a follow-up of 30 Navajo patients in the
        Fort Defiance Disulfiram Treatment Program. While
        many of the patients managed to avoid returning to
        binge drinking, few found other recreational outlets
        aside from the drinking peer group. However, obser-
        vation and interviews indicated that the drinking
        peer group would accept the explanation of "I'm on
        the pill" as determined abstinence and would not
        pressure the individual to resume drinking. For the
        study group a success rate of 75% is reported.

0746** Savard, Robert J.
1970 The Navajo Alcoholic: a Man Yearning for Social Competence. Unpublished paper, U.S. Public Health Service, Navajo Area Mental Health Division, 13p.

A summary of the author's dissertation (1968, citation #0744), discussing the hypothesis that Navajo males are more likely to be alcoholic if they cannot express anger or talk easily with other people.

0747 Savishinsky, Joel S.
1970 Stress and Mobility in an Arctic Community: The Hare Indians of Colville Lake, Northwest Territories. Ph.D. Dissertation, Cornell University, 646p. U.M. Order #70-12648.

An ethnographic account of the yearly cycle in the life of the Colville Lake Hare Indians in which factors both precipitating and mitigating stress are examined. Drinking is a major focus of the investigation because of the sociological significance and because of the emotional release which accompanies drinking. Drinking behavior is examined and the effect of drinking on inter-family relations is detailed. While drinking is a source of stress and friction, it also enhances the sociality of many village events.

0748 Savishinsky, Joel S.
1971 Mobility as an Aspect of Stress in an Arctic Community. *American Anthropologist* 73:604-618.

The use of aggression as a means of relieving stress is almost entirely restricted to periods of heavy drinking. Population mobility is a major factor in the control and release of stress.

0749 Savishinsky, Joel S. and S.B. Frimmer
1973 The Middle Ground: Social Change in an Arctic Community, 1967-1971. *National Museum of Man, National Museums of Canada, Ethnology Division Paper #7*.

Drinking provided a release from stress which would otherwise be repressed and the cultural view of drinking was that it excused people from responsibility for their actions. However, drinking also caused disruptive and abusive encounters between people which generated conflict and tension.

0750**   Schaefer, James M.
               1978   Alcohol Metabolism and Sensitivity Reactions
               among the Hindu Reddis of South India.
               Alcoholism: Clinical and Experimental Research
               2:61-69.

               While this study focuses on the metabolic reactions
               to alcohol among Hindus, it contrasts their reactions
               to data collected on Occidentals, Orientals, and Native
               Americans (specifically Eskimos and Ojibwas).

0751   Schaefer, Otto
               1962   Alcohol Withdrawal Syndrome in a Newborn Infant
               of a Yukon Indian Mother. *Canadian Medical Association
               Journal* 87:1333-1334.

               A case history is presented in which a newborn Native
               American infant displays withdrawal symptoms for
               5-6 days after his birth. The child, born with signs
               of alcohol intoxication to an alcoholic mother, was
               apparently normal in development following his with-
               drawal and subsequent placement in a foster home.

0752   Schaefer, Otto
               1975   Eskimo Personality and Society - Yesterday and
               Today. *Arctic* 28(2):87-91.

               Alcohol is noted as a contributing factor in the
               disintegration of the family. Drinking is believed
               to be particularly devastating to males, leading
               to violence, aggression, and suicide.

0753   Schmeiser, Douglas A.
               1968   Indians, Eskimos and the Law. *Saskatchewan Law
               Review* 33(1):19-40.

               Examines the difficulties and injustices associated
               with trying to apply a complex legal system to people
               living under primitive and harsh conditions and who
               utilize traditional codes to guide their behavior.
               Liquor is cited as a major problem, especially for
               Native Americans in the Yukon and Northwest Territories.

0754   Schmitt, N., L.W. Hole and W.S. Barclay
               1966   Accidental Deaths among British Columbia Indians.
               Canadian Medical Association Journal 94:228-234.

               A review of Native American fatalities during the three
               year period, 1961-1963 revealed that accidents were the
               leading cause of death among Native Americans, but ranked
               only fourth among non-Native Americans. Socioeconomic,

psychosocial, environmental factors and excessive drinking are thought to be the cause of the high rate of accidental deaths.

0755** Schnell, Jerome V.
1977 The Flushing Reaction to Alcohol and Patterns of Alcoholism. Unpublished paper, ALC 406, Alcohol Studies Program, Seattle University, 8p.

Reviews the current research regarding the alcohol flushing reaction in Asians and Native Americans and concludes that one cannot predict drinking behavior on the basis of physiological sensitivities to alcohol.

0756 Schoenfeld, Lawrence S. and Sheldon I. Miller
1973 The Navajo Indian: A Descriptive Study of the Psychiatric Population. *International Journal of Social Psychiatry* 19:31-37.

A descriptive study of 348 cases which were brought to the attention of mental health professionals working with the Navajos. Only 9 of the 348 received a primary diagnosis of alcoholism, a surprisingly small number given the fact that alcohol abuse is a widely acknowledged problem among the Navajo. The authors discuss possible reasons for the low diagnosis of alcoholism.

0757 Schusky, Ernest Lester
1975 *The Forgotten Sioux: an Ethnohistory of the Lower Brule Reservation.* Chicago: Nelson-Hall.

Liquor is only briefly discussed (p. 182, 216, 225) in terms of its effect on law enforcement in the 1920s and as an issue to be debated in tribal council meetings concerning whether taverns should be opened on the reservation.

0758 Scomp, Henry A.
1888 *King Alcohol in the Realm of King Cotton.* Chicago: Blakeley.

Includes a section which discusses the use of liquor among the Native Americans of South Carolina. The Creeks are reported to have manufactured a mildly intoxicating drink; however, the Creeks were sober until the introduction of liquor by Anglos. Examines the role of liquor in trade and attempts to promote temperance.

0759   Scott, Woodrow W.
          1954 Recorded Inebriacy in Wisconsin: An Analysis of
          Arrested Inebriates in Two Wisconsin Counties.
          Sociological and Social Research 39:96-102.

          This study reveals that in one county Native Americans
          were arrested 17 times more often per capita than any
          other group.

0760   Sears, William F.
          1967 Community Treatment Approach for Alcoholism.
          In *Alcoholism: Behavioral Research, Therapeutic
          Approaches* R. Fox, ed. Pp. 179-185. New York:
          Springer.

          The author describes a community treatment format
          based on the Gallup project and the interactions
          required on the part of staff members in order to
          produce an effective alcoholism treatment program.

0761** Sears, William F. and Eugene L. Mariani
          1964 Community Treatment Plan for Navajo Problem
          Drinkers. Unpublished report prepared by the
          McKinley County Family Consultation Service, Inc.
          for the National Institute of Mental Health, 26p.

          A review of the Gallup project, detailing methodology,
          client selection, staffing, treatment, and follow-up
          of the patients. The role of anthropologists is
          discussed and some tentative hypotheses concerning
          Navajo drinking are explored. Results of the project
          are presented in detail by Ferguson (1966, 1968, 1970,
          1972, 1976).

0762   Sells, Cato
          1914 The Greatest Present Menace to the American Indian.
          The Red Man 6(7):249.

          Sells indicates that whiskey is the greatest menace
          to Native Americans and that not until the Indian is
          sober can he take the "long step" toward citizenship.

0763** Sharplin, C.D.
          1964 The Indian Alcoholic: His Social Characteristics.
          Unpublished report, The Alcoholism Foundation of
          Alberta.

          An investigation of Native American alcoholics which
          seeks to clarify their perceptions of alcohol as
          related to (1) value conflicts, (2) personal and group
          deviance, and (3) social disorganization. Characteristics

of Native American alcoholics are summarized by residence, occupation, income, mobility, and social class.

0764   Sherwin, Duane and Beverly Mead
1975   Delirium Tremens in a Nine Year Old Child. *American Journal of Psychiatry* 132:1210-1212.

Reports the case of a nine year old boy, presumed to be Navajo, who was seen in a small northern New Mexico hospital. Upon admission the boy was found to be suffering from delirium tremens. It was determined that he had probably been drinking steadily (i.e. daily) since the age of six.

0765   Sherwood, Morgan B.
1965   Ardent Spirits: Hooch and the Osprey Affair at Sitka. *Journal of the West* 4:301-344.

Describes the introduction of alcohol to the Tlingit Indians and attempts to prohibit the liquor trade by U.S. officials. Europeans in Sitka and other southern Alaskan communities provided models of drinking behavior which Native Americans emulated. Whiskey became a generic term for all liquor; however, as importation of alcoholic beverages became increasingly difficult, due to U.S. imposed prohibition, the Tlingit turned to the manufacture of "hoochinoo" from which the word "hooch" is derived.

0766   Shimpo, M. and R. Williamson
1965   *Sociocultural Disintegration among the Fringe Saulteaux*. Saskatoon, Saskatchewan: Centre for Community Studies, University of Saskatchewan, Extension Division, Extension Publication 193.

Native American drinking is considered a symptom of a deep seated and complicated social pathology. Problem drinking is derived from (1) social and economic deprivation and isolation, (2) absence of adequate opportunities for constructive self-expression, and (3) social disorientation.

0767   Shore, James H.
1972   Suicide and Suicide Attempts among American Indians of the Pacific Northwest. *International Journal of Social Psychiatry* 18(2):91-96.

Reports that alcohol is often associated with suicide and suicide attempts.

0768   Shore, James H.
            1974 Psychiatric Epidemiology among American Indians.
            Psychiatric Annals 4(11):56-66.

            Notes that alcohol stands out as a major problem among
            Native Americans. However, many Native Americans do
            not define it as an illness and do not feel that
            psychiatric intervention is appropriate. The use of
            Native American counselors is crucial in any alcoholism
            program. Notes that misunderstandings brought about
            by cultural differences and negative stereotypes have
            contributed to false impressions concerning Native
            American mental health problems.

0769   Shore, James H.
            1975 American Indian Suicide - Fact and Fantasy.
            Psychiatry 38:86-91.

            Examines suicide patterns among coastal, plateau
            and intermountain tribes and indicates that alcohol
            is very often associated with suicide and suicide
            attempts.

0770**   Shore, James H., John F. Bopp, Thelma R. Waller and
            J.W. Dawes
                n.d. Suicide Prevention Center on an Indian Reser-
                    vation. Report of the Mental Health and
                    Social Services Office, Portland Area Indian Health
                    Service, 16p.

            A report on the steps taken to establish a suicide
            prevention center on a reservation with an exces-
            sively high suicide rate among adolescents. 75%
            of all admissions to a holding center for suicide
            threats or attempts were related to alcohol and/or
            inhalant abuse.

0771   Shore, James H., John F. Bopp, Thelma R. Waller and
            J.W. Dawes
                1972 A Suicide Prevention Center on an Indian Reser-
                    vation. *American Journal of Psychiatry* 128:1086-1091.

            Examines the background and development of a suicide
            prevention center on a reservation with a high suicide
            rate. Alcohol and inhalant sniffing were associated
            with most of the completed suicides.

0772   Shore, James H., J.D. Kinzie, J.L. Hampson and E.M.
            Pattison
                1973 Psychiatric Epidemiology of an Indian Village.
                Psychiatry 36(2):70-81.

Examination of a Makah Indian village indicates that alcoholism represented the major psychiatric problem.

0773   Shore, James H. and Dennis L. Stone
1973 Duodenal Ulcer among Northwest Coastal Indian Women. *American Journal of Psychiatry* 130:774-777.

Makah Indian women were found to have a high rate of duodenal ulcers, about four times the rate of non-Native American women. Differences in psychiatric and psychophysiologic disorders are manifest in higher rates of alcoholism and peptic ulcers.

0774   Shore, James H. and Billee von Fumetti
1972 Three Alcohol Programs for American Indians. *American Journal of Psychiatry* 128:1450-1454.

Three tribally sponsored alcohol rehabilitation programs are briefly reviewed against an overview of theories on Native American drinking behavior and previous treatment approaches. The three programs include: (1) the Ute Tribal program, (2) the Jicarilla Apache program, and (3) the Nevada Inter-Tribal Council program. Each has developed a treatment approach and philosophy compatible with the values of the community in which the program is located.

0775   Siegel, Bernard J.
1967 Suggested Factors of Culture Change at Taos Pueblo. In *Acculturation in the Americas: Proceedings and Selected Papers of the 29th International Congress of Americanists*, Sol Tax, ed. Pp. 133-140. New York: Cooper Square Publishers.

The mounting frustration felt by young Native Americans is often relieved by verbal aggression and/or intoxication. An alternative to drinking is the Peyote Cult.

0776   Sievers, Maurice L.
1966 Disease Patterns among Southwestern Indians. *Public Health Reports* 81:1075-1082.

Notes that alcoholism constitutes a major health problem among Native Americans.

0777   Sievers, Maurice L.
1968 Cigarette Smoking and Alcohol Usage by Southwestern American Indians. *American Journal of Public Health* 58:71-78.

An observation that lung cancer seldom occurs among southwestern Native Americans, while cirrhosis of the liver is widespread led to a study of cigarette and alcohol use. The hypothesis was confirmed that cigarette smoking is infrequent while consumption of alcohol is prevalent.

0778 Sievers, Maurice L.
  1973a Comparative Frequency of Gastric Carcinoma, Pernicious Anemia, and Peptic Ulcer in Southwestern American Indians. Paper presented at the 8th joint meeting of the Professional Associations of the U.S. Public Health Service.

Discusses the prevalence of gastric carcinoma, pernicious anemia, and peptic ulcer among southwestern Native Americans and compares their experience with that of Anglos. Excessive alcohol consumption was one of the characteristics of the Native American population. See also citation #0779.

0779 Sievers, Maurice L.
  1973b Unusual Comparative Frequency of Gastric Carcinoma, Pernicious Anemia, and Peptic Ulcer in Southwestern American Indians. *Gastroenterology* 65:867-876.

Compares the incidence of gastric carcinoma, pernicious anemia, and peptic ulcer in Native Americans to that of the general population. Rates for gastric carcinoma and pernicious anemia among Native Americans are similar to that of the general population; however, rates for peptic and gastric ulcers show a marked reduction. Except for the predominance of the blood group "O", southwestern Native Americans share general characteristics infrequently associated with ulcers, such as noncompetitiveness, rural residence, excessive alcohol use.

0780 Sievers, Maurice L.
  1976 Peptic Ulcer Factors in American Indians. *Annals of Internal Medicine* 84:755-756.

A letter to the editor in which the author reviews factors common to rural reservation residence which may contribute to the infrequent incidence of peptic ulcer and the moderate incidence of gastric carcinoma and pernicious anemia. Excessive consumption of alcohol is listed as one of the factors commonly observed.

0781   Sinclair, J. Grant
       1970   The Queen vs. Drybones: The Supreme Court of
       Canada and the Canadian Bill of Rights. *Osgoode
       Hall Law Journal* 8:599-619.

       Discussion of a case in which the Canadian Indian
       Act conflicted with the Canadian Bill of Rights.
       The author suggests that the Bill of Rights should
       be applied to all citizens equally, regardless of
       race.

0782   Skelley, Thomas and Gregory March
       1971   Rehabilitating the Alcoholic. *Rehabilitation
       Record* 12(5):23-24.

       Report on the Rehabilitation Services Administration
       grants to state agencies for the purpose of providing
       new financial resources to break the alcoholic cycle.
       Among programs cited as funded by the RSA is the
       community project initiated by the Gila River Indian
       community at Sacaton, Arizona. The program seeks to
       provide vocational rehabilitation for Pima Indian
       alcoholics. Program services were designed to be
       integrated into larger tribal goals of developing
       a skilled, fully employed work force and a wider
       economic base for the tribe.

0783   Skirrow, Jan
       1971   *The North American Indian and Alcohol: A
       Bibliography.* Edmonton: The Alberta Alcoholism
       and Drug Abuse Commission.

       A compilation of 120 citations deemed to make a
       significant contribution to the literature dealing
       with Native American alcohol use.

0784** Slater, Arthur D.
       n.d.   Procedures for Helping the Indian Problem
       Drinker. Unpublished paper prepared for the Western
       Region Indian Alcoholism Training Center, University
       of Utah, 7p.

       Examines the role available for non-professionals in
       assisting problem drinkers toward sobriety. Would-be
       helpers are encouraged to conduct a personal assessment
       regarding attitudes, patience, and understanding.
       Indicates that non-professionals can make significant
       contributions in their home communities with the right
       training.

0785**   Slater, Arthur D.
1967 A Study of Attitudes towards the Use of Alcoholic Beverages Found among the Ute Indians. Unpublished report for the Committee on Indian Studies, Brigham Young University, 11p.

Reports the results of a survey conducted on the Uintah-Ouray Reservation. Findings indicate that drinkers viewed alcohol as an escape from boredom, while non-drinkers indicated that drinking was a denial of responsibility. Of the drinkers, 53% reported that they would stop drinking if they knew how to do so. However, many people perceived drinking as a right to be exercised.

0786**   Slater, Arthur D.
1971 Which Step Are You on? Unpublished paper prepared for the Western Region Indian Alcoholism Training Center, University of Utah, 9p.

Outlines eight steps which the average Native American problem drinker is believed to pass through. Questions are posed and symptoms presented in order to assist individuals in determining which step one is on. Possible solutions to the alcohol problem are also summarized.

0787   Slater, Arthur D. and Stan L. Albrecht
1972 The Extent and Costs of Excessive Drinking among the Uintah-Ouray Indians. In *Native Americans Today: Sociological Perspective*, Howard M. Bahr, Bruce A. Chadwick and Robert C. Day, eds. Pp. 358-367. New York: Harper and Row.

Provides estimates of the cost of excessive drinking to the tribe, the individual, and the agencies involved. Factors contributing to problem drinking include lack of employment opportunities, poor education, and discrimination in hiring practices.

0788   Sloan, Mary Ellen
1973 Indians in an Urban Setting: Salt Lake County, Utah. *University of Utah, American West Center, Occasional Paper #2*.

Indicates that drunkenness accounts for 70% of all Native American arrests in Salt Lake City. Two programs have been developed to deal with Native American alcohol problems; however Native American acceptance has been minimal. Mentions the Western Region Indian Alcoholism Training Center and the American Indian Commission on Alcoholism and Drugs.

0789   Slotkin, J.S.
         1953 Social Psychiatry of a Menomini Community.
         Journal of Abnormal and Social Psychology 48:10-16.

         Violation of tribal mores is accomplished through
         witchcraft, gossip, and drinking. Alcohol is reported
         to release inhibitions and lead to irresponsible,
         boisterous, and quarrelsome behavior.

0790   Smith, Anne M.
         1966 New Mexico Indians. Santa Fe: Museum of
         New Mexico.

         A report prepared for the New Mexico State Planning
         Office which examines New Mexico's Native Americans.
         Topics covered include population trends, education,
         federal aid, and social problems. The report notes
         that alcohol abuse exists among both the Pueblo and
         Apache, but that the "...percentage of alcoholics is
         probably no higher than in the general population..."
         The report also indicates that there has been in-
         sufficient study of drinking among Native Americans
         in New Mexico.

0791   Smith, David W., Kenneth L. Jones and James W. Hanson
         1976 Perspectives on the Cause and Frequency of the
         Fetal Alcohol Syndrome. *Annals of the New York
         Academy of Sciences* 273:138-139.

         The frequency of the Fetal Alcohol Syndrome (FAS)
         would be expected to vary in accordance with the
         incidence of chronic alcoholism in women of repro-
         ductive age. In the Pacific Northwest a dispropor-
         tionately high number of babies with FAS are born
         to Native American women, and this is a reflection
         of the frequency of chronic alcoholism among women
         in this ethnic group.

0792   Smith, Derek G.
         1975 *Natives and Outsiders: Pluralism in the Mackenzie
         River Delta, Northwest Territories.* Ottawa:
         Northern Research Division, Department of Indian
         Affairs and Northern Development, publication
         #QS-8032-000-EE-A1 Mackenzie Delta Research Project,
         vol. 12 (also Information Canada Catalog #R72-142/1975).

         Describes the manufacture of home brew and reports
         that it is a "poor man's drink." Mentions that com-
         mercial beer is preferred over wine and distilled
         liquor. Notes that Native Americans often obtain
         alcohol from products such as vanilla extract, shaving

lotion, hair spray. Provides a detailed description of drinking behavior patterns and discusses five motives for drinking. Reports that Natives and Eskimos are often overrepresented, relative to Anglos and Metis, in arrests for offenses related to liquor.

0793   Smith, J.C.
       1971 Regina vs. Drybones and Equality before the Law. *Canadian Bar Review* 49:163-187.

       Discusses the conflict between the Canadian Bill of Rights and the Indian Act which was brought to light by the Drybones case. Indicates that legislation which discriminates should be eliminated. Examines the meaning of equality before the law.

0794   Smith, Valene Lucy
       1966 Kotzebue: A Modern Alaskan Eskimo Community. Ph.D. Dissertation, University of Utah, 170p. U.M. Order #66-09398.

       Reports that excessive drinking is believed to be the single most disruptive element in Kotzebue. Drinking exacerbates many social ills, such as divorce, child abuse and neglect, homicide, suicide. Most criminal offenses are alcohol-related.

0795   Smith, Valene Lucy
       1970 The Self-Perception of the Alaskan Native. In *Science in Alaska. Proceedings of the 20th Alaska Science Conference*, Eleanor C. Viereck, ed. Pp. 134-143. College, Alaska: Alaska Division, American Association for the Advancement of Science.

       Unequipped to deal with the outside world, the Alaskan Native follows a dismal pattern of job instability, drinking, and eventual return home. Boredom contributes to excessive drinking.

0796   Smith, William W.
       1862 Canadian Temperance and Emigration. In *Proceedings of the International Temperance and Prohibition Convention, London, 2-4 September, 1862*, J.C. Street, F.R. Lees and D. Burns, eds. Machester, England: United Kingdom Alliance.

       Indicates that the consumption of alcohol by Native Americans leads to noisy and untrustworthy behavior. Missionary efforts are seen as a solution to the evils of alcohol.

0797   Snyder, Peter Zane
         1968 The Social Assimilation and Adjustment of
         Navaho Indian Migrants to Denver, Colorado. Ph.D.
         Dissertation, University of Colorado, 230p. U.M.
         Order #68-12427.

         Describes drinking behavior and reports that migration
         and adjustment to an urban environment contributes
         to drinking and alcohol-related problems, but is
         not necessarily maladaptive behavior.

0798   Snyderman, George S.
         1949 The Case of Daniel P.: An Example of Seneca
         Healing. *Journal of the Washington Academy of
         Sciences* 39(7):217-220.

         Indicates that alcoholism and drunkenness is attributed
         to witchcraft among the Seneca.

0799** Soler, Janice
         1977 Alaskan Natives, Ethnicity and Alcohol: Alcohol
         Worker's Perspective. Unpublished paper prepared
         for ALC 406, the Alcohol Studies Program, Seattle
         University, 12p.

         Proposes the development of culturally and racially
         sensitive educational programs for workers who must
         deal with Alaskan Native drinking problems. The
         importance of considering Native attitudes toward
         drinking and alcohol is stressed.

0800   Sorkin, Alan L.
         1971 *American Indians and Federal Aid*. Washington,
         D.C.: The Brookings Institution.

         Alcoholism is cited as one of the three major health
         problems and it is recommended that the government
         provide additional funds for research and treatment.
         Discusses the devastating effects of alcohol on man-
         power training programs.

0801   Spaulding, Philip
         1967 The Social Integration of a Northern Community:
         White Mythology and Metis Reality. In *A Northern
         Dilemma: Reference Papers*, Arthur K. Davis, ed.
         Vol. 2. Pp. 90-111. Bellingham: Western Washington
         State College.

         Various contemporary and historic elements involved
         in Metis integration into the modern world are dis-
         cussed. Integration is accomplished largely through

opposition to Anglos, as well as kinship-based internal organization. The high incidence of activities which violate the standards of the larger society, such as alcohol abuse, are not seen as evidence of social disintegration, but rather as a major integrating factor.

0802   Spence, R.E.
1919 *Prohibition in Canada*. Toronto: Ontario Branch of the Dominion Alliance.

In a chapter entitled "Early History: the French Regime," Spence suggests that governmental prohibition of human vice is impossible. Cites the inability of the French and British to regulate liquor trade with the Native Americans of Canada.

0803   Spindler, George D. and Louise S. Spindler
1957 American Indian Personality Types and Their Sociocultural Roots. *Annals of the American Academy of Political and Social Science* 311:147-157.

The penchant for alcohol among the Tuscarora is seen as an "oral" trait and serves to counteract Anglo "anal-reactive" traits such as the accumulation of property. Abuse of alcohol is seen as a transitional behavior and a result of loss of traditional controls.

0804   Spradley, James Philip
1970 *You Owe Yourself a Drunk: An Ethnography of Urban Nomads*. Boston: Little, Brown.

An in-depth portrait of life on America's skid rows, drawn from interviews with the inhabitants of Seattle's Skid Road. Many of Seattle's Indians populate Skid Road, and are frequently arrested for drunkenness, whether they are intoxicated or not. Police attitudes concerning Native Americans and other urban nomads are detailed, as well as treatment received at the hands of the police.

0805   Staats, Elmer B.
1974 *Progress and Problems in Providing Health Services to Indians*. Report to the Congress, Government Accounting Office. Washington, D.C.: Government Printing Office (to be found under U.S. General Accounting Office).

A review of Indian Health Service management of Native American alcohol problems. Although the IHS claims a leadership role and technical support for the resolution of alcohol problems the GAO finds that the IHS only treats alcoholics, while the majority of preventive program funds come from the Office of Economic Opportunity and the National Institute of Alcohol Abuse and Alcoholism. IHS reporting is found to be incomplete and manpower is lacking to adequately deal with the problem.

0806   Staats, Howard E.
        1964 Some Aspects of the Legal Status of Canadian Indians. *Osgoode Hall Law Journal* 3:36-51.

Many laws, such as the liquor provisions, were passed for the protection of Native Americans who were considered incapable of managing their own affairs. Numerous Native American liquor cases are noted. Recommends that laws affecting Native Americans be repealed except where repeal would clearly be detrimental to Native Americans. Suggests that liquor laws serve to breed contempt and disrespect for the law.

0807   Stage, Thomas B. and Thomas J. Keast
        1966 A Psychiatric Service for Plains Indians. *Hospital and Community Psychiatry* 17(3):74-76.

Although alcoholism was prevalent, few alcoholic patients were referred to a psychiatric service. Suggests that Native Americans regard alcoholism as more of a social than a psychiatric problem and something to be handled by the police, courts, and A.A. The community tolerated alcoholism and other forms of mental illness to a greater extent than Anglo communities.

0808   Stanbury, W.T.
        1975 *Success and Failure: Indians in Urban Society.* Vancouver: University of British Columbia Press.

Indicates, in a chapter titled "The State of Indian Health: a Statistical Profile," that alcohol abuse is a major problem among Native Americans of British Columbia and a significant factor in accidental death and injury. Finds that 66% of all Native American accident fatalities were alcohol-related, 83% of all suicides were intoxicated, as were 100% of all homicides.

0809   Stands-in-Timber, John and Margot Liberty
        1967 *Cheyenne Memories.* New Haven: Yale University Press.

Mentions that whiskey and wine caused many problems for Native Americans. Various incidents related to the use of liquor are noted.

0810 Stauss, Joseph H., Gary F. Jensen and V. William Harris
   1977 Crime, Delinquency, and the American Indian. *Human Organization* 36:252-257.

Native Americans have the highest arrest rate of any ethnic group in the country and a majority of the arrests are for alcohol-related offenses. Behavior of students at boarding schools was examined in order to determine relationships between drinking and rule violations. Results appear to run counter to the traditional "disorganization" explanation of Native American drinking.

A810 Stein, Gary C.
   1974 A Fearful Drunkenness: The Liquor Trade to the Western Indians as Seen by European Travellers in America, 1800-1860. *Red River Valley Historical Review* 1:109-121.

Many European travellers to the United States commented in detail on the liquor trade among Native Americans. The European account decried the debasement of Native Americans which resulted from the liquor trade. Many Europeans castigated the federal government for failure to end the liquor trade. Numerous historical accounts are cited.

0811 Steiner, Stanley
   1968 *The New Indians*. New York: Dell.

Alcohol is mentioned as a destructive force in Native American society and examples are presented.

0812 Stevens, Joyce Ann
   1969 Social and Cultural Factors Related to Drinking Patterns among the Blackfeet. MA Thesis, University of Montana, 87p.

Formulates several hypotheses regarding the extent and form of sociocultural influence upon Blackfeet drinking behavior. Examines historic as well as contemporary data.

0813 Stevenson, D.S.
   1968 *Problems of Eskimo Relocation for Industrial Employment: a Preliminary Study*. Ottawa: Northern Science Research Group, Department of Indian Affairs and Northern Development.

Provides observations on Eskimo drinking behavior. Reports that excessive drinking among women is fostered by a lack of acceptance in the community. The least assimilated individuals seem to use alcohol to blot out reality.

A813   Stewart, Eugene R.
        1936 The Liquor Traffic among the Southern Plains Indians, 1835-1875. MA Thesis, University of Oklahoma, 107p.

Discusses the development and expansion of the trade in liquor among several tribes, including the Five Civilized Tribes, the Comanches, the Kiowas, and others. Provides documentation of the various laws pertaining to the provision of liquor to Native Americans.

0814   Stewart, Omer C.
        1964 Questions Regarding American Indian Criminality. *Human Organization* 23:61-66.

Research indicates that Native Americans are arrested far more frequently than the size of their population would warrant and that the bulk of arrests are for alcohol-related offenses.

0815   Stirling, Matthew W.
        1955 *National Geographic on Indians of the Americas.* Washington, D.C.: National Geographic Society.

The introduction of alcohol is briefly mentioned (p. 57) as a contributing factor in the breakdown of Native American pride and spirit. Additional notations indicate that alcohol has had little effect on the Pueblo Indians (p. 111) and that alcohol has negatively affected the Cree Indians.

0816   Stratton, John
        1973 Cops and Drunks: Police Attitudes and Actions in Dealing with Indian Drunks. *International Journal of the Addictions* 8:613-621.

Through interviews and observation the attitudes of police in "Bordertown" are assessed with respect to dealing with Navajo inebriates. Police attitudes ranged from sympathy to perception of the drunk as a moral degenerate. Police frustration was enormous, as 85%-90% of all arrests were for intoxication. A lack of cultural understanding underlies police attitudes.

0817   Stratton, Ray
            1977 Variations in Alcohol Problems within the Oklahoma
            Indian Population. *Alcohol Technical Reports* 6:5-12.

            Estimates that the alcoholism rate among Oklahoma Native
            Americans is five times higher than that of the Anglo
            population and four times greater than the Black
            population. However, differences between tribes do
            exist. For example the Cherokee, Creek, and Choctaw
            exhibit a high incidence of alcohol-related deaths
            and arrests, while the Pawnee and Cheyenne rates were
            comparatively low.

0818   Street, Pamela B., Ronald C. Wood and Rita C. Chowenhill
            1976 *Alcohol Use among Native Americans: A Selective,
            Annotated Bibliography.* Sacramento: State of
            California, Office of Alcoholism. (Prepared under
            contract by the Social Research Group, School of
            Public Health, University of California, Berkeley.)

            An annotated bibliography of published works. Un-
            fortunately no index is provided.

0819   Streissguth, Ann Pytkowicz
            1976 Psychologic Handicaps in Children with the
            Fetal Alcohol Syndrome. *Annals of the New York
            Academy of Sciences* 273:140-145.

            Reports the results of a perinatal collaborative
            study in which a racially mixed sample (50% Black,
            44% Anglo, 6% Native American) of mothers and their
            children were examined in order to illustrate the
            effects of the Fetal Alcohol Syndrome.

A819   Streit, Fred and Mark J. Nicholich
            1977 Myths versus Data on American Indian Drug Abuse.
            Journal of Drug Education 7(2):117-122.

            The prevalence of drug and alcohol use among 2,647
            Montana Native American youths, age 6 through 18, was
            surveyed in 1975. Results indicate that approximately
            50% of the children's fathers in the sample were either
            dead, not living at home, or unemployed. Native American
            youths who have lived on a reservation and speak or
            understand their native language were found to be
            heavier users of alcohol and other drugs. Concludes
            that research and evaluation findings from other
            cultures are not applicable to Native Americans.

0820   Strimbu, Jerry L., Lyle F. Schoenfeldt and O. Suthern
        Sims, Jr.

1973 Drug Usage in College Students as a Function of Racial Classification and Minority Group Status. *Research in Higher Education* 1:263-272.

Native Americans reported the most contact with drugs, differed significantly from other racial groups in 25 of 26 comparisons for drug use, and had the highest mean usage level for most items.

0821   Stull, Donald David
1973 Modernization and Symptoms of Stress: Attitudes, Accidents, and Alcohol Use among Urban Papago Indians. Ph.D. Dissertation, University of Colorado, 174p. U.M. Order #74-12412.

Attempts to determine the effect of modernization upon individual Papago Indians in Tucson, Arizona, through the measurement of psychological stress. Accidental injury and alcohol use provide the social indicators of stress. Relationships between occupation and alcohol use were investigated; however, no correlation was found. The drinking patterns of modern and traditional individuals did not differ significantly.

0822** Stull, Donald David
1975 Annotated Bibliography: Alcohol and Drug Treatment Programs among U.S. Ethnic Groups. Unpublished paper, School of Public Health, University of California, Berkeley, 6p.

A review of literature and a description of reported ethnic alcohol and drug treatment programs. Native American programs cited include the Gallup project (Ferguson 1968, 1970), the Mendocino program (Klein and Roberts 1973), and the Navajo programs (Levy and Kunitz 1974).

0823   Sue, Hiroko
1964 Hare Indians and Their World. Ph.D. Dissertation, Bryn Mawr College, 529p. U.M. Order #67-12673.

A portion of Chapter 7 reviews the place of intoxicants in the Hare lifestyle. Drinking accompanies feasts and festive occasions. Children as young as 2 years of age are given home brew. Drinking behavior is examined, as is the Hare view of alcohol consumption.

0824   Swan, James Gilchrist
1857 *The Northwest Coast.* New York: Harper. (Reprinted by the University of Washington Press, 1972, and by Harper and Row, 1969.)

In a journal kept during a three year residence in Washington Territory, the author describes Native Americans' fondness for liquor and their behavior while intoxicated.

0825   Swanson, David W., Amos P. Bratrude and Edward M. Brown
            1971 Alcohol Abuse in a Population of Indian Children.
            Diseases of the Nervous System 32:835-842.

            Examines the effects of excessive drinking among children on the Colville Indian Reservation. Estimates that 75% of the population drinks to impairment. Childhood drinking begins around the age of 12.

0826   Swanton, John R.
            1946 The Indians of the Southeastern United States.
            U.S. Bureau of American Ethnology Bulletin #137 (SUDOCS #SI 2.3:137).

            Pages 764-765 describe the ceremonies which accompany the brewing of alcoholic beverages among Native Americans of southeastern Florida.

0827**   Swett, Daniel H.
            1963 Characteristics of the Male Indian Arrest Population in San Francisco. Unpublished paper presented at the annual meeting of the Southwestern Anthropological Association, 37p.

            The majority of arrests (92.5%) involved drunkenness. Native Americans exhibited more drinking problems than Anglos or Blacks.

0828**   Szuter, Carl F., Robert J. Savard and John H. Saiki
            1964 The Use of Disulfiram in Treatment of Alcohol Problems. Report of the Fort Defiance
            Indian Hospital, Navajo Reservation, 8p.

            A preliminary report on 120 Navajo patients treated in an antabuse program at the Fort Defiance Hospital. Sixty-five patients were followed closely, and 50% of these were considered to have successfully overcome problem drinking. Major patient characteristics are noted, factors contributing to drinking are examined, and needs outside of drug therapy are briefly discussed.

0829   Szuter, Carl F., Robert J. Savard and John H. Saiki
            1965 The Use of Disulfiram in Treatment of Alcoholic Problems in an American Indian Population. *Lecture and Reports, 1965 Manual Supplement.* Salt Lake City: School of Alcohol Studies, University of Utah.

See citation #0828 for an annotation.

0830   Termansen, Paul E. and Joan Ryan
          1970 Health and Disease in a British Columbian Indian
          Community. *Canadian Psychiatric Association Journal*
          15:121-127.

       Investigates morbidity and mortality among Native
       Americans of British Columbia. Accidents are the
       leading cause of mortality and alcohol is cited as
       the primary precipitating factor in accidents.
       Psychotic episodes, assaults, and suicides are also
       associated with excessive alcohol consumption.
       Alcohol was a significant factor in 40% of all Native
       American admissions to the provincial mental hospital.

0831   Terrell, John Upton
          1972 *Apache Chronicle*. New York: World Publishing.

       Discusses the use of alcohol to debilitate the Native
       Americans and reduce their resistance to Anglo
       domination.

0832   Thompson, W.A.
          1942 The Treatment of Chronic Alcoholism. *American
          Journal of Psychiatry* 98:846-856.

       Indicates that "...it seems a well-known fact that
       they [Native Americans] show little tolerance for
       alcohol." Maintains that Native Americans manifest
       an "allergy of desire" for alcohol. Remarks that
       there is a greater incidence of alcoholism among
       urban residents as compared to reservation residents;
       however, the author also states that while susceptible
       to alcohol, Native Americans rarely develop chronic
       alcoholism.

0833   Thompson, William M. and Harold Ackerstein
          1975 Peptic Ulcer Disease in the Alaska Natives:
          a Four-Year Restrospective Study. *Alaska
          Medicine* 17(3):43-44.

       Postulates that the high incidence of psychogenic
       disturbance, social problems, and alcoholism might
       contribute to the genesis of peptic ulcers among
       Native Alaskans; however, this has not actually been
       demonstrated.

0834   Thunder, Right Hand
          1880 *The Indian and the White Man or the Indian in
          Self-Defense*. Indianapolis: Carlon and Hollenbeck
          (edited by D.W. Risher).

Reports that no Anglo will ever know how devastating the introduction of alcohol was to the Native Americans. Reviews the laws prohibiting liquor traffic among Native Americans and describes the actual practices where the liquor trade thrives. Quotations from Native American leaders plead for temperance and point out the evils associated with liquor.

0835   Toler, Fred M.
       1966 Developing a State Program for Indian Alcohol Problems. *Lectures and Reports 1966 Manual Supplement.* Salt Lake City: School of Alcohol Studies, University of Utah.

Drinking patterns constitute the primary difference between Native American and non-Native American drinkers. Native American drinking patterns are attributed to past prohibition. Describes the role of the Turquoise Lodge in Albuquerque, New Mexico, in treating problem drinkers. Language barriers constitute the greatest problem to effective rehabilitation.

0836** Topper, Martin D.
        1970 The Determination of Navajo Drinking Patterns by Police Policy and Behavior and by Racial Discrimination in Tuba City, Arizona, Cortez, Colorado, Monticello, Utah, and Kayenta, Arizona. Unpublished paper presented at the annual meeting of the Central States Anthropological Society, 12p.

Investigates factors which influence Navajo drinking behavior both on and off the reservation. Topper believes that the interpretation of the law by police and other authority figures greatly affects Navajo drinking behavior. On the reservation drinking behavior is influenced by three factors: (1) drinking occurs out of doors, (2) liquor is prohibited on the reservation, and (3) tribal police are relatively reluctant to enforce the prohibition laws. Drinking patterns off the reservation are determined by the following five factors: (1) drinking usually occurs indoors in bars, (2) liquor laws in off-reservation towns differ greatly from reservation laws, (3) liquor laws in off-reservation towns are strictly enforced by the police, (4) Navajo drinkers cannot control the composition of the drinking group, and (5) the bartender sets the limits of "acceptable behavior" within the bar. Off-reservation bars are often a hostile environment for Navajos, and as a result more effectively curtail the venting of frustration through the use of alcohol than does prohibition on the reservation.

0837**   Topper, Martin D.
          1971 Alcohol and the Young Navajo Male: A Study of
          Drinking and Culture Change. Unpublished paper, 34p.

          Navajo drinking is seen as a regulated set of behaviors
          by which the normative drinker releases psychic tensions
          and reinforces social ties. An alcoholic is an indi-
          vidual who frequently denies the social proprieties
          of drinking and becomes deviant by Navajo standards.

0838**   Topper, Martin D.
          n.d. Drinking and Male Adolescence: The Navajo
          Experience. Unpublished paper.

          Discusses adolescent drinking, problem drinking, and
          alcoholism from a cognitive as well as functional
          framework. Reviews the position of anthropologists
          and other social scientists regarding alcoholism.
          Attempts to define drinking in cultural, social, and
          individual contexts. Provides a taxonomy of Navajo
          drinkers and a description of drinking behavior for
          each taxonomic category. Views drinking as both socially
          cohesive and as an escape mechanism.

0839   Topper, Martin D.
          1972 The Daily Life of a Traditional Navajo House-
          hold: An Ethnographic Study in Human Daily
          Activities. Ph.D. Dissertation, Northwestern
          University, 357p. U.M. Order #73-10303.

          Indirectly refers to alcohol use. Notes that the
          study of the interaction between behavior and environ-
          ment is important when attempting to transfer activities
          from an appropriate to an inappropriate environment,
          such as when a reservation drinker attempts to drink
          off-reservation. Indicates that the Navajo perception
          of deviant drinkers does not coincide with Anglo
          definitions of deviant drinking.

0840**   Topper, Martin D.
          1973 Navajo Culture, Social Pathology and Alcohol
          Abuse: A Broad Interpretation. Unpublished paper
          presented at the 32nd annual meeting of the Society
          for Applied Anthropology, 21p.

          Navajo drinking is viewed as a response to extreme
          stress due to an inability of the cultural system
          to undergo rapid economic change.

0841   Topper, Martin D.
          1974 Drinking Patterns, Culture Change, Sociability and
          Navajo "Adolescents." *Addictive Diseases* 1(1):97-116.

Federal programs aimed at improving the economic status of Native Americans proliferated in the 1960s. These programs accelerated culture change, especially among the Navajo. Drinking patterns among Navajo youth have changed considerably as a result of the accelerated culture change. Topper examines the altered drinking patterns as well as the traditional patterns.

0842 Topper, Martin D.
   1975 Roundtable on Alcoholism. *Medical Anthropology Newsletter* 6(2):3-4.

   Reports on the group discussion on alcoholism held at the American Anthropological Association meetings in Mexico City. Several major points of agreement were reached: (1) alcoholism is a phenomenon which is differently defined by various cultures; (2) the native term for alcoholic was used to describe the solitary drinker, rather than the excessive drinker; therefore, drinking behavior may be seen as a socially cohesive activity in many cultures; (3) normative drinking often accompanied cultural events which stressed solidarity among kinsmen; and (4) medical personnel often view only the socially disruptive or "pathological" aspects of drinking behavior.

0843 Topper, Martin D.
   1976 The Cultural Approach, Verbal Plans, and Alcohol Research. In *Cross-Cultural Approaches to the Study of Alcohol*, Michael W. Everett, Jack O. Waddell and Dwight B. Heath, eds. Pp. 379-402. The Hague: Mouton.

   A description of the methodology employed in eliciting verbal plans for drinking behavior among the Navajo. Examines the implications of utilizing verbal plans and direct observations in cross-cultural counseling. A "plan therapy" or behavioral modification treatment approach which is based on the Native American perception of normative and deviant behavior is proposed.

0844 Torrey, E. Fuller
   1970 Mental Health Services for American Indians and Eskimos. *Community Mental Health Journal* 6:455-463.

   Past and present mental health services among Native Americans and Eskimos are surveyed and found to be inadequate. In addition to traditional causes of mental illness, alcohol abuse, suicide, and homicide are on the increase.

A844   Towle, Leland H.
       1975 Alcoholism Treatment Outcomes in Different Populations. In *Research, Treatment, and Prevention: Proceedings of the Fourth Annual Alcoholism Conference of the National Institute on Alcohol Abuse and Alcoholism.* Washington, D.C.: NIAAA (SUDOCS #HE 20.8314:974).

       Reports on the characteristics and outcomes of client populations served by 5 treatment programs, one of which was aimed at Native Americans. Compares the characteristics and success rates of the client populations. Native Americans and public inebriates exhibited the lowest improvement rates. Native American clients tended to be male, younger than average, less educated, and exhibited higher unemployment rates even after treatment.

0845   Trelease, A.W.
       1960 *Indian Affairs in Colonial New York: The 17th Century.* Ithaca: Cornell University Press.

       Reports that the coexistence of Native Americans and colonists was threatened by Native American drinking. Liquor traffic was a constant feature of interracial relations.

0846   Trice, Harrison Miller and David J. Pittman
       1958 Social Organization and Alcoholism: A Review of Significant Research since 1940. *Social Problems* 5:294-306.

       A review of alcoholism research and an attempt to identify major theoretical frameworks. Native American studies reviewed include Lemert (1954), Berreman (1956), and Devereux (1948).

0847   Trillin, Calvin
       1971 U.S. Journal - Gallup, New Mexico: Drunken Indian. *New Yorker* 47(32):108-114.

       Describes the problem faced by Gallup regarding alcohol abuse among the Navajo. Includes a popularized description of Navajo drinking patterns and explains the functional aspects of Navajo drinking.

0848   Trudell, John
       1975 Alcohol and Native Peoples. *Akwesasne Notes* 7(4):38-39.

A statement issued by the national chairman of the
American Indian Movement regarding the damaging
relationship which has developed between alcohol
and Native Americans.

0849** Truro, Lee F.
1970 Survey Report. Unpublished report prepared
for the Schurz Service Unit, Indian Health Service,
54p.

Compilation of results of a 43 question survey
administered to the Dresslerville and Woodfords
Indian Colonies (Washo) and the Fort McDermitt
Reservation (Paiute). The majority of respondents
reported that alcoholism was a pressing health problem.

0850** Turner, Ernest J.
n.d.a Position Statement. Unpublished paper prepared
for the National Indian Board on Alcoholism and Drug
Abuse, 3p.

Attempts to clarify the role and function of the
National Indian Board on Alcoholism and Drug Abuse.
Indicates that the major tasks of the Board are
(1) to strengthen Native American alcohol programs,
(2) to serve as a liaison between government and
tribal/Native American programs, (3) to encourage
active Native American involvement, and (4) to
provide an organized focus on Native American alcohol
problems and program needs.

0851** Turner, Ernest J.
n.d.b Summary of Indian Problems. In Readings
in Indian Alcoholism, unpublished text prepared by
the Alcohol Studies Program, Seattle University.

Reports that one in every four Native Americans is
said to be alcoholic. Discusses the complexity of
alcohol abuse and notes the difficulties associated
with cross-cultural counseling.

0852** Turner, Ernest J.
1976 Indian Alcoholism, Seattle - Written Testimony
Prepared for the American Indian Policy Review
Commission Hearings in Portland, Oregon, 18p.

A discussion of the components which constitute a
comprehensive alcoholism program, based on the needs
of Native American problem drinkers in Seattle, Washington
and the Seattle Indian Alcoholism Program. See also
citation #0867 for a summary of the entire hearings.

A852** Turner, Ernest J.
1977a At Christmas. Seattle. Unpublished paper, Seattle Indian Alcoholism Program, 3p.

Remarks by the program director to a new group of clients upon entering the Seattle Indian Alcoholism Program's halfway house. Notes the destructiveness of drinking among Native Americans.

B852** Turner, Ernest J.
1977b Unpublished Testimony Prepared for Hearings by the State House Institutions Subcommittee on Alcoholism and Drug Abuse, 15p.

Discusses the special assistance which Native Americans need in order to combat alcohol problems. Cites data which indicate that alcohol abuse begins early in life, and that Native Americans are arrested for alcohol-related offenses out of proportion to their population size. Calls upon the subcommittee to strengthen the state commitment to prison programs, provide rehabilitation for ex-offenders, and improve preventive education. Encourages state outreach agencies to employ Native American counselors.

0853** Turner, Ernest J., Rebecca Fain and Joan Kauffman
1977 Analysis of an Indian Alcoholism Program: A Case Study. Unpublished report prepared for the annual meeting of the National Council on Alcoholism, 15p.

Analyzes the Seattle Indian Alcoholism Program which operates a treatment facility for urban Native Americans. Services include outpatient services, a residential center, Native American staffed inpatient treatment, and programs for inmates in local penal institutions.

0854 Tyler, S. Lyman
1973 *A History of Indian Policy*. Washington, D.C.: Government Printing Office (SUDOCS #I20.2:H62).

Provides a detailed history of U.S. government policy regarding Native Americans from initial European/Native American contact through 1972. Alcohol is mentioned on pages 26-28, 42, 43, 46, 129, 181. Indicates that alcohol was used as a valuable trade item by fur traders. The federal government tried without much success to prohibit the sale of alcohol to Native Americans; finally in 1953 Public Law 277 repealed the federal prohibition of the sale of alcohol to Native Americans.

0855   Uecker, Albert E. and Lynn R. Boutilier
        1975 Knowledge of Alcoholism, Initial Attitudes and
        Attitude Change: Indian versus White Alcoholics.
        *Newsletter for Research in Mental Health and
        Behavioral Sciences* 17(1):13-16.

        Brief report on Native American and Anglo alcoholics
        with respect to (1) pretreatment attitudes towards
        alcoholism, social drinking, alcohol education, and
        treatment, (2) changes in attitudes after treatment,
        and (3) the relation of attitude changes to gains in
        knowledge.

0856   Uecker, Albert E. and Lynn R. Boutilier
        1976 Alcohol Education for Alcoholics: Relation to
        Attitude Changes and Posttreatment Abstinence.
        Journal of Studies on Alcohol 37:965-975.

        Report of an investigation into changes in attitude
        regarding use and misuse of alcohol as determined
        by the Passey and Pennington attitude scales. Of
        the 98 patients included in the study, 16 were Native
        Americans.

0857   Underhill, Ruth Murray
        1936 The Autobiography of a Papago Woman. *American
        Anthropological Association Memoirs #46.*

        Considers the ceremonial use of wine and its effect
        on Native Americans.

0858   Underhill, Ruth Murray
        1938 *Singing for Power.* Berkeley: University of
        California Press.

        A discussion of Papago song magic, including an
        examination of the Wine Feast, the principal Papago
        ceremonial. Describes the manufacture of the wine
        and the ritual consumption. Notes that Anglos
        encouraged the Papago to drink outside of ceremonial
        situations, thereby profaning ceremonial drinking.

0859   Underhill, Ruth Murray
        1939 *Social Organization of the Papago Indians.*
        New York: Columbia University Press (reprinted
        in 1969 by AMS Press).

        Considers the influences which may have contributed
        to destructive drinking.

0860**   Underhill, Ruth Murray
         1942   Acculturation at Santa Rosa Village. Unpublished
         manuscript located in the Arizona State Museum
         Library (A-263), 30p.

         Notes that ceremonial drinking persists, but has
         changed as a result of acculturation.

0861   Underhill, Ruth Murray
         1946   *Papago Indian Religion*. New York: Columbia
         University Press (reprinted in 1969 by AMS Press).

         Reports that rain-making magic consists of fermenting
         and drinking a liquor made from saguaro cactus
         (Cereus giganticus) and accompanies a festival which
         takes place in July. Includes a description of the
         manufacture of the liquor.

0862   Underhill, Ruth Murray
         1951   *People of the Crimson Evening*. Washington, D.C.:
         Bureau of Indian Affairs, Branch of Education.

         A book written for children which attempts to explain
         the traditional culture of the Papago Indians.
         Examines the place of the saguaro wine ceremony
         in the lifestyle of the Papagos.

0863   Underhill, Ruth Murray
         1957   Religion among American Indians. *Annals of
         the American Academy of Political and Social
         Sciences* 311:127-136.

         Notes that the Peyote Cult and the Native American
         Church help individuals to achieve and maintain
         sobriety. Ethical teachings compatible with Native
         American lifestyles are needed in order to turn
         the tide of liquor abuse and family disintegration.

0864   United Indians of All Tribes
         1977   *Adult Education Newsletter*. January, unpaged.

         Half of the January issue of the newsletter is devoted
         to articles written by G.E.D. students about alcoholism
         and available treatment facilities in the Seattle area.

0865   United States. Alcohol, Drug Abuse, and Mental Health
         Administration
         1976   *The Forward Plan for FY 1978-1982*. Rockville,
         Maryland: U.S. Alcohol, Drug Abuse, and Mental
         Health Administration.

Discussion of the decision to transfer Native American projects funded by the National Institute on Alcohol Abuse and Alcoholism to the Indian Health Service. The historical development of NIAAA Native American projects is reviewed, as are achievements of the projects to date. Recommends the transfer of "mature" programs, that is programs which have been in existence for six or more years, to the IHS while the NIAAA retains responsibility for all new projects.

0866   United States. American Indian Policy Review Commission. Task Force 6
1976 *Report on Indian Health. Task Force Six: Indian Health.* Washington, D.C.: Government Printing Office (SUDOCS #Y4.In 2/10-H 34).

A review of the accomplishments and problems of the Indian Health Service. Alcohol problems are noted as a major and prevalent illness which is poorly dealt with, if at all, by the IHS. Reports that 25% of the urban Native American center case load is generated by clients seeking help for alcoholism.

0867   United States. American Indian Policy Review Commission. Task Force 11
1976 *Report on Alcohol and Drug Abuse. Task Force Eleven: Alcohol and Drug Abuse. Final Report.* Washington, D.C.: Government Printing Office (SUDOCS #Y4.In 2/10-AL 1).

Concludes that alcohol abuse is a significant problem for Native American communities and that federal programs have not developed a comprehensive approach to deal with the problem. Problems are well identified; however, solutions are sketchy at best.

0868   United States. Bureau of Indian Affairs
1901 *Digest of Decisions Relating to Indian Affairs. Volume I. Judicial.* Washington, D.C.: Government Printing Office (reprinted in 1973 by Kraus Reprint Co.).

Brief summary of decisions by Congress, the Supreme Court, and lower courts regarding the regulation of Native American affairs, including sections pertaining to the sale, distribution, and licensing of liquor. See sections 20, 304, 305, 307, 371, 433, 467, 468, 472, 475, 560, 561, 562, 572, 573, 577, 578, 583, 584, 586, 617, 618, 619, 620, 621, 622, 623, 624, 625, 757, 758, 764, 767, 768, 840, 841, 995.

0869   United States. Commission on Civil Rights
        1973 *The Southwest Indian Report*. Washington, D.C.:
        Government Printing Office (SUDOCS #CR 1.2:In2).

        Examines a number of Native American concerns, including
        employment, education, water rights, law and justice,
        and health. In both the legal and health areas
        alcoholism was cited as a major problem. Points out
        the lack of federal and state programs to treat the
        alcoholic Native American. Alcohol abuse was singled
        out as the "...most important medical and social problem
        confronting the Indian community."

0870   United States. Commission on Civil Rights. Minnesota
        Advisory Committee
        1975 *Bridging the Gap: The Twin Cities Native American
        Community*. Washington, D.C.: Government Printing
        Office (SUDOCS #CR 1.2:N21).

        Examines Native American life in Minnesota. Eleven
        percent of all Minneapolis arrests are made on Native
        Americans and the majority of the arrests are alcohol-
        related. Native Americans represent 20.9% of all
        admissions to detoxification centers. About 10% of
        Native American households were found to have drug or
        alcohol problems.

0871   United States. Comptroller General
        1974 *Progress and Problems in Providing Health Services
        to Indians, Report to the Congress*. Washington, D.C.:
        Government Printing Office (also located under United
        States. General Accounting Office, SUDOCS #GA 1.13:
        H34/12).

        Briefly details the effort of the Indian Health Service
        to treat alcohol problems among Native Americans.
        Recommends that the Secretary of Health, Education,
        and Welfare direct the IHS to develop or help Native
        Americans develop information which (1) identifies
        the extent of the alcohol problem and factors leading
        to and resulting from the problem, (2) influences
        funding sources regarding the need for alcoholism
        programs, and (3) provides a basis for evaluating
        existing programs.

0872   United States. Congress. Senate. Committee on Interior
        and Insular Affairs
        1974 *Indian Health Care Improvement Act IV. Deficiencies
        in Indian Health Services*. Report 93-1283. Washington,
        D.C.: Government Printing Office.

Suggests that poverty, forced abandonment of traditional ways of life, inadequate schools, degradation of Native American family life, and a harsh physical environment are factors which result in the excessive use of alcohol and contribute to suicide, homicide, violence, family disorganization and child neglect.

0873   United States. Department of Health, Education, and Welfare
1973 *Alcohol and Health: Report from the Secretary of Health, Education, and Welfare.* New York: Charles Scribners.

Notes that Native Americans have an epidemic incidence of alcoholism (xvi), and that Native Americans are a priority population for research and services (p. 7, 9).

0874   United States. District Court. Wyoming
1976 Indian Civil Rights Act: Due Process. *Indian Law Reporter* 3:g-173-g-178.

The desire or expectation of an applicant for a tribal liquor license does not rise to the level of a property right protectable under the full due process requirements of the Indian Civil Rights Act; however, a tribe, in exercising its authority to regulate the introduction of liquor into Indian country, is required to apply its regulation uniformly to all persons and to give applicants at least adequate notice and opportunity to be heard at a meaningful time and in a meaningful manner. At issue is the definition of a "non-Indian" community within reservation boundaries.

0875** United States. Indian Health Service. Desert Willow Training Center
1970 A Descriptive Study of the Academic Achievement, Delinquency, and Alcohol Usage of the Teenage Population of the Reno-Sparks Indian Colony. Unpublished paper prepared by members of Training Course DTC-70-3, 23p.

An epidemiological study of the Reno-Sparks Indian Colony in which the only major health problem identified by community members was alcohol abuse. Of the teenagers studied, 46% had started drinking before the age of 14. Alcohol use was found to be related to school dropouts and arrests of youth.

0876** United States. Indian Health Service. Desert Willow Training Center
1973 Alcohol and the San Felipe Pueblo: A Study of the Problem with Recommendations for Change.

Unpublished paper prepared by members of the Health
Services Management Course, 49p.

In a population of 1692, alcohol-related arrests accounted
for 71 of 94 juvenile arrests and 230 of 344 adult
arrests. Of all hospital admissions, 50% are estimated
to be alcohol-related. Recommendations for treatment
and prevention programs are made.

0877** United States. Indian Health Service. Desert Willow
Training Center
1976 The Mescalero Apache Teen-Ager Needs and Influences.
Unpublished paper prepared by members of the Health
Services Research Course HSR-76-3, 45p.

Report of a project designed to identify the needs of
Mescalero Apache teenagers, with special emphasis on
social and mental health needs. Education is a tribal
priority, as a result the drop-out rate is of greater
concern than alcohol or drug abuse. However, 10%
of the adults surveyed indicated that teenage alcohol
abuse was a concern.

0878 United States. Indian Health Service. Task Force on
Alcoholism
1977 *Alcoholism: A High Priority Health Problem*.
Washington, D.C.: Government Printing Office
(DHEW Publication 77-1001, SUDOCS #HE 20.5302:al 1).

This publication is a combination of three separate
Task Force Reports (1969, 1970) issued by the Indian
Health Service discussing the problems of alcohol
abuse among Native Americans. The first section
develops background information and reviews factors
which may contribute to alcoholism in Native American
communities. The second section deals with the problems of prevention, control, and treatment, and
recommends a plan of action. The third section is
a reference guide for tribal programs which defines
terms and lists resources which may provide assistance
in planning and program implementation.

0879 United States. National Clearinghouse for Alcohol Information
1973 NIAAA Widens Role of Indians. *Alcohol and Health
Notes* April:1-5.

Reports that the NIAAA has attempted to give Native
Americans a more direct role in reviewing grant
proposals involving Native American alcoholism.

0880**   United States. National Institute on Alcohol Abuse and
            Alcoholism
                1972 Guide: Indian Program. Unpublished paper, 5p.

                Reviews the historical precedent for the authority to
                fund special Native American demonstration projects
                on a community-wide basis. Program guidelines are
                included and cover topics such as staff training,
                geographic service area, use of other resources, and
                directions for filing grant applications.

0881   United States. National Institute on Alcohol Abuse and
            Alcoholism
                1974 Self-Help Programs for Indians and Native
                Alaskans. *Alcohol Health and Research World*
                1974:11-16.

                Briefly discusses the extent of alcohol abuse among
                Native Americans. Reviews various agencies and
                programs working to reduce the rate of alcohol abuse.
                Describes the Alcohol Abuse Prevention Program
                utilized by the Chemawa Indian School, near Salem,
                Oregon.

0882   United States. Public Health Service
                1957 *Health Services for American Indians*. Washington,
                D.C.: Government Printing Office, DHEW Publication
                531 (SUDOCS #FS 2.2:In 25/2).

                A comprehensive survey of Native American health
                problems prepared at the request of the 84th Congress.
                Alcohol abuse is identified as a specific mental
                health problem requiring special attention. Alcohol
                abuse is felt to contribute to high unemployment,
                accidents, and desertion of children. Increased
                appropriations and staffing of preventive and curative
                programs is requested.

0883**   Upchego, Henry and Reynold Brown
                1970 The Ute Indian Tribal Court Alcoholism Program.
                Unpublished Report, Ute Indian Tribal Alcoholism
                Information and Counseling Program, 17p.

                Describes the involvement of the tribal courts in the
                rehabilitation and recovery of tribal problem drinkers.
                The court utilizes (1) pre-sentence evaluation, (2)
                weekly A.A. meetings, (3) a probation and parole
                program, and (4) direct court orders to assist problem
                drinkers.

0884   Useem, Ruth Hill and Carl K. Eicher
        1970 Rosebud Reservation Economy. In *The Modern
        Sioux: Social Systems and Reservation Culture*,
        Ethel Nurge, ed. Pp. 3-34. Lincoln: University
        of Nebraska Press.

        Alcohol is mentioned in regard to the work performance
        of Sioux laborers and in connection with urban re-
        location problems.

0885** Ute Tribal Business Council
        1970 Cooperative Management of Indian Health Programs.
        Unpublished proceedings of the Uintah and Ouray
        Training Workshop, Roosevelt Indian Health Center,
        76p.

        A discussion during a management training workshop
        between tribal representatives and agency personnel
        regarding health problems on the reservation. Alcohol
        and alcohol-related problems are mentioned frequently.

0886   Vachon, A.
        1968 L'eau-de-vie dans la Société Indienne. *Toxicomanies*
        1:205-215.

        The disintegration and depopulation of Native American
        society (the Montagnais and Illinois are specifically
        mentioned), as well as the resistance of Native
        Americans to conversion have traditionally been
        attributed, particularly by missionaries, to the desire
        for alcohol. Vachon suggests that alcohol cannot be
        held wholly accountable for the downfall of Native
        Americans. The author notes that drunkenness pro-
        duced a desirable trance-like state which often took
        on religious significance.

0887   Vall-Spinosa, A.
        1968 Antabuse Treatment of Alcoholism in Navajo
        and Hopi Indians. Unpublished paper presented
        at the 3rd joint meetings of the Clinical Society
        and Commissioned Officers Association of the U.S.
        Public Health Service.

        A program to reduce the high incidence of abusive
        drinking based on the administration of Antabuse was
        formulated and tested among Navajo and Hopi at the
        Tuba City Hospital. Results of the treatment with
        the first 82 patients revealed that 75% were not
        drinking or were drinking less than before going on
        the drug, and a definite decrease in hospitalization,
        arrests, and unemployment was noted.

0888   Van Stone, James W.
            1965 The Changing Culture of the Snowdrift Chipewyan.
            National Museum of Canada, Bulletin #209.

            An ethnographic account of culture change among the
            Snowdrift Chipewyan in which smoking and drinking
            behavior are specifically examined. Drinking behavior
            is described, as are various types of home brew.
            Notes that most of the people favored beer or commercial
            liquor. Reports that intoxication may be psychological
            as well as physiological and that pseudo-intoxication
            was observed. No instance of addiction was encountered
            in spite of frequent drinking bouts.

0889   Van Valkenburgh, Richard
            1937 Navajo Common Law. II. Navajo Law and Justice.
            Museum Notes 9:51-54 (*Plateau* is the present title
            of *Museum Notes*).

            Reports that homicide used to be rare among the
            Navajo, but has increased since the introduction of
            liquor, to the extent that today drinking is the cause
            of or associated with most Navajo homicides.

0890   Van Valkenburgh, Richard
            1938 Navajo Common Law. III. Etiquette, Hospitality,
            Justice. *Museum Notes* 10:39-46 (*Plateau* is the
            present title of *Museum Notes*).

            In the past no stigma accompanied the sale of alcohol
            to Native Americans, and traders supplied the Navajo
            with alcohol until prohibition. Prior to the intro-
            duction of Anglo law Navajos handled intoxicated
            individuals by tying them up and only turning them
            loose when they had sobered up.

A890   Vaughan, Frederick
            1970 The Case of Joseph Drybones: Legal Forces in
            the Bill of Rights. *Round Table* 238:213-216.

            Discusses the case of Drybones vs. the Queen in which
            Drybones, an Indian residing in the Northwest Ter-
            ritories of Canada, was arrested and found guilty
            under section 94(b) of the Indian Act. However, on
            appeal to the Territorial Court and the Supreme
            Court of Canada, Drybones's conviction was overturned
            and the Indian Act was found to be discriminatory
            and in violation of the Canadian Bill of Rights.

0891   Viola, H.J.
            1974 *Thomas L. McKenney: Architect of America's Early
            Indian Policy: 1816-1830.* Chicago: Sage Books.

McKenney was strongly opposed to the sale of liquor to Native Americans and his main goal was the passage of legislation which would drive whiskey peddlers out of Indian country (see especially p. 49-51 and 174-179).

0892   Vogt, Evon Z.
        1951 Navajo Veterans. *Peabody Museum of American Archaeology and Ethnology Papers* 41(1):3-223. (Reprinted by Kraus Reprint Co., 1973.)

A case study of John Nez, a Navajo veteran, is presented as part of a larger study which highlights many of the problems of Navajo acculturation. While in the Army, John learned to drink in a controlled manner so as not to get "sloppy drunk." However, John continued to drink after returning to the reservation in a manner which suggested that alcohol was used as an escape mechanism.

0893   Vollmann, Tim
        1974 Criminal Jurisdiction in Indian Country: Tribal Sovereignty and Defendant's Rights in Conflict. *Kansas Law Review* 22:387-412.

A review of the jurisdictional maze which complicates Native American legal cases. Two cases, Keeble vs. United States and United States vs. Kills Plenty, both involving alcohol-related offenses, are discussed. The National Commission on Reform of Criminal Laws has proposed that a complete revision of Title 18 of the *United States Code* be undertaken.

0894   Von Hentig, Hans
        1945 The Delinquency of the American Indian. *Journal of Criminal Law and Criminology* 36:75-84.

Reports that drunkenness is the most frequent offense for which Native Americans are arrested.

0895** Wacko, William J.
        1973 Observations and Recommendations Respecting Alcohol and Drugs in the Northwest Territories. Unpublished paper prepared for the Department of Social Development, Government of the Northwest Territories, 63p.

Report of alcohol problems in the Northwest Territories among both Native Americans and non-Native Americans. Indicates that Native Americans are a "psychologically hurt people" and that non-Native Americans who migrated north did not provide positive drinking role models. Existing services are reviewed and recommendations for proposed programs are discussed.

0896** Wacko, William J.
1974 Indian Alcohol and Drug Abuse in Alberta: Discussion Paper for Indian People and the Staff of Indian Affairs and Northern Development. Unpublished paper prepared for the Alberta Region of the Department of Indian Affairs and Northern Development, 68p.

An overview of the status of alcohol and Native Americans in the Alberta region, with a discussion of the cost of alcohol abuse, the current status of alcohol abuse in Alberta, historical factors contributing to Native American alcohol abuse, and suggestions for programs and future research.

0897 Waddell, Jack O.
1971 Drink Friend: Social Contexts of Convivial Drinking and Drunkenness among Papago Indians in an Urban Setting. In *Proceedings of the First Annual Alcoholism Conference of NIAAA*, M. Chafetz, ed. Pp. 237-251. Washington, D.C.: National Institute on Alcohol Abuse and Alcoholism (may be located under: Alcoholism Conference of the National Institute on Alcohol Abuse and Alcoholism, SUDOCS #HE 20.2430/2:971).

An initial report of the role which drinking and drunkenness play among Papago men, both on the reservation and in urban settings. Concludes that drinking and drunkenness are social ritual postures which create and maintain social bonds.

0898** Waddell, Jack O.
1972 Drinking and Friendship: The Urban Papago Experience. Unpublished paper, 80p.

An examination of the social context in which Papago drinking occurs, the cultural orientations operative in drinking situations, and the meanings attached to drinking experiences. Stresses that Papago definitions of appropriate drinking behavior must be considered in designing rehabilitation programs.

0899** Waddell, Jack O.
1973 The Place of the Cactus Wine Ritual in the Papago Indian Ecosystem. Unpublished paper presented at the IXth International Congress of Anthropological and Ethnological Sciences, 12p.

Suggests that the Wine Feast serves to emphasize
the basic egalitarian principles of Papago existence
and reaffirm inter-village solidarity. The feast
helps to maintain traditional values and a sense
of history.

0900   Waddell, Jack O.
1975   For Individual Power and Social Credit: The Use of Alcohol among Tucson Papagos. *Human Organization* 34:9-15.

The author asserts that two fundamental dimensions
of Papago social or cultural reality are related to
current drinking experiences. Drinking serves both
to maintain a system of social credit and to provide
a means whereby individuals may attain personal power
in an otherwise egalitarian social system.

0901**   Waddell, Jack O.
1976   The Use of Intoxicating Beverages among the Native Peoples of the Aboriginal Greater Southwest. Unpublished paper, 54p.

An ethnohistoric overview of alcohol use among Native
Americans of the greater southwest.

0902   Wagner, Roland M.
1975   Some Pragmatic Aspects of Navaho Peyotism. *Plains Anthropologist* 20:197-205.

Discusses and describes the rehabilitative effect
of the Peyote religion on alcoholics.

0903   Walker, Constance Georgene
1976   Influence of Parental Drinking Behavior on That of Adolescent Native Americans. MS Thesis, (nursing), University of Washington, 70p.

A study designed to survey the behavior and attitudes
of adolescent Native Americans toward drinking and
to determine how such behavior and attitudes are
influenced by parental drinking patterns.

0904   Walker, Deward E., Jr.
1967   Problems of American Indian Education. *Research Studies - Washington State University* 34(4):247-252. (Reprinted in *Hearings before the U.S. Senate Special Subcommittee on Indian Education of the Committee on Labor and Public Welfare*, 90th Congress, 1st and 2nd Sessions, p. 2002-2006, SUDOCS #Y4.L11/2:In 2/2.)

Recommends a culturally sensitive educational program as a solution to destructive drinking practices. Programs aimed at the major social problems confronting Native American students and designed to develop improved self-concepts would do much to prevent drinking and delinquency.

0905   Wallace, Anthony F.C.
        1951 Some Psychological Determinants of Culture Change in an Iroquoian Community. *U.S. Bureau of American Ethnology Bulletin* 149:55-76 (SUDOCS #SI 2.3:149).

        Discusses the "...chronic longing for alcoholic intoxication..." among the Tuscarora Indians. Indicates that in the 200+ years since the introduction of liquor the Tuscaroras have developed or adopted institutions, such as the Baptist Church and the Temperance Society, in order to maintain drinking behavior within socially tolerable levels.

0906   Wallace, Anthony F.C.
        1956 Revitalization Movements. *American Anthropologist* 58:264-287.

        Notes that the founder of the Handsome Lake Movement among the Seneca, a confirmed alcoholic, gave up drinking after founding the movement.

0907   Wallace, Anthony F.C.
        1959 The Institutionalization of Cathartic and Control Strategies in Iroquois Religious Psychotherapy. In *Culture and Mental Health*, Morris K. Opler, ed. Pp. 63-96. New York: Macmillan.

        Postulates that acculturation processes are apt to increase the complexity of native systems and at the same time drastically reduce their orderliness. Examines the strategies utilized by the various Iroquoian tribes (Huron, Seneca, Cayuga, Onondaga, Oneida, and Mohawk) to control alcohol abuse.

0908   Wallace, Anthony F.C.
        1970 *The Death and Rebirth of the Seneca*. New York: Alfred A. Knopf.

        A history of the Seneca at a time when they dominated the Iroquois Confederacy, with emphasis on the effect of the Handsome Lake Movement. Examines psychosocial aspects of Seneca drinking behavior and describes the social pathology which accompanied the increase in drunkenness among the Seneca. Notes that after his conversion Handsome Lake preached against liquor and established a cult of sobriety which restored the Seneca and revived their culture.

0909   Washburn, Wilcomb E.
       1971 *Red Man's Land - White Man's Law.* New York: Scribner's.

       Notes that drinking is one of the most serious problems facing Native Americans. Acculturation studies are cited in an effort to suggest that the more acculturated Native Americans have fewer drinking problems. The loss of traditional controls and the inability to share economic rewards of the new society are cited as contributing factors in Native American alcohol abuse.

0910   Washburne, Chandler
       1961 *Primitive Drinking: A Study of the Uses and Functions of Alcohol in Preliterate Societies.* New York: College and University Press.

       Pages 172-186 report on alcohol use among the Papago of southern Arizona. A wide variety of information is included. A brief outline of Papago culture is provided; the method of preparing alcoholic beverages is described, as is the membership of drinking groups. Drinking behavior is analyzed, as are the situations in which alcohol is consumed.

0911   Washburne, Chandler
       1968 Primitive Religion and Alcohol. *International Journal of Comparative Sociology* 9(2):97-105.

       An inquiry into the range and extent of alcohol use in connection with religion. Native American examples include the Papago (used in connection with religious rain making) the Oglala Sioux (used for contacting the supernatural).

0912   Washington (State). Department of Social and Health Services
       1977 *Washington State Comprehensive Alcoholism Plan, Fiscal Year 1978.* Olympia: Washington. Department of Social and Health Services, Alcoholism Office.

       Describes the history and goals of the Washington Indian Commission on Alcohol and Drug Abuse and indicates that Native Americans are involved in the planning of programs designed for Indians.

0913   Washington (State). Indian Commission on Alcohol and Drug Abuse
        1977 *Washington State Indian Acloholism Plan, fy 1978*. Olympia: Washington. Indian Commission on Alcohol and Drug Abuse (distributed through the State Office of Alcoholism).

        The first Indian State Plan for alcoholism programs provides a history of the Washington Indian Commission on Alcohol and Drug Abuse, a description of alcohol problems among Washington Native Americans, a set of objectives, and a detailed discussion of counselor certification guidelines.

0914   Watsky, Morris
        1955 Constitutional Law - Indians - Intoxicating Liquors. *Miami Law Quarterly* 9(4):484-486.

        Discussion of the arguments, both pro and con, concerning the sale of liquor to Native Americans. Suggests that laws aimed at protecting Native Americans were established 100 years ago and need to be re-examined.

0915   Watson, Jane
        1969 The Etiology of Suicide at Fort Hall. In *Hearings before the U.S. Senate Special Subcommittee on Indian Education of the Committee on Labor and Public Welfare*, 90th Congress, 1st and 2nd Sessions, p. 2367-2371 (SUDOCS #Y4.L11/2: In 2/2).

        Intoxication from alcohol, glue, gasoline, or other drugs is almost always associated with suicides and attempted suicides.

0916   Wax, Murray L.
        1971 *Indian Americans: Unity and Diversity*. Englewood Cliffs: Prentice-Hall.

        Indicates that Native Americans were often introduced to liquor by fur traders and that alcohol was used to divest Native Americans of their lands. The author distinguishes between chronic alcoholism, ritual drinking, social drinking, and binge drinking.

0917   Wax, Murray L., Rosalie H. Wax and R.V. Dumont, Jr.
        1964 Formal Education in an American Indian Community. *Social Problems* 11(4):supplement.

        The pervasive image of the "drunken Indian" influences many aspects of the educational system.

0918   Weast, Donald E.
        1969 Patterns of Drinking among Indian Youth: the
        Case of a Wisconsin Tribe. Ph.D. Dissertation,
        University of Wisconsin, 162p. U.M. Order #69-22508.

        A study of attitudes and drinking practices among
        Oneida Indian youth, utilizing the theoretical concepts
        of anomie and differential association to demonstrate
        that drinking behavior is positively related to
        anomie in Indian young people. The results indicate
        that the stereotype of Oneida adolescents as excessive
        drinkers is not warranted.

0919   Weaver, Thomas and Ruth Hughes Gartell
        1974 The Urban Indian: Man of Two Worlds. In *Indians
        in Arizona. A Contemporary Perspective*, Thomas
        Weaver, ed. Pp. 72-96. Tucson: University of
        Arizona Press.

        Alcoholism is postulated as the root cause of urban
        Native American health and social problems. Factors
        contributing to alcohol abuse are mentioned.

0920   Weightman, Barbara Ann
        1972 The Musqueam Reserve: A Case Study of the
        Indian Social Milieu in an Urban Environment.
        Ph.D. Dissertation, University of Washington,
        281p. U.M. Order #73-03801.

        A social geographic analysis of the changing space
        between Native Americans and Anglos. Notes that
        taverns play an important role in the social inter-
        actions of contemporary urban Native Americans, yet
        the stereotype of the Native American as a heavy
        drinker persists.

0921   Weil, R.
        1975 *The Legal Status of the Indian*. New York:
        AMS Press.

        Under its constitutional powers to regulate commerce
        with Native American tribes the Congress may prohibit
        the unlicensed introduction and sale of liquor into
        Indian country and it may extend such jurisdiction
        to adjacent territory.

0922   Weppner, Robert Stephens
        1968 The Economic Absorption of Navajo Indian Migrants
        in Denver, Colorado. Ph.D. Dissertation, University
        of Colorado, 160p. U.M. Order #69-04343.

Mentions alcohol in connection with employer interviews. Of the employers interviewed, 13% indicated that alcohol abuse among Navajo employees was a problem. Excessive drinking was the third most frequently mentioned negative trait associated with Navajo employees.

0923   Werden, Patricia K.
       1974a Health Education for Indian Students. *Journal of School Health* 44:319-323.

       A review of health and education problems on the Pine Ridge Reservation, with suggestions regarding the importance of health education among the Oglala Sioux. Alcohol abuse and suicide are cited as the two major mental health problems; both are employed as coping mechanisms. Alcohol abuse is blamed for 30% of acute chronic brain disorders diagnosed by U.S. Public Health Service physicians.

0924   Werden, Patricia K.
       1974b Health Education Needs of the Oglala Sioux. *School Health Review* 5(5):14-16.

       A condensed version of Werden (1974a); see citation #0923 for an annotation.

0926** Werner, V.W.
       1963 New Mexico State Alcoholism Program. Unpublished paper presented to the School of Alcohol Studies, University of Utah, 9p.

       Reviews the position of New Mexico regarding Native American alcoholism, and provides a brief description of the Shiprock pilot study, the Turquoise Lodge program, and the Gallup Community Council and Indian A.A. programs.

0927   Westermeyer, Joseph John
       1970 Alcohol Related Problems among the Ojibway People in Minnesota: a Social Psychiatry Study. Ph.D. Dissertation, University of Minnesota, 339p. U.M. Order #71-18837.

       Consists of epidemiological data which permit intra-group and cross-cultural comparisons. The author provides recommendations for primary, secondary, and tertiary treatment programs.

0928   Westermeyer, Joseph John
        1972a Chippewa and Majority Alcoholism in the Twin
            Cities: A Comparison. *Journal of Nervous and
            Mental Diseases* 155:327-332.

            A comparative study to determine whether
            there are any differences between Native American
            alcoholics and a sample of majority culture
            alcoholics. Marked similarities as well as some
            differences were found. Physiological and clinical
            traits were similar; the major differences were
            among sociocultural variables. There is no validity
            to distinguishing between majority alcoholism and
            Native American alcoholism as separate or differing
            entities.

0929   Westermeyer, Joseph John
        1972b Options Regarding Alcohol Use among the
            Chippewa. *American Journal of Orthopsychiatry*
            42:398-403.

            Chippewa people drink in "Anglo" or "Indian" style
            or abstain from drinking for various reasons.
            Their choices are related to individual factors
            such as age, sex, family role, and past experience
            with alcohol. There are advantages and disadvantages
            to each style of drinking, depending on the goals
            of the individual. However, "Indian" drinking
            functions as an entree to certain social activities
            and reinforces the corporate in-group of Native
            American people, thus contributing to the well-
            being of the Chippewa society and the individuals
            within that society.

0930   Westermeyer, Joseph John
        1974a Alcoholism from the Cross-Cultural Per-
            spective: A Review and Critique of Clinical
            Studies. *American Journal of Drug and Alcohol
            Abuse* 1(1):89-105.

            A review of methodology applied to cross-cultural
            research in alcoholism. Discusses problems which
            arise in definition, sampling, and research
            strategies.

0931   Westermeyer, Joseph John
        1974b "The Drunken Indian": Myths and Realities.
            Psychiatric Annals 4(11):29-36.

            Discusses the misconceptions and various political
            strategies associated with the stereotype of the

"drunken Indian." Data on alcohol use and alcohol-related problems which are common to Native Americans are examined. Concludes that there is a wide variation in alcohol use and abuse among the various tribes and subgroups within tribes. Also concludes that alcohol problems among Native Americans resemble alcohol problems common to other ethnic groups in the United States.

A931   Westermeyer, Joseph John
        1974c "Use of Halfway Houses by Indian Alcoholics." Minneapolis: Unpublished paper, University of Minnesota Hospitals, 10p. (National Clearinghouse for Alcohol Information Accession #019193.)

        Reports the results of a study that examined the subsistence and social behavior of urban Chippewa men, categorized by themselves and others as "drunks" or "alcoholics." Characteristics of the drinking lifestyle with respect to material and social resources within the area, circumstances under which the men moved to the city, and the role of the Indian-run halfway house in altering behavior were explored.

0932   Westermeyer, Joseph John
        1976a Clinical Guidelines for the Cross-Cultural Treatment of Chemical Dependency. *American Journal of Drug and Alcohol Abuse* 3(2):315-322.

        Clinicians are advised to develop skills in working with their own ethnic peers before attempting cross-cultural treatment. It is important for the clinician to maintain primary commitment to the patient rather than to an institution which is not responsible to the patient population. Observations are based on experience with Asian narcotic addicts and Native American alcoholics.

0933   Westermeyer, Joseph John
        1976b Cross-Cultural Studies of Alcoholism in the Clinical Setting: Review and Evaluation. In *Cross-Cultural Approaches to the Study of Alcohol*, Michael W. Everett, J.O. Waddell and Dwight B. Heath, eds. Pp. 359-377. The Hague: Mouton.

        A survey of the types of cross-cultural studies which have been conducted within clinical settings. Native American studies are cited to illustrate research on withdrawal signs, incidence of cirrhosis of the liver, and differential blood and tissue levels of ethanol.

0934 Westermeyer, Joseph John
1976c Use of a Social Indicator System to Assess Alcoholism among Indian People in Minnesota. *American Journal of Drug and Alcohol Abuse* 3(3):447-456.

A social indicator system employed to assess alcohol-related problems among the Native Americans of Minnesota revealed that Native Americans commonly encountered alcohol-related "events" which led to death or social institutions with a poor record of problem resolution (foster homes, jail and welfare.) However, Native Americans infrequently appeared at psychiatric facilities with alcohol-related "events." Institutional bias helps to direct Native Americans to problem-maintenance programs rather than to higher cost problem-solving resources.

0935 Westermeyer, Joseph John
1976d Erosion of Indian Mental Health in Cities. *Minnesota Medicine* 59(6):431-433.

Over the last two decades Native Americans have increasingly migrated from reservations to urban areas. Once away from home Native Americans encounter increased mental health problems including alcohol and drug abuse.

0936 Westermeyer, Joseph John and John Brantner
1972 Violent Death and Alcohol Use among the Chippewa in Minnesota. *Minnesota Medicine* 55:749-752.

Violent death occurs five times more often among Chippewa than among the general population of Minnesota and violent deaths are more often associated with alcohol among the Chippewa than among the general population.

0937 Westermeyer, Joseph John and Gretchen Lang
1975 Ethnic Differences in Use of Alcohol Facilities. *International Journal of Addictions* 10:513-520.

Native American and majority patient utilization of a detoxification center in Minneapolis is compared. Demographic characteristics, the nature of withdrawal symptoms, and readmission data are presented for the two groups. The data suggest that Native Americans make more appropriate use of facilities. Recommendations regarding the planning of treatment facilities are provided.

0938** Whear, James B.
n.d. Field Training Manual. Unpublished report, Western Region Indian Alcoholism Training Center, University of Utah.

A guide to conducting alcohol continuing education courses in the field, including directions for Native American counselors on developing workshops and seminars once they have returned to their home areas.

0939 White, Robert Anthony
1960 The Urbanization of the Dakota Indians. MA Thesis, St. Louis University, 302p.

Indicates that drinking is a problem for both transitional and traditional groups, but not for transpositional groups. "Camp Indians" who migrated to Rapid City often drink a great deal, while the rate for "transitional" families is less and "middle class" families even less.

0940 White, Robert Anthony
1970 The Lower-Class "Culture of Excitement" among Contemporary Sioux. In *The Modern Sioux*, Ethel Nurge, ed. Pp. 175-197. Lincoln: University of Nebraska Press.

The "culture of excitement" is described as the central factor which gives meaning to the life of the members of the lower socioeconomic groups. Alcohol, intoxication, and travel from bar to bar are elements of the "culture of excitement." Chronic drinking is characteristic of this lifestyle.

0941 Whitehead, Paul C. and Cheryl Harvey
1974 Explaining Alcoholism: An Empirical Test and Reformulation. *Journal of Health and Social Behavior* 15:57-65.

An explanation of alcoholism based on the structure and quality of social norms is tested with data from several preliterate non-European societies, including various Native American groups, such as Aleuts, Arapaho, Crow, Hopi, Navajo, Papago, and Zuni.

0942   Whiteside, Don
            1973 *Aboriginal People: A Selected Bibliography
            concerning Canada's First People.* Ottawa:
            National Indian Brotherhood.

            Citations concerning alcohol are included in
            Chapter XVII (p. 208-216) entitled "Health,
            Housing, Welfare - Poverty."

A942   Whittaker, James O.
            1961 *Alcohol and the Standing Rock Sioux Tribe.*
            Fort Yates, North Dakota: Commission on
            Alcoholism, Standing Rock Sioux Tribe.

            Represents the original research report upon
            which Whittaker's articles are based (1962, 1963,
            see citations #0943, 0944).

0943   Whittaker, James O.
            1962 Alcohol and the Standing Rock Sioux Tribe,
            I: the Pattern of Drinking. *Quarterly Journal
            of Studies on Alcohol* 23:468-479.

            A survey of drinking practices of 208 adult Sioux
            revealed that about 70% were drinkers. Drinking
            behavior is examined by age, sex, frequency,
            and symptoms of problem drinking and/or alcoholism.
            Comparisons are made to non-Native American
            populations.

0944   Whittaker, James O.
            1963 Alcohol and the Standing Rock Sioux Tribe,
            II: Psychodynamic and Cultural Factors in
            Drinking. *Quarterly Journal of Studies on
            Alcohol* 24:80-90.

            Consideration of the motivations and contributing
            factors behind Sioux drinking suggests that con-
            temporary Sioux culture is one in which pressures
            to drink are strong, there are few alternative
            means of alleviating such pressures, and social
            sanctions against heavy drinking are virtually
            nonexistent.

0945   Whittaker, James O.
            1966 The Problem of Alcoholism among American
            Reservation Indians. *Alcoholism* 2:141-146.

            A summary of findings of research into problem
            drinking among the Standing Rock Sioux. The
            environmental and sociocultural factors contributing

to high rates of excessive drinking are noted.
Causes of such drinking were attributed to high
stress, disintegration of culture, suppression
of agressive tendencies when sober, lack of
social sanctions against drinking, and an attitude
that drinking is utilitarian.

0946   Wilkinson, Rupert
        1970 *The Prevention of Drinking Problems: Alcohol
        Control and Cultural Influences.* New York: Oxford
        University Press.

        A sweeping program which the author believes might
        change the attitudes and patterns of American
        drinking. An example of changed drinking behavior
        is the Frobisher Bay Eskimo experience reported
        by John Honigmann (1965). Native Americans figure
        only slightly in this work; however, many of the
        suggestions could be applied to Native Americans.

0947   Williams, Arline K.
        1970 A Study of a Cross-Cultural Mental Health
        Program. MS Thesis, Sir George Williams College.

        In discussing a community mental health program
        on the Pine Ridge Sioux Reservation, the author
        briefly mentions that the CHMP Program proposed
        a community alcohol education program, but that
        the proposal did not come to fruition. Indicates
        that alcohol was a substitute for aggressive
        behavior and the inability to adapt to stress.

0948   Williams, John Robert
        1975 A Comparison of the Self-Concepts of Alcoholic
        and Non-Alcoholic Males of Indian and Non-
        Indian Ancestry in Terms of Scores on the
        Tennessee Self-Concept Scale. Ed.D. Dissertation,
        University of South Dakota, 127p. U.M. Order
        #76-02410.

        Alcoholics demonstrated a less adequate concept
        of self than the non-alcoholics; however, Native
        American alcoholics had a better self-concept
        than non-Native American alcoholics.

0949   Williamson, R.G.
        1974 Eskimo Underground. Sociocultural Change
        in the Canadian Central Arctic. Uppsala
        Universitet: *Institutionen för allmän och
        Jämförande Etnografi. Occasional Papers* 11:127-129.

Reports that contrary to expectations, drinking was not a problem for the Keewatin Eskimo in adapting to life in Rankin Inlet.

0950   Wills, James
        1969 Psychological Problems of Sioux Indians Resulting in the Accident Pheonomena. *Pine Ridge Research Bulletin* 8:49-65.

        Alcohol is frequently related to accidents on the Pine Ridge Reservation.

0951   Wilson, Benjamin D.
        1952 *The Indians of Southern California in 1852.* San Marino: Huntington Library.

        Examines the effects of alcohol on Native Americans in California.

0952   Wilson, Eugene B.
        1968 Misuse of Alcohol among Our Youth: Group III Report. Unpublished report, Indian Health Institute on Community Health Development. Fort Lewis College, and the Division of Indian Health.

        Examines the problems of alcohol abuse among Native American youth. Techniques for combating the problem are listed.

0953   Wilson, Lawrence G. and James H. Shore
        1975 Evaluation of a Regional Indian Alcohol Program. *American Journal of Psychiatry* 132:255-258.

        An analysis of follow-up data collected on 83 Native American alcoholic males who had been out of inpatient treatment an average of 18 months. A 44% improvement rate compares favorably with other treatment programs, especially in light of the fact that the patient selection process favored more difficult patients from the outset.

0954   Winkler, Allen M.
        1969 Drinking on the American Frontier. *Quarterly Journal of Studies on Alcohol* 29:413-445.

        A survey of drinking history, practice, and customs on the American frontier in the 19th century, particularly among fur trappers, miners, cowboys, soldiers, and Native Americans. Notes that Anglo trappers encouraged intoxication as the cheapest tool for swindling Native Americans. A recipe for "Indian whiskey" is provided.

0955** Winn, Wandal William
1977 American Indian Alcoholism: Etiology and Implications for Effective Treatment. Unpublished paper presented at the 12th annual meeting of the U.S. Public Health Service Professional Association.

Alcoholism has long been identified as a top priority health problem for Native American people, yet attempts to address the problem have been characterized by program fragmentation, interagency polarization, and low staff morale. The present impasse may be due to a lack of consensus regarding the definition and etiology of Native American alcoholism among those involved in the planning and delivery of services.

0956 Wissler, Clark
1940 *Indians of the United States*. New York: Anchor Books.

Europeans brought three gifts to North America which drastically changed the life of Native Americans: the horse, the gun, and liquor. Provides a brief discussion of the introduction of liquor and its effects on Native Americans. Stresses that alcohol reduced Native Americans to "debauchery." Emphasizes that the sale of alcohol to Native Americans was often prohibited, but that whiskey traders usually managed to circumvent such restrictions.

0957 Wolff, Peter H.
1973 Vasomotor Sensitivity to Alcohol in Diverse Mongoloid Populations. *American Journal of Human Genetics* 25(2):193-199.

Vasomotor flushing resulting from the ingestion of small quantities of alcohol is prevalent among native Japanese, Chinese, and Koreans. The same phenomenon is evident among American-born Japanese, Chinese, and at least one group of Native Americans. The author concludes that such flushing may reflect a genetic variation in vasomotor sensitivity; however, the implications for alcoholism remain unclear.

0958 Wolman, Carol
1970 Group Therapy in Two Languages, English and Navajo. *American Journal of Psychotherapy* 24: 677-685.

The treatment of alcoholism among Navajo Indians via psychological therapy is discussed. The author investigates the use of English-speaking therapists

to treat Navajo-speaking alcoholics, and the problems
posed by the language barrier.

0959** Wood, Ronald C.
1977 Legalization vs. Prohibition of Alcohol on the
Navajo Reservation. Unpublished paper prepared
for the 1st annual Native American Alcoholism
Conference, 29p.

Discusses alcohol use on the Navajo Reservation and
the traditional and contemporary controls on drinking.
Reviews the advantages of the legalization of alcohol
and recommends the repeal of prohibition.

0960** Woods, Richard G. and Arthur M. Harkins
1968 *Indian Americans in Chicago*. Training Center
for Community Programs, University of Minnesota.
Eric Document ED 027 108.

The location, funding, organization, goals and
activities of the St. Augustine's Center for American
Indians are described. Notes an apparent relationship
between alcoholism and increased education and marriage
of Native Americans to non-Native Americans.

0961** Workshop on American Indian Affairs
n.d. Federal Indian Legislation and Policies: A Study
Packet. Unpublished report, Department of Anthropology,
University of Chicago.

Presents the texts of public laws and congressional
bills affecting Native Americans, with discussion
by Native American students. Includes the text and
discussion of Public Law 83-277 which repealed the
federal prohibition against selling liquor to Native
Americans.

0962 Wyman, Leland and Betty Thorne
1945 Notes on Navajo Suicide. *American Anthropologist*
47:278-288.

Of 33 cases of suicide examined, only two involved
alcohol.

0963 Yatsushiro, Toshio
1960 The Changing Eskimo Economy. Unpublished paper
presented at the 59th annual meeting of the American
Anthropological Association.

The tensions which engulfed the Eskimo due to extensive
culture change increased social pathology, especially
excessive drinking.

0964   Yava, Aaron
        1975 *Border Towns of the Navajo Nation*. Alamo, California: Homgangers Press.

        Drawings made by a Native American artist reflecting the worst of the Native American in Gallup, Farmington, and Winslow. The sketches depict many perspectives of Native American drinking from the viewpoint of the Native American.

0965   Yawney, Carole D.
        1968 The Kenora Report. Unpublished report, Alcoholism and Drug Addiction Research Foundation of Ontario, substudy 2-Y-67, 40p.

        Report of an investigation into alcohol use by Native Americans in Kenora, Ontario and the attitudes of the community toward a proposed treatment and rehabilitation program. Problem drinking is said to be symptomatic of larger problems affecting Native American people.

0966   Young, Robert
        1961 *Navajo Yearbook (VIII)*. Window Rock, Arizona: Navajo Nation.

        Discusses, in the section entitled "Law Enforcement," the prohibition of alcohol and the traffic in bootleg liquor. Drinking constitutes the largest category of crime on the reservation, and is involved in most other crimes.

0967   Zentner, Henry
        1963 Factors in the Social Pathology of a North American Indian Society. *Anthropologica* 5:119-130.

        A consideration of historical and contemporary factors within a Native American community which contribute to extraordinarily high rates of social pathology, such as alcoholism, child neglect, truancy, etc.

0968   Zentner, Henry
        1967 Reservation Social Structure and Anomie: a Case Study. In *A Northern Dilemma: Reference Papers*, Arthur K. Davis, ed. Pp. 112-123. Bellingham, Washington: Western Washington State College.

        Similar to citation #0967. Examines the variables which contribute to the social pathology of an unnamed Native American society. The lack of moral compulsion within the reservation to render aid proved to be one of the downfalls of the A.A. group.

0969   Zwick, Gwen
             1940 Prohibition in the Cherokee Nation, 1820-1907.
             MA Thesis, University of Oklahoma.

             Chronicles the relationship between the Cherokee Indians and alcohol from 1820 to 1907. Examines the numerous laws, federal and tribal, which attempted to deal with alcohol abuse among the Cherokees.

AUTHOR INDEX

ABERLE, David F.
  (Anthropologist)
  0001

ABLON, Joan
  (Anthropologist)
  0002, 0003, 0004

ABRAMS, George H.J.
  (Anthropologist;
  Seneca Indian)
  0005

ACKERMAN, Lillian A.
  (Anthropologist)
  0006

ACKERSTEIN, Harold (Physician)
  0833

ADAMS, Alexander B.
  0007

ADLER, Nathan
  0008

ALASKA. Native Health Board
  0009, 0010, 0011

ALBAUGH, Bernard J. (Social
  Worker)
  0012, 0013, 0014, 0015

ALBRECHT, Stan L.
  0787

ALDAY, Rudy K.
  0016

ALLEN, James R. (Psychiatrist)
  0017

ANDERSON, P. (Pharmacist)
  0015

ANDRE, James M. (Psychiatrist)
  0018, 0019, 0020, 0021,
  0022, 0023, 0024, 0025,
  0026, 0027, 0028

ARCHIBALD, Charles W., Jr.
  0055

ARIZONA. Commission of Indian
  Affairs
  0056, 0057, 0058, 0059

ARTHAUD, Bradley (Physician)
  0060

ASSOCIATION OF AMERICAN INDIAN
  AFFAIRS, INC.
  0061, 0062

ATCHESON, J.D. (Psychiatrist)
  0063

ATTNEAVE, Carolyn L.
  (Psychologist)
  A063

AUBURN, F.M.
  0064

BACON, Margaret K.
  (Anthropologist)
  0065, 0066, 0167, 0168

BADCOCK, William T.
  0067

BADT, Milton B. (District
  Judge)
  0068

BAHA, Carla J. (Apache
  Student)
  0256, 0257

BAILEY, Pearce (Physician)
  0069

BAIZERMAN, Michael (Social
  Worker)
  0722

-290-

BIENVENUE, Rita M. (Sociologist)
0106

BITSUIE, Delphine
0143

BITTKER, Thomas E. (IHS Physician)
0107, 0108

BLAKESLEE, Clement
(Anthropologist)
0109

BLANCHARD, Evelyn Lance
(Social Worker)
0110

BLANCHARD, Joseph D.
(Psychologist)
0110

BLAUVETT, Hiram
0111

BLEVANS, Stephan Anthony
(Anthropologist)
0112

BLOOM, Joseph D. (Psychiatrist)
0113, 0114, 0474, 0475

BLOUW, R.
0115

BLUMENTHAL, L.M.
0116

BOAG, Thomas J. (Psychiatrist)
0117

BOATMAN, John Francis
(Sociologist)
0118

BOCK, George E. (Physician)
0119

BOCK, P.K. (Anthropologist)
0120

BOLLINGER, Henry E., Jr.
A120

BOLLINGER, J.
0489

BOLYAI, John Zoltan
0121

BOPP, John F. (Social Worker)
0770, 0771

BOURKE, John G. (Captain,
U.S. Army)
0122

BOUTILIER, Lynn R.
0855, 0856

BOWECHOP, Sandra
(Social Worker)
0123

BOWKER, W.F.
0124

BOWLES, R.P.
0125

BOWMAN, Norman L. (ONEO
Alcoholism Staff,
Navajo Tribe)
0126

BOYCE, George A.
(Superintendent, BIA
Intermountain School)
0127, 0128

BOYER, L. Bryce (Psychiatrist)
0129, 0130, 0131

BOYER, Ruth M.
(Anthropologist)
0132

BRAASCH, W.F. (Physician)
0133

BRADFORD, R. LaJeune
(Nutritionist)
0615

BRAKEL, Samuel J. (Lawyer)
0134

BRANTNER, John
0936

BRANTON, B.J. (Physician)
0133

BRATRUDE, Amos P.
0825

BREHM, Mary L.
A704

BAKER, James L. (Physician)
0070

BALES, Robert Freed (Sociologist)
0071, 0072

BALIKCI, Asen (Anthropologist)
0073, 0074

BALL, Julia A. (Indian Affairs Task Force Coordinator)
0103

BANFILL, B.J.
0075

BARCLAY, W.S.
0754

BARNOUW, Victor (Anthropologist)
0076, 0077

BARROW, Mark V. (Physician)
0078

BARRY, Herbert III (Psychologist)
0065, 0066, 0167, 0168

BARTER, Eloise R.
0079

BARTER, James T. (Physician)
0079, 0080

BASSO, Keith H. (Anthropologist)
0081, 0082, 0083

BEANE, Syd (Social Worker)
0100

BEARSS, Edwin C.
A083

BEATTY, Lamar
0649

BEEDE, Laurence Ivan (Anthropologist)
0084

BEIGEL, Allan (Physician)
0085, 0086

BEISER, Morton (Psychiatrist)
0087, 0100

BELL, Willis H.
0161, 0162

BELMONT, Francois Vachon de (Catholic Priest)
0088

BELSHAW, Cyril S. (Anthropologist)
0363, 0364

BEN-DOR, S.
0089

BENEDICT, Ruth (Anthropologist)
0090

BENGE, William B. (Chief, BIA Law & Order Division)
0091

BENNETT, Bob (Commissioner, Bureau of Indian Affairs)
0092

BENNETT, Michael C.
0093

BENNION, Lynn J. (Physician)
0094

BERG, Lawrence (Associate Director, IHS Office of Research & Development)
0095, 0096, 0097, 0098, 0298, 0377, 0378, 0379, 0619, 0620, A620

BERGMAN, Robert L. (Psychiatrist)
0099, 0100, 0119

BERREMAN, Gerald D. (Anthropologist)
0101, 0102

BERTOLUZZI, Renitia
0303

BESTOR, Frank H. (Indian Affairs Task Force Director)
0103, 0104

BETHESDA RESEARCH INSTITUTE
0105

BRELSFORD, Gregg
(Anthropologist)
0135, A135

BRENTS, Thomas E.
0136

BRICKNER, Philip W.
0461

BROD, Thomas M. (Physician)
0137

BRODY, Hugh (Anthropologist)
0138

BROWN, De Koven
0139

BROWN, Donald N.
(Anthropologist)
0140, 0141

BROWN, Edward M.
0825

BROWN, Paula (Anthropologist)
0142

BROWN, R. Chris
0143

BROWN, R.M.
0424

BROWN, Reynold W.
0144, 0650, 0883

BROWNING, Randall
(Anthropologist)
0145

BRUMAN, Henry John (Geographer)
0146

BRYDE, John F. (Psychologist)
0147

BUCKLEY, Patricia Lorraine
(Anthropologist)
0148

BUEHLMANN, John
0149

BURCK, Charles G.
0150

BURNAP, Donald W. (Physician)
0151

BURNS, M.
0152

BURNS, Thomas R.
0153

BUSHNELL, John H.
(Anthropologist)
0154

BUTLER, G.C. (Physician)
0155

BUTTERFASS, Theodore O.
0156

BYLER, William
0157, 0158

BYNUM, Jack
0159

CARLILE, William K.
(Physician)
0320, 0321

CARPENTER, Edmund S.
(Anthropologist)
0160

CASTETTER, Edward F.
0161, 0612

CAVANAUGH, Betty
A704

CHANCE, Norman A.
(Anthropologist)
0163, 0164

CHAPIN, Edwin H.
0085, 0086

CHAPMAN, Arthur
0165

CHERRINGTON, Ernest Hurst
0166

CHESKY, Jane
0451

CHESLEY, A.J. (Physician)
0133

CHILD, Irvin L. (Psychologist)
0065, 0066, 0167, 0168

CHINN, Dick (Director, Inter-Tribal Alcoholism Program)
0169

CHITTENDEN, Hiram Martin (Historian)
0170

CHOUDHURI, Adjit
0734

CHOWENHILL, Rita C.
0818

CHRISTENSEN, Ray
0649

CIPRIANO, Juan Joe (Alcoholism Counselor, Papago Tribe)
0097

CLAIRMONT, Donald H.J. (Anthropologist)
0171, 0172

CLARK, Norman H. (Historian)
0173

CLARKE, Frank (Physician, Walapai)
0174, 0175

COCKERHAM, William C. (Educational Sociologist)
0176, 0177

CODERE, Helen (Anthropologist)
0178

COFFEY, T.G.
0179, 0180

COHEN, Fay G. (Anthropologist)
0181

COHEN, Felix S. (Lawyer)
0182

COHEN, Samuel L.
0320, 0321

COHEN, Warren H.
0183

COLLINS, Thomas William (Anthropologist)
0184

COLORADO, Joseph
0185

COLTON, Harold S. (Anthropologist)
0186

COLYAR, Ardell B. (Physician)
0695

CONRAD, Rex Dwayne (Psychologist)
0187, 0188, 0189, 0455

COULT, Allan Donald (Anthropologist)
0190

COVINGTON, James W.
A190

CRAHAN, M.E. (Physician)
0191

CRAMER, John O.
0465

CRANKSHAW, Libbet
0192

CRANSTON, Virginia A.
0292

CRAWFORD, Mazie
0568

CRUZ, Justina
0258

CULL, John G.
0193

CURLEE, Wilson V.
0194

CURLEY, Richard T. (Sociologist)
0195

CUTLER, Ron E.
0196

-294-

DAILEY, R.C. (Anthropologist)
    0197, 0198, 0199
DAILY, J.M.
    0152
DANN, Jeffery Lewis
    (Anthropologist)
    0200
DAVIS, Edward H.
    0201
DAVIS, Laurence
    0202
DAVIS, Robert E. (Chief,
    Community Prevention
    Branch, NIAAA)
    0203
DAVIS, William N. (Psychologist)
    0569
DAWES, J.W. (Social Worker)
    0770, 0771
DEARDORFF, Merle H.
    0204
DeCLAY, Edwin
    0256, 0257
DELK, John L.
    0453
DELORIA, Vine, Jr. (Lawyer,
    Author, Sioux)
    0205, 0206, 0207
DeMONTIGNY, Lionel H.
    (Physician, Chippewa)
    0208
DENISON, B.W.
    0209
DENSMORE, Frances
    (Anthropologist)
    0210
DEVEREUX, George
    (Anthropologist)
    0211, 0212
DICKMAN, Phil
    0213

DIETHELM, Oskar (Physician)
    0214
DIZMANG, Larry H.
    (Physician)
    0215, 0216, 0217,
    0603, 0715
DODSON, John W.
    (Anthropologist)
    0218
DONNELLY, Joseph Peter
    0219
DOSMAN, E.J.
    0220
DOZIER, Edward P.
    (Anthropologist, Tewa)
    0221, 0222
DRILLING, Vern
    0223, 0224
DRIVER, Harold E.
    (Anthropologist)
    0225, 0226, 0227
DRUCKER, Peter
    0228
DUBBS, Patrick James
    (Anthropologist)
    0229
DUMONT, Robert V., Jr.
    0917
DUNCAN, Earle
    0230
DURGIN, Edward C.
    (Anthropologist)
    0231
DuTOIT, Brian M.
    (Anthropologist)
    0232
DYER, Dorothy T. (Teacher,
    Family Relations)
    0233

DYER, Morris E. (Health
    Educator, Choctaw)
    0234, 0235

EASTWOOD, M.R. (Psychiatrist)
    0535

EBRAHIMI, Fred
    0637

ECKERMAN, William C.
    A704

EDDY, R.
    0236

EDGERTON, Robert
    (Anthropologist)
    0567

EDUCATIONAL RESEARCH ASSOCIATES
    0237

EDWARDS, E. Daniel
    0238, 0239, 0240

EDWARDS, Margie E.
    0240

EGGLESTON, Elizabeth
    0241

EGOAK, John A.
    0665

EHN, Shirley E.
    0242

EICHER, Carl K.
    0884

EIDLIN, Harold
    0243

EMBRY, C.B.
    0244

ENDFIELD, Marilyn R.
    0256, 0257, 0258

ERICKSON, Gerald
    0245

ERVIN, Alexander M.
    (Anthropologist)
    0246, 0247

ESCALANTE, Fernando
    0248

EVERETT, Michael W.
    (Anthropologist)
    0249, 0250, 0251,
    0252, 0253, 0254,
    0255, 0256, 0257,
    0258, 0488, 0543

EWING, John A. (Psychiatrist)
    0259

FAHY, Agnes
    0260

FAIN, Rebecca
    0853

FAIRBANKS, Robert A.
    (Lawyer)
    0261

FAIRBANKS, Rulon R.
    (Marriage Counselor)
    0262

FARBER, W.O.
    0263, 0264

FARRIS, John J.
    0265

FENNA, D. (Biochemist)
    0266

FENTON, William N.
    (Anthropologist)
    0267

FERACA, Stephen A. (Program
    Analyst, Bureau of
    Indian Affairs)
    0268

FERGUSON, Frances Northend
  (Anthropologist)
  0269, 0270, 0271, 0272,
  0273, 0274, 0275, 0276,
  0277, 0278

FEY, H.E.
  0279

FIELD, Peter B. (Psychologist)
  0280

FINKLER, Harold W.
  0281

FINNEY, Frank F.
  A281

FISHER, Karen
  0282

FITZPATRICK, Darleen
  (Anthropologist)
  0283, 0284

FLANNERY, Regina
  0285

FLINT, Garry
  0477

FOGELMAN, Billye Y. Sherman
  (Anthropologist)
  0286

FOLSOM, R.D.
  0287

FONTANA, Bernard L.
  (Anthropologist)
  0288

FORSLUND, Morris A.
  (Sociologist)
  0289, 0290, 0291, 0292,
  0293

FORTUINE, Robert (Physician)
  0078

FOSTER, Ashley (Psychologist)
  0294

FOSTER, Kenneth W.
  0295

FOULKS, Edward F. (Physician)
  0296

FRANCISCAN FATHERS
  0297

FRANCISCO, Geraldine
  (Papago)
  0298

FREDERICK, Calvin J.
  0299

FREDERICKSON, Otto F.
  (Historian)
  0300, 0301

FREEMAN, Daniel M.A.
  (Physician)
  0302

FRENCH, Laurence
  0303

FRIEDMAN, M.
  0304

FRIMMER, S.B.
  0749

FRY, Alan
  0305, 0306

FUCHS, Estelle
  0307

FULLER, Lauren L.
  0308

FUTTERMAN, Sanford
  (Pharmacist)
  0686, 0687

GABE, Ruth Chase
  0309

GABOURIE, Fred W. (Lawyer, Seneca)
  0310

GALLAGHER, Mary M.
  (Anthropologist)
  0338

GALVEZ, Eugene (Mental Health Technician, Papago)
0097, 0454, 0455

GARBARINO, Merwyn S.
0311, 0312

GARDNER, Richard E. (Anthropologist)
0313

GARFIELD, Viola E. (Anthropologist)
0314

GARTELL, Ruth Hughes
0919

GEARING, Fred (Anthropologist)
0315

GEERTZ, Clifford (Anthropologist)
0316

GEIOGAMAH, Hanay (Playwright)
0317

GHACHU, Stanley (Mental Health Coordinator, Zuni)
0027, 0028

GIBBINS, Robert J.
0709

GILBERT, J.A.L. (Biochemist)
0266

GILES, David K.
A317

GILLIN, John
0318

GOLDEN, Sandra
0319

GOLDMAN, Stanford M.
0320, 0321

GOLDSTEIN, George
0455

GOLDSTEIN, Sol (Physician)
0322

GOLEMAN, Daniel
0008

GOODWIN, W.S.
0665

GORDON, Donald
0544

GRABURN, N.H.H.
0323

GRACIA, M.F.
0324

GRANT, Claude W.
0325

GRAVES, Theodore D. (Anthropologist)
0326, 0327, 0328, 0329, 0438

GREEN, Lillian
0330

GREENWALT, Naoma I. (Statistician)
0712

GREGORY, Dick
A330

GRIFFITHS, Kenneth A.
0325

GRINNELL, George Bird (Anthropologist)
0331

GROSSMAN, Peter Holmes (Clinical Psychologist)
0332

GROVE, Alvin R.
0162

GUIDOTTI, Lee L.
0333

GUILLEMIN, J.
0334

GURUNANJAPPA, Bale S.
0143

HAAS, Theodore H.
    0335, 0336
HACKENBERG, Robert A.
    (Anthropologist)
    0337, 0338
HADDAD, Susan
    0339
HAFEN, Brent Q.
    A339
HAFFNER, Marlene (Physician)
    0340
HAGAN, William T.
    0341
HALDEMAN, Jack C. (Physician)
    0342, 0343
HALE, L.
    0464
HALLOWELL, A. Irving
    (Anthropologist)
    0344, 0345, 0346
HALSWEIG, Mark
    0687
HALVERSON, Darrell R.
    0347
HAMER, John H. (Anthropologist)
    0348, 0349
HAMMERSCHLAG, Carl A.
    (Psychiatrist)
    0100
HAMPSON, John L. (Psychiatrist)
    0772
HANLEY, J.L.
    0125
HANLON, John J.
    0350
HANNA, Joel M. (Anthropologist)
    0351
HANO, Arnold
    0352

HANSON, Diane
    0383
HANSON, James W.
    0448, 0791
HANSON, Robert C.
    0438
HARDY, Richard E.
    (Psychologist)
    0193
HARKINS, Arthur M.
    0353, 0960
HARMER, Ruth Mulvey
    (Journalist)
    0354
HARRIS, V. William
    (Psychologist)
    0434, A434, 0810
HARROVER, May J.
    0741
HARTOCOLLIS, Peter
    (Psychiatrist)
    0355
HARVEY, Cheryl
    0941
HARVEY, Elinor B.
    0356
HASSRICK, Royal B.
    0357
HAUSER, Sol Frederick
    0358
HAVARD, V.
    0359
HAVIGHURST, Robert J.
    (Educator)
    0307, 0360, 0361
HAWK, Rodney T.
    0143
HAWORTH, David D.
    (Social Worker)
    0362

HAWTHORNE, H.B. (Anthropologist)
0363, 0364

HAYNER, Norman S. (Sociologist)
0365

HAYS, Hoffman Reynolds
(Drama Teacher)
0366

HAYS, Terence E. (Anthropologist)
0367

HEASTON, Michael D.
A367

HEATH, Dwight B. (Anthropologist)
0368, 0369, 0370, 0371

HEESCH, Jack R.
0695

HEGG, Theodore D.
0372

HEIDENREICH, C. Adrian
0373

HEIZER, Robert F.
(Anthropologist)
0374

HELM, June (Anthropologist)
0375, 0376

HELMICK, Edward
0095, 0096, A376, 0377,
0378, 0379, 0619, 0620,
A620

HENDERSON, Norman B.
(Clinical Psychologist)
0380, 0381, 0382

HENDRIE, Hugh C.
0383

HENK, Matthew L.
0384

HENNIGH, Lawrence
0504

HERTZBERG, H.W.
0385

HETRICK, Barbara
0536

HILDES, J.A. (Physician)
0115

HILL, C.A.
0671

HILL, Thomas Warren
(Anthropologist)
0386

HIPPLER, Arthur E.
(Anthropologist)
0387, 0388, 0389,
0390, 0391

HIROKAWA, Theodore
0392

HIRSCHFELD, Mervyn H.
0393

HOBART, C.W. (Sociologist)
0394

HODGINS, B.W.
0125

HOEBEL, E. Adamson
(Anthropologist)
0551, 0552

HOFFMAN, Helmut (Physician)
0395, 0396, A396

HOLE, L.W.
0754

HOLLOWAY, M.A.
(Registered Nurse)
0397

HOLLOWAY, Robert
0398

HONDA, Paul H. (Pharmacist)
0615

HONIGMANN, Irma (Anthropologist)
0406, 0407, 0408,
0409, 0410, 0411

HONIGMANN, John J.
(Anthropologist)
0399, 0400, 0401,
0402, 0403, 0404,
0405, 0406, 0407,
0408, 0409, 0410,
0411

-300-

HOOD, William R. (Psychologist)
0412

HORTON, Donald D.
(Anthropologist)
0413

HOWARD, James H.
(Anthropologist)
0414

HOWARD-CRAFT, A.
0415

HOWAY, F.W. (Historian)
0416

HOYT, Olga
0417

HRDLICKA, Ales
(Anthropologist)
0418, 0419

HUDSON, Peter J.
A419

HUFFAKER, Clair (Novelist)
0420

HUMMER, H.R. (Physician)
0421

HUMPHREY, J.A.
0491

HUNTER, E. James
0085, 0086

HURT, Wesley R.
(Anthropologist)
0422, 0423, 0424

HUSSEY, Hugh H. (Physician)
0425

HUTCHINSON, C.H.
0426

INDIAN HISTORIAN PRESS
0427

INDIAN RIGHTS ASSOCIATION
0428

IRVINE, Donald
0734

JACKSON, Douglas N.
0395

JACOBS, Wilbur R.
0429, 0430, 0431

JAMES, Bernard J.
(Anthropologist)
0432

JAMISON, S.M.
0363, 0364

JAYWARDENE, C.H.S.
(Criminologist)
0433

JEFFRIES, William R.
0104

JENSEN, Gary F. (Sociologist)
0434, A434, 0810

JEPSON, William W.
0435

JESSOR, Richard (Psychologist)
0436, 0437, 0438

JESSOR, S.L.
0438

JILEK, Wolfgang George
(Psychiatrist)
0439, 0440, 0441, 0442

JILEK-AALL, Louise (Physician)
0441, 0443

JOHNSON, Carmen A.
0444

JOHNSON, Clarence T.
0136

JOHNSON, Dale L.
(Psychologist)
0444, 0459

JONES, Ben Morgan (Physician)
0265

JONES, Dorothy M. (Sociologist)
    0445, 0446
JONES, Kenneth L. (Physician)
    0447, 0448, 0449, 0791
JORGENSEN, J.G.
    0450
JOSEPH, Alice (Anthropologist)
    0451
JOYCE, Kevin
    0452
JUSTICE, James W. (Physician)
    0713

KAHN, Marvin W. (Psychologist)
    0188, 0189, 0453, 0454, 0455
KALANT, Harold
    0709
KALIN, Rudolf (Psychologist)
    0569
KANE, Robert L. (Physician)
    0456
KANE, Rosalie A. (Social Worker)
    0456
KANE, Roslyn D.
    0698
KANE, Stephen L.
    0457
KAPLAN, Bert (Anthropologist)
    0458, 0459
KAPLAN, Gary J. (Physician)
    0695
KAPUR, Bushan M.
    0709
KATZ, Solomon (Anthropologist)
    0296
KAUFMAN, Arthur
    0460, 0461

KAUFFMAN, Joann (Resource Developer, Seattle Indian Health Board)
    0853
KEALEAR, Charles A. (Sioux)
    0462
KEAST, Thomas J.
    0807
KEHOE, Alice B. (Anthropologist)
    0463
KELBERT, M.
    0464
KELLY, Roger E.
    0465
KELSO, Dianne R. (Librarian)
    A063
KEMNITZER, Luis S. (Anthropologist)
    0466, 0467, 0468
KENEALLY, Henry J., Jr. (Health Educator)
    0469
KENNEDY, Donald A.
    0512
KESTER, F.E.
    0470
KICKINGBIRD, Kirke (Kiowa)
    0207
KILEN, Allan G.
    0471
KIM, Yong C.
    0472, 0473
KINZIE, J. David (Psychiatrist)
    0772
KLAPPENBACH, R.S. (Physician)
    0713
KLEINFELD, Judith (Educator)
    0474, 0475

KLINE, James A. (Psychologist)
0476, 0477

KLUCKHOHN, Clyde (Anthropologist)
0478

KNIGHT, Mary (VISTA Worker)
0479

KNISLEY, E.R.
0480

KOOLAGE, William W., Jr.
(Anthropologist)
0481

KRAUSE, Marilyn Louise
(Anthropologist)
0482

KRAUS, Robert F. (Physician)
0483, 0484

KRUTZ, Gordon V.
(Anthropologist)
0485

KUNITZ, Stephen J.
(Physician-Sociologist)
0486, A486, 0487, 0488,
0489, 0539, 0540, 0541,
0542, 0543

KUNSTADTER, Peter
(Anthropologist)
0490

KUPFERER, H.J.
0491

KUTTNER, Robert E. (Physician)
0492, 0493

LaBARRE, Weston (Anthropologist)
0494, 0495, 0496

LaBUFF, Stephen (Director,
Chemawa Alcohol Education
Program)
0497

LAGASSE, Jean H.
0498

LAING, A. (Canadian Minister
of Indian Affairs)
0499

LAL, Ravindra
0500, 0501

LAMOUREAUX, Calvin
(Sioux)
0502

LANG, Gretchen Mary Chesley
(Anthropologist)
0503, 0937

LANGNESS, Lewis L.
(Anthropologist)
0504, 0716

LATIF, A.H. (Sociologist)
0106

LAVALLEE, Mary Ann
0505

LAWRENCE, William J.
0506

LEAGUE OF WOMEN VOTERS / DALLAS
0507

LEAGUE OF WOMEN VOTERS /
MINNEAPOLIS
0508

LEAGUE OF WOMEN VOTERS /
MINNESOTA
0509

LEATHAM, Raymond Claude
(NIAAA Indian Desk)
A509

LECHNYR, Ronald Joseph
(Social Worker)
0510

LEIGH, L.H.
0511

LEIGHTON, Alexander H.
(Physician)
0512, 0513

LEIGHTON, Dorothea C.
0513

LEJERO, Linda (Mental Health Technician, Papago)
0097, 0455

LELAND, Joy Hanson (Anthropologist)
0514, 0515, 0516, 0517, 0518, 0519, 0520, 0521, 0522, A522

LEMERT, Edwin M. (Anthropologist)
0523, 0524, 0525, 0526, 0527, 0528, 0529

LEON, Robert L. (Psychiatrist)
0530, 0531

LEUPP, Francis E. (Commission of Indian Affairs)
0532

LEVI, M.C.
0533

LEVINE, Harry-Gene
0534

LEVINE, Saul V. (Psychiatrist)
0535

LEVITAN, Sar A.
0536

LEVY, Jerrold E. (Anthropologist)
0487, 0488, 0489, 0537, 0538, 0539, 0540, 0541, 0542, 0543, 0544

LEWIS, Claudia (Educator)
0545

LEWIS, Jesse
0454

LEWIS, Thomas H. (Psychiatrist)
0546

LI, Ting-Kai (Physician)
0094

LIBERTY, Margot (Anthropologist)
0809

LIEBER, Charles S. (Physician)
0547

LINDQUIST, G.E.E.
0548

LITTMAN, Gerard (Social Worker)
0549, 0550

LLEWELLYN, K.N.
0551, 0552

LOBBAN, Mary C. (Physician)
0553

LOCKLEAR, Herbert H.
A553

LOEB, E.M.
0554

LOOKOUT, F. Morris (Director, Tulsa Council on Alcoholism)
0555, A555

LORINCZ, Albert B. (Physician)
0492, 0493

LOUGHLIN, B.
0672

LOVRICH, Frank
0556

LOWERY, Mary J.
0085, 0086

LUBART, Joseph M. (Psychiatrist)
0557, 0558

LUEBBEN, Ralph A. (Anthropologist)
0559, 0560

LUMHOLTZ, Carl Sofus
0561

LUNGER, Harold L.
0562

LURIE, Nancy Oestreich (Anthropologist)
0376, 0563, 0564

LYSYK, K. (Lawyer)
0565, 0566

MacANDREW, Craig (Psychologist)
0567

McBETH, Kate C. (Missionary)
0568

McCABE, Thomas R. (Hospital Administrator)
0086

McCLELLAND, David C. (Psychologist)
0569

McCLURE, William J.
A376

MacCRACKEN, Robert Dale (Anthropologist)
0570

MacDONALD, John A. (Social Worker)
0571

McDONALD, David R. (Librarian)
B588

McDONALD, Thomas (Psychologist)
0572

MacGREEVY, Susan (Anthropologist)
0573

MacGREGOR, Gordon (Anthropologist)
0574

McGUNIGLE, Elizabeth R.
0575

MacKINNON, A.A. (Psychologist)
0576

MacKINNON, Victor S.
0577

MACKLIN, June
0578

MacLEOD, William C. (Historian)
0579

McNAIR, Crawford N.
0580

McNICKLE, D'Arcy (Anthropologist)
0581

McSWAIN, Romola Mae (Anthropologist)
0582

MADDEN, Michael A.
0714

MAIL, Patricia Davison (Health Educator)
0583, 0584, 0585, 0586, 0587, 0588, A588, B588

MANDELBAUM, D.G. (Anthropologist)
0589

MANGIN, William (Anthropologist)
0590

MANN, Marty
0591

MANNING, Leah (Social Worker)
0592

MANZOLILLO, Lola R. (Anthropologist)
0593

MARCH, Gregory
0782

MARCUS, R.
0097

MARGOLIN, Sydney G. (Psychiatrist)
0594

MARIANI, Eugene L. (Director, New Mexico Division of Mental Health)
0761

MARSDEN, Gillian (Health Planner)
0595

MARTINEZ, Frederic H. (Indian Field Representative, New Mexico Commission on Alcoholism)
0596, 0597

MARX, Herbert (Lawyer)
0598, 0599

MASHBURN, William
0461

MASON, Velma Garcia
0600

MASSEY, William C.
0227

MAUSE, Philip J.
0183

MAY, Philip A. (Sociologist)
0601, 0602, A602, B602, 0603

MAYNARD, Eileen (Anthropologist)
0604, 0605, 0606

MEAD, Beverley (Physician)
0764

MEAD, Margaret (Anthropologist)
0607

MEDICINE, Bea (Anthropologist)
0608

MEEKS, Donald E.
0609

MEMPHIS STATE UNIVERSITY
A609

MENDELSOHN, B.
0610

MENDEZ, Alfredo F. (Physician)
0611

MERCER, G.W.
0612

MERITT, Edgar B. (Assistant Commissioner of Indian Affairs, BIA)
0613, 0614

MERK, Frederick
A614

METZNER, Richard J.
0108

MEYERS, Ralph E.
0293

MICHAL, Mary L. (Physician)
0615

MILAM, James R. (Psychologist)
0616

MILLER, Maurice W.
0617

MILLER, Sheldon I. (Psychiatrist)
0095, 0096, 0377, 0378, 0379, 0618, 0619, 0620, A620, 0756

MILLIGAN, Donald (Social Worker)
0621

MINDELL, Carl E. (Physician)
0622, 0623, 0624, 0625, 0626

MINNIS, Mhyra S.
0627

MINNIS, Roberta
0104

MITCHELL, Patricia M.
A376

MITCHELL, T.V.
0665

MITO, Bob
0628

MIX, L. (Biochemist)
0266

MJELDE, Lee Ann
0629

MOHATT, Gerald (Psychologist)
0630

MOLINARI, Carol (Director, Center for Alcohol and Addiction Studies, University of Alaska)
0631

MONTANA. State Department of Health and Environmental Sciences
0632, 0633, 0634, 0635

MONTANA. State Department of Institutions
0636

MOORE, R. Paul
A704

MORGAN, Lael
A636

MORRIS, Joann S.
0637

MORSE, J.
0638

MORRISON, N.
0196

MOSHER, James F.
0639

MOSKOWITZ, H.
0152

MOSS, Fenton E. (Social Worker)
0325, 0640, 0641, 0642, 0643, 0644, 0645, 0646, 0647, 0648, 0649, 0650

MUGGIA, Albert L. (Physician)
0651, 0652, 0653

MUNZ, C. Stewart (Educator)
0654

MUNZ, Victor R.
0655

MURPHY, Jane M.
0656

MUSCHENHEIM, Carl (Physician)
0260

NAGEL, Gerald S. (English Teacher)
0657

NAGLER, M.
0658, 0659

NELSON, Leonard
A659

NELSON, Thurston D.
0660

NEUFELDT, A.H.
0576

NEUGARTEN, Bernice
0361

NEW YORK (STATE). Center for Migrant Studies
0661

NICOLICH, Mark
A819

NILSSON, Joel (Journalist)
0662

NISWANDER, Jerry D. (Dentist)
0078

NOBLE, Gaile P. (Social Worker)
0663

NOEM, Avis A.
0396, A396

NORICK, Frank A. (Anthropologist)
0664

NORIEGO, Julian L.
0665

NORTH PUGET SOUND HEALTH COUNCIL
0666

NOWAK, Jean
0667

NURGE, Ethel (Anthropologist)
0668

NUTTING, Paul A. (Physician)
0095, 0096, 0098, 0377,
0378, 0379, 0619, 0620,
A620

NYBROTEN, Norman
0669

ODEEN, Philip A.
0264

ODOROFF, Charles L. (Physician)
0489

OFFICER, James E.
(Anthropologist)
0670

OFTEDAL, Alfred
0136

OGDEN, Michael
0671

O'MEARA, James E.
A671

OMRAN, A.R. (Physician)
0672

OPLER, Morris Edward
(Anthropologist)
0673, 0674

OREGON. Division of Mental Health
0675

OREGON. Indian Commission on Alcohol and Drug Abuse
0676

OSTENDORF, Don
0617

OSWALT, Wendell H. (Historian)
0677, 0678

OXEREOK, Charles H.
0679

PALMER, Ina C.
(Psychiatric Nurse)
0680

PAMBRUN, Audra (Registered Nurse)
0681

PARISH, John C.
A681

PARKER, Seymour
(Anthropologist)
0682

PARKIN, Michael
0683

PARMEE, Edward A.
(Anthropologist)
0684, 0685

PASCAROSA, Paul
(Psychiatrist)
0686, 0687

PATTERSON, Harold L.
(School Superintendent)
0688

PATTISON, E. Mansel
(Psychiatrist)
0772

PELLIZZARI, E.D. (Chemist)
0259

PETRINKA, A. (Registered Nurse)
0115

PETTERSON, Jay R.
0689

PHELPHS, Graham Herbert
0309

PIERRE, George
0690

PINCOCK, T.A. (Physician)
0691

PINTO, Leonard J.
0692

PITTMAN, David J.   (Sociologist)
    0693,   0846
POPHAM, Robert E.   (Director,
    Research Addiction
    Foundation, Toronto)
    0694
PORTER, Margaret R.
    0695
PORVAZNIK, John   (Physician)
    0696
PRAGER, Kenneth M.   (Physician)
    0697
PRESS, Daniel S.   (Lawyer)
    0698
PRICE, John A.   (Anthropologist)
    0699,   0700
PRICE, Monroe E.
    0701
PROVINCIAL NATIVE ACTION COMMITTEE
    0702
PRUCHA, Francis Paul
    0703

QUERY, Joy M.
    0704
QUERY, William T.
    0704

RABIN, David A.   (Physician)
    0713,   0714
RACHAL, J. Valley
    A704
RAE-GRANT, Quentin   (Psychiatrist)
    0535
RANKIN, James G.
    0709

RASPA, G.
    0705
RATTRAY, Richard
    0706
RAWLYK, G.A.
    0125
REAGAN, Albert
    0707
REASONS, Charles H.
    0708
REED, T. Edward
    0709
REESE, Kenneth M.   (Lawyer)
    0710
REIFEL, Ben   (Congressman,
    Sioux)
    0711
REINHARD, Karl R.
    (Veterinarian,
    Statistician)
    0712,   0713,   0714
RESNIK, H.L.P.
    0715
RHODES, Robert J.   (Physician)
    0716
RICHARDS, W.
    0610,   0717
RIFFENBURGH, Arthur S.
    (Probation Officer)
    0718
RITZENTHALER, Robert
    0719
ROBBINS, Richard Howard
    (Anthropologist)
    0720,   0721
ROBERTS, Arthur C.   (Physician)
    0476,   0477
ROBERTSON, G.G.   (Psychiatrist)
    0722
ROBERTSON, Heather
    0723

ROBINSON, Doane (Secretary of State, South Dakota)
0724

ROBINSON, Shirley
0725

ROGG, E.W. (Physician)
0713

ROHNER, Evelyn C. (Anthropologist)
0726

ROHNER, Ronald P. (Anthropologist)
0726

ROLL, Samuel
0110

ROMANCE, G.L.
0727

ROSS, John Alan
0728

ROSS, W.G.
0729

ROTMAN, Arthur Edel (Anthropologist)
0730

ROUSE, Beatrice A.
0259

ROUSSEAU, Victor
0731

ROY, Chunilal (Psychiatrist)
0732, 0733, 0734

ROZYNKO, Vitali V.
0477

RUCK, James Allen
0309

RUDE, Douglas H.
0735

RYAN, Joan
0830

SAFFORD, W.E. (Economic Botanist)
0736

SAIKI, John H. (Physician)
0828, 0829

SAKIESTEWA, Douglas (Hopi)
0698

SALONE, Emile
0737

SALTONSTALL, Richard, Jr. (Journalist)
0738

SANCHEZ, Paul R. (Community Living Specialist, BIA)
0739

SANFORD, Nevitt
0740

SASLOW, Harry L.
0741

SATA, Lindbergh S. (Physician)
0628

SAUM, Lewis O. (Historian)
0742

SAVARD, Robert J. (Social Worker)
0743, 0744, 0745, 0746, 0828, 0829

SAVISHINSKY, Joel S. (Anthropologist)
0747, 0748, 0749

SCHAEFER, James M.
0750

SCHAEFER, Otto (Physician)
0266, 0751, 0752

SCHMEISER, Douglas A. (Lawyer)
0753

SCHMITT, N.
0754

SCHNELL, Jerome V. (Biochemist)
 0755

SCHOENFELD, Lawrence S.
 (Psychologist)
 0618, 0756

SCHOENFELDT, Lyle F.
 (Psychologist)
 0820

SCHUSKY, Ernest Lester
 0757

SCOMP, Henry A.
 0758

SCOTT, Woodrow W.
 0759

SEARS, William F. (Physician)
 0760, 0761

SELBY, Karen
 0256, 0257

SELLERS, Mary
 0719

SELLS, Cato (Commissioner of
 Indian Affairs, BIA)
 0762

SHARPLIN, C.D. (Sociologist)
 0763

SHEILDS, J.
 0717

SHERMAN, Gail H. (Statistician)
 0615

SHERWIN, Duane (Physician)
 0764

SHERWOOD, Morgan B.
 0765

SHIMPO, M.
 0766

SHORE, James H. (Psychiatrist)
 0544, 0767, 0768, 0769,
 0770, 0771, 0772, 0773,
 0774, 0953

SHORR, Gregory I. (Physician)
 0095, 0096, 0098, 0377,
 0378, 0379, 0619, 0620,
 A620

SIEGEL, Bernard J.
 (Anthropologist)
 0775

SIEVERS, Maurice L.
 (Physician)
 0320, 0321, 0776,
 0777, 0778, 0779,
 0780

SIMS, O. Suthern, Jr.
 (Educator)
 0820

SINCLAIR, J. Grant (Lawyer)
 0781

SKELLEY, Thomas (Director,
 Division of Special
 Problems, DHEW)
 0782

SKIRROW, Jan
 0783

SLATER, Arthur D.
 (Anthropologist)
 0784, 0785, 0786, 0787

SLOAN, Mary Ellen
 0788

SLOTKIN, J.S.
 (Anthropologist)
 0789

SMITH, Anne M.
 0790

SMITH, Arlene
 (Papago)
 0298

SMITH, Austin
 0393

SMITH, David W. (Physician)
 0447, 0448, 0449, 0791

SMITH, Derek G.
 0792

SMITH, J.C.
 0793

SMITH, Valene Lucy
 (Anthropologist)
 0794, 0795

SMITH, William W.
    0796
SNYDER, Charles R.
    (Sociologist)
    0066
SNYDER, Peter Zane
    (Anthropologist)
    0797
SNYDERMAN, George S.
    (Anthropologist)
    0798
SOLER, Janice
    0799
SORKIN, Alan L.
    0800
SPAULDING, Philip
    (Anthropologist)
    0801
SPECTOR, Mozart I.   (Statistician)
    0671
SPENCE, R.E.
    0802
SPICER, Rosamund B.
    0451
SPINDLER, George D.
    (Anthropologist)
    0803
SPINDLER, Louise S.
    (Anthropologist)
    0803
SPRADLEY, James Philip
    (Anthropologist)
    0804
STAATS, Elmer B.
    0805
STAATS, Howard E.   (Lawyer, Mohawk)
    0806
STAGES, Thomas B.
    0807
STANBURY, W.T.
    0808

STAND-IN-TIMBER, John
    0809
STARKEY, Vesta
    A120
STAUSS, Joseph H.
    (Sociologist)
    0434, A434, 0810
STEIN, Gary C.
    A810
STEINER, Stanley
    0811
STEVENS, Joyce Ann
    (Anthropologist)
    0812
STEVENSON, D.S.
    0813
STEWART, Eugene R.
    A813
STEWART. Omer C.
    (Anthropologist)
    0814
STIRLING, Matthew W.
    0815
STONE, Dennis L.
    0773
STRATTON, John R.
    0816
STRATTON, Ray
    0817
STREET, Pamela B.
    0818
STREISSGUTH, Ann Pytkowicz
    (Physician)
    0449, 0819
STREIT, Fred
    A819
STRIMBU, Jerry L.
    (Psychologist)
    0820
STUART, Paul
    (Social Worker)
    0625, 0626

STULL, Donald David
(Anthropologist)
0821, 0822

SUE, Hiroko (Anthropologist)
0823

SWAN, James Gilchrist
0824

SWANSON, David W.
0825

SWANTON, John R.
0826

SWETT, Daniel H.
0827

SZUTER, Carl F. (Physician)
0828, 0829

TAMERIN, John S. (Physician)
0085, 0086

TERMANSEN, Paul E.
0830

TERRELL, John Upton (Historian)
0831

THOMPSON, W.A.
0832

THOMPSON, William M.
(Physician)
0833

THORNE, Betty
0962

THUNDER, Right Hand
0834

TODD, Anne L.
0714

TODD, Norman
0442

TOLER, Fred M. (Director,
New Mexico Commission
on Alcoholism)
0835

TOPPER, Martin David
(Anthropologist)
0836, 0837, 0838,
0839, 0840, 0841,
0842, 0843

TORREY, E. Fuller
0844

TOWLE, Leland H.
A844

TRAUTMANN, Phillip R.
(Physician)
0322

TRELEASE, A.W.
0845

TRICE, Harrison Miller
(Sociologist)
0846

TRILLIN, Calvin (Journalist)
0847

TRUDELL, John
0848

TRURO, Lee F.
0849

TSCHETTER, Robert A.
0264

TSOSIE, Philip
A317

TURNER, Ernest J. (Director,
Seattle Indian
Alcoholism Program)
0850, 0851, 0852,
A852, B852, 0853

TWISS, Gayla
0606

TYLER, S. Lyman
0854

-313-

UECKER, Albert E. (Psychologist)
0855, 0856

ULLELAND, Christy N.
0449

UNDERHILL, Ruth Murray
(Anthropologist)
0857, 0858, 0895, 0860,
0861, 0862, 0863

UNITED INDIANS OF ALL TRIBES
0864

U.S. ALCOHOL, DRUG ABUSE AND
MENTAL HEALTH ADMINISTRATION
0865

U.S. AMERICAN INDIAN POLICY REVIEW
COMMISSION. TASK FORCE SIX
0866

U.S. AMERICAN INDIAN POLICY REVIEW
COMMISSION. TASK FORCE
ELEVEN
0867

U.S. BUREAU OF INDIAN AFFAIRS
0868

U.S. COMMISSION ON CIVIL RIGHTS
0869

U.S. COMMISSION ON CIVIL RIGHTS.
MINNESOTA ADVISORY COMMITTEE
0870

U.S. COMPTROLLER GENERAL
0871

U.S. CONGRESS. SENATE.
COMMITTEE ON INTERIOR
AND INSULAR AFFAIRS
0872

U.S. DEPARTMENT OF HEALTH,
EDUCATION AND WELFARE
0873

U.S. DISTRICT COURT. WYOMING
0874

U.S. INDIAN HEALTH SERVICE.
DESERT WILLOW TRAINING
CENTER
0875, 0876, 0877

U.S. INDIAN HEALTH SERVICE.
TASK FORCE ON ALCOHOLISM
0878

U.S. NATIONAL CLEARINGHOUSE
FOR ALCOHOL INFORMATION
0879

U.S. NATIONAL INSTITUTE ON
ALCOHOL ABUSE AND
ALCOHOLISM
0880, 0881

U.S. PUBLIC HEALTH SERVICE
0882

UPCHEGO, Henry (Ute Tribal
Judge)
0883

USEEM, Ruth Hill
0884

UTE TRIBAL BUSINESS COUNCIL
0885

VACHON, A. (Historian)
0886

VALL-SPINOSA, A.
0887

Van STONE, James W.
(Anthropologist)
0888

Van VALKENBURGH, Richard
(Anthropologist)
0889, 0890

VARNER, Richard
0461

VAUGHAN, Frederick
A890

VIEIRA, Theodore A.
0695

VIOLA, H.J.
0891

VOGT, Evon Z.
(Anthropologist)
0892

VOLLMANN, Tim (Lawyer)
    0893

Von FUMETTI, Billee
    (Psychiatric Nurse)
    0774

Von HENTIG, Hans (Criminologist)
    0894

WACKO, William J.
    0895, 0896

WADDELL, Jack O.
    (Anthropologist)
    0897, 0898, 0899, 0900,
    0901

WAGNER, Roland M. (Social Worker)
    0902

WALKER, Constance Georgene
    (Registered Nurse)
    0903

WALKER, Deward E., Jr.
    (Anthropologist)
    0904

WALLACE, Anthony F.C.
    (Anthropologist)
    0905, 0906, 0907, 0908

WALLER, Thelma R. (Social Worker)
    0770, 0771

WANNER, Eric (Psychologist)
    0569

WASHBURN, Wilcomb E.
    0909

WASHBURNE, Chandler
    (Anthropologist)
    0910, 0911

WASHINGTON (STATE). Department
    of Social and Health Services
    0912

WASHINGTON (STATE). Indian
    Commission on Alcohol and
    Drug Abuse
    0913

WATSKY, Morris
    0914

WATSON, Jane
    (Anthropologist)
    0915

WAX, Murray L. (Anthropologist)
    0916, 0917

WAX, Rosalie H. (Anthropologist)
    0917

WEAST, Donald Ellsworth
    (Anthropologist)
    0918

WEAVER, Thomas
    (Anthropologist)
    0919

WEIGHTMAN, Barbara Ann
    (Geographer)
    0920

WEIL, R.
    0921

WEIST, Katherine M.
    (Anthropologist)
    0080

WEPPNER, Robert Stephens
    (Anthropologist)
    0922

WERDEN, Patricia K.
    0923, 0924

WERNER, Vic W.
    0926

WESTERMEYER, Joseph John
    (Physician-
    Anthropologist)
    0927, 0928, 0929,
    0930, 0931, 0932,
    0933, 0934, 0935,
    0936, 0937

WHEAR, James B.
    0938

WHITE, Robert Anthony
    (Jesuit Priest)
    0939, 0940

-315-

WHITECROW, Jay C.
0242

WHITEHEAD, Paul C. (Sociologist)
0941

WHITESIDE, Don
0942

WHITTAKER, James O.
(Psychologist)
A942, 0943, 0944, 0945

WILKINSON, Rupert
0946

WILLIAMS, Arline K.
0947

WILLIAMS, Cecil (Chairman,
Papago Tribe)
0455

WILLIAMS, Jay R.
A704

WILLIAMS, John Robert (Educator)
0948

WILLIAMSON, R.
0766

WILLIAMSON, R.G.
0949

WILLS, James (Social Worker)
0950

WILSON, Benjamin D.
0951

WILSON, Eugene B.
0952

WILSON, Lawrence G.
0953

WINKLER, Allan M. (Historian)
0954

WINN, Wandal William
(Psychiatrist)
0955

WISSLER, Clark (Anthropologist)
0956

WOLFF, Peter H.
0957

WOLMAN, Carol (Physician)
0958

WOOD, Ronald C.
0818, 0959

WOODS, Richard G.
0353, 0960

WORKSHOP ON AMERICAN INDIAN
AFFAIRS
0961

WYMAN, Leland
0962

YATSUSHIRO, Toshio
0963

YAVA, Aaron (Artist)
0964

YAWNEY, Carole D.
0694, 0965

YOUNG, Robert
0966

ZENTNER, Henry (Sociologist)
0967, 0968

ZUAZUA, P.A.
0665

ZWICK, Gwen W.
0969

SUBJECT INDEX

A.A. see ALCOHOLICS ANONYMOUS
ABERDEEN AREA 0151
ABORIGINAL ALCOHOL USE 0161,0253,
    0258,0758,0901
ABORIGINAL LAW 0142
ABSTINENCE
    see also TEMPERANCE
        0034,0048,0052,0071,0165,
        0284,0286,0330,0614,0740,
        0742,0745,0856,0920
    Alcoholics Anonymous
        see ALCOHOLICS ANONYMOUS
    Native American Church 0001,
        0015,0099,0226,0268,0302,
        0385,0496,0686,0687,0733,
        0734,0902
    Religious aspects
        see also HANDSOME LAKE
            RELIGION, INDIAN
            SHAKER CHURCH,
            NATIVE AMERICAN
            CHURCH, WINTER
            CEREMONY
        0139,0140,0154,0204,0283,
        0284,0390,0391,0414,0439,
        0440,0441,0442,0450,0803,
        0905,0906,0918
ACCIDENTS
    see also DRIVING, INTOXICATED
        0006,0022,0104,0183,0228,
        0257,0362,0534,0757,0968
    Alcohol related 0143,0196,0338,
        A339,0350,0372,0522,0570,
        0603,0615,0657,0672,0696,
        0697,0754,0808,0821,0830,
        0882,0885,0950
    Incidence of 0026,0196,0322,
        0338,0342,0343,0455,0666
    Mortality 0026,0143,0196,
        0342,0343,0372,0603,0615,
        0653,0666,0671,0696,0754,
        0830,0870

Sex differences 0196
ACCULTURATION 0076,0102,
    0109,0112,0137,0163,
    0178,0184,0187,0216,
    0252,0272,0273,0286,
    0316,0318,0326,0345,
    0348,0353,0388,0389,
    0394,0411,0432,0465,
    0479,0486,0489,0492,
    0493,0503,0514,0539,
    0541,0542,0543,0559,
    0593,0605,0610,0630,
    0663,0664,0699,0706,
    0730,0734,0766,0773,
    0797,0860,0892,0907,
    0911,0920,0960
ACHKINHESHACKY INDIANS 0111
ADAPTATION 0089,0229,0247,
    0286,0402,0405,0410,
    0422,0446,0467,0481,
    0503,0557,0558,0574,
    0699,0720
ADDICTION RESEARCH FOUNDATION
    TORONTO, ONTARIO 0197,
    0580,0609,0612
ADJUSTMENT 0071,0072,0163,
    0327,0444,0467,0478,
    0582,0605,0654,0813
ADOLESCENTS
    see also YOUTHS
        0097,0128,0214,0242,
        0256,0258,0444,0475,
        0497,0544,0610,0665,
        0692,0877
    Arrests A046,0084,0454,
        0605,0627,0685,0875,
        0876,0903
    Drinking, behavioral aspects
        0017,0045,0084,0171,
        0176,0177,0237,0257,
        0289,0332,0352,0353,
        0398,0409,0583,0584,

-317-

0741,0812,0841,0875,0903,
0918,0952
Drinking, etiology
   see ETIOLOGY, of drinking
Drinking, familial aspects
   0257,A819,0903
Drinking, prevention
   see PREVENTION PROGRAMS, for
      adolescents
   ALCOHOL EDUCATION, for
      adolescents
Drinking, sex differences
   0176,0237,0289,0291,0292,
   0302,0356,A704
Drinking, sociological aspects
   0054,0084,0118,0127,0128,
   0237,0255,0298,0402,0474,
   0522,A704,0756,A819,0825,
   0875,0918
Drinking, treatment 0454,0710
Drug Use, behavioral aspects
   0013,0054,0177,0217,0234,
   0290,0291,0352,0460,0695,
   0735,A819
Drug Use, sex differences
   0237,0695
Suicide, alcohol related
   0217,0360,0484,0710
Suicide, etiology
   see ETIOLOGY OF SUICIDE,
      Among Adolescents
Suicide, familial aspects
   0110,0217,0307,0360
Suicide, incidence of
   0028,0110,0217,0255,0307,
   0322,0352,0356,0360,0544,
   0610,0681,0770,0771
Suicide, psychological aspects
   0110,0217,0255,0307
Suicide, sex differences
   0356,0360
AGAVE 0162,0227
AGGRESSION
   see also VIOLENCE
   0063,0089,0114,0129,0160,
   0171,0257,0302,0316,0348,
   0349,0358,0406,0424,0478,
   0527,0530,0545,0580,0594,
   0618,0622,0623,0625,0647,
   0697,0704,0726,0748,0752,
   0775,0924,0945,0947

AKLAVIK (N.W.T., CANADA)
   0171,0172,0409
ALASKA 0011,0038,0060
   see also FAIRBANKS, ANCHORAGE,
      NOME, ALASKAN
      NATIVES, ESKIMO,
      ALEUT, ATHABASCAN
   0135,0163,0164,0166,0185,
   0228,0229,0325,0342,0343,
   0353,0356,0366,0388,0389,
   0390,0391,0470,0474,0483,
   0548,0610,0620,A620,0636,
   0656,0664,0677,0683,0725,
   0765,0794
   Treatment programs in
   0009,0010,0095,0377,0378,
   0379,0619,0620,A620,0631
ALASKA NATIVE HEALTH BOARD
   0620,A620
ALASKAN NATIVES
   see also ESKIMO, ALEUT,
      ATHABASCAN
   0060,0209,0295,0342,0343,
   A376,0610,0725,0866
   Arrests among 0480
   Detox program 0185
   Drinking among 0377,0378,
      0379,0389,0445,0480,0664,
      0679,0695,0765,0795,0799
   Health problems of 0833
   Mortality 0470
   Suicide among 0483,0683
   Treatment programs among
      0620,A620
ALBERTA, CANADA 0116,0896
ALBERTA ALCOHOLISM AND DRUG
   ABUSE COMMISSION 0116
ALBUQUERQUE, NEW MEXICO
   0596,0835
ALCOHOL
   Education 0062,0193,0238,
      0304,A553,0675
   Attitude changes 0307,
      0816,A852,0855,0856
   Efficacy and evaluation
      0144,0596,0740,0856,0904
   For adolescents
      0047,0127,0128,0233,0235,
      0398,0454,0923,0924
   For community members
      0947

-318-

For families 0047
For law enforcement officials
  0047,0816
For paraprofessionals 0047,
  0799,0938
For tribal officials 0047,
  0126
Materials 0047,0128,0600,
  0938
Planning aspects 0047,
  0127,0144,0648,0700,0760,
  B852
Program design 0497,0643,
  0675,0722,0881
Historical aspects 0024,
  0156,0191,0236
Intoxication
  see DRUNKENNESS
Metabolism
  see METABOLISM OF ALCOHOL
Programs, transfer of Indian
  0319,A522,0865
Research
  see also DATA COLLECTION AND
    ANALYSIS
  Methodology 0066,0167,
    0249,0436,0437,0843
  Planning aspects 0112,
    0249,0381,0437,0504,0512,
    0514,0540,0740,0933
ALCOHOL AND DRUG FOUNDATION,
  ONTARIO 0580
ALCOHOL FOUNDATION OF BRITISH
  COLUMBIA 0196
ALCOHOLIC BEVERAGES
  see BEER, BRANDY, HOMEBREW,
    LIQUOR DISTILLED, MAIZE
    BEER, MOONSHINE, NATIVE
    INTOXICATING BEVERAGES,
    PIVA, RUM, TISWIN, TULAPAI,
    WHISKEY, WINE
ALCOHOLIC PSYCHOSIS
  see PSYCHOSIS, ALCOHOL INDUCED
ALCOHOLICS ANONYMOUS
  0042,0044,0067,0119,0126,
  0264,0271,0299,0441,0598,
  0686,0706,0807
  Efficacy and evaluation
    0029,0362,0415,0508,0592,
    0596,0723,0835,0883,0968

Historical aspects 0650
Program design 0926
ALCOHOLISM
  Behavioral aspects 0019,
    0238,0337
  Complications
    see also DIABETES,
      DIPHTHERIA, LUNG
      CANCER, TUBERCU-
      LOSIS, ULCERS
    0347,0652,0653,0691,0696,
    0714,0755,0773,0776,0778,
    0779,0780,0833,0923,0928,
    0933
  Definitions and typologies
    see also STAGING CONCEPT
      OF ALCOHOLISM
    0024,0249,0258,A330,0520,
    0540,0786,0839,0842,0928,
    0941,0955
  Diagnosis A330,0619
  Epidemiology
    see EPIDEMIOLOGY OF
      ALCOHOLISM
  Etiology
    see ETIOLOGY OF
      ALCOHOLISM
  Familial aspects 0013,0123,
    0396,0746,0763,0919,0960
  Mortality 0060,A120,A330,
    0343,0350,0470,0653,A659,
    0666,0696,0713,0817
  Nutritional aspects
    see NUTRITIONAL ASPECTS
      OF ALCOHOLISM
  Philosophical and ethical
    issues 0055,0061,0062,
    0240,0244
  Prevention
    see PREVENTION OF
      ALCOHOLISM
  Psychological aspects
    0013,0019,0039,0061,0065,
    0071,0337,0395,0396,0468,
    0477,0704,0763
  Sex differences 0343,0470,
    0713,0772,0773,0924,0928
  Sociological aspects 0018,
    0071,0072,0073,0092,0333,
    0337,0351,0693

-319-

ALCOHOLISM COMMISSION OF
  SASKATCHEWAN
  see SASKATCHEWAN, ALCOHOLISM
    COMMISSION
ALEUT 0356,0941
  Alcohol production among 0101
  Alcoholism among 0296,0342,
    0525
  Arrests among 0480
  Drinking among 0101,0102,
    0168,0446,0480,0695
  Homicide among 0342
  Psychological aspects 0102
  Suicide among 0342
ALGONKIAN INDIANS 0197,0401,
  0405,0662,0796
ALLERGIC REACTION TO ALCOHOL
  0575
ALTERNATIVES TO DRINKING
  see also SOLUTIONS TO ALCOHOL
    PROBLEMS
  0039,0080,0134,0138
AMERICAN INDIAN COMMISSION ON
  ALCOHOLISM AND DRUG ABUSE
  0788
AMERICAN INDIAN MOVEMENT (A.I.M.)
  0048,0181,0848
AMERICAN INDIAN POLICY REVIEW
  COMMISSION TASK FORCE
  0867
AMPHETAMINES 0054
ANADARKO, OKLAHOMA 0637
ANCHORAGE, ALASKA 0229,0445,
  0695
ANGER 0083,0147,0341,0647,0682,
  0697,0744,0745,0746,0884
ANGLOS
  see WHITES
ANOMIE, RELATION TO DRINKING
  0012,0102,0118,0295,0436,
  0439,0538,0541,0542,B602,
  0708,0918,0968
ANTABUSE
  see DISULFIRAM
ANTHROPOLOGISTS, ROLE IN POLICY
  MAKING A522
ANXIETY 0008,0211,0238,0246,
  0272,0273,0295,0318,0413,
  0523,0558,0949

APACHE INDIANS 0007,0057,
  0059,0066,0094,0122,0146,
  0162,0214,0227,0248,0297,
  0321,0359,A367,0434,0489,
  0554,0596,0617,0674,0777,
  0790,0810,0831,0901
  Alcohol production 0359,
    0554,0673,0707
  Behavioral aspects 0083,
    0250,0252,0253
  Chiricahua 0569,0673
  Cibicue 0082
  Delinquency among 0434
  Drinking among 0082,0083,
    0248,0250,0251,0253,0254,
    0255,0257,0367,0486,0490,
    0569,0583,0584,0585,0587,
    0673,0777,0790,0810
  Drunkenness among 0007,
    0122,0129,0131,0195,0567,
    0661,0674
  Familial aspects 0256,0257
  Health problems 0321,0490
    0776,0777
  Historical aspects 0146,
    0490,0588,0674,0831
  Homicide among 0252,0253,
    0539
  Jicarilla 0718,0774
  Mescalero
    see also RESERVATION,
      Mescalero Apache
    A120,0129,0130,0131,0195
    0285,0387,0490,0877
  Native Beverages
    see TISWIN, TULAPAI
  Psychological aspects
    0129,0131,0250,0251
  Religious aspects
    0081,0082,0122,0227
  San Carlos 0056,0252,0367,
    0419,0583,0584,0585,0587,
    0588,0661,0684,0685,0707,
    0882
  Sociological aspects 0082,
    0083,0490
  Suicide among 0250,0252,
    0253,0387,0539,0661
  Violence among 0250,0251,
    0684

-320-

White Mountain 0081,0082,
    0249,0250,0251,0252,0253,
    0254,0255,0256,0257,0258,
    0418,0486,0539,0542,0707
APATHY 0102,0251
ARAPAHOE INDIANS 0012,0015,
    0049,0066,0176,0667,0817,
    0941
  Alcoholism among 0686
  Drinking among 0218,0261,
    0289,0290,0291,0293
  Drunkenness among 0462
ARCTIC 0408,0411,0576,0729,
    0748,0749,0949
ARCTIC NATIVE PEOPLES
    0063,0117,0350,0747
ARIZONA 0036,0056,0057,0058,
    0059,0085,0086,0105,0243,
    0359,0420,0465,0561,0665,
    0862,0909,0919
  Treatment programs in
    0050,0105
ARIZONA COMMISSION ON INDIAN
    AFFAIRS 0056,0057,0058,0059
ARRESTS
    0021,0028,0033,0051,0064,
    0111,0124,0152,0181,0216,
    0224,0270,0274,0277,0291,
    0475,0480,0731,0781,0870,
    0887
  Age differences 0084,0263,
    A330,0454,0605,0627,0685,
    0875,0876,0903
  Alcohol related 0018,0038,
    0043,0044,0051,0067,0084,
    0093,0106,A120,0181,0223,
    0241,0281,0287,0293,0309,
    0327,A330,0354,0364,0380,
    0382,0388,0402,0407,0411,
    0434,0454,0472,0490,0513,
    0559,0583,0593,0601,0602,
    0605,0612,0624,0627,0642,
    0658,0660,0669,0685,0689,
    0706,0708,0759,0788,0792,
    0794,0804,0810,0814,0816,
    0817,0827,0875,0876,0894,
    0903,0916,0966
  Incidence of 0018,0051,
    0067,0084,0106,0223,0241,
    0263,0264,0309,0310,0327,
    0328,0329,A330,0364,0380,
    0382,0402,0411,0434,0490,
    0559,0601,0624,0759,0814,
    0827,0869,0894
  Sex differences 0106,0624
ASIANS 0259,0347,0755,0932,
    0957
ASSIMILATION 0171,0183,0465,
    0545,0556,0581,0593,0699,
    0797,0813
ASSINIBOIN INDIANS 0638
ASSOCIATION FOR AMERICAN
    INDIAN AFFAIRS 0260
ATHABASCAN
    0135,0375,0400,0683,0749,
    0901
  Alcoholism among 0296,0390,
    0391
  Drinking among 0135,0390,
    0405
  Sociological aspects 0135
ATKINS, EDMOND 0430
ATTAWAPISKAT, N.W.T., CANADA
    0401
ATTITUDE CHANGE
  See ALCOHOL, education,
    attitude changes
    TRAINING, attitude
    changes
ATTITUDES 0002,0071,0072,
    0087,0088,0096,0113,0160,
    0207,0209,0211,0226,0268,
    0269,0374,0413,0423,0465,
    0471,0503,0550,0554,0592,
    0658,0674,0698,0702,0718,
    0766,0804,0821,0918,0920,
    0932,0946
  Towards alcohol
    among adolescents 0118,
      0176,0256,0258,0294,
      0298,0361,0375,0398,
      0663,0903
    among alcoholics 0855,
      0856
    among community members
      0086,0171,0233,0245,
      0517,0518,0519,0794,
      0804,0917,0944,0945
    among Indians 0042,0046,
      0082,0086,0119,0148,
      0171,0172,0198,0256,
      0258,0370,0397,0426

-321-

0473,0517,0518,0519,0785,
0799,0807,0823,0825,0849,
0855,0864,0876,0917
  among students 0036,0352,
0502,0654
  among whites 0046,0119,
0855
  sex differences 0176
Towards alcoholics 0020,0199
  among alcohol workers
0095,0096,0245,0271,0383,
0530,0597,0622,0680,0784
  among community members
0025,0965
  among health workers
0020,0096,0108,0245,0621,
0842
  among Indians 0271
  among non-Indians 0046,
0597,0816
Towards delinquency
  among Indians 0627
Towards drunkenness
  among Indians 0464
  effects on drinking 0203
Towards health
  among adolescents 0294
Towards homicide
  among Indians 0551,0552
Towards Indians
  among non-Indians
0087,0574,0597,0621,0690
Towards prohibition
  among Indians 0556
Towards suicide
  among Indians 0215

BAFFIN ISLAND 0407,0408
BALTIMORE, INDIAN ALCOHOLISM
  CENTER A553
BANNOCK INDIANS
  see also SHOSHONE INDIANS
0159
BAPTIST RELIGION 0803,
0905
BARLEYCORN, JOHN 0165
BARROW, ALASKA 0353

BARS
  see TAVERNS
BEER 0081,0082,0089,0120,0237,
0312,0370,0399,0432,0494,
0656,0792,0858,0888,0949
  corn beer 0673,0674
  malt beer 0399
BEOTHUK INDIANS 0678
BETHEL, ALASKA A636
BEVERAGES, ALCOHOLIC
  see BEER, BRANDY, HOMEBREW,
LIQUOR DISTILLED, MOONSHINE,
NATIVE INTOXICATING BEVERAGES,
PIVA, RUM, TISWIN, TULPAI,
WHISKEY, WINE
BIBLIOGRAPHIES
  see also LITERATURE REVIEWS
A063,0078,0427,A588,0621,
0694,0783,0818,0822,0942
BILINGUALISM 0215,0274,0958
BIOLOGICAL DIFFERENCES
  see GENETIC DIFFERENCES
BLACK DRINK 0736,0826,0956
BLACKFOOT INDIANS 0207
  Drinking among 0125,0331,
0602,0812
  Suicide among 0681
BLACKOUTS 0289,0764,0943
BLACKS 0069,0084,0223,0224,
0309,0347,0351,0434,0563,
0708,0810,0817,0819,0827
BLESSING WAY 0192
BLOOD INDIANS
  see BLACKFOOT INDIANS
BOARDING SCHOOLS
  see SCHOOLS, boarding
    schools
BOOTLEGGING 0075,A083,0091,
0165,0352,0364,0506,0533,
0568,0613,0678,0766,0809,
0847,0966
BOSTON, MASSACHUSETTS 0334
BRANDY 0088,0111,0120,0416,
0429,0845
BREATHALYSER 0266
BREMERTON, WASHINGTON 0444
BREW
  see HOMEBREW

BREW PARTIES
  see DRINKING, sociological
    aspects
    NATIVE INTOXICATING
    BEVERAGES, sociological
    aspects
BRIGHAM CITY, UTAH   0654
BRITISH COLUMBIA, CANADA
    0196,0228,0305,0363,0364,
    0439,0441,0527,0726,0754,
    0808,0830
BUREAU OF INDIAN AFFAIRS
    0128,0261,0288,0325,0339,
    0354,0420,0506,0670,0767,
    0848,0854,0891,0917
  Recommendations for   0133,
    0530,0555,0614
BYLAS, ARIZONA   0584

CACTUS   0146,0161,0561,0899
CAHUILLA INDIANS   0678
CALGARY, CANADA   0125
CALIFORNIA
  see also LOS ANGELES
          SAN DIEGO
          SAN FRANCISCO
  Indians in   0036,0041,0333,
    0358,0374,0866,0951
  Treatment programs in   0105
CALIFORNIA INDIANS EDUCATION
  ASSOCIATION   0174,0175
CAMP 10 (MANITOBA, CANADA)
    0500,0501
CANADA
  see also TORONTO, NORTHWEST
          COAST
    0067,0073,0074,0088,0089,
    0093,0106,0115,0116,0117,
    0125,0138,0148,0155,0171,
    0172,0196,0197,0220,0228,
    0231,0245,0246,0247,0259,
    0281,0305,0306,0345,0363,
    0364,0365,0366,0375,0376,
    0398,0399,0400,0401,0402,
    0403,0405,0406,0407,0408,
    0409,0410,0411,0439,0441,
    0442,0443,0463,0472,0473,
    0481,0498,0500,0501,0524,
    0525,0527,0535,0545,0553,
    0557,0558,0576,0580,0609,
    0656,0658,0659,0662,0678,
    0691,0702,0720,0721,0723,
    0726,0731,0732,0733,0734,
    0737,0747,0748,0749,0753,
    0754,0792,0796,0802,0806,
    0808,0825,0830,0888,A890,
    0895,0896,0920,0942,0965
  Treatment programs in
    0193,0535,0612,0702,0895,
    0896
CANADIAN ARCTIC
  see ARCTIC NATIVE PEOPLES
CANADIAN BILL OF RIGHTS
    0064,0124,0511,0565,0566,
    0571,0577,0599,0781,0793,
    A890
CANADIAN INDIAN ACT
  see INDIAN ACT
CANADIAN RESEARCH CENTER FOR
  ANTHROPOLOGY   0411,0658
CANTON, SOUTH DAKOTA   0421
"CARBONATE CITY", COLORADO
    0559,0560
CARNEGIEA GIGANTEA
  see SAGUARO
CAROLINAS   0736
CASE HISTORIES   0070,0099,
    0131,0415,0442,0447,0467,
    0472,0482,0507,0680,0730,
    0735
CATAWABA INDIANS   0736
CAUCASIAN
  see WHITES
CEREMONIAL USES OF ALCOHOL
  see DRINKING, CEREMONIAL USES
      RAIN CEREMONY
      WINE CEREMONY
      WINTER CEREMONY
CHEMAWA INDIAN SCHOOL
  see also SCHOOLS
    0497,0881
CHEROKEE INDIANS
    A083,0122
  Alcoholism among   0817
  Drinking among   0303,0491,
    0969
  Homicide among   0491
  Suicide among   0491

-323-

   Violence among 0491
CHEYENNE INDIANS 0012,0015,
     0066,0080,0159,0215,0261,
     0551,0552,0817
   Alcoholism among 0710,0722,
     0807,0817
   Drinking among 0261,0417,
     0602,0809
   Drunkenness among 0551,0552
   Homicide among 0551,0552
   Northern Cheyenne 0080,0417,
     0602,0667,0710,0722,0807,
     0809
   Southern Cheyenne 0015
   Suicide among 0159,0215,0551
CHICAGO, ILLINOIS 0241,0312,
   0339,0549,0550,0960
CHICKASAW INDIANS A083
CHILD NEGLECT
   see also ALCOHOLISM, Familial
       aspects
   Alcohol related 0006,0063,
     0157,0158,0247,0394,0446,
     0531,0643,0794,0872,0882,
     0950,0967,0968
   Incidence of 0446,0950,
     0967
CHILD REARING 0065,0131,
   0153,0349,0915
CHILD REMOVAL 0157,0158
CHILDREN 0004,0157,0158,0208,
   0231,0235,0312,0361,0365,
   0375,0394,0410,0411,0447,
   0448,0449,0460,0481,0574,
   0588,0600,0614,0623,0643,
   0665,0679,0695,0710,0752,
   0764,0823,0825,0867
CHILOCCO INDIAN SCHOOL
   see also SCHOOLS
   0036
CHIPPEWA INDIANS
   0053,0076,0142,0318,A396,
   A931,0936
   Alcoholism among 0395,0396,
     0435,0509,0928,0937
   Drinking among 0481,0500,
     0501,0503,0509,0533,0593,
     0678,0719,0888,0929
   Health problems among 0435
   Historical aspects 0533,0678,
     0742

   Psychological aspects
     0500,0501
CHOCTAW INDIANS A083,A419,
   0817
CHOSA, MIKE 0339
CHURCHES
   Christian 0109,0139,0142,
     0154,0390,0391,0524,A671,
     0758
   Indian Shaker Church
     0104,0139,0283,0284,0479,
     0523,0863,0920
   Native American Church
     0012,0015,0099,0119,0226,
     0268,0686,0687,0863
   Yankton Dakota Church
     0422
CHURCHILL, MANITOBA, CANADA
   0115,0213,0481,0500,0501
CIBICUE, ARIZONA 0082
CIRRHOSIS 0104,0234,0251,
   0320,0321,0522,0544,0611,
   0651,0652,0680,0712,0714,
   0777,0825,0876,0933
   Mortality 0026,0060,0488,
     0603,0615,0653,0666,0671,
     0713,0870,0872,0885
   Sex differences 0488,0489,
     0776
CIVIL RIGHTS
   see also CANADIAN BILL OF
       RIGHTS
   0068,0874
COEUR D'ALENE INDIANS 0053,
   0417
COGNITIVE DISSONANCE 0467
COLORADO
   see also DENVER, COLORADO
   Indians in 0438,0559,0560,
     0594,0797
COLVILLE LAKE, N.W.T., CANADA
   0747,0749
COMANCHE INDIANS 0066,0414,
   A813
COMMUNICATION 0117,0163,
   0324,0500
COMMUNITY ALCOHOLISM PROGRAMS
   0641,0644,0649,0702,0760,
   0761

COMMUNITY CENTERS
  see PREVENTION PROGRAMS
COMMUNITY EDUCATION
  0085,0086,0641
COMMUNITY HEALTH AIDES
  see INDIGENOUS AIDES
       PARAPROFESSIONALS
COMMUNITY PLANNING 0085,
  0086,0617,0727
COMMUNITY RELATIONS WITH
  TREATMENT PROGRAMS
  see TREATMENT PROGRAMS,
       Community relations
COMMUNITY RESOURCES 0020,0025,
  0086,0110,0149,0235,0760
COMPREHENSIVE ALCOHOL ABUSE &
  ALCOHOLISM PREVENTION,
  TREATMENT, AND REHABILITATION
  ACT 0873
CONFLICT 0254,0255,0257
  Avoidance of 0251
COPING BEHAVIOR 0253,0503,0510
CORTEZ, COLORADO 0836
COSTS OF DRINKING
  see DRINKING, costs of
COUNCILS (TRIBAL, VILLAGE, ETC.)
  0163,0308,0506
COUNSELING
  see also ETHNIC THERAPY
           PEER COUNSELING
           THERAPY, Group
  0012,0123,0233,0238,0239,
  0272,0273,0274,0299,0457,
  0586,0587,0593,0646,0661,
  0706,0710,0768,0799,0843,
  0851
  Cultural aspects 0130,0238,
    0373,0628
  Native Language, use of
    0274,0959
  Program design 0093,0586
  Psychological aspects 0130,
    0621,0799,0851
  Techniques 0237,0238,0239,
    0262,0675,0843,0932
COURTS 0341,0405,0411,0612,0701
  Circuit Court of Appeals 0568
  Idaho Supreme Court 0040
  Overrepresentation of Indians
    0223,0224,0241,0287,0309,
    0870

Tribal Courts 0051,0134,
  0142,0341,0506,0883
U.S. Supreme Court
  0568,0868,0893
CREE INDIANS 0115,0732
  Alcoholism among 0732,0734
  Drinking among 0401,0638,
    0815,0957
  Historical aspects 0638
CREEK INDIANS
  Alcoholism among 0817
  Drinking among 0758
CRIME 0051,0067,0068,0070,
  0075,0084,0089,0106,0134,
  0141,0142,0183,0220,0310,
  0374,0410,0433,0506,0522,
  0543,0449,A614,0627,0660,
  0669,0702,0810,0814,0825,
  0876,0894,0962,0968
  Alcohol related 0018,0026,
    0041,0045,0141,0287,0434,
    0638,0708,0718,0794,0966
CRISIS 0100,0187,0215,0544,
  0625,0681
CROSS CULTURAL STUDIES
  0371,0381,0387,0395,0396,
  A396,0398,0413,0434,0435,
  0436,0443,0470,0512,0515,
  0525,0528,0529,0536,0542,
  0543,0549,0589,0656,0659,
  0691,0693,0704,0708,0709,
  0732,0750,0755,0792,0810,
  0817,0843,0855,0927,0928,
  0930,0932,0933,0937,0943,
  0947
CROW INDIANS 0066,0667,0941
  Alcoholism among 0710,
    0722,0807
  Drinking among 0602
  Historical aspects 0742
COLTACHICHES INDIANS 0736
CULTURAL CONFLICT
  see also STRESS
  0262,0263,0659,0671,0708,
  0718
CULTURAL DEPRIVATION
  see DEPRIVATION
CULTURAL DIFFERENCES 0048,
  0071,0072,0123,0768

CULTURAL DISINTEGRATION
see also ACCULTURATION
ASSIMILATION
0287,0288,0358,0656,0945
CULTURAL THERAPY
see ETHNIC THERAPY
CULTURE CHANGE
see also ACCULTURATION
ASSIMILATION
0073,0163,0181,0231,0338,
0545,0558,0631,0656,0711,
0730,0732,0772,0775,0821,
0837,0841,0859,0888,0905,
0906,0963
CUMBERLAND COUNTY 0033
CURING CEREMONIES
see also DRINKING, Ceremonial
uses
0083,0283
CUSHMAN INDIAN HOSPITAL 0103

DAKOTA INDIANS
see SIOUX INDIANS
DALLAS, TEXAS 0286,0506
DATA COLLECTION AND ANALYSIS
see also ALCOHOL, research
0085,0086,0153,0188,0540,
0698,0827,0941
Methodology 0272,0277,0309,
0377,0378,0379,0380,0402,
0412,0436,0438,0485,0486,
0517,0540,0542,0637,0655,
0761,0787,0839,0843,0855,
0918,0930,0933,0934,0937,
0960
Surveys 0245,0457,0469,0485,
0785,0807,0849,0933,0943
DELAWARE INDIANS 0111,0300
DELAWARE (STATE) 0111
DELINQUENCY
see also ATTITUDES, Towards
delinquency
Alcohol related 0045,A046,
0084,0255,0293,A317,0562,
0810,0851,0894,0904
Familial aspects 0006,0026,
0434,0684,0685

Incidence of 0022,0045,0243,
0247,0263,0290,0293,0434,
A434,0454,0627,0875,0950,
0967
Sex differences 0291,0292,0607
DELIRIUM TREMENS 0527,0764,0825,
0943
DENE VILLAGE 0213
DENVER, COLORADO 0136,0165,
0327,0570,0582,0797,0922
DEPARTMENT OF INDIAN AND
NORTHERN AFFAIRS (CANADA)
0193,0281,0558,0792,0896
DEPARTMENT OF NORTHERN AFFAIRS
AND NATIONAL RESOURCES
0073,0171,0172,0376
DEPENDENCY 0002,0065,0108,
0238,0240,0349,0387,0430,
0503,0623,0629,0950
DE PERE, WISCONSIN 0035
DEPRESSION 0022,0216,0439,
0453,0475,0558,0623
DEPRIVATION 0005,0063,0149,0198
DETOXIFICATION PROGRAMS
see TREATMENT PROGRAMS,
Detoxification programs
DEVELOPMENTAL RETARDATION
see also FETAL ALCOHOL
SYNDROME
0014
DEVIANCE 0171,0172,0367,0436,
0438,0458,0466,0482,0487,
0763,0801,0963
DIABETES, ALCOHOL RELATED
0714,0776
DIAGNOSIS 0117,0153,0251,
0705,0786
DIET 0259,0266,0575,0578,0668
DIPHTHERIA 0121,0340
DISCRIMINATION 0181,0197,
0244,0262,0263,0357,0364,
0366,0389,0415,0422,0450,
0533,0560,0571,0629,0665,
0700,0787,0836,0854,0869,
0894,0961
DISORDERLY CONDUCT
see DRUNK AND DISORDERLY
DISTILLED LIQUOR
see LIQUOR, DISTILLED
DISULFIRAM THERAPY
see also FORT DEFIANCE
ANTABUSE TREATMENT
PROGRAM

0055,0119,0269,0271,0272,
0273,0274,0384,0476,0622,
0653,0706,0743,0745,0746,
0828,0829,0887,0933
DOGRIB INDIANS 0376,0400
D-Q UNIVERSITY 0426
DREAM QUEST 0160
DRESSERVILLE INDIAN COLONY,
NEVADA 0849
DRINKING
  Age differences 0017,0045,
    0084,0135,0171,0176,0177,
    0257,0289,0332,0334,0352,
    0353,0398,0409,0509,0518,
    0519,0583,0584,0608,0712,
    0726,0741,0812,0841,0875,
    0903,0918,0943,0952
  Behavioral aspects 0009,
    0010,0011,0021,0022,0074,
    0117,0120,0125,0135,0140,
    0141,0147,0148,0171,0172,
    0175,0176,0178,0190,0197,
    0198,0214,0218,0229,0231,
    0246,0254,0264,0273,0286,
    0303,0315,0332,0334,0346,
    0349,0351,0357,0364,0368,
    0369,0370,0371,0376,0393,
    0411,0418,0424,0443,0445,
    0446,0450,0458,0459,0466,
    0486,0487,0489,0492,0516,
    0517,0518,0519,0520,0521,
    0525,0528,0542,0545,0622,
    0629,0642,0645,0663,0664,
    0690,0692,0693,0716,0738,
    0739,0740,0744,0745,0747,
    0755,0765,0786,0789,0792,
    0796,0835,0836,0837,0838,
    0840,0841,0847,0858,0860,
    0888,0895,0897,0898,0909,
    0916,0920,0929,0931,0943
  Binge 0003,0117,0172,0203,
    0260,0269,0270,0353,0622,
    0739,0745,0847,0916
  Blitz 0021,0195
  Ceremonial uses
    0041,0065,0081,0090,0191,
    0201,0210,0314,0349,0439,
    0440,0441,0442,0443,0446,
    0451,0496,0524,0546,0561,
    0645,0687,0736,0823,0826,
    0857,0858,0860,0861,0862,
    0897,0899,0901,0911,0916

  Costs of 0026,0135,0787,
    0800
  Epidemiology
    see EPIDEMIOLOGY DRINKING
  Etiology
    see ETIOLOGY OF DRINKING
  Familial aspects 0006,0065,
    0074,0140,0311,0410,0481,
    0521,0570,0747,0752,0789,
    0928,0929,0950
  Functions of 0120,0129,
    0220,0222,0270,0280,0316,
    0328,0337,0348,0370,0375,
    0376,0386,0413,0458,0466,
    0504,0509,0527,0563,0564,
    0589,0590,0693,0719,0837,
    0838,0841,0842,0909,0944,
    0945
  Historical aspects 0005,
    0021,0024,0026,0032,0088,
    0140,0141,0150,0166,0173,
    0178,0179,0190,0197,0258,
    0279,0304,0305,0348,0355,
    0371,0374,0416,0429,0430,
    0457,0527,0534,0546,0548,
    0554,0575,0579,0591,0601,
    0629,0639,0737,0739,0742,
    0765,0824,0845,0888,0954,
    0956
  Legal aspects
    see also ARRESTS, Alcohol
        related
        LIQUOR LAWS,
        enforcement
        RESERVATIONS,
        Law enforcement
    0134,0197,0241,0263,0264,
    0602,0700,0701
  Myths about Indians
    see also DRUNKEN INDIAN
        STEREOTYPE
    0230,0482,0517,0520,0591,
    0917,0931,0965
  Parties 0466
  Patterns of 0021,0127,0135,
    0140,0141,0148,0150,0168,
    0171,0172,0178,0218,0229,
    0231,0232,0295,0298,0303,

0312,0332,0334,0368,0369,
0424,0443,0445,0464,0481,
0482,0486,0487,0489,0498,
0504,0514,0516,0517,0518,
0519,0521,0523,0527,0535,
0542,0563,0564,0580,0593,
B602,0642,0658,0662,0691,
0700,0726,0740,0744,0765,
0792,0836,0838,0841,0847,
0888,0916,0918,0940,0943
Psychological aspects
   0002,0073,0074,0100,0137,
   0147,0315
Public   0218,0277,0280
Recreational   0272,0273,
   0348,0443,0622,0658,0677
Religious aspects   0006,
   0090,0122,0160,0201,0302,
   0349,0422,0886,0910,0918
Sex differences   0135,0140,
   0141,0168,0171,0190,0334,
   0358,0368,0369,0409,0479,
   0518,0519,0521,0583,0584,
   0606,0608,0677,0726,0777,
   0812,0813,0821,0837,0841,
   0924,0929,0943,0949
Sexual aspects   0368,0493,
   0557,0558
Sociological aspects   0002,
   0022,0024,0065,0071,0072,
   0073,0074,0077,0080,0081,
   0083,0101,0112,0140,0141,
   0148,0167,0173,0178,0179,
   0184,0211,0212,0214,0221,
   0229,0231,0248,0250,0251,
   0253,0254,0256,0305,0349,
   0357,0358,0367,0369,0371,
   0393,0403,0404,0405,0406,
   0407,0409,0411,0413,0423,
   0432,0513,0523,0528,0545,
   0567,0569,0589,0608,0629,
   0783,0898,0900,0901,0916,
   0944,0964
Solitary   0120,0140,0489,
   0492,0842
Surreptitious   0041
DRIVING, INTOXICATED
   0045,0194,0327,0950
Legal aspects   0134,0183,
   0627,0893,0903
Mortality   0143,0893

DROP-IN CENTERS   0116,0185
DROP-OUT, SCHOOL   0610,
   0685,0875,0877
DRUGS
   see also SUBSTANCE SNIFFING
   0054,0110,0155,0177,0191,
   0226,0290,0291,0298,0440,
   0442,0461,0475,0495,0600,
   0618,0692,0695,0717,0820,
   0915
DRUNK AND DISORDERLY
   see also DRUNKENNESS
   0038,0045,0559,0627,0660,
   0685
DRUNKEN INDIAN STEREOTYPE
   see also DRINKING, myths
      about Indians
   0123,0147,0604,0718,0917,
   0931,0964
DRUNKENNESS   0021,0075
Adolescents   0462
Behavioral aspects   0076,
   0088,0135,0147,0211,0246,
   0358,0368,0375,0386,0406,
   0424,0567,0718,0726,0744
Etiology
   see ETIOLOGY OF DRUNKEN-
      NESS
Historical aspects   0088,
   0147,0374,0579,0925
Legal aspects   0134,0241,
   0263
Management   0083,0528,0529
Sociological aspects   0168,
   0195,0232,0280,0299,0304,
   0344,0365,0375,0407,0413,
   0528,0529
DRYBONES CASE   0064,0124,
   0511,0565,0566,0571,0577,
   0598,0599,0781,0793,A890
DUCK LAKE, MANITOBA, CANADA
   0500,0501
DUODENAL ULCER
   see ULCERS, Duodenal
DUTCH   0111,0156,0236,
   A685,0737,0845

EAGLE BUTTE, SOUTH DAKOTA
0637,0697
ECONOMICS AS CAUSE OF DRINKING
see also ETIOLOGY OF ALCOHOLISM
ETIOLOGY OF DRINKING
ETIOLOGY OF DRUNKENNESS
0197,0218,0261,0262,0326,
0329,0372,0640,0648,0657,
0700,0708,0718,0721
EDUCATION
see also ALCOHOL EDUCATION
HEALTH EDUCATION
0027,0041,0046,0047,0062,
0093,0105,0126,0127,0128,
0133,0143,0144,0149,0163,
0169,0197,0203,0224,0233
0235,0239,0255,0262,0271,
0274,0304,0307,0325,0343,
0353,0362,0373,0417,0426,
0457,0471,0476,0497,0516,
0588,0596,0597,0598,0603,
0636,0641,0643,0644,0648,
0657,0666,0675,0685,0689,
0700,0722,0740,0752,0760,
0784,0787,0790,0799,0800,
0835,0851,0855,0856,0869,
0904,0917,0919,0923,0924,
0947,0960
EDUCATORS, ROLE IN ALCOHOLISM
PREVENTION 0127,0128
ELDERLY 0149,0484,0509,0636,
0712,0734
EMPLOYMENT
see also UNDEREMPLOYMENT
UNEMPLOYMENT
0028,0046,0132,0164,0190,
0195,0220,0274,0284,0307,
0312,0423,0465,A486,0508,
0585,0634,0642,0643,0657,
0688,0692,0711,0719,0782,
0787,0800,0813,0821,0884,
0922,0928
ENGLISH 0156,0170,0236,A685,
0802,0845
EPIDEMIOLOGY
of accidents 0672,0754,0955
of alcoholism 0052,0056,0085,
0174,0175,0190,0230,0261,
0269,0270,0271,0272,0273,
0274,0275,0276,0277,0278,
0299,0302,0363,0373,0395,
0427,0492,0622,0631,0633,
0705,0732,0786,0790,0851,
0869,0873,0927,0928,0931,
0945,0960
of delinquency 0084,0290,
0454,0605,0627,0685,0875,
0876,0903
of drinking 0049,0140,
0149,0152,0163,0164,0176,
0178,0190,0197,0198,0199,
0212,0218,0223,0224,0247,
0248,0250,0251,0255,0256,
0257,0258,0289,0290,0291,
0314,0356,0371,0382,0386,
0404,0417,0423,0424,0457,
0485,0509,0574,0593,0622,
0623,0669,0697,0787,0820,
0884,0910,0922,0923,0940,
0943,0944,0950,0952,0965
of drinking, age differences
0017,0045,0084,0135,0171,
0176,0177,0257,0289,0332,
0334,0352,0353,0398,0409,
0509,0518,0519,0583,0584,
0608,0712,0726,0741,0812,
0841,0875,0903,0918,0952
of drunkenness 0344,0642,
0943
of homicide 0252,0299,0338,
0936
of suicide 0151,0155,0159,
0187,0188,0189,0194,0216,
0250,0252,0266,0299,0338,
0356,0360,0392,0445,0483,
0484,0544,0624,0625,0626,
0767,0915,0923,0924,0936
ESCAPE 0004,0233,0244,0260,
0302,0337,0348,0353,0443,
0446,0467,0647,0718,0785,
0813,0837,0838,0841,0903,
0915
ESKIMO 0089,0114,0137,0155,
0163,0164,0172,0203,0229,
0246,0247,0259,0266,0281,
0323,0342,0353,0356,0387,
0388,0394,0401,0402,0403,
0405,0408,0410,0433,0474,
0475,0480,0483,0484,0553,
0557,0558,0576,A636,0656,
0664,0677,0683,0691,0695,
0717,0729,0750,0752,0753,

0792,0794,0813,0844,0864,
0963
Aklavik   0171,0172
Alcohol, effects on   0259,
0266
Alcoholism among   0342,
0557
Arrests among   0388,0402,
0480
Behavioral aspects   0060,
0089
Drinking among   0163,0171,
0209,0353,0388,0401,0407,
0408,0411,0474,0475,0480,
0553,0557,0558,0664,0677,
0717,0729,0792,0794,0813,
0963
Frobisher Bay
0281,0401,0408,0497,0946
Historical aspects   0164,
0281,0656,0729
Homicide among   0114,0342
Inuvik   0171,0172,0246,0247,
0402,0403,0410,0553
Sociological aspects   0060,
0089,0163,0209,0752,0753,
0949
Suicide among   0155,0342,
0386,0483,0717
Violence among   0433
ESOPHAGEAL VARICES   0320,0321,
0651,0652,0653,0776
ETHNIC THERAPY
see also PREVENTION PROGRAMS
0001,0099,0268,0283,0284,
0385,0453,0686,0687,0733,
0775
Efficacy and evaluation
0015,0016,0439,0440,0441,
0442,0443,0459
Familial aspects   0468
Philosophical and ethical
issues
0012,0048,0063,0192,0221,
0319,0324,0555,0585,0799,
0822,0907
Techniques   0012,0439,0440,
0441,0442,0450,0455,0468
ETIOLOGY
of accidents   0950,0968

of alcoholism
see also ACCULTURATION
ANOMIE
ASSIMILATION
SELF IMAGE
STAKE THEORY
STRESS
0004,0006,0008,0013,0019,
0023,0024,0039,0041,0052,
0063,0065,0069,0071,0072,
0079,0100,0119,0123,0131,
0132,0137,0148,0159,0171,
0172,0174,0175,0183,0190,
0199,0214,0220,0237,0244,
0248,0254,0260,0261,0263,
0264,0269,0270,0271,0272,
0273,0274,0275,0276,0277,
0278,0280,0287,0288,0296,
0302,0308,0315,0326,0329,
0337,0351,0366,0373,A376,
0377,0386,0390,0395,0396,
0409,0412,0417,0424,0436,
0437,0438,0444,0446,0452,
0457,0468,0489,0490,0492,
0498,0500,0507,0509,0523,
0525,0527,0535,0541,0549,
0550,0569,0575,0580,0585,
A588,0597,0605,0616,0627,
0628,0630,0631,A636,0640,
0645,0647,0648,0657,0659,
0662,0665,0666,0679,0693,
0694,0697,0704,0711,0730,
0734,0738,0739,0745,0746,
0755,0763,0768,0772,0787,
0792,0795,0837,0840,0872,
0878,0919,0924,0941,0952,
0955,0965,0966,0967,0968
of delinquency   0045,0084,
0097,0247,0255,0290,0291,
0292,0434,0604,0689,0710,
0894,0967,0968
of drinking
0080,0084,0089,0101,0102,
0117,0118,0120,0123,0129,
0131,0132,0135,0137,0140,
0145,0147,0148,0160,0163,
0167,0168,0171,0172,0178,
0179,0184,0190,0195,0199,
0205,0208,0211,0213,0214,
0218,0222,0229,0231,0233,

0236,0244,0246,0247,0248,
0250,0251,0253,0254,0255,
0258,0263,0264,0269,0270,
0271,0272,0295,0302,0303,
0316,0323,0327,0328,0329,
0332,0334,0345,0348,0349,
0358,0365,0366,0367,0368,
0369,0370,0371,0375,0376,
0386,0392,0393,0394,0401,
0404,0405,0406,0407,0409,
0411,0412,0413,0417,0424,
0426,0432,0436,0443,0458,
0466,0467,0473,0478,0482,
0487,0492,0498,0504,0522,
0523,0527,0542,0545,0549,
0554,0563,0564,0567,0569,
0574,0575,0580,0581,0597,
0606,0608,0609,0622,0623,
0630,0663,0677,0684,0692,
0693,0700,0713,0718,0719,
0720,0721,0723,0730,0739,
0740,0742,0744,0747,0752,
0766,0775,0792,0795,0801,
0803,0812,0820,0821,0825,
0837,0838,0841,0847,0884,
0886,0892,0897,0898,0899,
0900,0903,0911,0915,0918,
0923,0929,0940,0944,0945,
0947,0952,0966
of drinking, age differences
  0097,0311,0332,0352,0353,
  0356,0409,0444,0474,0475,
  0581,0604,0605,0610,0623,
  0677,0684,0825,0838,0841,
  0903,0915,0918,0952
of drinking, among reservation
  Indians 0190,0233,0608,
  0622,0624,0625,0660,0661,
  0692,0711,0713,0723,0739,
  0746,0757,0836,0839,0884,
  0885,0897,0943,0950,0959,
  0965
of drinking, among urban
  Indians 0003,0138,0200,0206,
  0213,0220,0229,0246,0247,
  0286,0310,0312,0313,0317,
  0327,0328,0329,0334,0354,
  0386,0389,0415,0423,0445,
  0465,0467,0480,0481,0486,
  0492,0503,0507,0509,0522,
  0549,0550,0570,0582,0593,
  0595,0616,0628,0657,0658,
  0659,0712,0716,0719,0720,
  0741,0797,0804,0821,0827,
  0897,0900,0934,0935,0940,
  0960,0965
of drunkenness 0137,0172,
  0194,0195,0218,0220,0270,
  0280,0313,0329,0332,0353,
  0357,0368,0386,0387,0412,
  0413,0425,0463,0504,0567,
  0569,0700,0886,0897,0929,
  0944,0945
of drunkenness, among
  adolescents 0322,0332
of substance sniffing 0735
of substance sniffing, among
  adolescents 0013,0234,
  0460,0735
of suicide 0023,0026,0027,
  0028,0089,0110,0155,0156,
  0159,0187,0189,0194,0288,
  0307,0360,0387,0445,0483,
  0484,0538,0539,0541,0618,
  0665,0671,0681,0683,0688,
  0715,0769,0872,0915,0923
of suicide, age differences
  0028,0110,0217,0255,0307,
  0322,0352,0356,0360,0484,
  0544,0610,0681,0710,0770,
  0771
of violence 0063,0194,0433,
  0478,0535,0539,0540,0541,
  0543,0563,0671,0708
EUROPEAN(S)
  see also WHITES
  0076,0267,0429,0464,0523,
  0567,0656,0679,0703,0765,
  A810,0845,0888,0911,0956
EVALUATION 0009,0065,0098,
  0105,0149,0153,0325,0377,
  0378,0379,0469,0471,0617,
  0619,0620,0635,0637,0644,
  0654,0705,0774,0805,0871,
  0933,0934,0953
EXCESSIVE DRINKING
  see also DRUNKENNESS
  0056,0057,0058,0059,0163,
  0164,0172,0248,0498,0500,
  0517,0662,0711,0780,0787,
  0794,0803,0813

FAIRBANKS, ALASKA 0325,0683
    Treatment programs in 0325
FAMILIES
    see also ADOLESCENTS, Drinking,
            familial aspects
        ALCOHOL EDUCATION,
            for families
        ALCOHOLISM, Familial
            aspects
        CHILD NEGLECT
        DELINQUENCY, Familial
            aspects
        DRINKING, Familial
            aspects
        FEMALES, Role in family
        PARENTAL DRINKING,
            effect on children
        SUBSTANCE SNIFFING,
            Familial aspects
        SUICIDE, Familial
            aspects
        TREATMENT PROGRAMS,
            Familial aspects
    0100,0123,0140,0157,0158,
    0238,0247,0271,0457,0545,
    0608,0710,0763,0813,0903
    Disintegration of
    0092,0187,0360,0531,0665,
    0752,0863,0872
FARMINGTON, NEW MEXICO 0954
FEDERAL POLICIES
    see also LIQUOR LAWS
    0062,0183,0240,0318,0703,
    0868
FEMALE ALCOHOLISM
    see also FETAL ALCOHOL SYNDROME
    0014,0045,A120,0210,0353,
    0416,0470,0518,0519,0608,
    0611,0677,0681,0709,0713,
    0726,0772,0773,0776,0777,
    0791,0812,0813,0853,0924,
    0928,0949
    Mortality 0343
    Treatment 0324,0476,0572
FEMALE ARRESTS 0106,0624
FEMALE DELINQUENCY 0291,0292,
    0607
FEMALE DRINKING
    Age differences 0176,0289,
    0291,0292,0302,0356,0607,
    0696

Behavioral aspects 0135,
    0140,0141,0168,0190,0237,
    0311,0358,0368,0369,0493,
    0521,0557,0558,A704
Historical aspects 0374
Sociological aspects 0237,
    0394,0479,0521,0607
FEMALE DRUG USE
    Age differences 0695
FEMALE SUICIDE
    Age differences 0356,0360
    Alcohol related 0028,0080,
    0155,0187,0188,0189,0196,
    0216,0356,0360,0583,0603,
    0618,0625,0683
FEMALES
    see also ACCIDENTS, Sex
            differences
        ATTITUDES, Towards
            alcohol, Sex
            differences
        CIRRHOSIS, Sex
            differences
        FETAL ALCOHOL
            SYNDROME
        METABOLISM OF
            ALCOHOL, Sex
            differences
    Psychological aspects
    0510,0521,0772
    Role in alcoholic beverage
    production 0285,0418,
    0673,0674
    Role in alcoholism control
    0570,0582
    Role in family 0006,0132,
    0505
    Sociological aspects 0493,
    0505,0527,0607,0773
FERMENTED BEVERAGES 0122,
    0161,0166,0191,0419
FETAL ALCOHOL SYNDROME 0014,
    0447,0448,0449,0522,0791,
    0819
    Incidence of 0791
    Mortality 0447,0522
    Physiological aspects 0014,
    0447,0448,0449,0819
FIRLAND TUBERCULOSIS
    SANATORIUM 0347

FIVE CIVILIZED TRIBES 0166,
    0428,A813
FLAGSTAFF, ARIZONA 0465
FLORIDA 0611,0736
FLUSHING REACTION 0755
FOLK TAXONOMY 0516,0517,0518,
    0519
FOLLOW-UP TREATMENT
    see TREATMENT PROGRAMS,
        Follow-up studies
FORT DEFIANCE ANTABUSE TREATMENT
    PROGRAM 0119,0743,0745,0828,
    0829
FORT GOOD HOPE, N.W.T., CANADA
    0231
FORT HALL RESERVATION
    see also RESERVATIONS
    Delinquency on 0627
    Substance sniffing on 0735
    Suicide on 0915
    Treatment programs on 0450
FORT MACKENZIE, CANADA 0409
FORT MEADE V.A. HOSPITAL 0856
FORT PIERRE, SOUTH DAKOTA 0724
FORT SMITH, ARKANSAS A083
FOSTER HOMES 0157,0158,0751,
    0934
FOX INDIANS 0300,0678
FRANKLIN, BENJAMIN 0534
FRASER VALLEY, BRITISH COLUMBIA
    0441
FREMONT COUNTY, WYOMING 0289
FRENCH 0156,0429,A685,0737,
    0802,0845
FROBISHER BAY, N.W.T., CANADA
    0281,0401,0407,0408,0409,
    0946
FRONTIER
    Culture of 0403,0411
    Style of drinking 0178,0409
FUNCTIONS OF DRINKING
    see DRINKING, Functions of
FUR TRADE, RELATION TO LIQUOR
    TRADE 0101,0147,0170,0430,
    0464,0533,A614,0629,0638,
    A671,0724,0728,0742,0888,
    0916,0925,0954

GALLUP, NEW MEXICO
    Arrests in 0382
    Indians in 0270,0272,0382,
        0488,0816,0847,0926,0964
GALLUP COMMUNITY TREATMENT
    PROGRAM 0119,0269,0270,
        0272,0273,0274,0275,0276,
        0277,0380,0381,0760,0761,
        0822
GALLUP INDIAN MEDICAL CENTER
    0652
GAMBLING 0172,0403,0802
    Psychological aspects
        0008,0513
    Relation to alcohol use
        0008,0963
    Sociological aspects 0008
GASTROINTESTINAL DISORDERS
    see also ULCERS
    0251,0320,0321,0651,0652,
    0653,0696,0776
GENETIC DIFFERENCES
    see also RACIAL DIFFERENCES
    0048,0244,0266,0351,0357,
    0412,0425,0575,0616,0709,
    0755,0814,0894,0957
GERONIMO 0007
GONZALES CASE 0124
GOVERNOR'S TASK FORCE
    (WASHINGTON STATE) 0104
GREAT WHALE RIVER, N.W.T.,
    CANADA 0401
GREEN BAY, WISCONSIN 0035
GROUP DRINKING
    see also DRINKING,
        Behavioral
        aspects
    DRINKING,
        Patterns of
    0021,0120,0172,0248,0255,
    0367,0549,0593
GROUP THERAPY
    see THERAPY

HALFWAY HOUSES 0029,0299,
    0415,0788,A931

-333-

Community based programs
  0050,0507,0508,0573,A852
  Efficacy and evaluation 0573
  Planning aspects 0457
  Program design 0050,0573
HANDSOME LAKE RELIGION 0160,
  0204,0863,0906,0907,0908
HARE INDIANS 0231,0748,0749
  Drinking among 0747,0823
HASKELL INDIAN JUNIOR COLLEGE
  see also SCHOOLS
  0036
HAVASUPAI INDIANS 0056,0057,
  0058,0059,0665
  Alcohol production among
  0554
HAYES, IRA 0279,0811
HEADSTART PROGRAMS 0722
HEALTH BOARDS 0062,0509,0698
HEALTH EDUCATION 0115,0143,
  0740
  Planning aspects 0294,0923,
  0924
HEALTH PROBLEMS
  see also ACCIDENTS
           DIABETES, Alcohol
             related
           DIPHTHERIA
           ESOPHAGEAL VARICES
           HOMICIDE
           HYPOGLYCEMIA
           LUNG CANCER
           MENTAL HEALTH
           PSYCHOSIS, Alcohol
             induced
           RESERVATION INDIANS,
             Health problems
           SUICIDE
           TRACHOMA
           TUBERCULOSIS
           ULCERS
           URBAN INDIANS, Health
             problems
  0062,0078,0115,0133,0333
  0372,0615
HEYOKA CEREMONY 0546
HOLTZMAN INKBLOT TEST 0704
HOMEBREW 0073,0089,0101,0120,
  0172,0231,0323,0364,0376,
  0400,0406,0678,0747,0792,
  0823,0888

HOMICIDE 0186,0250,0253,
  0299,0338,0342,0544,0553,
  0872
  Alcohol related 0070,0114,
  0142,0252,A339,0343,0344,
  0346,0421,0491,0522,0539,
  0543,0551,0552,0657,0794,
  0808,0811,0889,0936
  Incidence of 0022,0026,
  0070,0114,0196,0343,0541,
  0671,0844
HOMOSEXUALITY 0131
HOPI INDIANS 0056,0057,0058,
  0066,0252,0361,0696,0740,
  0941
  Alcoholism among 0072,
  0489,0541,0887
  Delinquency among 0186,
  0434
  Drinking among 0186,0486,
  0489,0678,0777,0810
  Health problems 0321
  Legal aspects 0186
  Suicide among 0541
  Violence among 0541
HOSTILITY 0167,0168,
  0171,0238,0623,0726,0905
HOUSING 0046,0213,0220,0312,
  0372,0465,0508,0671,0851
HUDSON BAY, CANADA 0729
HUDSON BAY COMPANY 0213,0323
HUPA INDIANS 0154,0237
HYPOGLYCEMIA 0578

IBAPAH 0068
IDAHO 0040
IDAHO INDUSTRIAL TRAINING
  SCHOOL
  see also SCHOOLS
  0069
IDENTITY 0002,0017,0145,0184,
  0312,0322,0353,0366,0385,
  0409,0441,0474,0563,0564,
  0610,0622,0623,0629,0662,
  0676,0686,0720,0721,0723,
  0738,0741
ILIAKA VILLAGE 0446

ILLEGITIMACY 0133,0967,0968
ILLINOIS, see also CHICAGO
   A190
ILLINOIS INDIANS 0886
INCEST, ALCOHOL RELATED 0570
INCOME, USED FOR PURCHASING
   ALCOHOL
   see also ECONOMICS AS CAUSE
      OF DRINKING
   0026,0190,0432,0463,0465,
   0492,0513,0642,0658,0739,
   0747,0787,0944,0949
INDIAN ACT (CANADA)
   0124,0499,0565,0566,0577,
   0598,0599,0781,0793,0806,
   A890
INDIAN BARS
   see TAVERNS
INDIAN CENTERS 0206,0465,0960
INDIAN COURTS
   see COURTS, TRIBAL
INDIAN COUNSELLOR PROGRAM 0093
INDIAN HEALTH BOARDS
   see HEALTH BOARDS
INDIAN HEALTH SERVICE 0151,
   0261,0319,0452,0456,0490,
   0698,0714,0805,0865,0866,
   0867,0871,0872,0877,0878,
   0882
INDIAN HERITAGE SCHOOL, see also
   SCHOOLS 0054
INDIAN LEADERS
   see TRIBAL OFFICIALS
INDIAN REORGANIZATION ACT
   0142,0506
INDIAN RIGHTS ASSOCIATION 0428
INDIAN SELF-DETERMINATION AND
   EDUCATION ACT (P.L. 93-638)
   0051
INDIAN SERVICE (BIA)
   0031,0036,0136,0562,0762,
   0889
INDIAN SHAKER CHURCH 0104,0139,
   0283,0284,0479,0523,0863,
   0920
INDIANA 0030
INDIGENOUS AIDES
   see also PARAPROFESSIONALS
   0062,0093,0095,0096,0116,
   0255,0392,0453

INFANTS, ALCOHOL EFFECTS ON
   see FETAL ALCOHOL SYNDROME
INHALANTS
   see also DRUGS
      ETIOLOGY, of
         substance
         sniffing
      SUBSTANCE
         SNIFFING
   0054,0217,0770,0771
INPATIENT SERVICES
   0362,0383,0384,0930
INTERCOURSE ACTS A083,
   A367,0703,0724,0891
INTERMOUNTAIN SCHOOL
   see also SCHOOLS
   0654
INTERPERSONAL RELATIONSHIPS
   0073,0163,0254,0721
INTER-TRIBAL ALCOHOLISM
   TREATMENT CENTER 0667
INTERTRIBAL COUNCIL 0471
INTERVENTION 0044,0061,0107
INUIT
   see ESKIMO
INUVIK
   see ESKIMO
INUVIK, N.W.T., CANADA
   0171,0172,0246,0247,0402,
   0403,0405,0410,0411,0553,
   0753
INVOLVEMENT 0022,0062,0103,
   0194,0206,0281,0469,
   0471,0591,0592,0596,0600,
   0675,0685,0698,0702,0725,
   0767,0771,0774,0850,0935
IOWA (STATE)
   0386,0706
   Treatment programs in
   0706
IOWA INDIANS 0300
IROQUOIS CONFEDERACY 0156,
   0907,0908
IROQUOIS INDIANS 0156,
   0204,0845
   Drinking among 0088,0197,
   0199,0464,0678,0796,0905,
   0907,0908
   Historical aspects 0157,
   0160,0464,0907,0908
   Suicide among 0267

ISOLATION 0444,A636,0715,0718,
    0738,0748,0766,0780
ITALIAN 0148

JAILS, OVERREPRESENTATION OF
    INDIANS
    0223,0224,0241,0287,0309,
    0870
JEFFERSON, THOMAS 0336
JELLINEK PROGRESSION OF ALCOHOLISM
    0024,0514,0515,0520
JESUIT, RELATIONS 0199
JESUITS A671,0802
JOHN HOWARD SOCIETY 0093
JOHNSON, WILLIAM E. "PUSSYFOOT"
    0038,0165,0568,0731
JUDGES 0134,0650
JURISDICTION 0049,0053,0091,
    0182,0202,0341,0506,0689,
    0702,0710,0893,0921
JUVENILE DELINQUENCY
    see DELINQUENCY

KAGAN'S INTERPERSONAL PROCESS
    RECALL TECHNIQUE
    0108
KAKTOVIK, ALASKA 0163
KANSA INDIANS 0300
KANSAS 0036,0070,A281,0300,
    0301,0355
    Treatment programs in 0105
KANSAS, TERRITORY OF 0355
KANSAS CITY 0573
KASKA INDIANS
    Alcohol production among
    0399
    Drinking among 0401,0580
KAYENTA, ARIZONA 0836
KEEBLE VS. UNITED STATES 0893
KENORA, INDIANS IN 0609,0895
KENORA WAY STATION 0612,0965
KICKAPOO INDIANS 0300

KING COUNTY, WASHINGTON
    0084,0655
KIOWA-APACHE INDIANS 0302,
    A813
KLALLAM INDIANS 0207
KLAMATH INDIANS 0066,0207
    Alcoholism among 0525
    Drinking among 0232,0365
KNOWLEDGE OF ALCOHOL
    among alcoholics 0855,0856
    among Indians 0397,0398,
    0855,0856
    among students 0654
KOTZEBUE, ALASKA 0353,0794
KUTCHIN INDIANS 0401
    Vunta Kutchin 0073,0074
KWAKIUTL INDIANS 0526,0726

LABRADOR 0089,0203
LAC LA MARTE, N.W.T., CANADA
    0376,0400
LAGUNA, NEW MEXICO 0637
LANGUAGE BARRIERS 0029,
    0510,0512,0631,0835
LANGUAGE, RELATION TO
    ALCOHOL ABUSE A819
LA PAS, MANITOBA, CANADA
    0245
LARSON, HENRY A. 0165
LAW 0030,0035,0037,0040,
    0051,0064,0067,0091,0093,
    0124,0129,0142,0170,0178,
    0182,0183,0186,0197,0202,
    0228,0261,0263,0264,0281,
    0308,0310,0335,0336,0364,
    0368,0370,0407,0408,0423,
    0462,0498,0499,0508,0511,
    0548,0551,0552,0556,0562,
    0565,0566,0571,0577,0598,
    0599,0602,0627,0629,0639,
    0659,0669,0700,0701,0710,
    0731,0753,0781,0793,0806,
    A813,0834,0854,0868,0874,
    0889,0890,A890,0893,0911,
    0914,0921,0959,0961,0965,
    0969

LAW ENFORCEMENT
  see also ARRESTS
           COURTS
           COURTS, TRIBAL
           LIQUOR LAWS,
             enforcement
           RESERVATIONS, law
             enforcement
  0041,0186,0203,0689
LAW ENFORCEMENT OFFICIALS
  see also POLICE 0043
  Indians 0341,0562
  Relations with Indians
    0051,0106,0382,0388,0389,
    0392,0411,0794,0804,0816
  Training 0047,0816
LEARNED BEHAVIOR
  0150,0191,0248,0393,0444,
  0525,0534,0567,0575,0639,
  0726
LEAVENWORTH, KANSAS 0070
LEWISTON COUNTY, IDAHO 0568
LIQUOR, DISTILLED
  0039,0120,0385,0792
LIQUOR CONTROL OFFICERS
  0031,0038,0136,0165,0731
LIQUOR LAWS
  see also DRYBONES CASE
           GONZALES CASE
  Enforcement 0031,0033,0038,
    0049,0051,0064,0067,0075,
    0134,0136,0165,0181,0182,
    0183,0197,0202,0203,0228,
    0263,0264,0330,0335,0341,
    0364,0366,0450,0462,0506,
    0513,0565,0566,0577,0598,
    0599,0602,0700,0701,0703,
    0724,0753,0757,0806,0836,
    0847,0869,0891,0893
  Historical aspects 0021,
    0030,0111,0165,0170,0173,
    0182,0202,0207,0279,0330,
    0336,0548,0601,0602,0629,
    0639,0670,0703,0724,0737,
    0762,A813,0834,0854,0868,
    0890,0891,0914,0951,0954,
  Possession restrictions
    0124,0207,0308,0336,0602,
    0874
  Purchasing and selling
    restrictions

    0031,0033,0035,0040,0049,
    0053,0202,0207,0228,0308,
    0336,0355,0357,0407,0408,
    0462,0463,0498,0506,0532,
    0556,0562,0571,0598,0602,
    0728,0731,0806,0868,0874,
    0890,0914,0921,0961
  Tribal Statutes A602
LIQUOR LICENSE
  0049,0053,0868,0874
LIQUOR SUPPRESSION CAMPAIGN
  see also PROHIBITION
           0613
LIQUOR TRADE
  see also FUR TRADE
           TRADE
           TRADERS
  0031,A190,0300,0301,0330,
  0579,A685,0728,0731,0762,
  A810
  Historical aspects
    0031,0156,0157,0165,0170,
    0182,A190,0219,0300,0301,
    0330,0331,0335,0355,0365,
    0416,0428,0429,0430,0431,
    0464,0532,0568,0579,0613,
    0638,A685,0703,0724,0728,
    0729,0731,0737,0742,0758,
    0762,0802,A810,A813,0834,
    0845,0854,0891,0916,0956,
    0961,0969
  White involvement in
    0156,0157,0170,0219,0331,
    0344,0365,0428,0429,0533,
    0613,0639,A671,0737,0742,
    0891,0916,0954
LIQUOR TRAFFIC
  see also FUR TRADE
           TRADE
           TRADERS
  A083,0136,0156,0165,0170,
  0182,0202,0331,0335,0428,
  0506,0513,0533,0568,0703,
  0724,0731,0737,0802,A813,
  0834,0845,0868
LITERATURE REVIEWS
  see also BIBLIOGRAPHIES
  0112,0137,0473,0522,B588
LOCAL OPTION
  see PROHIBITION

LOS ANGELES
  Indians in   0152,0313,0354,
    0699
  Treatment programs in   0310
LOUISIANA PURCHASE   A685
LOWER POST, BRITISH COLUMBIA
  0401,0580
LUMBEE INDIANS   0491
LUNG CANCER   0060
LYBROOK, NEW MEXICO   0029,0596
LYNX POINT   0375

MACKENZIE DISTRICT, N.W.T., CANADA
  0376,0400,0403,0557,0558,
  0792
MAGUEY   0122,0227,0419
MAINE   0738
MAIZE BEER
  see also BEER
  0146,0227,0419,0673,0674
MAKAH INDIANS   0207,0772,0773
MAKKOVIK, LABRADOR   0089
MALES   0028,0045,0106,0109,
  0121,0131,0132,0133,0137,
  0140,0141,0154,0155,0168,
  0176,0187,0188,0189,0190,
  0201,0216,0237,0265,0270,
  0275,0277,0278,0291,0292,
  0302,0324,0345,0352,0356,
  0358,0360,0362,0368,0376,
  0395,A396,0407,0409,0415,
  0424,0454,0458,0477,0479,
  0486,0488,0489,A509,0518,
  0519,0542,0543,0584,0603,
  0605,0606,0608,0611,0618,
  0624,0630,0677,0680,0692,
  0709,0711,0713,0714,0730,
  0735,0744,0746,0752,0764,
  0767,0771,0772,0773,0777,
  0788,0812,0827,0829,0837,
  0838,0841,0858,0902,0948,
  0950,0953
MALFORMATION   0014,0448,0449
MANITOBA, CANADA   0106,0245,
  0398,0498,0723
MANHATTAN, NEW YORK   0579

MANUFACTURE OF ALCOHOLIC
  BEVERAGES
  0007,0073,0122,0129,0146,
  0161,0166,0172,0225,0226,
  0227,0282,0285,0359,0376,
  0399,0418,0561,0673,0707,
  0758,0765,0792,0826,0861,
  0901,0909,0954
MANY FARMS, ARIZONA   0352
MARGINALITY AS CAUSE OF
  DRINKING
  see also ETIOLOGY, of Alcoholism
          ETIOLOGY, of Drinking
          ETIOLOGY, of Drunkenness
  0113,0159,0231,0246,0327
MARICOPA INDIANS   0359
MARIJUANA   0054,0177,0237,0352,
  0695
MARITAL INSTABILITY   0006,0538,
  0717,0963
MASONIC RITUAL   0139
MASSACHUSETTS
  see BOSTON, MASSACHUSETTS
MCKENNEY, THOMAS L.
  0891
MEANS-GOAL DISJUNCTION
  0171,0172,0231
MEDICAL RECORDS   0295,0378,
  0705,0713,0714,0734
MEDICINE MEN (NATIVE
  PRACTITIONERS)
  0082,0426,0442,0768
  Role in alcoholism treatment
  0192,0535,A555,A659
  Role in mental health
  0129,0439,0440,0453,0455,
  0535,0536,0844
MENDOCINO STATE HOSPITAL
  0476
MENOMINI INDIANS
  Drinking among   0789
  Historical aspects   0035
MENTAL DISORDERS
  Incidence of   0732,0734
MENTAL HEALTH
  see also DELINQUENCY
          DEPRESSION
          HEALTH PROBLEMS
          HOMICIDE
          SUICIDE

A063,0069,0078,0079,0087,
0099,0107,0117,0137,0153,
0295,0322,0338,0345,0444,
0453,0454,0455,0475,0536,
0576,0609,0610,0617,0619,
0624,0626,0729,0768,0844,
0877,0923,0935,0947
Historical aspects 0421
Philosophical and ethical issues
0061,0062,0623
MENTAL ILLNESS 0061,0062,0063,
0069,0095,0096,0251,0260,
0296,0459,0512,0657,0705,
0732,0807
MERRITT, EDGAR B. 0613
MESCALERO APACHE
see APACHE, Mescalero
METABOLISM OF ALCOHOL
see also GENETIC DIFFERENCES
RACIAL DIFFERENCES
Age differences 0351
Ethnic differences 0094,
0259,0265,0266,0351,0357,
0393,0412,0547,0616,0709,
0755,0957
Indians 0094,0259,0265,0266,
0412,0425,0547,0575,0616,
0709,0755,0832,0894,0911,
0931,0957
Sex differences 0351
METIS 0115,0193,0220,0246,
0247,0405,0410,0576
Alcoholism among 0383,0472
Drinking among 0398,0402,
0403,0498,0792,0801
MEXICAN-AMERICANS 0085,0086,
0436
MEXICO AND MEXICANS
0031,0122,0146,0162,0166,
0225,A367,0419,0561
MICCOSUKEE INDIANS 0611
MICMAC INDIANS 0120,0334
MILWAUKEE, WISCONSIN 0719
MINI-WAKAN (LIQUOR) 0608
MINNEAPOLIS, MINNESOTA
Indians in 0223,0224,0508,
0593,0870,0928
Law enforcement in 0181,0870
Treatment programs in
0206,0508,0937

MINNESOTA
Health care facilities in
0133
Indians in 0036,0395,
0396,0509,0543,0870,0927,
0928,0934,0936
Treatment programs in
0395,0396
MINNESOTA MULTIPHASIC
PERSONALITY INVENTORY
0477
MISSIONARIES 0088,0209,0219,
0390,0464,0524,0737,0796,
0886
MISSISSIPPI RIVER
A190
MISSISSIPPI VALLEY
A685
MISSOURI 0916
MIXED BLOOD 0045,0046,0510,
0574,0606,0625,0884
MODELS
see ROLE, models
MODERNIZATION
see ACCULTURATION
ASSIMILATION
CULTURAL CONFLICT
CULTURE CHANGE
STRESS
MODOC INDIANS 0333
MODOC-LASSEN INDIAN
DEVELOPMENT COMMITTEE
0333
MOHAVE INDIANS 0159,0211,
0212,0248,0846
MOIETY SYSTEM 0074
MONTAGNAIS INDIANS 0886
MONTANA
Health care facilities in
0133
Indians in 0080,0632,
0633,0634,0635,0636,A819
Treatment programs in
0324,0632,0633,0634,0635,
0636,0722
MONTANA INDIAN COMMISSION ON
ALCOHOL AND DRUG ABUSE
0632,0633,0635
MONTICELLO, UTAH 0836
MOONSHINE 0075,0209,A367

-339-

MORNING STAR LODGE   0573
MORTALITY
   see also ACCIDENTS, mortality
         ALCOHOLISM, mortality
         CIRRHOSIS, mortality
         DRIVING, mortality
         FEMALE ALCOHOLISM,
           mortality
         FETAL ALCOHOL SYNDROME,
           mortality
         MULTIPLE DRUG USE,
           mortality
         SUBSTANCE SNIFFING,
           mortality
         VIOLENCE, mortality
   Correlates   0394,0652,0653,
     0679.0696,0713,0936
MOTOR VEHICLES ACT   0067
MOUNT EDGECUMBE SCHOOL, see also
     SCHOOLS   0356
MUCKLESHOOT INDIANS   0372,0479
MUD BAY, WASHINGTON   0139
MULTIPLE DRUG USE
   among adolescents   0177
   mortality   0110
MURDER
   see HOMICIDE
MUSQUEAM INDIANS   0920
MYTHOLOGY ABOUT INDIAN DRINKING
   see DRINKING, Myths about
        Indians

NA IH ES   0081
NASKAPI INDIANS   0677,0720,0721
NARRANGANSETT INDIANS   0030
NATCHEZ INDIANS   0678
NATIONAL CONGRESS OF AMERICAN
   INDIANS   0052
NATIONAL HEALTH INSURANCE   0595
NATIONAL INDIAN BOARD ON
   ALCOHOLISM AND DRUG ABUSE
   0052,0850
NATIONAL INSTITUTE ON ALCOHOL
   ABUSE AND ALCOHOLISM
      0319,A522,0632,0725,0782,
      0805,0865,0879

NATIONAL MUSEUM OF CANADA
   0120,0375,0749,0888
NATIVE ALCOHOL COUNCIL
   (SASKATCHEWAN)
   0193
NATIVE ALCOHOLIC BEVERAGES
   see NATIVE INTOXICATING
      BEVERAGES
NATIVE AMERICAN CHURCH
   Abstinence from alcohol
     see ABSTINENCE, Native
        American Church
   Ceremonies   0015,0268,
     0686,0687,0902
   Efficacy and evaluation
     0015,0099,0268,0302,0385,
     0496,0686,0733,0734
   Historical aspects   0268,
     0385,0863
   Sociological aspects
     0001,0775
NATIVE BEVERAGES
   see NATIVE INTOXICATING
      BEVERAGES
      PIVA
      TESVINO
      TISWIN
      TULAPAI
NATIVE BROTHERHOOD MOVEMENT
   0067,0228
NATIVE COUNSELORS
   see COUNSELORS, Indian
      INDIGENOUS AIDES
      PARAPROFESSIONALS
NATIVE INTOXICATING BEVERAGES
   see also PIVA
        TESVINO
        TISWIN
        TULAPAI
   0166,0225,0226,0299,0406
   Production   0073,0146,0161,
     0162,0191,0225,0282,0359,
     0375,0376,0399,0406,0418,
     0419,0494,0554,0561,0678,
     0736,0765,0792,0823,0826,
     0861,0956
   Sociological aspects   0323,
     0375,0385,0399,0494,0561,
     0747,0857,0858,0861,0862,
     0888,0901

NATIVE PERSONNEL
  see COUNSELORS, Indian
    INDIGENOUS AIDES
    PARAPROFESSIONALS
    TREATMENT PROGRAMS, Staff
      training
NATIVE POLICE
  see LAW ENFORCEMENT OFFICIALS,
    Indians
NATIVE PRACTITIONERS
  see MEDICINE MEN
NATIVISTIC MOVEMENTS 0179,
  0221,0441
NAVAJO INDIANS 0001,0029,0041,
  0043,0056,0057,0058,0059,
  0066,0083,0099,0119,0143,
  0167,0192,0252,0297,0329,
  0352,0361,0362,A367,0459,
  0465,0478,A486,0512,0537,
  0582,0651,0653,0654,0663,
  0696,0699,0743,0761,0777,
  0788,0822,0837,0902,0941,
  0964,0966
  Alcohol production among
    0299
  Alcoholism among
    0380,0381,0382,0384,0456,
    0488,0541,0596,0672,0730,
    0744,0745,0746,0756,0760,
    0828,0829,0887,0958
  Arrests among 0380,0381,0382,
    0434,0513,0559,0560
  Delinquency among 0434
  Drinking among 0094,0248,
    0269,0270,0271,0272,0273,
    0274,0275,0276,0277,0278,
    0316,0327,0328,0368,0369,
    0370,0417,0458,0486,0487,
    0488,0489,0513,0538,0542,
    0559,0570,0672,0764,0797,
    0810,0816,0836,0838,0839,
    0840,0841,0843,0847,0889,
    0890,0892,0922,0959
  Health problems among
    0321,0340,0513,0652,0756
  Homicide among 0543,0889
  Ramah 0316,0368,0458
  Suicide among 0159,0458,0538,
    0541,0543,0618,0962
  Tribal Council 0126

  Violence among 0368,0369,
    0458,0459,0541,0890
NAVAJO-CORNELL FIELD HEALTH
  RESEARCH PROJECT
    0672
NAWAIT RITUAL 0899
NEGROS
  see BLACKS
NEVADA 0036,0471,0518
  Indians in 0457,0516,
    0517,0519
  Treatment Programs in
    0169,0592
NEVADA INTER-TRIBAL
  ALCOHOLISM PROGRAM
    0169,0774
NEW FRANCE 0088,A671,A813
NEW HARBOR VILLAGE 0446
NEW MEXICO
  see also ALBUQUERQUE
    GALLUP
    TAOS PUEBLO
  0022,0027,0029,0090,0105,
  0359,A367,0562,0764,0790
  Indians in 0022,0090,0140,
    0141,0562,0775,0790
  Treatment programs in
    0105,0637,0835,0926
NEW MEXICO STATE COMMISSION
  ON ALCOHOLISM
    0362,0596
NEW MEXICO STATE COMMISSION
  ON INDIAN AFFAIRS
    0562
NEW NETHERLANDS 0111
NEW SPAIN 0146
NEW YORK (STATE) 0005,0309,
  0845
NEZ, JOHN 0892
NEZ PERCE INDIANS
  0006,0207,0568,0669
NIKOLSKI, ALASKA
  0101,0102
NISQUALLY INDIANS 0207
NOME, ALASKA 0388
NOOTKA INDIANS 0145
NORTH CAROLINA 0491
NORTH DAKOTA 0133
NORTHEASTERN WOODLAND INDIANS
  0072,0344,0346,0738

NORTHWEST COAST
 0042,0054,0065,0066,0075,
 0084,0093,0103,0104,0121,
 0139,0145,0148,0173,0196,
 0200,0207,0219,0228,0231,
 0232,0284,0314,0322,0347,
 0360,0363,0364,0366,0372,
 0397,0439,0440,0441,0442,
 0443,0444,0479,0482,0497,
 0524,0526,0527,0545,0586,
 0595,0628,0655,0666,0688,
 0690,0726,0728,0747,0753,
 0754,0767,0769,0772,0773,
 0791,0804,0808,0825,0830,
 0846,0852,0853,0881,0903,
 0912,0913,0920
 Alcoholism among 0314,0315,
  0523,0525
 Drinking among 0178,0248,0365
 Historical aspects 0365,0416,
  0824
 Suicide among 0769
NORTHWEST TERRITORIES
 0064,0155,0281,0400,0753,
 0781,0792,A890,0895
NURSES 0245,0680
NUTRITIONAL ASPECTS OF ALCOHOLISM
 0041,0575,0578,0688

OKLAHOMA CITY, OKLAHOMA 0241
OLD CROW, YUKON TERRITORY,
 0073,0401
OLYMPIC PENINSULA INDIANS
 0444
OMAHA, NEBRASKA 0492
OMAHA INDIANS 0168,0417,
 0492
ONEIDA INDIANS
 Drinking among 0719,0907,
  0918
 Historical aspects 0035
ONONDAGA COUNTY, NEW YORK
 0309
ONTARIO, CANADA 0067,
 0197,0535,0609,0612
ORATAM, CHIEF 0111
OREGON 0207,0219,0232,0497,
 0675,0676,0881
OSAGE INDIANS A083,A281,
 0300,0495
OTTAWA INDIANS 0300
OUTPATIENT TREATMENT
 0055,0362,0383,0384,0930
OUTREACH EFFORTS
 0079,0116,0193,0476,0497,
 0518,0633,0935
OVERDOSE 0110,0155,0786

OAKLAND, CALIFORNIA
 0827
OFFICE OF ECONOMIC OPPORTUNITY
 0805
OFF-RESERVATION
 see URBAN INDIANS
OHIO 0030,0429
OJIBWA INDIANS 0432,0709,0750
 Drunkenness among 0682
 Homicide among 0142
 Psychological aspects
  0345,0682,0723
OKLAHOMA 0017,0036,0037,0165,
 A281,A330,0287,0428,0817,
 0866
 Treatment programs in
  0105,0637

PAIUTE INDIANS 0420,0849
PAN-INDIAN CHURCH 0313
PAN-INDIANISM 0002,0015,
 0200,0313,0334,0385,0414,
 0422,0450
PAPAGO INDIANS 0056,0057,
 0059,0066,0097,0146,0161,
 0162,0187,0189,0201,0210,
 0227,0282,0298,0361,0451,
 0941
 Accidents among 0455
 Alcohol production among
  0554,0561,0860,0861,0862,
  0909
 Alcoholism among 0455,
  0713,0714

Drinking among 0248,0288,
 0338,0588,0590,0712,0777,
 0821,0857,0858,0859,0862,
 0897,0898,0899,0900,0909,
 0910
Health problems 0321,0712
Historical aspects 0588
Psychological aspects 0590
Suicide among 0189,0288
PAPAGO INDIAN RESERVATION
Treatment programs on
 0453,0454,0455
PARAPROFESSIONALS 0019,0022,
 0047,0048,0062,0096,0105,
 0116,0119,0193,0362,0392,
 0455,0487,0510,0536,0550,
 0609,0617,0625,0626,0628,
 0681,0700,0702,0706,0725,
 0760,0784,0849,0935
Efficacy and evaluation
 0646,0706,0760,0768,0774,
 0849,0932
Role in alcoholism management
 0662,0760,0784,00853,0912,
 0958
Training 0047,0239,0646,
 0700,0702,0799,0917,0938
PARENTAL DRINKING
Effects on children
 0026,0361,0394,0396,0410,
 0411,0460,0481,0484,0588,
 0643,0684,0685,0710,0752,
 0764,0825,0877,0882,0903,
 0917
PARENTS 0047,0158,0257,0903
PATTERNS, PERSISTENCE
see also DRINKING, Patterns of
 0369,0370,0539,0541,0542,
 0645,0812,0860
PAWNEE, OKLAHOMA
 0637
PAWNEE INDIANS 0678,0817
PEER COUNSELING
see also COUNSELING
 COUNSELORS, Indian
 0497,B852,0938
PEER GROUP
 0050,0176,0184,0257,0270,
 0271,0272,0278,0444,0474,
 0475,0745,0915,0917,0932

PEER PRESSURE 0163,0248,
 0273,0661,0662,0665,0700
PEER SUPPORT 0283
PENNSYLVANIA 0030,0036
PEORIA, ILLINOIS A190
PEPTIC ULCER
see ULCERS, Peptic
PERSONALITY 0076,0077,
 0344,0345,0476,0477,0589,
 0590,0719,0752,0803
PEYOTE 0001,0015,0099,0133,
 0165,0227,0268,0302,0385,
 0495,0496,0548,0686,0687,
 0733,0734,0775,0863,0902
PEYOTE CULT
see NATIVE AMERICAN CHURCH
PHILADELPHIA, PENNSYLVANIA
 0543
PHILADELPHIA ANTI-SALOON LEAGUE
 0032
PHOENIX, ARIZONA 0241,0279
PHOENIX INDIAN MEDICAL CENTER
 0320,0321,0776,0777
PIEGAN INDIANS
see BLACKFOOT INDIANS
PIMA INDIANS 0146,0161,
 0162,0227,0279,0321,0359,
 0554,0777,0782,0901
Alcohol production among
 0359,0554,0901
Alcoholism among 0782
Drinking among 0146,0161,
 0162,0227,0279,0777
Health problems 0321
PIMA COUNTY ALCOHOLISM TASK
FORCE 0085,0086
PINE RIDGE RESERVATION
see also RESERVATIONS
 0045,0046,0051,0466,0468,
 0606,0608
Drinking on 0622,0624,0625,
 0950
Prevention programs on
 0917,0923,0924,0947
PITAHAYA FRUIT 0146,0161
PIVA 0101
PLAINS INDIANS 0012,0017,
 0365,0414,0422,0601,0667,
 0687,0807,A813,0925
Alcoholism among 0687

Drinking among 0366,0414
Historical aspects 0925
Violence among 0366
PLANTS
see MANUFACTURE OF ALCOHOLIC
BEVERAGES
PLATEAU TRIBES 0283,0769,0903
PNEUMONIA 0060,0707
POISONING 0155,0267
POLICE
see also LAW ENFORCEMENT
OFFICIALS
0402,0405,0411,0450,0562,
0642,0759,0807,0816,0836,
0870,0969
Discrimination by
0106,0181
POMO INDIANS 0358
PONCA INDIANS 0492
POSTON, ARIZONA 0050
POTAWATOMI INDIANS
Drinking among 0248,0348,
0349
Historical aspects 0300
Sociological aspects 0349
POTLATCH 0314,0443
POVERTY 0079,0446,0493,0503,
0535,0615,0624,0666,0772,
0773,0811,0851,0872
PREJUDICE 0130,0244,0262,
0432,0560,0604,0665,0681
PREVENTION
Education 0126
of alcoholism 0011,0013,
0027,0061,0097,0105,0110,
0133,0143,0188,0203,0217,
0235,0277,0343,0362,0505,
0543,0584,0661,0697,0746,
0805,0856,0944
of delinquency 0243,0741
of suicide 0151,0299,0307,
0392,0544,0603,0625,0626,
0688,0770,0771
PREVENTION PROGRAMS
Community based 0373,0644
Community involvement 0600,
0675,0767,0844
Economic aspects 0544
Efficacy and evaluation 0544
Ethnic programs 0242,0725

For adolescents 0242,0243,
0298,0497,0675,0741,0904,
0952
Models 0242,0531,0881,0895
Planning aspects 0039,
0104,0113,0149,0151,0153,
0242,0260,0531,0537,0591,
0600,0631,0648,0649,0676,
0702,0725,0727,0738,0754,
0785,0844,0852,0876,0877,
0878,0882,0895,0927,0931
Program design 0169,0256,
0600,0649,0675,0676,0850,
0881,0946,0947,0960
Reservation programs 0535,
0641,0643,0644,0648,0649,
0770,0771,0917,0923,0924,
0947
Urban programs 0079,0206,
0572,0595
PRISONS 0033,0067,0070,0090,
0274,0299,0642,0643,0717,
0770,0804,0890,0934
Counseling programs in
0093,B852
Group therapy programs in
0067
Indians in 0018,0067,0093,
0287,0708,0853
Treatment programs in
0853
PROHIBITION 0038,0039,A083,
0111,0124,0133,0134,0156,
0163,0166,0170,0178,0207,
0263,0264,0310,0331,0358,
0364,A367,0393,0442,0463,
0524,0532,0534,0556,A602,
A671,A685,0701,0703,0728,
0765,0802,0806,0845,0891,
0956
Effects on drinking behavior
0068,0070,0183,0369,0370,
0408,0500,0501,0506,0560,
0562,0574,0583,0602,0629,
0645,0672,0708,0744,0746,
0810,0814,0835,0847,0969
Historical aspects 0005,
0030,0035,0037,0040,0068,
0157,0165,0173,0179,0183,
0236,0300,0301,0318,0355,
0357,0365,0428,0430,0464

0499,0533,0548,0579,0601,
0613,0614,0656,A671,0724,
0739,0834,0854,0890,0914,
0925,0956,0969
Local options
0308,0336
Philosophical and ethical
issues
0068,0070,0183,0499,0533,
0701,0914,0921
Repeal of 0179,0182,0264
Reservations 0038,0039,0041,
0182,0183,0202,0222,0308,
0336,0366,0506,0568,0574,
0584,0602,0718,0740,0744,
0810,0921,0959,0961,0966
Tribal 0090,0253,0440,
0568,0740
PROJECT SHOSHONWUA 0298
PROMISCUITY 0129,0353,0368,
0374,0401,0475,0493,0558
PROSTITUTION 0213,0493
PROTECTIVE CUSTODY
see ARRESTS
PSEUDO-INTOXICATION 0432
PSYCHOPATHOLOGY
0100,0114,0117,0251,0395,
0459,0554
PSYCHOSIS, ALCOHOL INDUCED
0350,0682,0830
PUBERTY CEREMONY 0081
PUBLIC HEALTH SERVICE
see U.S. PUBLIC HEALTH SERVICE
PUBLIC LAW 277
0961
PUBLIC DRINKING
see DRINKING, Public
PUEBLO INDIANS
0028,0041,0043,A367,0901
Drinking among 0090,0110,
0140,0141,0417,0596,0740,
0790,0815,0876
Psychological asepcts 0542
Substance sniffing 0460
PULQUE 0162
PUYALLUP INDIANS 0207

QUAKERS 0204
QUALLA CHEROKEE INDIANS
see also CHEROKEE INDIANS
0303
QUANTITY-FREQUENCY-
VARIABILITY INDEX
0152
QUEBEC PROVINCE, CANADA
0720,0721
QUINAULT INDIANS 0207
Suicide among 0322,0360,
0688

RACIAL DIFFERENCES
0175,0179,0222,0259,0263,
0265,0266,0316,0351,0393,
0412,0547,0616,0709,0750,
0755,0819,0820,0827,0832,
0937,0957
RAIN CEREMONY 0210,0282,0451,
0910
RANKIN INLET, CANADA 0949
RAPID CITY, SOUTH DAKOTA
0461,0556,0939,0940
RECREATION 0041,0176,0197,
0198,0233,0248,0272,0273,
0286,0298,0307,0322,0358,
0375,0376,0401,0406,0411,
0446,0476,0479,0548,0585,
0659,0665,0688,0692,0739,
0745,0794,0823,0847
RECREATIONAL DRINKING
see DRINKING, Recreational
RECREATIONAL FACILITIES
0041,0046,0264,0417,0465,
0584,0719,0877
RED LAKE, MINNESOTA 0506
RED LAKE COURT OF INDIAN
OFFENSES 0506
REGINA, SASKATCHEWAN
0064,0124,0472
REGINA VS. DRYBONES CASE
see DRYBONES
REGINA VS. GONZALES CASE
see GONZALES

REHABILITATION
    0012,0020,A046,0051,0104,
    0113,0135,0169,0193,0255,
    0284,0287,A317,0325,0362,
    0392,0471,0476,0493,0503,
    0536,0550,0596,0635,0641,
    0643,0644,0648,A659,0660,
    0706,0774,0782,0785,0835,
    0848,B852,0898,0958,0965
REHABILITATION SERVICES
  ADMINISTRATION 0782
RELOCATION 0002,0213,0312,0327,
    0328,0354,0415,0444
  Effects on drinking behavior
    0102,0213,0262,0339,0354,
    0388,0465,0481,0500,0501,
    0572,0699,0797,0813,0884,
    0939
  Psychological aspects
    0004,0354,0388,0415,0467,
    0593,0699,0922,0935
RENO-SPARKS INDIAN COLONY 0485,
    0875
RESERVATION INDIANS
  Health problems 0056,0057,
    0058,0059,0121,0536,0606,
    0615
RESERVATIONS
  Ak-Chin Reservation 0056,0057,
    0058
  Blackfoot Reservation 0125
  Camp Verde Indian Reservation
    0056,0057,0059
  Cheyenne River Reservation
    0194,0608,0697
  Cocopah Reservation
    0056,0057,0059
  Colorado River Reservation
    0050,0056,0057,0058,0859
  Colville Reservation 0042,
    0365,0690,0728,0825
  Crow Creek Reservation 0109
  Fort Apache Reservation
    0056,0057,0059
  Fort Hall Reservation
    0216,0392,0360,0450,0544,
    0627,0669,0735,0770,0771,
    0915
  Fort McDermitt Reservation
    0849
  Fort McDowell Reservation
    0056,0058

  Gila River Reservation
    0056,0058,0059,0146,0782
  Havasupai Reservation
    0056,0057,0058,0059
  Hopi Reservation 0056,0057,
    0058,0186
  Hualapai Reservation 0056,
    0058,0059,0190
  Kaibab-Paiute Reservation
    0056,0057
  Lame Deer Reservation 0426
  Mescalero Apache Reservation
    0285,0490
  Muckleshoot Reservation
    0479
  Navajo Reservation 0056,
    0057,0058,0059,0126,0143,
    0192,0456,0966
  Papago Reservation
    0056,0057,0059
  Pine Ridge Reservation
    0045,0046,0051,0466,0468,
    0574,0606,0608,0622,0626,
    0917,0923,0924,0947,0950
  Quinault Reservation 0688
  Rocky Boy Reservation 0053
  Rosebud Sioux Reservation
    0044,0608,0884
  Salt River Reservation 0056
  San Carlos Reservation
    0056,0587,0684,0707,0882
  San Xavier Reservation 0288
  Standing Rock Reservation 0233,
    0608,0660,0943,0944,0945
  Uintah-Ouray Reservation
    0643,0785,0787,0885
  Ute Mountain Reservation 0450
  Umatilla Reservation 0675
  Wind River Reservation
    0049,0176,0218,0290,0291,
    0292,0293,0450,0874
  Yavapai-Prescott Reservation
    0056
RESERVATIONS
  Alcoholism on
    0675,A819,0945
RESERVATIONS
  Crime on
    0018,0045

RESERVATIONS,
 Drinking on 0190,0233,0608,
  0622,0624,0625,0660,0661,
  0692,0711,0713,0723,0739,
  0746,0757,0836,0839,0884,
  0885,0897,0943,0950,0959,
  0965
RESERVATIONS,
 Law Enforcement
  0091,0134,0142,0183,0341,
  0874,0966
RESERVATIONS,
 Liquor Laws
  see LIQUOR LAWS
RESERVATIONS,
 Prevention Programs
  see PREVENTION PROGRAMS
RESERVATIONS,
 Prohibition
  see PROHIBITION,
   Reservations
RESERVATIONS,
 Suicide on
  see also SUICIDE
  0288,0624,0625,0626,0723,
  0767,0770,0771
RESERVATIONS,
 Treatment Programs on
  0116,0126,0453,0454,0455,
  0490,0592,0643,0644,0650,
  0675,0722,0725,0774,0782,
  0883,0887,0946
RESERVATIONS,
 Tribal Courts
  see COURTS, TRIBAL
RESERVES, CANADIAN
  0197,0463,0545,0723
 Blackfoot Reserve 0125,0723
 Musqueam Reserve 0920
 Norway House Reserve 0723
 Pas Reserve 0723
 Rapid Lake Reserve 0662
 Roseau Reserve 0723
RESIDENTIAL TREATMENT
  0476,0572,0573,0596,0637,
  0667,0853
REVITALIZATION 0048,0414,0450,
  0906,0908
RISK ANALYSIS
  0011,A376,0377,0378
RISK FACTORS, SUICIDE
  0189,0387
RITUAL DRINKING
  see DRINKING, Ceremonial

ROLES 0092,0128,0129,0195,0240,
  0432,0446,0662,0720,0738,
  0739,0839,0895
 Confusion 0013,0647
 Female 0006,0132,0479,0911
 Male 0006,0132,0682,0911
 Model 0251,0254,0255,0257,
  0286,0386,0765
ROSEBUD, SOUTH DAKOTA
  0637,0884
RUM 0236,0399,0429,0430,0431,
  0534,0729,0742,0845,0888,
  0916

SAC INDIANS 0300
SAGUARO CACTUS
  0146,0161,0201,0227,0282,
  0561,0857,0861,0862
SALISH
 Ceremonies 0439,0440,0441,
  0442,0524
 Drinking among 0148,0443,
  0524,0527,0545
 Health problems 0442
SALT LAKE CITY, UTAH 0788
SALT LAKE COUNTY, UTAH 0788
SANCTIONS
 see also SOCIAL CONTROLS
 Against alcohol 0160,0270,
  0413,0789
 Supernatural 0142,0682
SAN DIEGO, CALIFORNIA 0572
SAN FELIPE PUEBLO 0876
SAN FRANCISCO, CALIFORNIA 0827
SAN FRANCISCO BAY AREA
  0002,0467
SALTEAUX 0734
SANTA ROSA, ARIZONA 0860
SASKATCHEWAN, CANADA
  0067,0463,0473,0732,0733,
  0734
SASKATCHEWAN ALCOHOLISM
 COMMISSION 0193
SASKATOON, CANADA 0220
SCHIZOPHRENIA 0070,0296,0732,
  0734
SCHOOLS
 see also ALCOHOL EDUCATION
   EDUCATORS

0126,0128,0291,0298,0304,
0307,0332,0356,0360,0410,
0481,0623,0684,0685,0695,
0741,0872
  Boarding schools 0262,0352,
    A376,0434,0474,0475,0484,
    0654,0767,0810
  Chemawa Indian School
    0497,0881
  Chilocco Indian School
    0036
  Haskell Indian Junior College
    0036
  High School 0114,0289,A376,
    0454,0474,0604,0695
  Idaho Industrial Training School
    0669
  Indian Heritage School 0054
  Intermountain School 0654
  Many Farms 0352
  Mt. Edgecumbe School 0356
SEATTLE, WASHINGTON
  0054,0084,0121,0200,0397,
  0628,0803
  Treatment programs in
    0616,0655,0852,0853,0864
SEATTLE INDIAN ALCOHOLISM PROGRAM
  0103,0655,0852,0853
SEATTLE INDIAN HEALTH BOARD
  0103,0595
SELF-CONCEPT
  0097,0145,0147,0187,0244,
  0307,0423,0432,0479,0580,
  0647,0688,0795,0851,0904,
  0923,0924,0948
  among adolescents 0097,
    0307,0603,0610,0904,0923
  among alcoholics 0395,A509,
    0510,0647,0666,0706,0948
  among drinkers 0145,0147,
    0187,0215,0479,0647,0964
SELF-DETERMINATION
  0023,0205,0446,0530,0531,
  0603,0617,0698
SELF-ESTEEM
  see also SELF-CONCEPT
  0215,0244,0480,0510,0666,
  0706
SELF-HELP 0181,0725
SELS, CATO 0136,0165,0330,0762

SELS SERVICE UNIT 0714
SEMINOLE INDIANS
  Drinking among 0311
  Health problems among 0611
SENECA INDIANS
  Drinking among 0798,0906
  Historical aspects 0005,
    0907,0908
SETTLERS 0089,0150,0331,
  0355,0756
SHAKER RELIGION
  see INDIAN SHAKER CHURCH
SHAWNEE INDIANS 0300
SHERIDAN, WYOMING 0637,
  0667
SHIPROCK, NEW MEXICO 0488
  Treatment programs in
    0362,0926
SHOALWATER BAY, WASHINGTON
  0824
SHOSHONE INDIANS
  see also ARAPAHOE INDIANS
               BANNOCK INDIANS
  0159,0218,0289,0291,0293,
  0667
  Arrests among 0627
  Delinquency among 0627
  Drinking among 0049,
    0176,0218,0289,0290,0291,
    0669
  Suicide among 0159,0216,
    0360,0392,0544,0915
SHOSHONE, WESTERN 0068
SIOUX INDIANS
  0044,0045,0046,0051,0066,
  0109,0147,0159,0233,0248,
  0268,0361,0386,0395,0417,
  0463,0466,0467,0468,0492,
  0509,0593,0604,0608,0668,
  0697,0757,0939,0940,0950
  Alcoholism among 0395,0492,
    0622,0623,0945
  Ceremonies of 0546
  Cheyenne River
    see RESERVATIONS, Cheyenne
         River Reservation
  Drinking among 0044,0248,
    0386,0417,0422,0423,0424,
    0463,0467,0509,0535,0574,
    0593,0608,0622,0623,0668,

0697,0884,0910,0923,0924,
0939,0940,0943,0944,0950
Historical aspects 0147,0574,
0660,0757
Lower Brule 0417,0574,0757
Mental health among 0623
Oglala 0046,0051,0468,0546,
0574,0604,0606,0622,0623,
0624,0625,0626,0910,0923,
0924
Rosebud 0044,0608,0622,0884
Santee 0386
Standing Rock 0660,A942,
0943,0944,0945
Suicide among 0159,0624,
0625,0626,0923,0924
Teton 0066,0268,0546,0630
Yankton 0149,0422,0423,0424
SIOUX CITY, IOWA 0386,A509
SIOUX LOOKOUT PROJECT 0535
SITKA, ALASKA 0765
SIVOKOK VILLAGE, CANADA 0656
SKID ROAD 0121,0138,0200,0220,
0492,0616,0628,0716,0804,
0827
SLOWM, JOHN 0139
SNAKE INDIANS
see also SHOSHONE INDIANS
0207
SNIFFING
see SUBSTANCE SNIFFING
SOBRIETY 0139,0270,0271,0272,
0273,0302
SOCIAL CHANGE
see CULTURE CHANGE
SOCIAL CONTROLS
see also SANCTIONS
0112,0142,0164,0181,0269,
0375,0390,0391,0409,0436,
0528,0529,0700,0890
SOCIAL DISINTEGRATION
see also ACCULTURATION
ASSIMILATION
CULTURE CHANGE
0061,0092,0101,0173,0295,
0365,0401,0538,0575,0624,
0763,0766,0801
SOCIAL DRINKING
see DRINKING, Sociological
aspects

SOCIAL ORGANIZATION
0072,0082,0092,0277,0280,
0387,0484,0490,0627
SOCIAL STRUCTURE
see SOCIAL ORGANIZATION
SOCIAL WORKERS
0157,0158,0240,0245,0621
SOCIOCULTURAL CONDITIONS
0131,0137,0179,0194,0195,
0197,0211,0218,0221,0231,
0236,0252,0424,0438,0442,
0525,0564,0581,0587,0629,
0679,0715,0734,0766,0803,
0949
SOCIOECONOMIC CONDITIONS
0084,0106,0140,0141,0184,
0248,0260,0394,0395,0436,
0463,0479,0481,0507,0597,
0605,0606,0618,0660,0669,
0710,0754,0840,0940
SOLITARY DRINKING
see DRINKING, Solitary
SOLUTIONS TO ALCOHOL PROBLEMS
0048,0149,0166,0221,0222
0244,0264,0308,0324,0363,
0390,0391,0444,0457,0498,
0563,0587,0605,0625,0629,
A636,0648,0663,0665,0676,
0680,0700,0710,0784,0786,
0796,0816,0851,0944,0946,
0967
SONORAN DESERT 0161,0210,
0451,0561
SOTAL 0227,0673
SOUTH CAROLINA 0758
SOUTH DAKOTA
0036,0051,0149,0466,A509
Health care facilities in
0133
Indians in 0151,0421,
0856,0948
Law enforcement in 0263,0264
Treatment programs in 0151,
0461,0637
SOUTHWEST INDIAN YOUTH CENTER
A046,A317
SOUTHWESTERN INDIANS, HEALTH
PROBLEMS 0320,0321
SPANISH A367,0438,0561

-349-

SPECIAL OFFICERS 0031,0038,0136
SPIRIT DANCING 0439,0440,0441
SPIRITUALISM 0048,0686,0851
  0864
STAFF OF TREATMENT PROGRAMS
  see TREATMENT PROGRAMS, Staff
STAGE OF INTOXICATION 0135
STAGING CONCEPT 0009,0010,
  0011,0619,0786
STAKE THEORY 0275,0276,0278,
  0409
STATUS 0006,0113,0348,0424,
  0630,0720
  Deprivation 0118
STEREOTYPE
  see also DRINKING, Myths about
      Indians
    DRUNKEN INDIAN
      STEREOTYPE
  0117,0123,0125,0159,0206,
  0233,0239,0303,0381,0382,
  0457,0519,0533,0604,0642,
  0768,0917,0920
STRESS
  see also ETIOLOGY, of Alcoholism
    ETIOLOGY, of Drinking
    ETIOLOGY, of Drunken-
        ness
  0006,0061,0101,0102,0123,
  0137,0153,0229,0262,0273,
  0316,0328,0338,0353,0392,
  0396,0483,0489,0531,0538,
  0539,0557,0581,0593,0605,
  0608,0656,0657,0664,0730,
  0744,0747,0748,0749,0773,
  0775,0821,0840,0935,0945,
  0947
STUDENTS
  see also SCHOOLS
  0036,0054,0127,0128,0176,
  0352,0356,A376,0434,0475,
  0497,0502,0581,0604,0654,
  0685,0695,0820
STUYVESANT, PETER 0111
STYLES OF DRINKING
  see DRINKING, Binge
    DRINKING, Blitz
    DRINKING, Patterns of
SUBSTITUTION
  see ALCOHOL, Substitution for

SUBSTANCE SNIFFING
  0235,A317,0352,0353,0669,
  0695,0915
  Age differences 0735
  Etiology
    see ETIOLOGY, of
        substance sniffing
  Familial aspects 0013,0460
  Mortality 0217,0234
  Psychological aspects
    0013,0234
SUDDEN DEATH SYNDROME
  0196
SUGLUK, DRINKING IN 0323
SUICIDE
  0021,0022,0078,0100,0104,
  0114,0194,0211,0212,0215,
  0243,0250,0253,0299,0323,
  0338,0342,0445,0455,0475,
  0541,0671,0700,0722,0872,
  0923,0924,0936
  Age differences
    see also ADOLESCENTS,
        Suicide
  0028,0110,0217,0255,0307,
  0322,0352,0356,0360,0544,
  0610,0681,0770,0771
  Alcohol related 0027,0028,
  0142,0151,0155,0156,0159,
  0187,0189,0216,0252,0266,
  0288,0307,A339,0343,0360,
  0387,0392,0458,0483,0484,
  0491,0522,0538,0539,0543,
  0551,0552,0583,0603,0618,
  0625,0626,0653,0657,0661,
  0665,0683,0688,0710,0715,
  0735,0752,0767,0770,0808,
  0830,0915,0962
  Epidemiology
    see EPIDEMIOLOGY, of
        suicide
  Etiology
    see ETIOLOGY, of suicide
  Familial aspects 0028,0156,
    0538,0717,0770,0771
  Historical aspects 0080,
    0159,0267,0544
  Incidence of 0026,0027,0028,
    0105,0151,0155,0156,0159,
    0189,0196,0322,0343,0360,
    0444,0483,0484,0536,0538,

0606,0618,0679,0717,0723,
0767,0769,0844
Prevention
see PREVENTION, of suicide
Sex differences 0028,0080,
0155,0187,0189,0196,0216,
0356,0360,0583,0603,0618,
0624,0625,0681,0683,0962
SUN DANCE 0450
SUQUAMISH INDIANS 0207
SWINOMISH INDIANS 0666

TAHLTAN INDIANS 0580
TAOS PUEBLO 0140,0141,0775
TAVERNS 0002,0203,0286,0370,
0568,0583,0757
Drinking behavior
0125,0190,0200,0313,0334,
0424,0560,0719
Social interaction 0190,0286,
0313,0334,0423,0836,0920,
0940
Violence in 0836
TAXONOMY OF DRINKING
0253,0838,0895
TEACHERS
see EDUCATORS
TEENAGERS
see ADOLESCENTS
TEMPERANCE
see also ABSTINENCE
0036,0139,0204,0209,0283,
0284,0301,0304,0385,A419,
0429,0450,0758,0762,0796,
0803,0834,0954,0969
Temperance ships 0729
Temperance society 0905
TEQUILA 0162
TERMINATION 0815
TESQUINO REGION 0146
TESVINO 0418,0419
THEATER
0039,0242,0317
THEORIES REGARDING INDIAN
DRINKING
0006,0024,0065,0069,0112,
0148,0179,0404,0406,0413,
0424,0434,0436,0437,0438,

0466,0467,0492,0504,0510,
0514,0515,0520,0522,0525,
0540,0541,0547,0563,0564,
0567,0569,0570,0573,0575,
0578,0589,0590,B602,0616,
0640,0645,0663,0693,0744,
0746,0761,0774,0812,0846,
0847,0941,0955
Culture of excitement theory
0940
Culture of poverty theory
0220
THERAPY
see also COUNSELING
0117,0439,0440,0441,0442,
0687,0717,0843
Group therapy 0179,0273
0454,0476,0572,0958
THOMAS, ALEX 0145
THUNDERBIRD FELLOWSHIP HOUSE
see HALFWAY HOUSES
TISWIN 0129,0146,0210
Production of 0007,0122,
0201,0285,0673,0674,0707
Religious aspects 0122,0201
TLINGIT INDIANS 0678
"TOKAWAKA" INDIANS 0075
TOPE, HOMER W. 0032
TORONTO, CANADA 0658
TRACHOMA 0133
TRADE
see also FUR TRADE
LIQUOR TRADE
0111,0156,0335,0366,A367,
0416,0429,0430,0431,0523,
A614,0638,0639,0703,0758,
A813,0854,0891
TRADERS
see also FUR TRADE
LIQUOR TRADE
0076,0150,0219,0236,0314,
0344,0366,0406,0429,0639,
0729,0742,0747,088,0890,
0916,0954
TRADITIONS 0022,0048,0063,
0100,0138,0140,0192,0324,
0455,0723,0726,0892
TRAINING
see also TREATMENT PROGRAMS,
Staff training
0016,0095,0722,0880

Empathy training 0510
Program design 0510,A609,
0649,0788,0938
TRAINING OF ALCOHOLISM PERSONNEL
0093,0149,0510,0530,0555,
A609,0640,0641,0642,0644,
0645,0646,0647,0648,0649,
0702,0760,0784,0788,0938
Attitude changes 0096,0530
Techniques 0680,0938
TRANQUILIZER USE 0461
TRANSFER OF INDIAN ALCOHOL
PROGRAMS
0319,A522,0865
TRAPPERS 0150,0728,0729
TREATIES 0005,0111,0166,0207,
0236,0261,0420,0472,0533,
0568,0854,0921,0967
TREATMENT
see also ALCOHOLICS ANONYMOUS
COUNSELING
DISULFIRAM THERAPY
ETHNIC THERAPY
FORT DEFIANCE ANTABUSE
TREATMENT PROGRAM
GALLUP COMMUNITY
TREATMENT PROGRAM
HALFWAY HOUSES
KENORA WAY STATION
MEDICINE MEN
NEVADA INTER-TRIBAL
ALCOHOLISM PROGRAM
SIOUX LOOKOUT PROJECT
URBAN INDIANS,
Treatment programs
0012,0015,0042,0095,0105,
0107,0108,0109,0119,0126,
0175,0179,0217,0221,0224,
0242,0255,0270,0271,0273,
0278,0283,0284,0364,0392,
0395,0396,0439,0440,0442,
0472,0492,0495,0536,0550,
0555,0572,0573,0588,0612,
0623,0651,0668,0686,0687,
0743,0783,0799,0800,0825,
0828,0829,0832,0843,0855,
0856,0869,0873,0887,0931,
A931
Inter-Tribal Alcoholism
Treatment Center
0637,0667

Philosophical and ethical
issues 0240,0261,0264,
0274,0275,0276,0277,0299,
0441,0443,0445,0522,0584,
0585,0587,0663,0848,0851,
0878,0932
Religious aspects 0390,
0391,0864
Sex differences 0324,0476
Techniques 0020,0055,0192
TREATMENT PROGRAMS
0029,0048,0050,0062,
0180
Community based
0085,0086,0373,0518,0592,
0617,0631,0644,0650,A659,
0760,0761,0774,A844,0880,
0883
Community involvement
0025,0469,0471,0485,0592,
0844,
Community relations
0086,0965
Detoxification programs
0116,0185,0362,0870,0937
Economic aspects 0325,0455,
0586,0631,0632,0633,0634,
0635,0782,0805,0871,0879,
0880
Efficacy and evaluation
0009,0010,0098,0238,0239,
0272,0325,0362,0378,0379,
0380,0381,0384,0454,0455,
0471,A553,0586,0617,0619,
0620,A620,0635,0637,0644,
0655,0697,0745,0774,A844,
0853,0871,0930,0952,0955
Ethnic therapy
see ETHNIC THERAPY
Family therapy 0717,0746
Follow-up studies
0025,0272,0362,0377,0378,
0379,0383,0384,0442,0457,
0476,0586,0619,0620,A620,
0761,A844,0953
for adolescents 0454,0710
Inpatient and hospital
programs 0055,0362,
0383,0384,0461,0476,0667,
0691,0853,0930,0933,0937,
0953

-352-

Legal aspects 0965
Multimodality approach 0477
Outpatient approach
 0055,0362,0383,0384,0853,
 0930
Patient characteristics
 0324,0377,0380,0476,0477,
 0490,0839,0853,0932,0933,
 0937,0953,0958
Planning aspects
 0010,0085,0098,0113,0153,
 0240,0261,0269,0382,0444,
 0512,0537,A555,0591,0617,
 0619,0620,A620,0622,0626,
 0743,0648,0698,0702,0725,
 0727,0768,0774,0785,0822,
 0835,0842,0865,0866,0867,
 0876,0878,0882,0896,0897,
 0898,0912,0913,0931,0955
Political aspects
 0319,0698,0702,0805,0850,
 0865,0866,0867,0879
Probation programs 0883
Program design 0016,0151,
 0169,0180,0185,0245,0269,
 0444,0461,0471,0535,0596,
 0648,0649,0655,0667,0706,
 0722,0774,0822,0850,0852,
 0926,0965
Risk analysis 0011,0377,0378,
 0379
Staff 0324,0325,0380,0471,
 0655,0667,0680,0725,0760,
 0761,0852,0932,0958
Staff training 0016,0149,
 0510,0530,0621,0625,0626,
 0702,0784,0880
TRIBAL ALCOHOL STATUTES
 see LIQUOR LAWS
  Tribal statutes
TRIBAL COURTS
 see COURTS, Tribal
TRIBAL OFFICIALS
 0047,0126,0527
TRIBAL SOVEREIGNTY 0893
TRIBAL TAX 0049
TRUANCY
 0243,0967,0968
TSIMSHIAN INDIANS 0314
TUBA CITY, ARIZONA
 0836,0841,0887

TUBERCULOSIS
 0055,0133,0483,0484,0502,
 0691,0707,0776
 Incidence of
  0060,0347
TUCSON, ARIZONA
 0085,0086,A317,0900
TULAPAI
 0007,0081,0122,0201,0210,
 0285,0418,0673,0674,0707
TULSA, OKLAHOMA 0242
TURQUOISE LODGE
 0029,0362,0596,0835,0926
TUSCARORA INDIANS 0803,0905

ULCERS
 see also GASTROINTESTINAL
  DISORDERS
 0651,0778
 Duodenal
  0320,0773,0776,0833
 Peptic
  0776,0779,0780,0833
UMATILLA INDIANS 0675
UNDEREMPLOYMENT
 see also EMPLOYMENT
  UNEMPLOYMENT
 0021,0023
UNEMPLOYMENT
 0021,0120,0231,0437,0500,
 0535,0657,0681,0715,0851,
 0904,0919
 Alcohol related
  0262,0606,0643,0666,0734,
  0882,0944
U.S. BUREAU OF ALCOHOL,
 TOBACCO AND FIREARMS 0053
U.S. COMMISSION ON CIVIL
 RIGHTS 0869
U.S. PUBLIC HEALTH SERVICE
 0133,0269,0322,0362,A636,
 0680,0697,0743
UNIVERSITY OF BRITISH COLUMBIA
 0148,0439,0808
UNIVERSITY OF COLORADO 0722
UNIVERSITY OF UTAH
 0649,0938

UPPER STALO REGION, BRITISH
  COLUMBIA 0439
URBAN INDIANS
  see also names of individual
    cities
    0054,0084,0085,0086,0106,
    0152,0241,0242,0373,0408,
    0414,0417,0508,0509,0522,
    0556,0559,0560,0573,0596,
    0655,0695,0717,0808,0810,
    0813,0816,0817,0836,0847,
    0853,0866,0870,0884,0898,
    0920,0929,0939
  Alcoholism among
    0002,0079,0103,0220,0223,
    0224,0397,0492,0507,0570,
    0595,0628,0832,0919,0928
  Cultural conflicts
    0004,0247,0262,0334,0389,
    0415,0467,0481,0507,0549,
    0550,0628,0699
  Drinking among
    0003,0138,0200,0206,0213,
    0220,0229,0246,0247,0286,
    0310,0312,0313,0317,0327,
    0328,0329,0334,0354,0386,
    0389,0415,0423,0445,0465,
    0467,0480,0481,0486,0492,
    0503,0507,0509,0522,0549,
    0550,0570,0582,0593,0595,
    0616,0628,0657,0658,0659,
    0712,0716,0719,0720,0741,
    0797,0804,0821,0827,0897,
    0900,0934,0935,0940,0960,
    0965
  Economic aspects
    0003,0079,0138,0246,0247,
    0329,0415,0492,0582,0659,
    0922
  Familial aspects
    0002,0003,0481,0570,0919
  Health problems
    0103,0107,0121,0397,0615,
    0628
  Law enforcement 0181,0310
  Prevention programs
    0079,0206,0572,0595
  Psychological aspects
    0079,0339,0415,0510,0549,
    0572,0719
  Social interaction
    0002,0138,0200,0206,0286,
    0312,0493,0804

  Sociological aspects
    0445,0480,0493,0503,0699,
    0788,0919,0934,0960
  Suicide among 0445
  Treatment programs 0103,0104,
    0362,0572,0616,0655,0712,
    0788,0852,0853,0864,0926,
    0934,0937,0960
  Violence among 0310,0919
URBANIZATION
    0200,0423,0658,0817,0939
UTAH 0650,0787,0788
UTE INDIANS
    0144,A367
  Drinking among
    0450,0594,0642,0643
  Historical aspects 0642
  Uintah-Ouray 0043,0184,
    0785,0787
UTE TRIBAL ALCOHOLISM PROGRAM
    0650,0774,0883

VALUES 0004,0012,0016,0077,
    0102,0112,0147,0158,0171,
    0240,0270,0294,0323,0345,
    0426,0446,0455,0458,0467,
    0468,0479,0484,0503,0528,
    0529,0593,0594,0600,0610,
    0656,0659,0664,0671,0675,
    0693,0715,0719,0763,0766,
    0848,A852,0892,0899,0900
VANCOUVER, CANADA 0920
VANCOUVER ISLAND 0093,0545
VETERANS 0154,0533
VIKITA CEREMONY 0201
VIOLENCE
    0063,0120,0129,0186,
    0194,0255,0267,0343,0435,
    0500,0539,0563,0638,0666,
    0684,0788,0866,0872,0890,
    0969
  Age differences 0543
  Alcohol related 0002,0070,
    0076,0089,0142,0215,0237,
    0254,A339,0344,0358,0368,
    0369,0406,0432,0433,0458,
    0459,0470,0478,0491,0527,
    0534,0535,0543,0603,0625,

-354-

0697,0708,0752,0830,0894,
   0905,0924,0936
  Incidence of 0114
  Mortality 0470
  Sex differences 0543,0936
  Sociological aspects 0089
VISION QUESTS, RELATION TO
  ALCOHOL USE
   0006,0090,0302
VISTA WORKERS/PROGRAMS 0722
VUNTA KUTCHIN
  see KUTCHIN, Vunta

WALLA WALLA 0207
WASHINGTON INDIAN COMMISSION
  ON ALCOHOLISM AND DRUG ABUSE
   0912,0913
WASHINGTON STATE
  Indians in
   0042,0103,0104,0121,0139,
   0173,0372,0444,0621,0690,
   0912,0913
  Treatment programs in
   0103,0444,0912,0913
WASHINGTON TERRITORY
  0824
WASHO INDIANS 0849
WELFARE 0274,0415,0432,0463,
  0508,0642,0904,0934
WESTERN REGIONAL INDIAN ALCOHOL
  TRAINING CENTER
   0510,0640,0641,0642,0644,
   0645,0646,0647,0648,0649,
   0788,0938
WHALERS 0729
WHISKEY 0039,0091,0164,0165,
  0209,0297,0312,0331,0399,
  0419,0614,0703,0724,0731,
  0762,0765,0809,0916
WHISKEY TRADE
  see LIQUOR TRADE
WHITE MOUNTAIN APACHE TRIBAL
  ALCOHOL PROGRAM 0258
WHITEHORSE 0348

WHITES
  0084,0085,0086,0094,0101
  0102,0106,0109,0118,0145,
  0148,0150,0155,0157,0165,
  0170,0171,0172,0173,0177,
  0178,0183,0199,0223,0224,
  0237,0247,0251,0258,0265,
  0266,0289,0290,0291,0292,
  0301,0304,0305,0309,0316,
  0318,0326,0342,0347,0348,
  0351,0353,0358,0360,0361,
  0364,0365,0388,0395,0396,
  A396,0399,0406,0431,0434,
  0437,0438,0443,0445,0450,
  0527,0529,0533,0550,0556,
  0559,0563,0574,0576,0579,
  0604,0617,0627,0629,0639,
  0676,0679,0683,0690,0691,
  0704,0708,0709,0716,0723,
  0738,0765,0766,0777,0778,
  0779,0792,0794,0801,0803,
  0810,0817,0819,0827,0834,
  0836,0841,0855,0911,0915,
  0918,0920,0928,0929,0937,
  0950,0954
WIITIKO PSYCHOSIS 0682
WIND RIVER RESERVATION
  Drinking on 0176,0218,0290,
   0291,0293
  Treatment programs on 0450
WINE 0041,0082,0120,0161,0312,
  0399,0432,0494,0792,0809
  Saguaro wine, see also SAGUARO
                           CACTUS
   0282,0561,0857
WINE CEREMONY 0161,0210,0282,
  0858,0862,0897,0899
WINNEBAGO INDIANS 0066,0386,
  0492
WINNIPEG, CANADA 0106,0691
WINSLOW, ARIZONA 0465,0964
WINTER CEREMONY
  0439,0440,0441,0442,0443,
  0523,0524
WINTERROCK 0043
WISCONSIN 0005,0031,0035,0036,
  0118,0423,0759,0918
WITCHCRAFT 0478,0789,0798,
  0889
WITHDRAWAL 0004,0447,0751,
  0928,0933,0937

WOODFORDS INDIAN COLONY, NEVADA
    0849
WORCHESTER CASE 0091
WYOMING 0218,0293,0462,0874
  Health care facilities in
    0133
  Indians in 0289,0290
  Treatment programs in
    0637,0667

YAKIMA INDIANS 0207,0283,0284,
    0365,0482
YANKTON, SOUTH DAKOTA 0948
YANKTON DAKOTA CHURCH 0422
YAQUI INDIANS 0248
YAVAPAI INDIANS 0056,0420
YELLOWKNIFE, N.W.T.
    0064,0565
YOUTHS
  see also ADOLESCENTS
    0026,0034,0041,0045,0047,
    0084,0149,0171,0176,0185,
    0195,0205,0216,0217,0233,
    0240,0243,0290,0291,0293,
    0294,0298,0307,0322,0360,
    0398,0402,0437,0484,0522,
    0584,0606,0623,0636,0661,
    0663,0669,0675,0684,0688,
    0692,0709,0735,0741,0775,
    0866,0915,0918,0952
YUKON TERRITORY
    0073,0074,0155,0306,0580,
    0751,0753
YUMA INDIANS 0359,0901
YUWIPI CEREMONY 0468

ZETA-TYPE DRINKING PATTERN
    0198
ZIA INDIANS 0361
ZUNI INDIANS 0027,0066,0072,
    0077,0090,0234,0235,0316,
    0361,A659,0941